GANDHI AS DISCIPLE AND MENTOR

THOMAS WEBER
La Trobe University

CAMBRIDGE
UNIVERSITY PRESS

CAMBRIDGE UNIVERSITY PRESS
Cambridge, New York, Melbourne, Madrid, Cape Town,
Singapore, São Paulo, Delhi, Tokyo, Mexico City

Cambridge University Press
The Edinburgh Building, Cambridge CB2 8RU, UK

Published in the United States of America by Cambridge University Press, New York

www.cambridge.org
Information on this title: www.cambridge.org/9780521174480

First published 2004
First paperback edition 2011

A catalogue record for this publication is available from the British Library

ISBN 978-0-521-84230-3 Hardback
ISBN 978-0-521-17448-0 Paperback

ctions
turn,
focus
social
these
lected
Polak,
no are
n and
vated
olstoy
Johan
ıtma's
h his
ne life
res of

Trobe
s life,
clude
eshua
hy of
i Sena
dhian
ement

Contents

NOTE: for Gandhi's own writings only the date and title of the relevant article is given rather than the standard of the date plus the volume and page reference in the *Collected Works of Mahatma Gandhi*. This is because there are now two versions of the *CWMG* and they do not correspond. The original 100 volumes included several volumes of supplementary material that was unearthed after the publication of the volume covering the dates of the new material. In the CD-ROM version of the *CWMG* this material has been integrated into the body of the work. The date and title should make a required item relatively easy to find in whichever version is used. Where no full date is available, the pages in the hard copy version of the *CWMG* are provided. The item can be located in the CD-ROM version through the word search facility.

Note: The publisher has used its best endeavours to ensure that the URLs for external websites referred to in this book are correct and active at the time of going to press. However, the publisher has no responsibility for the websites and can make no guarantee that a site will remain live or that the content is or will remain appropriate.

Preface

In a sense this whole project started when I was researching Gandhi's Salt March to Dandi in the early 1980s. I worked in the library of the Sabarmati Ashram for many weeks and walked the ashram grounds daily. While there, a significant question arose for me: how could Gandhi have left this utopia – or at least a place that must have been a rural utopia in 1930 rather than the small oasis surrounded by a very noisy and dirty urban sprawl it is now – vowing (in effect) never to return? Simplistic explanations of sacrificing his home on the altar of the national cause were not totally satisfying. I completed my Salt March work and went on to look at other aspects of Gandhi's nonviolence, but the question never really went away.

In 1996, when, for a short time, I was at the Peace Research Institute in Oslo (PRIO), I had the good fortune of getting to know Arne Næss. I had long admired his Gandhi-related writings and we had lengthy talks on matters Gandhi. When he stayed with us in Australia the following year, I realised how deeply he was influenced by Gandhi. After reading some of his writings on deep ecology, although the issue was not often commented on, and certainly not in any detail, it became obvious to me how much that work also owed to the Mahatma. As a teacher of peace studies, I was aware of the Gandhian philosophical feel of Johan Galtung's brand of peace research, especially his views on the definitions of violence. The expanded definition that comes through his writings as structural and cultural violence clearly seemed to me to owe much to Gandhi. And I had the same feeling years before when I read E. F. Schumacher's classic book *Small is Beautiful*. In 1999, I spelled out these connections in an article on the Gandhian underpinnings of deep ecology, peace research and Buddhist economics by looking at Gandhi's influence on the three leading figures in the respective fields: Næss, Galtung and Schumacher.

Following discussions on the different approaches to nonviolence in my honours class on nonviolent activism over the years, I decided to spell out the similarities and differences between the approaches of the 'idealists', represented by Gandhi, and the 'pragmatists', represented by Gene Sharp, the main contemporary nonviolence theoretician. Following the acceptance for publication of that article, I decided that my next task should be going back and finally looking seriously at Gandhi's abandonment of the Sabarmati Ashram in 1930 and seeing if it might have had anything to do with his 'nephew' Maganlal Gandhi. As I started this work, it dawned on me that this was not another article but a chapter of a book on the influences on Gandhi, and about Gandhi's influence on others. The paper on Næss, Galtung and Schumacher formed the core for three much lengthier sections looking at each in turn to add to the work on Sharp. This would make up the bulk of the Gandhi's influence side of the ledger. The Maganlal Gandhi work was really just one of the studies that would make up the other, the influenced, side.

The influenced and influential Gandhi give us another valuable insight into the Mahatma and his philosophy. The most well-known recent biographies of Gandhi tend to be political biographies. He is the main player in India's freedom struggle, the eventual 'father of the nation'. His fight for the rights of Indians in South Africa and his three major political movements in India are generally the centre pieces of his story. The years between political campaigns – and the ones in India came at roughly ten-yearly intervals – spent on self-discovery or anti-untouchability and other social work, are often glossed over. But different biographies of Gandhi could be written. How about a spiritual or constructive work biography with the political campaigns being mere extensions to these more fundamental projects which are far more than periods of marking time? A different picture of Gandhi would emerge, and certainly not a less accurate picture. By examining the influences that went into making the Mahatma, we see Gandhi the spiritual seeker, the Gandhi who wanted to find the meaning of life through various 'New Age' experiments and philosophies and through service to others without which he could not find his true Self. If we examine Gandhi this way, his most important relationships are not necessarily the ones he has with the usually recorded political co-workers (such as Jawaharlal Nehru and Sardar Vallabhbhai Patel) but those with social work colleagues and fellow seekers and soulmates who tend to disappear from the record, especially the English-language record. In short, if we look at a different Gandhi to the one who is usually portrayed, different influences can be found and different relationships come to the fore.

The influential Gandhi shows us the parts of his quest and discovery that have been found useful by others, and thus gives us a picture of his legacy – and, as seen here, again it is not necessarily a political activist legacy. This exploration of Gandhi is not presented in a strictly chronological way (although the order of the influences on him are given more or less in the sequence in which they occurred), rather it is presented through his relationships and through those who had relationships with him or his thought.

The first section sets the scene by looking at the phenomenon we call influence. I examine what is meant by it and how it differs from determinism, conversion and chance. This is followed by a discussion of whether the moments at which life-changing influences take hold can be pinpointed or whether influence tends to move more in an incremental fashion. Why was Gandhi so influential? He is examined in light of the literature on power and authority. Influence is inextricably tied in with relationships and of course it does not only flow in one direction – Gandhi was also influenced by his close friends, some of whom can best be described as soulmates, and even by those who owed their allegiance to him as disciples.

The next section of the book, about influences on Gandhi, contains six chapters. The first details the usually discussed examples of influences on the making of the Mahatma. Short case studies look at his relationships with a childhood friend, religious and New Age fellow travellers, the key books that Gandhi himself discusses as having a great impact on him, and his political guru. This is followed by four chapters that look at Gandhi's relationship with Henry Polak, Hermann Kallenbach, Maganlal Gandhi and Jamnalal Bajaj. All of these four relationships, even though Gandhi may have been the senior partner in them and at times the completely dominant one, had a great influence on Gandhi himself. I argue that it is not possible to understand why Gandhi set up Phoenix Settlement, why he moved to Tolstoy Farm, why he left Sabarmati Ashram, and why he ended up at Sevagram without understanding these relationships. Interestingly, in the English-language (mainly political) Gandhi biographies, these relationships, especially the ones concerning Maganlal and Bajaj, barely rate a mention even though I argue that they were crucial in Gandhi's life. The sixth chapter looks at Gandhi himself. Who was the person that grew out of these influences? What do his influencers tell us about him?

The final section, on Gandhi's influence, mirrors the previous section and it also consists of six chapters. It again details the people whose names generally come up in discussions of Gandhi's (again, generally political) influence. The case studies look at his relationships with his co-workers in India's freedom struggle and international figures from three continents who are famously known, and self-described, as Gandhians. The four following chapters look at Gandhi's influence on the philosophies of the intellectuals and social activists Arne Næss, Johan Galtung, E. F. Schumacher and Gene Sharp. The final chapter examines the question of why he had the power to influence so many others. What do those he influenced tell us about the legacy of his philosophy?

For the chapters that conclude each of the two substantive sections of what follows, I have used the analogy of an hourglass. By way of personal history, most of us can be represented by a funnel – a utensil for concentrating liquids so that they can be fed into a small opening. In the analogy, a great many influences are captured by the cone of a funnel. They are combined as they flow through the narrowing outlet to give a blended output – the personality and behaviour traits of the individual who is the end product. This seems to be a fair representation of how most of us get to be who we are – and probably for many of us the funnel analogy is sufficient. However, some individuals also have more than a passing influence on others (beyond their children).

For those who strongly influence many others or whose influence is significant in shaping the world in an objectively discernible way, the analogy does not go far enough – the appropriate analogy may be the hourglass rather than the funnel. An hourglass is like a funnel standing on its apex on a mirror. Sand from the top compartment flows through a narrow opening to the bottom compartment. The influence that is concentrated at the narrows, the 'waist' between the two glass compartments representing the individual, spreads again to influence many others. Gandhi is such an individual. Countless influences, like sands in an hourglass, flowed into the making of the Mahatma. Some of them are identifiable as those of friends and notable thinkers who went before him. But influences also flowed from him (and many through him) to the bottom chamber, the broad spectrum of others who, either personally or by way of a system of thought or style of activism, in a recognisable way became who they did become at least partly as a result of his influence. The concluding chapter of the influenced section examines the 'top of the hourglass' while the concluding chapter of the influential section examines the 'bottom of the hourglass'.

In this work, I have been helped by many. They include Robin Jeffrey, who (as often seems to be the case) was part of the process of formulating the idea for this book; James D. Hunt and Surendra Bhana, who assisted me with my investigations into Gandhi's days in South Africa and helped me track down important sources; Shahed Power, who shared his manuscript about Gandhi's influence on Arne Næss with me; Peter Lawler who kindly gave me copies of Galtung's unpublished papers on Gandhi; Johan Galtung, Ralph Summy, Brian Martin, Graham Dunkley and Arne Næss who read sections of the manuscript and gave me valuable advice; Delene Hutchins who read the entire manuscript, too often pointing out poor punctuation or grammatical indelicacies; and the librarians at La Trobe University's Borchart Library, who so efficiently managed to procure obscure documents for me. In India, I would like to thank Amrutbhai Modi of the Sabarmati Ashram in Ahmedabad for guiding me in my search for Maganlal Gandhi and for making my stay at the ashram as pleasant as it was, Rambhauji Mhaskar, Kanakmal Gandhi and Hirabhai at Sevagram for organising my programme there, and Tulsidas Somaiya for bookending my 2003 India visit at the Bombay Sarvodaya Mandal. Jyotibhai Desai, Michael and Anand Mazgaonkar assisted me with translations of Gujarati material concerning Maganlal Gandhi. I would also like to thank Narayan Desai, who helped me clarify my thinking about seeing Gandhi in a more holistic way than he so often comes across in English-language biographies. And, of course, thanks to Marja and Hanna for being there.

Glossary

Ahimsa	Nonviolence
Ashram	Religious community; hermitage; centre for social service
Beti	Daughter
Bhai	Brother; as a suffix to a proper name it connotes respect
Bhagavad Gita	Sacred Hindu book containing Krishna's dialogues before battle
Bhoodan	Land gift. Vinoba Bhave's movement aimed at securing land for the landless by asking the wealthy to donate it voluntarily
Brahmacharya	Celibacy; control of the senses as a spiritual discipline
Charkha	Spinning wheel
Charotar	A fertile, dark soiled area of the Kaira District of Gujarat, which is the stronghold of the Patidar (Patel) caste
Chhotabhai	Younger brother
Chipko	To hug. The name of the world-renowned Himalayan conservation movement
Dacoits	Bandits
Darshan	View of auspicious object or person from which the viewer gains merit
Dhoti	Long cloth, tied at the waist and wrapped around the legs. A common north Indian male garment
Gramdan	Village gift. Vinoba Bhave's plan for villagers to pledge to run their village on a cooperative and communal basis
Gram Swaraj	Village self-government

Harijans	Literally 'Children of God'. Gandhi's term for dalits, known in his time as 'untouchables'
Hanuman	The monkey god. A popular Hindu deity and a hero of the epic tale, the *Ramayana*
Karmayogi	One practising the yoga of selfless action as a path to union with God
Khilafat	Hindu-supported Muslim movement in 1919–20 against the harsh terms imposed on Turkey by Britain following the Great War in which the Turkish Sultan, who was also the Caliph of Islam, was to be deposed
Khadi	Hand-spun, hand-woven cloth
Krishna	Most popular incarnation of the Hindu god Vishnu
Kurta	Long, long-sleeved collarless Indian shirt
Lok Sabha	The Lower House in the Indian parliament
Mahatma	Literally 'great soul'. A title of great respect
Mahila	Women
Malguzar	Important landowner
Mandal	Association or conference
Moksha	Liberation from the cycle of birth, death and rebirth. Unity with the Supreme
Purdah	The custom of keeping women in seclusion or under the veil
Sangh	Association or congregation
Sangha	The Buddhist monastic order
Sannyasa	Renunciation of normal life in a religious quest
Sannyasi	One who has taken *sannyasa*
Sardar	Chief. An honorific title
Sarva Seva Sangh	Association for the service of all. An umbrella grouping of most of the major Gandhian organisations
Sarvodaya	Literally the 'welfare of all'. Gandhi's social philosophy
Sati	The ritual self-immolation of a widow on the funeral pyre of her deceased husband
Satyagraha	'Truth Force' or 'Soul Force'. Gandhi's term for nonviolent resistance
Saurashtra	Literally land of a hundred states. Peninsular Gujarat.

Seth	Merchant; wealthy man
Seva	Service
Sastra	An authoritative text, usually religious
Shanti Sena	Peace brigade
Swadeshi	Made in one's own country, local production. Self-sufficiency
Swaraj	Self-rule; independence
Upanishads	A collection of holy Hindu treatises
Yajna	Religious sacrifice
Yatra	Journey, pilgrimage
Zamindar	Important landowner

PART I

Influence

CHAPTER I

The nature of influence

INTRODUCTION

We all come to times in our lives when we change our beliefs or ways of living. How do these changes come about? Why at one particular time rather than at another? To what degree do such changes come about because of contact with persons and ideas that have the power, at that particular point in time, to alter our destiny? William James noted that 'Our ordinary alterations of character, as we pass from one of our aims to another, are not commonly called transformations, because each of them is so rapidly succeeded by another in the reverse direction; but whenever one aim grows so stable as to expel definitely its previous rivals from the individual's life, we tend to speak of the phenomenon, and perhaps to wonder at it, as a "transformation".[1] Where this transformation is a religious one, especially if it is preceded by crisis or is sudden, James calls it 'conversion'. This means that 'religious ideas, previously peripheral in [the] consciousness, now take a central place, and that religious aims form the habitual centre of [the person's] energy'. This self-surrender, while to James more interesting and with more abundant and startling subconscious effects, is not the only form of conversion. And, by and large, it is the other form that is of more concern to us here. In the 'volitional' type of conversion 'the regenerative change is usually gradual, and consists in the building up, piece by piece, of a new set of moral and spiritual habits'.[2] Gandhi, and those who were his followers in various senses, did change deeply as a result of their interactions, sometimes suddenly but more often as a 'final straw' in an evolutionary process. In exploring causal antecedents of the changes that grew out of these relationships, possibly the word that best sums up what I am trying to convey is 'influence'.

[1] William James, *The Varieties of Religious Experience: A Study in Human Nature* (Glasgow: Collins, 1960), p. 199.
[2] *Ibid.*, pp. 201, 209.

The first definition of influence in the Oxford dictionary is an astrological one. It informs us that influence is an ethereal fluid that flows from the stars in a way as to affect a person's character, personality and destiny. Of course the Oxford dictionary does not leave it there. Further definitions, perhaps more immediately relevant for my task, include the flowing into a person of 'any kind of divine, spiritual, moral, immaterial, or secret power or principle'; and the 'exertion of action of which the operation is unseen ... by one person or thing upon another'; and most pertinently, 'the capacity or faculty of producing effects by insensible or invisible means without the employment of material force, or the exercise of formal authority; ascendency of a person or social group; moral power *over* or *with* a person; ascendency, sway, control, or authority, not formally or overtly expressed.' In short, influence is also an agency of power, without the overt exercise of power in any political sense, that can affect and modify something or someone else.

When someone changes their attitudes or behaviour as a result of some sort of physical sanction, we call the process the exercise of power. Although psychologists may also use the term 'influence' as synonymous with more surreptitious techniques of persuasion, for the purposes of this study I am not interested in mass communication and in influence as the formation of public opinion or manipulation (where someone, for example a clever salesperson, pressures another to do something they would not otherwise do, such as purchasing a product they may not really want; or pressures someone to do something that builds up a debt relationship that may later compel an act of reciprocity). Nor am I using it in the way it is employed in the social psychology literature where the influence is often a synonym for the word 'power' and generally concerns the questions about how agreement is actively elicited from others (through rewards or punishments) and about the dynamics of social groups where members tend to hold similar views. I am using the term in the sense that it is used in sociological parlance, where the process occurs voluntarily or unconsciously without the necessary presence of an active influencer. The issue for me is best encapsulated by the sorts of answers that can be expected to be given when someone is asked: 'who have been the main influences in your life?' In short, for my purposes the astrological metaphors are more apt than the psychological explanations concerning the use of overt power in relationships.

Influence can come from formal institutions such as schools and the mass media (where often it does amount to manipulation), from other individuals or informal groups. Although he lived at a time before the advent of mass media as we know it, Gandhi of course must have been greatly influenced by family members and school. The influence of family and school are more or less given to all of us, but there are other influences that strike cords with some of us and not with others, some that affect us at some times in our lives where they would not at other times. What really concerns me here is the seemingly selective influence of individuals, personally or through notable books, or by way of informal groups, on the making of the Mahatma. This includes the relationships that prompted or legitimated changes he made or gave him the social support necessary for taking innovative risks – the top of the hourglass. Equally, I am also interested in the bottom of the hourglass, the influence of Gandhi in shaping the lives of others who went on to make substantial contributions in their chosen fields in ways that can, at least to a discernable degree, be said to have come about because of this influence.

CHANCE, CHOICE AND DETERMINISM

Of course we should not totally overlook chance as a determinant of history, especially personal history. There has been a tendency to see the march of history as somehow inevitable, however, in the words of Merriman, chance, and equally we could add 'coincidence' here, 'has not always received its due from historians seeking to explain world events'.[3] At the individual level most of us accept the role played by chance in our personal lives, why, then, not in the life of Gandhi? Perhaps it was pure chance that he went to England to study law, that he stumbled upon a certain vegetarian restaurant, that he ended up in South Africa to practise his new profession, having failed at it at home, or that Henry Polak and Hermann Kallenbach were introduced to him. Of course chance played a role in the life of the Mahatma, and of course so did many other factors – and far too many for them all to be put down to mere chance. Gandhi chose to do things that most of those around him simply did not choose to do.

The determinists tell us that every event has a cause or a series of determining causes and that we are victims of a past which has conditioned us to choose in a certain way. At times we may not be able to trace the sequence of cause and effect, and at times there may be many contributory causes to an effect. If an event happens where we cannot pinpoint any cause, we may call it a chance happening and if the happening seems to have been caused by ourselves, we say that we chose it by our own free will. Whatever

[3] See John M. Merriman's introduction to his edited book, *For Want of a Horse: Choice and Chance in History* (Lexington: The Stephen Green Press, 1985), p. ix.

the driving determinants of our choices are, differing possibilities present themselves to us and we continually have to make choices regarding them. The degree to which our choices are free is still debated by philosophers and psychologists. In any case, the choices we make can have profound consequences for our lives. Whether the choices made by Gandhi were 'hard determined' by his previous history, including his interactions with the others described in this book, cannot be settled here. However, there is ample evidence that the relationships discussed had a profound influence on him, encouraging his evolution in certain directions, perhaps being 'soft derminants' in his development. While it is undoubtedly true that small causes can have large effects and that no one can tease out all the possible determining variables in any given life, I am trying to understand Gandhi's own life journey by attempting to piece together what probably were determining conditions, by attempting to distinguish significant connections between events and less significant ones.

What I have attempted here is not to write counterfactual history of Gandhi's life: if this did not happen, or if this person had not met Gandhi, or if Gandhi had not read this particular tract, what shape would his future have taken? Possibly, perhaps even probably, Gandhi would not have become the Mahatma if he had not gone to England to study, or, even more importantly, to South Africa as a failed Indian lawyer. But could he have become the Mahatma without the circumstances that led him to write articles on Indian recipes for London vegetarian journals? Other counterfactual questions could include: If Gandhi had not met Raychand would he have become a Christian? And then what? If he had not met Polak would he not have founded an intentional rural community based on simplicity and spirituality? Would he have remained an urban lawyer or would his ashram days merely have come a little later – or perhaps even earlier? If Maganlal Gandhi had not died when he did, would Gandhi have returned to Sabarmati after the Salt March and continued with its unruly (or in that case perhaps less unruly) inhabitants? Without meeting Gandhi could Rajendra Prasad have become President of India and Vallabhbhai Patel Deputy Prime Minister? Would Kenneth Kaunda have been a believer in nonviolence for as long as he was without his reading of Gandhi? And without such a reading, what different path would the American Civil Rights Movement have taken with a non-Gandhi-influenced Martin Luther King Jr.? Without meeting Gandhi, would Shantidas have set up Gandhian ashrams in the south of France? Would there be no philosophy of deep ecology, or concepts of structural violence and Buddhist economics if their founders had not undertaken a careful reading of Gandhi? While these questions may be interesting to speculate upon, no definitive answers are possible. Nevertheless, as Ferguson suggests, such counterfactual scenarios need not be mere fantasy, they can be 'simulations based on calculations about the relative probability of plausible outcomes in a chaotic world'.[4] I will leave these speculations to others who may wish to engage in them. Although the plausibly causal, or at least influencing, connections in the four substantive chapters in each half of what follows have not previously been commented on at any length, the connections and their consequences explored here *were* made and *did* happen and although chance and coincidence may have played their parts, the people and philosophies Gandhi came into contact with at more than a superficial level, generally through seemingly conscious decisions on his part, also had a very strong influence on his personal future development. And it is argued that he also had similar strong influences on the personal history and intellectual development of those portrayed here who came into contact with him or his ideas.

EVOLUTION, TIPPING POINTS AND TRIGGER EVENTS

Life is a progression of one thing after another. We learn from our mistakes, we are inspired by people and events, we change our world views as we mature. Short of accidents, major illnesses, wars or other significant catastrophes, only rarely does something momentous happen that alters our lives in an instant. Most changes are gradual, or volitional conversion in James' terminology. They tend not to occur on the road to Damascus. Sometimes, however, although probably coming out of a later realised nurturing groundwork, change seems sudden. How often does it happen that we may be interested in something or want to go somewhere but do very little about it until, suddenly (and possibly very suddenly to the outside observer), one day a decision to follow through on the interest is taken and we change our lives? Why did it happen then, not before or later? Out of what dynamics do seemingly rapid changes emerge?

Although the word 'conversion' usually refers to religious change, it also has a wider meaning and can, at the less dramatic end of the scale, grow out of the phenomenon that I have been calling influence. There is a dearth of empirical studies on the unconscious and psychic mechanisms involved in conversion, and the literature that does exist is very general. However, from it can be concluded that conversion manifests itself as a change in

---

[4] Niall Ferguson, 'Introduction' to Naill Ferguson (ed.), *Virtual History: Alternatives and Counterfactuals* (London: Paperback, 1988), p. 85.

personal thoughts, feelings and actions, often preceded by 'anguish, turmoil, despair, conflict, guilt, and other such difficulties'.[5] It is generally agreed that almost all conversion follows upon some kind of crisis where previous standards, goals and beliefs cease to function well and the conversion can be described as a coping mechanism. The crisis need not be spiritual, but may be political, psychological or cultural. Gandhi certainly had times of deep spiritual crisis in his life, and at these times his way forward tended to come out of the interaction with someone close to him. For example, the counsel of Raychand when Gandhi was questioning his own faith at a time when his Christian friends believed that his conversion, in the traditional religious sense of the word, was imminent. But there does not always seem to be a crisis before a rapid change, and this can make abrupt changes seem inexplicable.

Recently there has been much written about 'tipping points' where suddenly an idea, trend or behaviour pattern reaches a 'take-off' point the way that a present but managed disease suddenly and inexplicably becomes a full-scale epidemic or the way a subculture's emblematic clothing becomes the height of popular fashion almost overnight.[6]

Decades ago, the dispute formation and conflict resolution theorists were talking about 'trigger events' where an incident (or one too many) or perhaps some annoying or irritating behaviour suddenly brings on a new realisation that pushes the person acted against into the arena of overt and public dispute. The trigger event forces a person to consciously analyse his or her experience of an action, or may cause them to reinterpret previously seemingly insignificant actions in a way that imbues them with added meaning, causing them to see the world differently. In the area of disputes this may mean that they realise that they have been wronged and that this requires some reaction.[7]

Analogous situations occur in the lives of individuals outside the context of disputes or trend changes. At times it may be hard to define the tipping points and trigger events that make sudden changes possible, but they are there. Gandhi, for example, was experimenting with different 'New Age' philosophies and practices and working at simplifying his life, then, literally overnight, after having read John Ruskin's book *Unto this Last*, he

5 Lewis R. Rambo, 'Conversion', in Mircea Eliade (ed.), *Encyclopedia of Religion* (New York: Macmillan, 1987), vol. IV, p. 74.
6 On this see Malcolm Gladwell, *The Tipping Point: How Little Things Can Make a Big Difference* (London: Abacus, 2000).
7 On this see Jeffrey M. Fitzgerald, David C. Hickman and Richard L. Dickins, 'A Preliminary Discussion of the Definitional Phase of the Dispute Process', unpublished paper presented at the 1980 Conference of the 'Law and Society' Association in Madison, Wisconsin, pp. 4–5.

purchased a property and set up a communal farm run along the lines of the dictates of his till then more or less armchair philosophy. The tipping point may have been the reading of the book, or the final straw in a lengthy evolutionary process may have started with the forming of a relationship with Polak who was to give him the book, or even with the chain of events that led him to claim Polak as a friend. In the other geographical and lifestyle shifts that Gandhi undertook, the trigger events may have grown out of special relationships or may have been provided by the sudden ending of such a relationship through death, or even by the lengthy pleading of a soulmate/disciple in search of a surrogate father that could no longer be ignored.

MENTORS, FELLOW TRAVELLERS, SOULMATES AND DISCIPLES

No inventor, including the inventor of the self, works alone. We all make ourselves in interaction with others. How do our relationships influence our future directions and even future selves? In relationships sometimes it is difficult to determine who influences whom – even if one partner is clearly the senior one. Relationships, if they are not totally one-sided (and possibly even then), are dialectical. The more influenced party, if in a direct relationship with the object of influence, can still affect the more influencing one – and, even if the dominant party is or becomes a world figure, the flowing back of influence can have profound significance.

Four terms spring to mind in this connection: mentor, fellow traveller, soulmate and disciple. Mentors are experienced and trusted advisers who are also friends. Although the term 'fellow traveller' is often used to describe communist sympathisers, more generally it refers to those responsive to a certain point of view without being fully paid-up members of the organisation propagating that view. The term 'soulmate' is predominantly used to describe the relationship between two people, usually of the opposite sex, who are temperamentally well suited to each other or have a strong affinity with each other, often at a deep spiritual and intellectual level. Disciples are the dedicated followers of a leader.

While Gandhi may have seen himself as a disciple of Raychand, Ruskin and Leo Tolstoy and considered Gopal Krishna Gokhale as his mentor, he was also a mentor to many others and an undisputed leader to still others who can be classed as his disciples. In Hindu tradition, the guru is a religious teacher who undertakes to give personal instruction to a disciple, the chela. The relationship between master and pupil is a close one with utmost reverence and obedience required of the chela. An ashram is a community where a holy man and his disciples live. And it is the presence of the guru that gives the ashram its importance. Four of the major influential relationships discussed here are inextricably tied up with Gandhi's four ashrams.

Gandhi was a guru for many, but regardless of Ved Mehta's characterisation of some of those that worked with him as apostles[8] most of the best-known political ones such as Jawaharlal Nehru, Rajendra Prasad and Vallabhbhai Patel were clearly more than that, being co-workers in India's freedom struggle. Of course, although Gandhi's philosophy in action actively rejected the hierarchical dependence and 'inequality of the master-disciple relationship in favour of a dialectic between equals',[9] this did not necessarily mean that all could step out of Gandhi's shadow and operate as fully independent and creative, albeit influenced, individuals (as Shantidas could, but Mirabehn and Hermann Kallenbach could not). Disciples generally try to carry on the work of the master, often following the holy writ without the ability to marshal the creativity necessary to meet new situations. These disciples do not interest me in this particular study.

Gandhi was a fellow traveller with the South African Christian missionaries who became his close friends and in his school years, although early on the junior partner, with his childhood friend Sheikh Mehtab. Henry Polak and Kallenbach, and especially Saraladevi Chaudhurani, whom in 1920 Gandhi called his 'spiritual wife', were clearly for a time his soulmates[10] rather than mere political co-workers. Maganlal Gandhi and Jamnalal Bajaj, who I have included in the list of those who influenced him, were clearly disciples – but on the death of what sort of disciple does the master claim that he has been widowed? What sort of disciple is adopted as a son whose death leaves the leader in a state of utter desolation? Maganlal Gandhi and Bajaj were not the equals of Gandhi on a common quest as friends earlier in the Mahatma's life may have been, but nevertheless their discipleship was tinged with something of the soulmate relationship. Perhaps Moore's definition of the soulmate as someone 'to whom we feel profoundly connected, as though the communication and communing that takes place between us were not the product of intentional efforts, but rather a divine grace'[11] is nearer the mark than the more bland definition given above. Several of Gandhi's relationships I examine here seem to be of this order. Moore

---

[8] See Ved Mehta, *Mahatma Gandhi and his Apostles* (London: Andre Deutsch, 1977).

[9] Richard Lannoy, *The Speaking Tree: A Study of Indian Culture and Society* (London: Oxford University Press, 1971), p. 381.

[10] Gandhi seems to have had a platonic but sexually charged love affair with Saraladevi, see Martin Green, *Gandhi: Voice of a New Age Revolution* (New York: Continuum, 1993), especially pp. 273–85.

[11] Thomas Moore, *Soul Mates: Honoring the Mysteries of Love and Relationship* (New York: Harper Perennial, 1994), p. xvii.

speaks of these relationships when he notes, that 'The point in a relationship is not to make us feel good, but to lead us into a profound alchemy of soul that reveals to us many of the pathways and openings that are the geography of our own destiny and potentiality.'[12] This is the very point of some of the explorations of relationship I attempt here. Further, Moore believes that 'slight shifts of imagination have more impact on living than major efforts at change', and that 'deep changes in life follow movements in imagination'.[13] Several slight shifts of imagination that led to deep changes in Gandhi's life came out of the dialectical processes of interactions within his close relationships. The influence of those, often shared, slight shifts frequently proved profound.

Of those who Gandhi influenced by his personal presence most were disciples. Prasad, Patel and Vinoba Bhave clearly were disciples, but more than mere disciples and less than soulmates. Because of the mentoring of Gandhi their political guru, and because they retained the ability to act independently of their master, they achieved the highest positions in newly independent India. Shantidas, for whom Gandhi was a guru/mentor, went on to become more of a fellow traveller than obedient disciple, and the others, who did not know Gandhi personally (for example Kaunda and King) were fellow philosophical travellers who learned important political lessons from their illustrious predecessor. Perhaps Sunderlal Bahuguna is somewhere in between. Of the four major figures discussed in the section exploring Gandhi's influence on others, Arne Næss, Johan Galtung and E. F. Schumacher are fellow travellers with Gandhi, not political disciples. Gene Sharp became one after starting off as a disciple. The web of influences is a complicated one.

CHARISMA AND AUTHORITY

As noted above, Gandhi, like the rest of us, was heavily influenced by various elements of his childhood situation and the people and philosophies he came into contact with. However, unlike most of the rest of us, he was also extremely influential. A glance at a Gandhi bibliography will readily turn up books with titles that attest to this: *Under the Shelter of Bapu, In the Shadow of the Mahatma, At the Feet of Bapu, At the Feet of Mahatma Gandhi, Homage to Gandhi, The Saint of Human Rights: Gandhi, A Saint at Work, Mahatma Gandhi: The Man Who Became One with the Universal Being, World's Homage to Mahatma, Gandhi-Mahatma: An Anthology of*

---

[12] *Ibid.*, p. 257.   [13] *Ibid.*, p. viii.

Appreciations from all Quarters of the Globe, Mahatma Gandhi: The World Significance, Humanity's Homage to Gandhiji, Mahatma Gandhi: Essays and Reflections on His Life and Work, *Gandhi as Others See Him, Mahatma Gandhi and the U. S. A., Gandhi and the American Scene, Mahatma Gandhi as Viewed by Foreigners, Gandhi Through Western Eyes, Mahatma Gandhi (The World's Greatest Man), Gandhi on World Affairs, Gandhi and the Nuclear Age, Gandhi Today, Gandhi: His Relevance for Our Times, Gandhi and Stalin, Gandhi and Marx,* and countless thousands of others, including many hundreds of biographies. Anthologies of his works or articles about him promote his relevance, explain why he should be an influence for the rest of us (and even claim that we ignore him not just to our individual peril, but at the risk of the annihilation of the planet).

For Gandhi's seventieth birthday, India's leading philosopher (and later President of the Republic) Sarvepalli Radhakrishnan edited a volume of essays of reflections on Gandhi's life and work by extremely eminent persons. A second edition, that was to be presented to Gandhi on his eightieth birthday appeared after the Mahatma's assassination as a memorial volume with a section containing essays of appreciation and shorter homages from world statesmen and moral leaders.[14] In short, it is hard to think of too many people who were more influential than the Mahatma.

Why *was* Gandhi so influential? It has often been remarked that Gandhi provided a signpost for moral living, leaving us with some valuable insights about the way life should be oriented so as not to become dysfunctional to the self, society or planet. For many of those who knew him he was influential as a father figure or charismatic leader, and for those who did not come under his personal sway there was the great world-renowned moral authority he wielded and example and teachings he left behind. In short, Gandhi had power.

Power comes in many forms. It can be coercive or manipulative or stem from legitimate authority – where obedience is voluntary rather than forced or wielded in a way not visible to the obedient. For the great sociologist Max Weber, legitimate authority is of three types: the traditional (where obedience stems from tradition), legal-rational (where obedience stems from the legal legitimation of the ruler), and charismatic (where obedience is exchanged for the possibility of the leader transforming the life of the follower). Charismatic leaders are the most legitimate of rulers for they have no hold over their followers other than the faith the followers voluntarily

---

[14] S. Radhakrishnan (ed.), *Mahatma Gandhi: Essays and Reflections on his Life and Work* (Bombay: Jaico, 1956).

invest the leader with. The religious prophet who defies tradition in the name of divine command, such as Christ or Mohammad, is the archetypical charismatic leader. It is not overly presumptuous to include Gandhi in this list of charismatic leaders.

In Weber's scheme, the charismatic leadership style is characterised by a guru-disciple relationship in which the leader creates his or her own structures in keeping with the religious nature of their 'calling', rather than relying on more traditional ones.[15] Willner notes that followers effectively relinquish their autonomy to the will of the charismatic leader.[16] In a similar vein, Kohut describes the messianic leader with whom followers identify because 'his self has largely merged with the idealized superego'.[17] The values and 'meaningful, high ideals' of the leader provide a potential for psychological growth in the followers.[18]

Other theorists of leadership have produced different typologies. In his examination of political groupings, Graham Little analyses the ways individual selves come into relationship with other selves in his classification of leadership types. His 'strong leader' is engaged in a project of competition (the self *vs* other), his 'group leader' is concerned with group solidarity (self in other), while the project of his 'inspiring leader' is one of mutuality or communion (self and other).[19] In the latter group, the leader and followers interrelate through communication, and the relationship is one of shared visions and ideas where, even if the leader is the first to see the vision, the response of the followers is also an internal one.

While Little's inspiring leader and followers 'are distinguished by their equality under the authority of an idea',[20] rather than the authority of the leader under Weber's charismatic leadership or Kohut's messianic leadership, they share similarities. For Gandhi's Indian co-workers, whom I examine in the introductory chapter to the Gandhi's influence section of what follows, and also in the case of the two Indians in the major case studies in the Gandhi influenced section the relationship was one of charismatic leader and followers. However, in the case of the two Jewish fellow seekers of

[15] Max Weber, *The Theory of Social and Economic Organisations* (New York: The Free Press, 1964), pp. 360–1.

[16] Ann R. Willner, *The Spellbinders: Charismatic Political Leadership* (New Haven: Yale University Press, 1984), pp. 243–9.

[17] Heinz Kohut, 'Creativeness, Charisma, Group Psychology: Reflections on the Self-Analysis of Freud', in Paul H. Ornstein (ed.), *The Search for Self: Selected Writings of Heinz Kohut, 1950–1978* (New York: International Universities Press, 1990), vol. II, p. 828.

[18] *Ibid.*, p. 801.

[19] Graham Little, *Political Ensembles: A Psychosocial Approach to Politics and Leadership* (Melbourne: Oxford University Press, 1958), pp. 6–8.

[20] *Ibid.*, p. 134.

Gandhi's South Africa days and the activists who saw Gandhi as a spiritual and social reformist guru, the relationship is best seen as one of inspirational leader and followers. For the four people detailed in the major case studies in the Gandhi's influence section there is strong intellectual influence rather than leadership.

CONCLUSION

What I am attempting here is not a chronological biography of Gandhi – there have been enough of those already. Yet, in order to undertake a thorough examination of the major turning points in anyone's life and the interior processes that went into bringing them about, as I attempt to do here with Gandhi's, what may be required are the tools of psychoanalysis. Even then, when the Freudian process is applied to long dead individuals through their writings or recollections of those who knew them, the enterprise is one that many view with more than a little scepticism: the arenas of psycho-history and psycho-biography remain controversial.[21] In looking for clues in Gandhi's private life that throw light onto his public one,[22] I am not in any way attempting to belittle the admirable public political Gandhi. Having said this, there is the possibility, especially given that I am not a psychoanalyst, that I am merely selecting small instances from a very full life, snippets of conversation that may have been inadequately remembered years later, or lines of correspondence that may not have had the deep meanings I invest them with, and stretching them to provide a very subjective interpretation of Gandhi's movements, both intellectual/emotional and geographical. I may be guilty of elevating chance encounters or small influences to the status of the major influence on a life, or in Gay's words of explaining 'too much by too little'.

And I may even be doing the same with those I claim were influenced by Gandhi. Of course everyone's life is composed of many influences – but was Gandhi an influence among many equally minor influences or a great one, and even perhaps the greatest one? It is not always possible to tell, and in what I am doing here there is danger of peddling a conspiracy theory of sorts, one that sees the Mahatma lurking under every bed, as the inspiration behind almost every social movement with a peace/justice/ecological bent.

---

[21] See Peter Gay, *Freud for Historians* (New York: Oxford University Press, 1985).
[22] For the best example of such a study of Gandhi, see Erik H. Erikson's chapter 'On the Nature of "Psycho-Historical" Evidence' in his book *Life History and the Historical Moment* (New York: Norton, 1975), pp. 113–68.

Nevertheless, I strongly believe that in examining Gandhi's life in light of those who (to me, clearly) influenced him, we get a far clearer idea of who the Mahatma was and why he did and thought what he did. Also, in looking at his influence, we can see which parts of his complex and (especially to the western mind) at times confusing philosophy have stood the test of time, what of Gandhi's thought has proved to be the most enduring and having the greatest relevance after his death. Further, in examining the antecedents, I believe, we get not only a far clearer idea of the life and thought of the several significant others in the political and social movement arena that I have chosen to examine, but also of the movements themselves.

PART II
Gandhi influenced

CHAPTER 2

The influenced Gandhi

INTRODUCTION

Most people come to several crossroads in their lives. Why is one path taken rather than another? Many experience 'dark nights of the soul'. Some emerge strengthened with clear purpose, others, presumably not the ones who write about such experiences, are possibly crushed. When, in June 1893, en route from Durban to Pretoria to assist Dadda Abdulla and Company in a legal case, the young barrister Mohandas Gandhi was thrown off the train at Pietermaritzburg station because a white passenger did not want to sit next to a 'coloured man', Gandhi was at one of these crossroads. That winter night, shivering in the dark waiting room, Gandhi had to decide whether he should fight for his rights or return to India defeated.[1] It could have gone either way. Gandhi had been a shy, nondescript school student whose main characteristic seemed to be truth telling, even when it caused him and others problems. Although still extremely shy, he discovered some self-respect in London when he found friends who were interested in what he had to say, but back in India he proved to be a failure as a lawyer. He was more or less escaping a future of hopelessness by taking the job in South Africa. Here he was, after only one week in the country, already facing defeat in life. He rose to the challenge and by the time he arrived back in India for good, in 1915, he returned as a 'Mahatma', a 'great souled' person, awaited by a cheering multitude. Something in the combination of the inheritances of the past that went into his make-up pushed him along one path rather than the other when faced with this trigger event.

Everyone is influenced by their parents, close relatives and friends, their culture, their religion, their education and the time in which they live. This is the background from which we all emerge. In the case of Gandhi this has been written about in numerous sources. To know the Mahatma

---

[1] See M. K. Gandhi, *An Autobiography Or The Story of My Experiments With Truth* (Ahmedabad: Navajivan, 1940), pp. 80–1.

well enough to attempt to pass judgement on why he did what he did, one must understand the social and religious traditions of Kathiawad, his native region,[2] know the folk tales of peninsular Gujarat and have read the *Bhagavad Gita* and some of the key Upanishads (especially the short *Isha* Upanishad) which may have been crucial in determining his make-up. Psychological probing may also throw some light on that night at Pietermaritzburg, but probably we will never know what really happened and why. However, there are generally other strong influences which seem to impact directly on our lives that can be far more easily traced. We cross paths with someone, or pick up a book, or attend a lecture, or become involved with some event that alters the direction of our lives.

There will always be some debate on just how strong an influence a particular text or close associate has had on another individual. This is no less true for Gandhi. It is however revealing to see, for example, how often themes and phrases from the western texts that Gandhi read, especially during the time of his early philosophical explorations in London and South Africa (when he still had time to be building his intellectual capital), crop up in his speeches and writings even decades later. Reading Tolstoy's *The Kingdom of God is Within You*, Ruskin's *Unto this Last*, Thoreau's *On the Duty of Civil Disobedience*, or Plato's dialogues of Socrates (especially the *Apology* and *Crito*) are genuine eye-openers in this regard – many of Gandhi's favourite sayings or examples, and even whole areas of his philosophy, have been taken almost verbatim from these sources.

In the final analysis, because of his voluminous preserved writings, Gandhi himself would appear to be of great assistance in determining the influence of others on him. However, given the perhaps surprising lack of insight (not to mention deliberate obfuscation) in much autobiographical writing, how much weight should be put on Gandhi's own words, especially when he never set out to write a comprehensive autobiography at all, merely instructive snippets for the readers of his newspapers that were later bound together as *An Autobiography*? And what do we make of the claim by George Woodcock, for example, that the influences of Tolstoy and Ruskin on Gandhi can be exaggerated, and indeed that Gandhi himself was inclined to do so because of his humility, and that these authors merely

---

[2] See for example Howard Spodek, 'On the Origins of Gandhi's Political Methodology: The Heritage of Kathiawad and Gujarat', *Journal of Asian Studies* 30 (1970–1), pp. 361–72; and Stephen N. Hay, 'Jain Influences on Gandhi's Early Thought', in Sibnarayan Ray (ed.), *Gandhi, India and the World* (Melbourne: The Hawthorn Press, 1970), pp. 29–38.

strengthened concepts he had held into convictions,[3] and the claims of others who have gone so far as to call Tolstoy the 'founder of Gandhism'?[4] Choices have to be made and the following seem to me to be the texts and people who have had the greatest influence on the development of, or the strategic choices taken by, the young man who would become the Mahatma.

Some well-known influences upon Gandhi, such as Ruskin and Tolstoy, as well as Thoreau, various South African Christian missionaries, and Raychand, are discussed in his own writings. Others are more ephemeral. Erik Erikson and Victor Wolfenstein have written about the psychological influences that have gone into constructing Gandhi's nonviolent philosophy[5] and revolutionary personality,[6] Sudir Kakar about the psycho-sexual determinants of his behaviour,[7] and some new scholarship, for example the writings of Martin Green, looks at the influence of New Age intellectuals who helped to shape the Mahatma's persona.[8] Perhaps there is still something more to add.

I will briefly introduce the more or less well-known personal or textual influences. However my reading of Gandhi tells me that as complete as this list seems to be, somehow something seems to be missing. Gandhi had many other colleagues in his life, without whom his work could not have gone on. For example, one could not imagine Gandhi without his faithful secretary, and possibly alter-ego, Mahadev Desai. But Desai was an assistant to an already made Mahatma. Others who interacted closely with him, causing him joy and disappointment, were generally disciples who were influenced by him more than the other way around. Following the brief introduction to the better-known influences, I want to look at four figures in a little more depth. I believe that they were integral to the formation of Gandhi's philosophy in action yet are given insufficient attention in the Gandhi literature, seemingly because the Gandhian philosophy they influenced was not Gandhian political philosophy – the component of his overall philosophy that is too often elevated above the other important elements in the literature. They are instructive for a glimpse of the whole Gandhi, the combined political, social and spiritual, not merely the political, Gandhi.

[3] George Woodcock, *Gandhi* (London: Fontana, 1972), p. 25.
[4] Pyarelal, *Mahatma Gandhi, volume 1: The Early Phase* (Ahmedabad: Navajivan, 1965), p. 707.
[5] Erik H. Erikson, *Gandhi's Truth: On the Origins of Militant Nonviolence* (New York: Norton, 1969).
[6] E.Victor Wolfenstein, *The Revolutionary Personality: Lenin, Trotsky, Gandhi* (Princeton University Press, 1971).
[7] Sudhir Kakar, *Intimate Relations: Exploring Indian Sexuality* (The University of Chicago Press, 1989).
[8] Green, *Gandhi*.

In Gandhi's *Autobiography* there are chapters entitled 'A Tragedy' and 'A Tragedy (*Contd.*)'. These do not concern themselves with death of parents or some other large disaster. They are about his best friend in childhood. He calls this friendship 'a tragedy in my life'.[9] His friend, who was still alive at the time when the book was published, is not mentioned by name, yet, along with his wife Kasturbai, Sheikh Mehtab formed the major relationship in the life of the pre-London Gandhi.

Mehtab, whom Gandhi seems to have inherited as a friend from his elder brother Karsandas, was three years older than Mohandas, and a Muslim. By all accounts he was handsome, outgoing, fearless and a star athlete – everything that Gandhi was not. As Robert Payne puts it, he 'was the first friend he ever had, the first Muslim he had ever encountered, and the first person who ever made him eat meat. Their friendship was to have lasting consequences'.[10] Martin Green adds that 'because we know so little about Mehtab, and perhaps because what we do know is "merely" personal or anecdotal, he has been overlooked by most biographers. But he is surely one of the three or four keys to Gandhi's emotional development.'[11]

As a Muslim, Mehtab ate meat, and whether to merely corrupt his young friend or because he really believed that meat eating was necessary for strength so that the powerful, fearless and non-vegetarian Englishmen who dominated their country could be overcome, he induced Gandhi to do the same. Gandhi at first hated the experience and suffered nightmares. Later he quite relished the outings to a restaurant and did not suffer too greatly at these feasts if the dishes sufficiently disguised what it was that he was eating. What really upset Gandhi was that he had to do this in secret, knowing that his parents would be horrified if they found out. His sense of guilt turned him back to being a vegetarian.[12]

It seems that the virile Mehtab also decided that Gandhi was too devoted to his wife, that he did not have the freedom and power that men should have. He paid for his friend to visit a brothel, but the timid, tongue-tied Gandhi was rendered impotent and therefore saved when the prostitute 'naturally lost patience with me, and showed me the door, with abuses and insults'.[13] Before Gandhi set sail for England a cousin made a vague offer to help finance the trip. Sheikh Mehtab put pressure on this cousin by

---

[9] Gandhi, *An Autobiography*, p. 14.
[10] Robert Payne, *The Life and Death of Mahatma Gandhi* (London: The Bodley Head, 1969), p. 37.
[11] Green, *Gandhi*, p. 133.   [12] Gandhi, *An Autobiography*, pp. 15–17.   [13] *Ibid.*, p. 17.

reminding him of the promise in a letter he wrote and sent under Gandhi's forged signature. The cousin backed down, and from then on 'always acted the part of an enemy, speaking ill of me before everyone'.[14]

As a successful lawyer in South Africa, Gandhi had a large household and entertained often. He needed someone to oversee his household staff. Gandhi invited Mehtab from India to fill this role. Soon he had undermined the position of an innocent law clerk, who was also living in the household and of whom seemingly he was jealous. He 'managed to poison' Gandhi's mind against the clerk to the point where Gandhi suspected his honesty and dismissed him. The clerk 'left heart-broken'. Although on discovering the truth, Gandhi tried to make amends, the clerk never forgave him.[15] Apparently soon after, Gandhi caught Mehtab with a prostitute in the house and finally broke off the friendship.

Why did Gandhi have a friendship with such a person? According to Gandhi himself, he formed the friendship in the spirit of a reformer. He claims that he calculated wrongly in that 'a reformer cannot have close intimacy with whom he seeks to reform. True friendship is an identity of souls rarely to be found in this world. Only between like natures can friendship be altogether worthy and enduring. Friends react on one another. Hence in friendship there is very little scope for reform.'[16] That the friendship was formed in the spirit of a reformer can be doubted. Mehtab seemed to be a hero figure to young Gandhi and this particular gloss on the relationship came from an instalment of his instructive 'Experiments with Truth' *Autobiography*. Erik Erikson, in his psycho-political analysis of Gandhi, claims that Mehtab's role in Gandhi's life was one of elemental significance 'not only because the young Muslim was such a "devil," but because Mohandas chose him and stubbornly held onto him in order to test . . . the devil in himself'.[17]

To the timid mother's boy, Mehtab must have provided an 'adolescent haven where young men can be both dismissive and fearful of women and heterosexual love, where in the vague homoeroticism of masculine banter and ceaseless activity a youth can gradually come to terms with the femininity within and without him'.[18] However, there may have been more to it than that. Gandhi was warned of Mehtab's bad influence, his family disliked him, and he often quarrelled with his friend. It almost seems as though Gandhi was addicted to him.

---

[14] Pyarelal, *Mahatma Gandhi, volume I: The Early Phase*, p. 221.   [15] *Ibid.*, p. 492.
[16] Gandhi, *An Autobiography*, p. 14.   [17] Erikson, *Gandhi's Truth*, p. 135.
[18] Kakar, *Intimate Relations*, p. 88.

Erikson notes that in his writings Gandhi could feel the need to make an example of Mehtab to warn youth against false friends (and he does so in a way that protected his anonymity), and adds that if Mehtab had not existed he would have to have been invented.[19] Nevertheless, this relationship coloured Gandhi's views of future relationships. Green sees that a pattern of 'suspicion, jealousy, conspiracy, accusation . . . was the life of the emotions, of the "exclusive relationship," as Gandhi knew it. It is no wonder that he had to renounce that life.' He adds that 'Gandhi remained suspicious of exclusive relationships ever after, even in friendship.'[20]

In his high school days, Gandhi had only two intimate friends and one of these did not last long. Although Gandhi claims never to have forsaken this friend, the friend left because of Mehtab.[21] In his writings Gandhi implies a divide and rule approach by Mehtab who could dominate Gandhi in a way as to cause him confusion and turn him against innocent friends who would then leave. Soon Mehtab was causing problems between Gandhi and his spouse Kasturbai[22] when he 'fanned the flame of my suspicions about my wife'. Mehtab persuaded the teenager Gandhi that he had to exercise dominance over her, controlling her life totally and forcing her to tell him of all her movements. He claims to have often pained his wife 'by acting on his information'. Perhaps worse, although Kasturbai did not like Mehtab and the hold he had over her husband, when studying in London Gandhi sent letters to his young illiterate wife via Mehtab to read to her. He drove his wife to the point where, in a state of desperation, she threatened to leave. Looking back, even forty years later, he could still write that he never forgave himself for his actions. He adds, 'Whenever I think of those dark days of doubts and suspicions, I am filled with loathing of my folly and my lustful cruelty, and I deplore my blind devotion to my friend.'[23]

This relationship with his manipulative friend really did seem to haunt Gandhi. In 1940 there were problems at Sevagram Ashram while he was present. A pen and letter were stolen from his wife's room. Gandhi was obviously distressed, he was suspicious of his co-workers and there was quarrelling in the Ashram. Green notes that his anger 'swelled out of all control and reason,' and that the nervous agitation that Gandhi had occasionally exhibited returned.[24] Gandhi claimed to be a 'wholly incompetent person' – if such things can occur while he is in the Ashram his

[19] Erikson, *Gandhi's Truth*, p. 135.   [20] Green, *Gandhi*, p. 131.
[21] Gandhi, *An Autobiography*, p. 14.
[22] When she became a mother Kasturbai became known as Kasturba, or, as head of Gandhi's household, simply Ba (grandmother).
[23] Gandhi, *An Autobiography*, p. 18.   [24] Green, *Gandhi*, pp. 207, 356.

penance must have been defective.[25] The incident was relatively trivial and Gandhi's response was out of all proportion. He threatened to go on a fast until the responsible person confessed. Following protests from his secretaries Mahadev Desai and Pyarelal, Gandhi finally called off his intention to fast. 'What is of most interest in this incident', notes Green, 'is that Gandhi traced his storm of the nerves and emotions to the way the incident had evoked in him traumatic memories of Sheikh Mehtab: he had thought someone was making him suspect someone else, just as Mehtab had so successfully done, in Rajkot, and in Durban.'[26] In a note to his colleagues, Gandhi is reflective of his troubled relationship with Mehtab, and consequently with his wife:

You know what a terrific quarrel I had with Ba over my suspicion: she stayed away from me for a whole year. How shall I say what other things I did. But Ba showed courage. In the end, after four or more years, my suspicion was dispelled. It was not a matter of stealing. It was something worse. You do not know me! How could I have told you all this? Sheikh Mehtab was behind this. He kept me under his thumb for more than ten years. On his suggestion, I came to doubt the character of Ba. I broke her bangles, refused to have anything to do with her and sent her away to her parents. The hatchet was buried only after my return from England. It was then that I realized fully after many years how wicked Sheikh Mehtab was. He threatened me many times.[27]

At the age of thirty-seven Gandhi was to take a vow of celibacy and went on to become an ardent advocate of chastity, even within marriage. Some of this had to do with Hindu approaches to spirituality, some with his own psychological problems with sexuality,[28] but they also had to do with the exclusivity of an overly close relationship. Gandhi, who was striving to devote his life to the service of humanity, saw a close bond, such as that usually found in marriage, an impediment. If one devotes oneself to a life partner 'a boundary wall' will be created 'around their love' which prevents them from looking 'upon all mankind as kith and kin'.[29] These sentiments, which were originally penned in relationship to marital bonds, seem to have been taken to heart by Gandhi in connection with other relationships

---

[25] See 'To Segaon Workers', 3 June 1940.
[26] Green, *Gandhi*, p. 356. During this incident, Gandhi refers to Sheikh Mehtab several times. See 'Note to Pyarelal and Mahadev Desai', 7 June 1940; and 'Note', 8 June 1940.
[27] See 'A Note', written sometime after 3 June 1940, *CWMG*, LXXII, p. 127.
[28] See Lloyd I. Rudolph and Susanne Hoeber Rudolph, *The Modernity of Tradition: Political Developments in India* (University of Chicago Press, 1967), pp. 200–16; and Vinay Lal, 'Nakedness, Non-Violence and the Negation of Negation: Gandhi's Experiments in *Brahmacharya* and Celibate Sexuality', *South Asia* 22 (1999), pp. 63–94.
[29] M. K. Gandhi, *From Yeravda Mandir* (Ahmedabad: Navajivan, 1932), p. 7.

also. After Mehtab, Gandhi did have very intense other relationships, but while the friendships often endured for lengthy periods the intensity that could have slipped into exclusiveness never again did. The relationship with Henry Polak in 1904–5 seemed to be heading that way and again so did the relationship with Hermann Kallenbach a few years later, but they did not. Following this, with the exception of Gandhi's seeming infatuation, and the spiritual turmoil it caused, with Saraladevi Chaudhurani in 1920, Gandhi contented himself with many co-workers and disciples. It could be said that he loved some of these associates but no one was ever again the exclusive object of his affection. This could be almost inevitable in the development of an increasingly famous person who tends to attract followers rather than equals but also it could be at least partly the legacy of the troubled relationship that the young Gandhi had with Sheikh Mehtab.

LONDON NEW AGERS AND SELF-RESPECT

Devanesan, the chronicler of the elements that went into changing Mohandas Gandhi into the Mahatma, poses the question: 'Could Gandhi have become a Mahatma if he had never gone to England, never walked the streets of London?'[30] Before Gandhi embarked for London to obtain the qualifications of an English barrister, he had solemnly vowed to his mother that he would abstain from alcohol, meat and women during his overseas sojourn. At first he was intent on being a proper English gentleman by way of the expensive lodgings he stayed at, the fashionable clothes he wore and the dancing, French, elocution and violin lessons he took. Soon he realised that he could not afford the extravagance of his lifestyle, and that on an English diet, minus the meat, he was slowly starving. He could have modified his lifestyle to make some savings and taken to an English diet like many of his young Indian contemporaries in London, but, instead, he kept his vow and his life took a path that could not have been predicted just months before.

In 1888, a few days short of his nineteenth birthday, having left his wife and infant son behind, Gandhi arrived in a strange and exotic London at perhaps the most impressionable stage of his life. Soon he was mixing in a circle of New Agers, talking with them and writing for their periodicals. Many of them, and many of the currents that flowed through their social groups, had a profound impact on the young student.

---

[30] D. S. Devanesen, *The Making of the Mahatma* (New Delhi: Orient Longmans, 1969), p. 219.

Devanesan notes that some biographers state that the discovery of vegetarian restaurants and vegetarianism started Gandhi on his 'life of ascetic
holiness and a return to the religious and moral ideas enshrined in the
Vaishnava practice of vegetarianism'[31] of his family and his own youth. He
adds that it also did two other things for Gandhi: it started him on his
career of an organiser (when he set up a vegetarian club in Bayswater),
speaker, journalist and propagandist, as well as bringing him into contact
with all sorts of intellectuals, writers and free thinkers, most influenced
by Ruskin (and Tolstoy and Thoreau, priming him for the great impact
these writers would have on his life in the years to come), and many in
some way reacting radically against industrialism and western civilisation
and expressing sympathy for the working class. Vegetarianism gave him the
'habit of meeting prominent people' and 'the germ of the Indian agitation in
South Africa lay in the young Gandhi's experience of Vegetarian activities in
England'.[32]

The first year of Gandhi's stay in London was not academically rigorous
and his time was spent acquainting himself with English life and current
affairs through his daily reading of several newspapers. Following a period
of much more intense study, he passed his Bar Finals in December 1890.
Although the formal part of his studies was over, he was required to remain
in London until June, attending the required dinners, known as 'keeping
terms'. This gave him an uncommitted half year, 'the most free, and perhaps
the happiest and most social period of his time in London',[33] which he
applied to increasing the frugality of his living and deepening his activities
with the Vegetarian Society (of which he had been a member since his early
days in the city) and the Theosophists.

When Gandhi heard that there were vegetarian restaurants in London,
he went in search of them: 'I would trot ten or twelve miles each day,
go into a cheap restaurant and eat my fill of bread, but would never be
satisfied' until he finally stumbled across *The Central*. 'The sight of it filled
me with the same joy that a child feels on getting a thing after its own
heart.'[34] Here, about a month after his arrival in England, he had his first
hearty meal and purchased Henry Salt's booklet, *A Plea for Vegetarianism*,
the tract that made him a vegetarian by choice. Soon he was eating regularly
at the various vegetarian restaurants that he had come to know, reading the
vegetarian papers and the books they recommended.

[31] *Ibid.*, p. 180.   [32] *Ibid.*, p. 185.
[33] James D. Hunt, *Gandhi in London* (New Delhi: Promilla, 1978), p. 27.
[34] Gandhi, *An Autobiography*, p. 35.

Gandhi became a member of the London Vegetarian Society Executive Committee in September 1890, and wrote articles for *The Vegetarian* on Indian vegetarians and Indian festivals. In May 1891, just over a month before he sailed for home, Gandhi was invited as a delegate to the Vegetarian Federal Union conference in Portsmouth. His paper on 'The Foods of India', shortly to be published in the *Vegetarian Messenger*, evoked great interest and discussion and was admired by vegetarians much senior to himself[35] and he even helped design the badge of the Society.[36] The shallow, uncertain youth trying to further his personal ambition was finally starting to show the signs of competence which would become his hallmark in later years.

His time in London was spent among nonconformists and radicals, the people Martin Green calls New Agers. As a leading force in this progressive movement, vegetarianism, as much about idealistic thinking and action as about diet options,[37] took on the proportions of a religious sect for Gandhi. It offered him fellowship and identity, as well as an ethic which naturally incorporated dietary prescriptions.[38]

One of the currents flowing through this New Age quasi sect was the work of Shelley. The metaphysical poet, Percy Bysshe Shelley was also a political rebel and he influenced Thoreau's writing on civil disobedience and thus indirectly had some impact on Gandhi in South Africa. Was there also a more direct link? Gandhi does not mention Shelley very often in his writings, although he does seem to know Shelley's poem the *Masque of Anarchy*, which encapsulates his ideas of bringing about the conversion of a foe through self-suffering, and quotes it in later life.[39] Shelley's political ideas revolve around two principles: first, that the individual changes society, rather than the other way around; and, second, a fundamental belief in the dictates of the individual conscience, even if it goes against government rules.[40] These ideas are recurrent themes in Gandhi's own writings throughout his life.

In the vegetarian circles in which he moved, and in the vegetarian books and journals he read, Shelley and his ideas on nonviolence were often topics of discussion. Salt's booklet was his entré into the world of vegetarianism, journalism and public speaking. While he did not know Salt well, he was

[35] Pyarelal, *Mahatma Gandhi, volume I: The Early Phase*, p. 265.
[36] Henry S. L. Polak, 'Some South African Reminiscences', in Chandrashanker Shukla (ed.), *Incidents of Gandhiji's Life* (Bombay: Vora, 1949), p. 241.
[37] Green, *Gandhi*, p. 95.   [38] Hunt, *Gandhi in London*, p. 30.
[39] See 'Discussion with Christian Missionaries', *Harijan*, 14 December 1938. The poem exhorted those opposing tyranny to resist their oppressors nonviolently, by shaming them through self-suffering.
[40] Madhu Benoit, 'The Mahatma and the Poet', *Gandhi Marg* 19 (1997), p. 307.

an avid reader of Salt's writings. And, amongst other things, Salt was an authority on Shelley (and Thoreau). It has been claimed that 'It is practically impossible that Gandhi did not imbibe Shelley's ideas in some form or other during his contacts with all these people.'[41] After concluding that Gandhi was indeed influenced by Shelley, Benoit asks why Gandhi, who was characterised by honesty and readily acknowledged his intellectual debts, did not count Shelley among his mentors. She claims that it may have had to do with their diametrically opposite views on sexuality: while Shelley sought to abolish sexual taboos, Gandhi sought to abolish sex. Shelley rejected sexless love and loveless sex. For Gandhi love and sex inhabited different universes.

Gandhi was in London during a Shelley revival, the functioning of the Shelley Society more or less corresponded with Gandhi's stay, and many members of the Vegetarian Society were also members of this society. Shelley's views on birth control were hotly debated in Salt's circle and his views on 'free love' were frequent topics of conversation. Possibly Gandhi was influenced, even deeply influenced, but perhaps he did not want to direct people to read Shelley, the way he later directed them to read Plato, Ruskin, Tolstoy and Thoreau, in case they took the wrong message from the poet.[42]

The vegetarians also had an interest in theosophy, and although Gandhi was not very impressed with its occult teachings, he found in it a welcome message of universal brotherhood, of the unity at the core of all religious teachings, and of the high regard in which Hinduism was held. While his serious study of his own religion did not commence until his days in South Africa, under the guidance of Raychandbhai, it was the theosophists who first encouraged in him the desire to read the *Bhagavad Gita* (in the form of Edwin Arnold's translation titled *The Song Celestial*). During his London days, Gandhi was in a state of spiritual seeking. He visited churches and listened to sermons, but the theosophists touched him most closely. Hunt concludes that Gandhi initially suffered under the 'colonial mentality' which took him from his heritage to adopt the ways of the west, but 'was stimulated by this eccentric but lively group of Westerners to value his own heritage.'[43] He became an associate member of the London

[41] *Ibid.*, p. 313.

[42] Gandhi has held up others as models while not informing his audience of everything the models may have done. For instance, he occasionally lauded the commitment and actions of the English suffragettes as models of satyagraha while omitting references to their destruction of property. See for example James D. Hunt, 'Suffragettes and Satyagraha', *Indo-British Review* 9 (1981), p. 70.

[43] Hunt, *Gandhi in London*, p. 34.

Theosophical Society by joining the Blavatsky Lodge three months before leaving London.

Gandhi's life seems to have struck a deep chord with a great many Christians. They supported him and even saw him as one of their own, and on his death he was hailed as someone who was more Christian than many of those who had been christened into the faith. And in turn, throughout his life, the Sermon on the Mount and the message of Christ's life were often mentioned in his speeches as examples of the way to live. He lauded the Christian approach to service to humankind, and his abiding love for Christian hymns ensured that they were often sung at his ashram prayer meetings. There was a lot about Gandhi that seemed Christian and to a large degree it originated in his first year in South Africa.

The Reverend Joseph Doke, an English Baptist minister who was one of Gandhi's close friends during his middle period in South Africa, and who later became Gandhi's first biographer, noted that Gandhi 'is not a Christian in any orthodox sense'.[44] He lays the blame for this at the feet of an orthodox Christianity which practised discrimination against Indians, and with Tolstoy. Doke notes that, 'Undoubtedly Count Tolstoi has profoundly influenced him. The old Russian reformer, in the simplicity of his life, the fearlessness of his utterances, and the nature of his teaching on war and work, has found a warmhearted disciple in Mr. Gandhi. I think, too, very probably, the Count's representation of the Christian Church has had its weight with him, and his own experience of Christian Churches has not been sufficiently happy to withstand it.'[45]

In other words, Gandhi was close to converting to Christianity in his South Africa days but was a committed Hindu (with some Christian trimmings) by the time he returned to India. Between the serious spiritual questing engendered by the London New Agers, and solace he received from Raychandbhai, the Protestant Christians left their mark on the Mahatma-to-be.

From his limited encounters with Christian missionaries as a child, Gandhi had a low regard for Christians.[46] On his second day in Pretoria, where he was to undertake the work which brought him to South Africa,

---

[44] Joseph J. Doke, *M. K. Gandhi: An Indian Patriot in South Africa* (The London Indian Chronicle, 1909), p. 148.
[45] *Ibid.*, p. 134.   [46] Gandhi, *An Autobiography*, pp. 24–5.

he met and befriended the attorney retained by Abdulla, Albert Weir Baker. Besides being a lawyer, Baker was the local head of the South African General Mission and committed lay preacher. It did not take him long to ascertain Gandhi's religious views. Gandhi informed him that: 'I am a Hindu by birth. And yet I do not know much of Hinduism, and I know less of other religions. In fact I do not know where I am, and what is and what should be my belief. I intend to make a careful study of my own religion and, as far as I can, of other religions as well.'[47]

What proselytising Christian could ask for more? Baker immediately invited Gandhi to his daily prayer circle, and the next day Gandhi was present. Hunt believes that Gandhi must have attended more than 100 of these meetings in the coming months. The participants knelt and asked God for peace or to open their hearts (at times with specific reference to Gandhi's).[48] Gandhi was young, impressionable and alone in a foreign land without family or friends. These people cared for him in a land of colour prejudice, they 'seemed attractive as sponsors into the life of the white world, and he was open to their arguments'.[49]

At his first prayer meeting Gandhi made the acquaintance of Quaker Michael Coates. Coates took over Gandhi's religious education, taking him to meet other Christians, giving him Christian literature, engaging him in religious discussion and even reading Gandhi's religious diary every week. Coates became his guide, 'almost an elder brother'.[50] Baker, in the hope that 'the enthusiasm and earnestness of the people attending it, would inevitably lead me to embrace Christianity',[51] took Gandhi to a Protestant revival convention in Wellington. Many at the convention were praying for Gandhi, however he could not understand why his salvation depended on him becoming a Christian – and when he 'said so to some good Christian friends, they were shocked. But there was no help for it.'[52] Hunt notes that the excitement of the convention was obviously one of the highlights of Gandhi's year in Pretoria, and probably the climax of Baker's efforts at securing his conversion.[53] With some humour, Gandhi reports that they desired his conversion so fervently that they would have become vegetarians if it had influenced him to become a Christian.[54]

This intensive encounter with the South African General Mission members, which lasted from June to October 1893, left a lasting impression on

---

[47] *Ibid.*, p. 87.
[48] James D. Hunt, *Gandhi and the Nonconformists: Encounters in South Africa* (New Delhi: Promilla, 1986), p. 29.
[49] *Ibid.*, p. xii. [50] *Ibid.*, p. 30. [51] Gandhi, *An Autobiography*, p. 97. [52] *Ibid.*, p. 98.
[53] Hunt, *Gandhi and the Nonconformists*, p. 35. [54] Doke, *M. K. Gandhi*, p. 58.

Gandhi. His friends and events such as the Wellington convention whetted his appetite for knowledge and maintained his interest in religion. Of this period, Gandhi recalls that he shared his 'mental churning' with his Christian friends 'whenever there was an opportunity, but their answers could not satisfy me'.[55]

Gandhi notes that, although he took a path that his Christian friends had not intended for him, he was to remain forever indebted to them 'for the religious quest that they awakened'.[56] The missionaries pushed for his conversion but in the end he was to reject Christianity because he could not accept the claimed uniqueness of Christian revelation, which in turn made him reject the missionary way of inducing conversion – because he believed in rebirth, because he felt that Hinduism better exemplified renunciation, and because, as Doke had noted, he could not reconcile religion with the racism of a majority of the white population.

While the efforts of his early Christian contacts did not yield the results they desired, they did have other outcomes. As Devanesan notes, these discussions and the reading of the 'heavy works' they directed him to, 'provided a rigorous discipline which sharpened and stimulated Gandhi's mind', and helped him marshal his arguments against Christianity and for Hinduism.[57] And a result of this religious ferment was that he read Tolstoy's *The Kingdom of God is Within You* and started corresponding with Raychandbhai.

During his second year in South Africa, Gandhi was finding more interest in alternative interpretations of Christianity which seemed capable of accommodating his strengthening belief system in a way that seemed to provide a bridge between himself and his Christian friends. He was again writing articles for *The Vegetarian*, and soon selling books by Anna Kingsford and Edward Maitland as the 'Agent for the Esoteric Christian Union and the London Vegetarian Society'.[58] Kingsford and Maitland had been leaders of the British Theosophical Society but eventually left because of their overwhelming interest in Christianity and formed the sect of the ECU. Gandhi had carried on a long correspondence with Maitland and as a result joined the movement. Maitland sent him a copy of his and Kingsford's book, *The Perfect Way or the Finding of Christ*, and his own *The New Interpretation of the Bible*. Gandhi liked the books because 'they seemed to support Hinduism'.[59] The books accepted the rebirth and the essential

[55] Gandhi, *An Autobiography*, p. 99.   [56] *Ibid.*, p. 100.
[57] Devanesen, *The Making of the Mahatma*, p. 258.
[58] See ads in the *Natal Mercury*, 28 November 1894; and *Natal Advertiser*, 2 February 1895.
[59] Gandhi, *An Autobiography*, p. 99.

unity of God and the individual soul, reconciling Christianity with other religions. Now he prepared to distribute ECU literature in South Africa. In a letter from Durban, he states that

During my stay here I intend to spread as much as possible information about theosophy. (To me there is little difference between Theosophy and Esoteric Christianity). I have therefore sent out letters to the President of the Vegetarian Society and Mrs. Besant. I propose that the E.C.U. should send me a selection of books to be sold here. I would sell the books at cost price plus the postage and 5% commission to be kept by me.[60]

This is as near as he came to formal affiliation with a brand of Christianity (although one which orthodox Christians would not have recognised). Soon after this time we find a Gandhi more secure in his own faith who 'no longer considered being a theosophist, or an Esoteric Christian, or even an evangelical Christian'.[61]

RAYCHANDBHAI AND GANDHI'S CERTAINTY ABOUT HIS RELIGION

When Gandhi arrived in London on 27 October 1888 to undertake his legal studies, he carried with him four letters of introduction. One was to fellow Gujarati Dr P. J. Mehta. Gandhi had cabled him from Southampton and he called on the somewhat confused and out of place young Oriental. He gave Gandhi some basic advice for survival in the strange land: 'Do not touch other people's things. Do not ask questions as we usually do in India on first acquaintance; do not talk loudly; never address people as "sir" whilst speaking to them as we do in India; only servants and subordinates address their masters that way.'[62] But Dr Mehta was to do Gandhi an even larger favour next time Mohandas got off a ship after a long voyage. On 6 July 1891, Gandhi's elder brother met the returning lawyer in Bombay. He then took him to stay at Dr Mehta's house (now the Bombay Gandhi museum Mani Bhavan) and informed him of their mother's death. Through Mehta, Gandhi met Shrimad Rajachandra (whom Gandhi affectionately called Raychandbhai), a relative of the doctor's by marriage. Raychand worked in the family jewellery business and was known for his good character

---

[60] Letter to Mrs A. M. Lewis, one of the founders of the ECU whom Gandhi knew from his London days, 4 August 1894.
[61] James D. Hunt, 'Gandhi and the Theosophists', in V. T. Patil (ed.), *Studies on Gandhi* (New Delhi: Sterling, 1983), p. 170.
[62] Gandhi, *An Autobiography*, p. 32.

and learning and for his photographic memory. While his feats of memory did not greatly impress Gandhi, Raychand's wide knowledge of the scriptures and 'burning passion for self-realization' did.[63] Soon they were fast friends – after all they both came from Saurashtra, were of the same caste, spoke the same language, were close in age and in interests were kindred spirits.

Raychand would engage Gandhi in 'conversations of a serious religious nature' and would become his 'refuge' in times of spiritual crisis. In his *Autobiography*, Gandhi notes that 'Three moderns have left a deep impress on my life, and captivated me: Raychandbhai by his living contact; Tolstoy by his book, *The Kingdom of God is Within You*, and Ruskin by his *Unto This Last*.'[64] Further, Gandhi states that during his time of spiritual questing he tried to meet the heads of various faiths and since then had met many spiritual leaders and teachers, yet 'no one else has ever made on me the impression that Raychandbhai did. His words went straight home to me.'[65]

As noted above, in his earliest days in South Africa Gandhi came into close contact with devoted proselytising Christians and spent much time in religious debate with them. His religious yearnings had these friends see Gandhi as a potential convert (and it seems that his Muslim friends also had the same idea), and it appears that he came close. However Gandhi felt that, until he had studied the teachings of his own faith and decided that they did not satisfy his longings, he should not renounce it. He started reading religious books widely, and for clarity he placed his doubts before them and 'entered into correspondence with every person in India in whom I had some trust, Raychandbhai being the chief among them'.[66] Gandhi and the anti-clerical Jain Raychand, whom some considered to be the twenty-fifth tirthankara (sage or master) and someone who had attained moksha, kept up a correspondence on religious matters until the latter's death.[67] Raychand advised him to be patient and to study Hinduism more deeply.[68]

---

[63] For Raychand's life, see Gandhi's lengthy 'Preface' to *Shrimad Rajchandra*, the second edition of Raychand's letters and writings, written on 5 November 1926; Digish Mehta, *Shrimad Rajchandra – A Life* (Ahmedabad: Shrimad Rajchandra Janama Shatabdi Mandal, 1978); and Green, *Gandhi*, pp. 81–4.

[64] Gandhi, *An Autobiography*, pp. 63–5. 'I have said elsewhere that in moulding my inner life Tolstoy and Ruskin vied with Kavi [the poet, a name by which Raychand was known]. But Kavi's influence was undoubtedly deeper if only because I had come in closest personal touch with him.' See 'A Great Seer', *Modern Review*, June 1930.

[65] Gandhi, *An Autobiography*, p. 64.   [66] Gandhi, 'Preface', *CWMG*, XXXII, pp. 1–13 at p. 4.

[67] In Jain tradition Mahavira, a contemporary of the Buddha, was the twenty-fourth tirthankara.

[68] Gandhi, *An Autobiography*, p. 99.

Raychand gave Gandhi 'peace of mind' in his time of spiritual turmoil and gave him the reassurance that Hinduism could give him 'what
I needed'.[69] He no longer had to consider changing his faith because, 'I
became convinced that those [religious ideas] we can accept are found in
Hinduism. Raychandbhai was responsible for bringing me to this position.
The reader can thus imagine how much my respect for him must have
increased.'[70] In a letter to his friend Henry Polak, Gandhi recommends
that everyone at the Phoenix Settlement should read Tolstoy and that the
Gujaratis among them should also read Raychand because

The more I consider his life and his writings, the more I consider him to have
been the best Indian of his times. Indeed, I put him much higher than Tolstoy in
religious perception. The books I have read have afforded me the highest solace.
They should be read over and over again. So far as English books are concerned,
Tolstoy is incomparable in my opinion in chastity of thought. His definition of
the purpose of life is unanswerable and easy to understand. Both Kavi and Tolstoy
have lived as they have preached.[71]

It seems that Raychand was also instrumental in implanting in Gandhi
seeds of a thought that would lead, for the Mahatma-to-be, to the logical
conclusion of celibacy even within marriage[72] – one which he finally took in
the year of Raychand's death and when he had become a father for the fourth
time, and one that led to his various experiments in diet when Raychand first
informed him that 'milk stimulated animal passion'.[73] In fact Gandhi noted
that Raychand had written that 'unadulterated brahmacharya' (celibacy)
requires the giving up of milk.[74]

At about the time Gandhi was starting his independent legal career and
entering the public political arena, on 20 October 1894, Raychand wrote
him a lengthy letter in reply to Gandhi's twenty-seven questions about
matters spiritual. They broached such topics as: What is the soul? What
is God? What do you think of Christianity? Can anyone remember past
lives? Can salvation be attained through faith in Krishna? And an answer
to a question that would have practical consequences for Gandhi and his
later Tolstoy Farm community as they embarked on a rural life in a snake-
infested location: 'If a snake is about to bite me, should I allow myself to

---

[69] Gandhi, 'Preface', p. 4.
[70] Quoted in Hay, 'Jain Influences on Gandhi's Early Thought', p. 35.
[71] Letter to H. S. L. Polak, 26 April 1909. See also 'Speech at Rajchandra Birth Anniversary, Ahmedabad,
The Bombay Chronicle, 23 November 1915.
[72] Gandhi, *An Autobiography*, p. 149.
[73] *Ibid.*, p. 242.   [74] Letter to Maganlal, sometime in 1914, see *CWMG*, xcvii, pp. 7–8.

be bitten or should I kill it, supposing that that is the only way in which I can save myself?' Raychand answered:

One hesitates to advise you that you should let the snake bite you. Nevertheless, how can it be right for you, if you have realized that the body is perishable, to kill, for protecting a body which has no real value to you, a creature which clings to it with love? For anyone who desires his spiritual welfare, the best course is to let his body perish in such circumstances. But how should a person who does not desire spiritual welfare behave? My only reply to such a question is, how can I advise such a person that he should pass through hell and similar worlds, that is, that he should kill the snake? If the person lacks the culture of Aryan character, one may advise him to kill the snake, but we should wish that neither you nor I will even dream of being such a person.[75]

In the battle for Gandhi's soul, Raychand defeated the South African General Mission. Even after Raychand's death in 1901, his presence continued to be felt in Gandhi's life. Gandhi referred to him and his influence throughout his life, one of Raychand's Ahmedabad disciples, the businessman Punjabhai Shah, found the land for the ashram at Sabarmati and administered its finances,[76] and the religious teacher's compositions were included among the Ashram *bhajans* (devotional songs).[77]

JOHN RUSKIN AND GANDHI'S ECONOMIC PHILOSOPHY

In a Johannesburg vegetarian restaurant, Gandhi met two of his closest early colleagues – Albert West and Henry Polak. At a request from Gandhi, West took charge of *Indian Opinion*, a money losing paper published in Durban that Gandhi had been financing and writing for before he finally took it over. West's first report to Gandhi was that the paper was in even worse financial shape than feared. On 1 October 1904 Gandhi set off to put things right. It was a twenty-four-hour train trip from Johannesburg to Durban and when Polak saw Gandhi off at the station he gave him a book that he 'was sure to like' to read on the journey.

That book was John Ruskin's classic political tract, *Unto This Last*. Gandhi couldn't put it down. The book resonated with some of the deep convictions that Gandhi was gradually coming to. It caused him a sleepless night and, there and then, he made a resolution to 'change my life in accordance with the ideals of the book'. Gandhi claimed that the book 'brought

---

[75] Gandhi wrote to Raychand sometime before June 1894 with a list of 27 questions, *CWMG*, I, pp. 90–1, and Appendix I in *CWMG*, xxxiii, pp. 593–602.
[76] See 'Long Live Punjabhai!', in 'Diary 1932', 23 October 1932.
[77] See Letter to Krishnachandra, 15 January 1946.

about an instantaneous and practical transformation in my life'.[78] He later translated (or more accurately, paraphrased) the book into Gujarati under the title of *Sarvodaya* (the welfare of all) and sarvodaya was to become a central plank of Gandhi's philosophy.[79] In short, through this book, it may not be a great exaggeration to call Ruskin the father of Gandhian economic thought.[80]

Gandhi summarised the teachings of the book under three truths:

(1) The good of the individual is contained in the good of all.
(2) That a lawyer's work has the same value as the barber's inasmuch as all have the same right of earning their livelihood from their work.
(3) That a life of labour, i.e., the life of the tiller of the soil and the handi-craftsman is the life worth living.[81]

Gandhi added: 'The first of these I knew. The second I had dimly realized. The third had never occurred to me.[82] *Unto This Last* made it clear as daylight for me that the second and the third were contained in the first.' The chapter in his *Autobiography* where Gandhi recounts this conversion, he titles 'The Magic Spell of a Book'.

The thirty-five-year-old Gandhi immediately took steps to remove the press to a rural setting where all involved should labour for the same living wage and attend the press in their spare time. In his seventies, Gandhi was to recall that the book 'transformed me overnight from a lawyer and city-dweller into a rustic living away from Durban on a farm, three miles from the nearest railway station'.[83] And so in 1904, Phoenix Settlement was founded. Gandhi the wealthy lawyer started simplifying his life and moving towards self-sufficiency while still keeping his flourishing legal practice going.

In the introduction to the English retranslation of Gandhi's paraphrase of Ruskin's tract (by Gandhi's colleague Valji Govind Desai), the Mahatma tells us that in the West physical and economic well-being is sought in disregard of morality and that this is contrary to divine law, 'as some

---

[78] Gandhi, *An Autobiography*, p. 220.
[79] See M. K. Gandhi, *Sarvodaya (The Welfare of All)* (Navajivan: Ahmedabad, 1954).
[80] Elizabeth T. McLaughlin, *Ruskin and Gandhi* (Cranbury, NJ: Associated University Presses, 1974). p. 25.
[81] Gandhi, *An Autobiography*, p. 221.
[82] Ashe maintains that Gandhi misunderstood the book because the second maxim was not there and the third only doubtfully. He adds that he 'read them into the text himself' out of his dim realisation which in turn was 'an amalgam of Tolstoy, Edward Carpenter's Simple Life doctrine, the memory of Mariann Hill [the Trappist monastery near Durban that he was very impressed by when he visited it in April 1895], the theory of Ashram in Hindu religion, and the theory of corporate property in Hindu Law.' See Geoffrey Ashe, *Gandhi: A Study in Revolution* (Heinemann: London, 1968), p. 83.
[83] Letter to American Friends, 3 August 1942.

wise men in the West have shown'. Of course here Gandhi is referring to
Ruskin who proclaimed that 'men can be happy only if they obey the moral
law'.[84]

John Ruskin, who had died four years before the founding of the
settlement, had achieved fame as the leading European authority on art and
architecture. In later life he gave up his art work to concentrate on issues of
social justice. He renounced his ancestral property, and advocated 'social
affection' and compassion instead of exploitation.[85] He believed in self-
sacrifice for the sake of community welfare and championed social reforms
such as old age pensions, universal free education and better housing, and
he always regarded *Unto This Last* as the central book of his life and 'the
truest, rightest-worded, and most serviceable'.[86]

McLaughlin, in her impressive study of Ruskin and Gandhi, points out
that 'Ruskin influenced Gandhi's conception of soul-force as a substitute
for physical force; he was the chief source of Gandhian economic idea; but
above all, he changed Gandhi as a person'[87] and this was far more than
influence – the suddenness of this change was more akin to an instantaneous religious conversion. She adds that 'Gandhi's discovery of Ruskin's
book was as significant a contribution to his development and as genuine
an encounter between two deeply concerned human beings as any actual
meeting could have been.' McLaughlin further notes that Ruskin once told
an admirer that he did not care whether the person had enjoyed his books
or not, the important question was 'Have they done you any good?' She
concludes that, although Ruskin was to suffer bouts of insanity in his later
life, partly because of his own inconsistencies in living up to his own beliefs,
Unto This Last did Gandhi, and through him the world, good.[88]

TOLSTOY AND GANDHI'S LAW OF LOVE

In response to the question, asked during an interview in London with
Evelyn Wrench, the editor of *The Spectator*, 'Did any book ever affect you
supremely and was there any turning point in your life?', Gandhi replied
that he changed the whole plan of his life after reading Ruskin's *Unto This
Last*, adding that 'Tolstoy I had read much earlier. He affected the inner

---

[84] M. K. Gandhi, *Ruskin: Unto This Last A Paraphrase* (Navajivan: Ahmedabad, 1951), p. 1; and 'John
   Ruskin', (Gujarati) *Indian Opinion*, 16 May 1908.
[85] See Benudhar Pradhan, *The Socialist Thought of Mahatma Gandhi* (Delhi: GDK, 1980), vol. 1, p. 24.
[86] McLaughlin, *Ruskin and Gandhi*, pp. 21–2. See also Amalendu Bose, 'Gandhi and Ruskin: Ideological
   Affinities', in C. D. Narasimhaiah (ed.), *Gandhi and the West* (University of Mysore Press, 1969),
   pp. 128–44.
[87] McLaughlin, *Ruskin and Gandhi*, p. 15.   [88] *Ibid.*, p. 22.

being'.[89] Gandhi's chief biographer and secretary in later life, Pyarelal, claims that so deeply was Gandhi's thinking 'impregnated with Tolstoy's that the changes that took place in his way of life and thinking in the years that followed [his reading of Tolstoy] can be correctly understood and appreciated only in the context of the master's life and philosophy'.[90]

When late in his life, his inner conflicts became unbearable, Count Lev Nikolayevich Tolstoy, the great Russian novelist, gave his estate to his family, disposed of much of his personal belongings and attempted to live the life of a poor and celibate peasant. In this attempt to put his personal philosophy into practice, he denounced authority and all violence, and became a vegetarian. Although this caused a rift with his wife and family and consequently his later life was embittered, his Christian anarchist life and moral and religious writings were to influence many people – not least of whom was the young Gandhi.[91]

A year after he landed in South Africa, Gandhi went through a time of religious ferment, engaging in wide-ranging religious discussions and reading eclectically among the religious texts that came his way. One of these texts was Tolstoy's book on living an authentic Christian life. Gandhi commented: 'Tolstoy's *The Kingdom of God is Within You* overwhelmed me. It left an abiding impression on me. Before the independent thinking, profound morality, and the truthfulness of this book, all the books given me by Mr. Coates seemed to pale into insignificance.'[92] In that book, subtitled *Christianity not as a Mystical Doctrine but as a New Understanding of Life*, Tolstoy portrayed Christ as a teacher and moral example rather than as 'a divine savior atoning for the sins of mankind and offering eternal life'.[93] Here Tolstoy emphasises the law of love as the moral core of Christianity and accuses the majority of Christians of not acknowledging 'the law of nonresistance to evil by violence' which he sees as being at the central core of the faith. And these interpretations of Christian teachings by Tolstoy in no way contradicted Gandhi's growing understanding of his own Hindu faith. Further, from his reading of Tolstoy, Gandhi realised that the best way to help the poor was to get off their backs and practise 'bread labour', 'the divine law that man must earn his bread by labouring with his own hands',[94] which was to be central to his economic and social philosophy. The book became mandatory reading for members of Phoenix Settlement. When, in

---

[89] Published in the *The Spectator*, 24 October 1931.
[90] Pyarelal, *Mahatma Gandhi, volume I: The Early Phase*, p. 628.
[91] For Gandhi's own summary of Tolstoy's beliefs, see 'Count Tolstoy', (Gujarati) *Indian Opinion*, 2 September 1905.
[92] Gandhi, *An Autobiography*, p. 99.   [93] Hunt, *Gandhi and the Nonconformists*, p. 42.
[94] Letter to Narandas Gandhi, 14/16 September 1930.

1908 and 1909, Gandhi started his regular rounds of imprisonment as part of his political campaigns, Tolstoy's book was a constant companion. And when, with the assistance of another Tolstoyan, his close friend Hermann Kallenbach, Gandhi established his next community in 1910, it was called Tolstoy Farm and was to be run on Tolstoyan principles.

As Gandhi's nonviolent political activities were becoming known outside South Africa, some revolutionaries saw campaigns such as his doomed to failure and worse. The Vancouver-based Bengali revolutionary Taraknath Das, who was editing the insurrectionary underground journal *Free Hindustan*, was attacking Indian moderates who were in favour of the gradual attainment of self-government achieved with the agreement of the British rulers. In May 1908, Das wrote to Tolstoy as a great champion of the oppressed, asking the Count to contribute an article to his journal and, in effect, to bless the true revolutionaries, like himself, who could deliver the goods.[95] While condemning British colonialism, Tolstoy's reply 'bluntly rebuked the young correspondent for his audacity'[96] and reminded him that only the law of love could bring happiness to individuals and humanity. The central theme of Tolstoy's letter concerned how India was to achieve independence. He made it clear that he saw nonviolence as the only legitimate means available to the morally upright conscience and accused Das of repeating 'the amazing stupidity indoctrinated in you by the advocates of the use of violence . . . your European teachers'[97] and instructed him and his fellow travellers to 'Free your minds from those overgrown, mountainous imbecilities which hinder your recognition of [the law of love], and at once the truth will emerge from amid the pseudo-religious nonsense that has been smothering it.'[98] He urged the revolutionaries to remain true to their traditions of nonviolence rather than 'adopting the irreligious and profoundly immoral social arrangements under which the English and other pseudo-Christian nations live today'.[99] The appropriate way of struggle was not violence but a rejection of state administration: a refusal to use the courts, pay taxes or serve in the army.[100] Such sentiments would become music to Gandhi's ears.

---

[95] For a detailed history of writing of the letter see Alexander Shifman, *Tolstoy and India* (New Delhi: Sahitya Akademi, 1969), pp. 68–83.

[96] Anthony J. Parel, 'Editor's introduction' to M. K. Gandhi, *Hind Swaraj and other writings* (Cambridge University Press, 1997), p. xxix. See also Anthony J. Parel, 'Gandhi and Tolstoy', in Bindu Puri (ed.), *Mahatma Gandhi and His Contemporaries* (Shimla: Indian Institute of Advanced Study, 2001), pp. 41–3. For the full text of the 'Letter to a Hindoo', see Appendix A to Kalidas Nag, *Tolstoy and Gandhi* (Patna: Pustak Bhandar, 1950), pp. 78–98; or Christian Bartolf (ed.), *Letter to a Hindoo: Taraknath Das, Leo Tolstoi and Mahatma Gandhi* (Berlin: Gandhi Informations Zentrum, 1997).

[97] Tolstoy, 'Letter to a Hindoo', in Nag, *Tolstoy and Gandhi*, p. 92.

[98] *Ibid.*, p. 98.   [99] *Ibid.*, p. 82.   [100] *Ibid.*, p. 93.

While the reply was not printed in *Free Hindustan*, when Gandhi came across a typed copy of the 'Letter to a Hindoo' in London on his 1909 visit to lobby for the interests of South African Indians the letter helped him crystallize his arguments against the Indian revolutionaries he was meeting. It would form the central thesis of his seminal work, *Hind Swaraj*, which he wrote on board ship on his way back to South Africa. Simultaneously, he wrote an English preface and translated it into Gujarati. In his 'Foreword' to *Hind Swaraj*, Gandhi makes the point that the views expressed in the slim volume are his and at the same time not his. They are his because he is integrating them into his being, yet not his because they are not original but were formed after reading several books. In an appendix he recommends a number of books to those who are interested in taking the arguments further. Of the twenty books listed, the first six are by Tolstoy (with *The Kingdom of God is Within You* heading the list).

At the beginning of October 1909, he wrote his first letter to Tolstoy, seeking to authenticate the 'Letter to a Hindoo' and to obtain permission to print it. He also took the opportunity to inform Tolstoy of his own activities in South Africa.[101] The permission was quick in coming and it led, not only to efforts to privately print 20,000 copies of the document, but also to a close and mutually admiring correspondence that lasted until Tolstoy's death on 20 November 1910.

Just a few months before he died, in the last long letter he was to pen, Tolstoy wrote to Gandhi commenting on how important his work in the Transvaal was in providing practical proof of the law of love in action.[102] And in turn, over thirty years later, Gandhi was able to state that

Russia gave me in Tolstoi, a teacher who furnished a reasoned basis for my nonviolence. He blessed my movement in South Africa when it was still in its infancy and of whose wonderful possibilities I had yet to learn. It was he who had prophesied in his letter to me that I was leading a movement which was destined to bring a message of hope to the downtrodden people of the earth.[103]

During a speech at Gandhi's Sabarmati Ashram on 10 September 1928, to mark the birth centenary of Tolstoy, Gandhi reminisced about the impact of *The Kingdom of God is Within You*, and recounted its message:

The title means that God's Kingdom is in our heart, that if we search for it outside we shall find it nowhere. I read the book forty years ago. At that time, I was sceptical about many things and sometimes entertained atheistic ideas. When I

---

[101] Letter to Tolstoy, 1 October 1909.
[102] Tolstoy's letter to Gandhi, 7 September 1910, reproduced as an appendix in *CWMG*.
[103] Letter to American Friends, 3 August 1942.

went to England, I was a votary of violence, I had faith in it and none in non-violence. After I read this book, that lack of faith in non-violence vanished.

On the effect of Tolstoy's life on him, he added:

I attach importance to two things in his life. He did what he preached. His simplicity was extraordinary; it was not merely outward; outward simplicity of course he had. Though he was born in an aristocratic family and had all the good things of life to enjoy, had at his disposal all that wealth and possessions could give a man, he changed the direction of his life's voyage in the prime of youth. Though he had enjoyed all the pleasures and tasted all the sweetness which life can offer, the moment he realized the futility of that way of life he turned his back on it, and he remained firm in his new convictions till the end of his life. I have, therefore, stated in some message I have sent that Tolstoy was the very embodiment of truth in this age. He strove uncompromisingly to follow truth as he saw it, making no attempt to conceal or dilute what he believed to be the truth. He stated what he felt to be the truth without caring whether it would hurt or please the people or whether it would be welcome to the mighty emperor. Tolstoy was a great advocate of non-violence in his age.

Here Gandhi is almost talking of himself. The parallels are clear. A little later he laments the lack of such men in India, perhaps indicating that he may be the heir of Tolstoy:

I know of no author in the West who has written as much and as effectively for the cause of non-violence as Tolstoy has done. I may go even further and say that I know no one in India or elsewhere who has had as profound an understanding of the nature of non-violence as Tolstoy had and who has tried to follow it as sincerely as he did.

We do not have among us men who, like Tolstoy, would speak out the plain truth irrespective of whether or not that would please the people or the society in which they work. Such is the pitiable condition of this our land of non-violence. Our non-violence is an unworthy thing. We see its utmost limit in refraining somehow from destroying bugs, mosquitoes and fleas, or from killing birds and animals. . . . Non-violence means an ocean of compassion, it means shedding from us every trace of ill-will for others. It does not mean abjectness or timidity, or fleeing in fear. It means, on the contrary, firmness of mind and courage, a resolute spirit. We do not see this non-violence in the educated classes in India.[104]

THOREAU AND GANDHI'S POLITICAL OBLIGATIONS

Although Americans particularly like to claim that Henry David Thoreau, anti-slavery and anti-war protester and withholder of taxes from a government he saw as unjust, and of course the author of the classic text

---

[104] 'Speech on Birth Centenary of Tolstoy', *Young India*, 20 September 1928.

'Civil Disobedience', had a formative influence in the development of the Mahatma,[105] Gandhi himself has claimed that 'The persons who have influenced my life as a whole in a general way are Tolstoy, Ruskin, Thoreau and Raychandbhai.' Then quickly he added, 'Perhaps I should drop Thoreau from this list.'[106]

On 11 September 1906, 3,000 Indians gathered at the Empire Theatre in Johannesburg to protest against the discriminatory Indian Registration Ordinance which required them to be registered, fingerprinted and to carry registration cards at all times under fear of heavy punishment for a breach. During the meeting a resolution was passed calling all present to defy the provisions of the legislation. The seconder of the resolution, Seth Haji Habib, wanted the resolution passed with God as witness. Such a pledge had great significance for Gandhi who pointed out to the assemblage that a vow taken in God's name could not be broken even to save one's own life. This meeting is seen in the Gandhian saga as the 'birth of satyagraha', where Gandhi embarked on civil disobedience.

In his essay 'Civil Disobedience', Thoreau reminds his reader that 'Unjust laws exist' and then asks: 'shall we be content to obey them, or shall we endeavor to amend them, and obey them until we have succeeded, or shall we transgress them at once?' His answer to the question is surely one that had great appeal to Gandhi:

If the injustice is part of the necessary friction of the machine of government, let it go, let it go: perchance it will wear smooth . . . but if it is of such a nature that it requires you to be the agent of injustice to another, then, I say, break the law. Let your life be a counter friction to stop the machine. What I have to do is to see, at any rate, that I do not lend myself to the wrong which I condemn.[107]

And, again, in words that would have undoubtedly received Gandhi's enthusiastic approval when he read them, Thoreau instructs his reader to 'Cast your whole vote, not a strip of paper merely, but your whole influence', and proclaims that 'under a government which imprisons any unjustly, the true place for a just man is also in prison'.[108]

It has often been assumed that Gandhi's speech at the Empire Theatre was inspired by his reading of 'Civil Disobedience'.[109] However, it appears

---

[105] See for example A. L. Hermann 'Satyagraha: A New Indian Word for Some Old Ways of Western Thinking', *Philosophy East and West* 19 (1969), pp. 123–42.
[106] Letter to Premabehn Kantak, January 17, 1931.
[107] Henry David Thoreau, *Walden and Civil Disobedience* (New York: Harper and Row, 1965), pp. 258–9.
[108] *Ibid.*, pp. 260–1.
[109] See C. Seshachari, *Gandhi and the American Scene* (Bombay: Nachiketa, 1969), p. 17.

that although Gandhi may have known of Thoreau since his London days, in fact did not read the seminal essay until over half a year after the historical meeting.[110] The essay, by a well-respected westerner and kindred spirit, certainly seemed to legitimise what he was doing and he was to go on mentioning Thoreau's dictum for the rest of his life. However, this was backing support not causal influence.[111]

Gandhi published extracts from the essay in his paper *Indian Opinion* on 7 and 14 September 1907 and a week later the two extracts were combined and printed as a pamphlet. On 9 November the paper announced an essay contest on 'The Ethics of Passive Resistance' for which submitted papers had to contain an examination of Thoreau's essay, Tolstoy's book and 'also the application of the "Apology of Socrates" to the question'. However, as Gandhi pointed out in 1935:

The statement that I had derived my idea of Civil Disobedience from the writings of Thoreau is wrong. The resistance to authority in South Africa was well advanced before I got the essay of Thoreau on Civil Disobedience. But the movement was then known as passive resistance. As it was incomplete I had coined the word *satyagraha* for the Gujarati readers. When I saw the title of Thoreau's great essay, I began to use his phrase to explain our struggle to the English readers.[112]

Henry Polak, who not only introduced Gandhi to Ruskin but was also probably the person who gave him a copy of Thoreau's essay, wrote to the American press that:

I cannot recall whether, early in 1907, he [Gandhi] or I first came across the volume of Thoreau's Essays . . . but we were both of us enormously impressed by the confirmation of the rightness of the principle of passive resistance and civil disobedience that had already been started against the objectionable laws, contained in the essay 'On the Duty of Civil Disobedience.'[113]

---

[110] The confusion seems to stem from some authors placing the Empire Theatre meeting in 1907, a year later than when it actually took place. See for example George Hendrick, 'Influence of Thoreau and Emerson on Gandhi's Satyagraha', *Gandhi Marg* 3 (1959), pp. 165–78. And perhaps in addition it has resulted from 'a sense of western superiority'. See James D. Hunt, 'Thoreau and Gandhi: a re-evaluation of the legacy', *Gandhi Marg* 14 (1970), pp. 325–32.

[111] See George Hendrick, 'The Influence of Thoreau's "Civil Disobedience" on Gandhi's Satyagraha', *New England Quarterly* 29 (1956), pp. 462–71; and Hendrick, 'Influence of Thoreau and Emerson on Gandhi's Satyagraha'. The same could be said for Gandhi's encounter with the English Suffragettes in London just weeks after the Empire Theatre meeting. See Hunt, 'Suffragettes and Satyagraha'. It seems that the feminists have not had as strong a need to stake a claim to having helped shape the Mahatma as some Americans did.

[112] Letter to P. Kodanda Rao, 10 September 1935

[113] Letter to the New York *Evening Post*, 11 May 1931. In a letter to Henry Salt, dated 12 October 1929, Gandhi says that a friend sent him a copy of the essay.

By way of summary, Seshachari points out that although satyagraha was well advanced when Gandhi came across Thoreau's writings, 'Thoreau helped Gandhi gain greater insight into the tremendous potential of non-payment of taxes and non-cooperation'. He continues by pointing out that Thoreau did more than merely provide 'intellectual sustenance to Gandhi's beliefs', but possibly directly inspired Gandhi's tactic of boycotting government institutions such as schools and law courts, and the tactic of making bonfires of registration cards and later foreign cloth.[114] It should be noted that the careful scholar James Hunt doubts even this. He points out that both these tactics were well known in India in Gandhi's time and did not have to be imported from the West.[115] In short, the purported influence of Thoreau on Gandhi is nowhere near as great as is often claimed. However, the words of the title of the printed version of Thoreau's lecture, 'civil disobedience', certainly were a boon to Gandhi who had come to reject the phrase 'passive resistance' (there was nothing passive about what he was doing) and understood that 'satyagraha' was going to be a little mystifying for his western audience.

GOKHALE AND GANDHI'S POLITICAL TUTELAGE

Following his graduation in 1884, Gopal Krishna Gokhale became a professor of history and political economy at Fergusson College in Poona, rising to the position of principal. He remained on the staff until 1902 when he resigned to dedicate his life undividedly to politics. In 1899 he became a member of the Bombay Legislature and was elected to serve as a member of the Imperial Legislature in 1902. He was a most effective member of the Legislature, well-read and always well prepared, he was quick in debate and spoke eloquently. He was also a member of the Indian National Congress from the beginning, serving as President of the 1905 session. In that year he founded his Servants of India Society (SIS) whose members took vows of poverty and lifelong service to their country and its underprivileged in a religious spirit. In announcing his death, the Calcutta *Statesman*, wrote that 'Mr. Gokhale was the greatest leader that India has ever produced – perhaps her greatest man.'[116]

---

[114] See Seshachari, *Gandhi and the American Scene*, pp. 22–3.
[115] Hunt, 'Thoreau and Gandhi', p. 329.
[116] Quoted in B. R. Nanda, *Gokhale, Gandhi and the Nehrus: Studies in Indian Nationalism* (London: Allen and Unwin, 1974), p. 11. For Gandhi's own hagiographical life sketch of Gokhale, see 'A Splendid Record', *Indian Opinion*, 24 August 1912.

Gandhi's political manifesto, *Hind Swaraj*, is presented as a dialogue between the 'reader' and the 'editor'. The protagonists quite obviously represent the young Indian revolutionaries he had been recently debating in London and himself, and also the 'extremists' in the Congress, led by Tilak, and the 'moderates', led by Gokhale. He has the impatient Reader criticising the cautious Gokhale 'as a great friend of the English' who insists that their political wisdom must be mastered before the issue of home rule can be taken up. For the defence the Editor responds by explaining that

> We believe that those, who are discontented with the slowness of their parents and are angry because the parents would not run with their children, are considered disrespectful to their parents. Professor Gokhale occupies the place of a parent. What does it matter if he cannot run with us? A nation that is desirous of securing Home Rule cannot afford to despise its ancestors. We shall become useless, if we lack respect for our elders. Only men with mature thoughts are capable of ruling themselves and not the hasty-tempered. Moreover, how many Indians were there like Professor Gokhale, when he gave himself to Indian education? I verily believe that whatever Professor Gokhale does, he does with pure motives and with a view to serving India.

This, of course did not mean following him in every respect, the Editor explains. 'If we conscientiously differed from him, the learned Professor himself would advise us to follow the dictates of our conscience rather than him.'[117]

Although Gokhale was only a few years older than Gandhi, he was a father figure and clearly Gandhi's political mentor. The passage in *Hind Swaraj* is an accurate picture of their relationship. When, during 1896, on a visit to India, Gandhi first met Gokhale, he notes that 'his manner immediately won my heart'.[118] At the Calcutta Congress in December 1901, Gokhale championed Gandhi's South Africa cause. In the following February, Gandhi stayed with Gokhale in Calcutta for a month and was introduced to a range of interesting and important people. Gandhi took on the role of worshipful student.[119] When it came time to leave, 'The separation was a wrench.' And for the time that Gandhi practised as a lawyer in Bombay, before being called back to South Africa, Gokhale kept a close eye on his protégé.[120]

---

[117] M. K. Gandhi, *Hind Swaraj or Indian Home Rule* (Ahmedabad: Navajivan, 1939), p. 22. Polak presented Gokhale with a translation of the booklet during his 1909 visit to India. In 1912, when Gokhale was in South Africa he told Gandhi that he thought that the ideas in it 'were so crude and hastily conceived that . . . Gandhi himself would destroy the book after spending a week in India.' See Mahadev Desai's 'Preface' to the 1938 edition.

[118] Gandhi, *An Autobiography*, p. 128.

[119] See for example his description of Gokhale at work, Gandhi, *An Autobiography*, p. 169.

[120] Gandhi, *An Autobiography*, pp. 174, 183.

Years later, when the differences between him and the SIS were at the greatest, Gandhi bristled at the suggestion that he was an impostor 'in claiming to be politically a disciple of Gokhale'. In an article in his paper, he points out that being a disciple is more than being a son, it 'is a second birth, it is a voluntary surrender' and although early on he had met many of India's great politicians, he could only say that he had 'many heroes, but no king'. That is until he met Gokhale:

It was different with Gokhale, I cannot say why. I met him at his quarters on the college ground. It was like meeting an old friend, or, better still, a mother after a long separation. His gentle face put me at ease in a moment. His minute inquiries about myself and my doings in South Africa at once enshrined him in my heart. And as I parted from him, I said to myself, 'You are my man.' And from that moment Gokhale never lost sight of me. In 1901 on my second return from South Africa, we came closer still. He simply 'took me in hand', and began to fashion me. He was concerned about how I spoke, dressed, walked and ate. My mother was not more solicitous about me than Gokhale. There was, so far as I am aware, no reserve between us. It was really a case of love at first sight, and it stood the severest strain in 1913.[121] He seemed to me all I wanted as a political worker – pure as crystal, gentle as a lamb, brave as a lion and chivalrous to a fault. . . . Not, therefore, that we had no difference. We differed even in 1901 in our views on social customs, e.g., widow remarriage. We discovered differences in our estimate of Western civilization. He frankly differed from me in my extreme views on non-violence. But these differences mattered neither to him nor to me. Nothing could put us asunder. It were blasphemous to conjecture what would have happened if he were alive today. I know that I would have been working under him.[122]

Gokhale had become Gandhi's chief political supporter in India, pub-licising his causes and raising funds for him. In 1912 Gokhale visited him in South Africa and Gandhi devoted himself to serving his honoured guest in a way that irritated some of his colleagues. He admitted that he wanted to see Gokhale 'as perfect a being as possible. He is my political teacher. For that reason also I would like to contemplate him in his perfection.'[123] Gokhale was kind, a dedicated, tireless and selfless worker, he was truthful, considerate of others, he was religious without having to 'wear his religion on his sleeve',[124] and he was a patriot. In short, Gokhale was the living embodiment of what Gandhi hoped to be.[125] And when his work in South

---

[121] When rather than co-operating with a Government commission of inquiry, as Gokhale advised, Gandhi initiated another mass campaign which Gokhale was strongly against. See M. K. Gandhi, *Satyagraha in South Africa* (Madras: S. Ganesan, 1928), pp. 489–91.

[122] 'A Confession of Faith', *Young India*, 13 July 1921.

[123] Letter to Hermann Kallenbach, 17 February 1913.

[124] Speech at Bombay Provincial Conference, Poona, 11 July 1915.

[125] See S. P. Aiyar, 'Gandhi, Gokhale and the Moderates', in Ray, *Gandhi, India and the World*, p. 100.

Africa was over, Gandhi stated that he wanted to return to India to work under Gokhale's guidance.[126] He wrote to his political guru in February 1914: 'I do not know whether you still want me to live at the Servants of India Society quarters in Poona.' However, he points out that he is completely in Gokhale's hands and wants 'to learn at your feet and gain the necessary experience . . . to have the real discipline of obeying someone whom I love and look up to.'[127]

On the way to India he visited London where again he could spend time with Gokhale who was there as part of his work for the Royal Commission on the Public Services in India. During September and October 1914 they met almost daily.[128] This friendship was to provide Gandhi's political base in India: towards the end of his life, Gandhi claimed that 'I was to have the honour of being Gokhale's successor'.[129]

When he finally did return to India, his South African work behind him, Gokhale was keen for him to join the SIS and it appears that he did indeed have Gandhi firmly in mind as his successor. Gokhale had offered financial support to establish an ashram in Gujarat and Gandhi was overjoyed 'to feel free from the responsibility of raising funds, and to realize that I should not be obliged to set about the work all on my own, but that I should be able to count on a secure guide whenever I was in difficulty. This took a great load off my mind.'[130] Thus, at ease, he set off to join his Phoenix colleagues (who had gone directly to India from South Africa rather than via London with him) at Rabindranath Tagore's school at Shantiniketan in Bengal. While there, not much more than a month after he had returned to his native land, he received the news of the sickly Gokhale's death. Gokhale was only forty-eight.

Gandhi immediately had differences with the SIS[131] and decided to act upon the promise he had made to Gokhale long before – to travel the country for a year, while observing political silence, to become acquainted with Indian conditions first hand, something he decided to do barefooted despite the inconvenience,[132] before plunging into national politics. It seems that Gokhale thought that this would temper the radicalism of his anointed heir, and 'prevent him making early blunders out of ignorance and enthusiasm which would lessen his potential for public work'.[133]

[126] Gandhi, *Satyagraha in South Africa*, p. 509.   [127] Letter to Gokhale, 27 February 1914.
[128] Sushila Nayar, *Mahatma Gandhi, volume V: India Awakened* (Ahmedabad: Navajivan, 1993), p. 18.
[129] See Gandhi's 'Foreword', to V. S. Srinivasa Sastri, *My Master Gokhale* (Madras: Model Publications, 1946).
[130] Gandhi, *An Autobiography*, p. 277.   [131] See Sastri, *My Master Gokhale*, pp. 220–1.
[132] Kaka Kalelkar, *Stray Glimpses of Bapu* (Ahmedabad: Navajivan, 1960), p. 14.
[133] Judith M. Brown, *Gandhi: Prisoner of Hope* (New Haven: Yale University Press, 1989), p. 71.

Gandhi could no longer count on the Society for funding as many members were uneasy about his critique of western education and 'modern' civilisation and probably had concerns about what would happen to the SIS if he took a leading role now that the founder was gone. On his return from his year of travel, the new leadership seems to have tactfully suggested that Gandhi not seek formal admission to the organisation and they were relieved when he did not force the issue. In this way, Gandhi's hoped-for initial Indian power-base did not eventuate. As Judith Brown notes: 'None of the contacts which were his stepping-stones from African to Indian politics led to a permanent road; and by the beginning of 1917 he was still more of a freelance preacher and social worker than a recognized politician.'[134]

The relationship with Gokhale is a strange one. Although Gandhi was sympathetic to the aims of the Servants of India Society, and admired the dedication of Gokhale and its workers, it was not long before he was questioning their championing of western education and their 'indifferent imitation of the West'.[135] At the 1901 Calcutta Congress session, he confirmed his suspicions that the westernised middle-class leadership was out of touch with the India masses. And already, by his mass campaigns in South Africa, which Gokhale disapproved of, Gandhi could no longer be classed as a 'moderate'. Yet Gokhale was an elitist moderate – why then the close bond? Stanley Wolpert claims that these 'superficial' differences in dress and manner may have obscured 'the deeper currents of mental and moral identity which bound the *guru* and his disciple'.[136] Srinivasa Sastri, Gokhale's successor at the SIS, noted that although Gandhi and Gokhale differed in their outer lives, theories, politics and that while 'their modes of approach to public questions were diverse and even contradictory', they 'were attracted to each other by some inner magnetism'.[137] From Gokhale's point of view it is quite understandable: he saw Gandhi's potential for greatness and saw a possible successor for his SIS work. There was of course also much in the relationship for Gandhi. He profited from the interest Gokhale took in him, the statesman's championing of the South African Indian activist gave Gandhi credibility and sowed 'the thought in Gandhi's mind that he was destined to play a role in the national movement in India'.[138]

[134] Judith M. Brown, *Gandhi's Rise to Power: Indian Politics 1915–1922* (London: Cambridge University Press, 1972), p. 50.
[135] Letter to Maganlal Gandhi, 27 January 1910.
[136] Stanley Wolpert, *Tilak and Gokhale: Revolution and Reform in the Making of Modern India* (Berkeley: University of California Press, 1962), p. 143.
[137] Sastri, *My Master Gokhale*, p. 220.   [138] Devanesen, *The Making of the Mahatma*, p. 352.

Gandhi needed this support, but perhaps it also fed his ego. Kalelkar, a close confidant of Gandhi's during his Ahmedabad years, noted that Gokhale came into Gandhi's life at a time when psychologically he needed a mentor, when he was at 'the right age for hero-worship'. On the other side, Gokhale was sympathetic and appreciative of Gandhi and Gandhi's 'grateful heart promptly invested Gokhaleji's politics with his own ideals' even though it was 'difficult to find any similarity between them'.[139]

Some recent works show that in South Africa a politically ambitious Gandhi actively pushed his way to leadership positions[140] in a manner that is not reflected in either his *Autobiography* or *Satyagraha in South Africa*. The Doke biography seems to have been more or less dictated by Gandhi to the writer, and it was Gandhi himself who arranged for its publication.[141] And as soon as he had a printed copy, he sent it to Tolstoy. And certainly a relationship with Gokhale would be a great asset in fulfilling his ambitions. But, as noted above, such purely utilitarian considerations do not suffice.

At the 1909 Lahore Congress session, Gokhale said of Gandhi:

A purer, a nobler, a braver and a more exulted spirit has never moved on the earth. Mr. Gandhi is one of those men who, living an austerely simple life themselves and devoted to all the highest principles of love to their fellow-beings and to truth and justice, touch the eyes of their weaker brethren as with magic and give them a new vision. He may be described as a man among men, a hero among heroes, a patriot among patriots, and we may say that in him Indian humanity at present has really touched its high-water mark.

On another occasion he went even further: 'Only those who have come in personal contact with Mr. Gandhi as he is now, can realise the wonderful personality of the man. He is without doubt made of the stuff of which heroes and martyrs are made. Nay more. He has in him the marvelous spiritual power to turn ordinary men into heroes and martyrs.'[142]

All of this may have proved to be true, but it still must be difficult not to like someone seen as a superior who praises one so highly even if there

---

[139] Kalelkar, *Stray Glimpses of Bapu*, p. 77.
[140] See for example, Maureen Swan, *Gandhi: The South African Experience* (Johannesburg: Ravan Press, 1985).
[141] See T. K. Mahadevan, *The Year of the Phoenix: Gandhi's Pivotal Year* (New Delhi: Arnold-Heinemann, 1982), pp. 159–64.
[142] Quoted in P. Kodanda Rao, 'Gokhale and Gandhi', in G. Ramachandran and T. K. Mahadevan (eds.), *Quest for Gandhi* (New Delhi: Gandhi Peace Foundation, 1970), p. 344.

are philosophical differences. Gandhi and Gokhale were very different, but Gandhi was the political heir-apparent. Gandhi and Maganlal Gandhi were quite different, yet Maganlal was anointed as heir. Later, although Gandhi and Nehru were also very different, Nehru, too, became the political heir. Many are still puzzled how, given the philosophical gap between Gandhi and Nehru on so many key issues, this could have been possible. While the pupil may take what he or she needs from a mentor and then move beyond the horizons of the wise and friendly adviser, a utility argument generally does not seem to be quite enough to explain such relationships and certainly does not explain these relationships in Gandhi's life. In order to make the best possible sense of them, invoking the concept of 'love' may prove instructive. Perhaps Gandhi needed to be a son again (and this time not let his 'father' down the way the young Mohandas had let his own dying father down in his last moments by seeking sexual union with his wife when he should have been massaging his parent's legs[143]) and perhaps he needed to be a father to those who could stand up to him, not live in his shadow the way his own sons did. Gandhi loved Gokhale, Maganlal, Jamnalal Bajaj and Jawaharlal Nehru. And this, in the nature of genuine mentoring, seemed to dissipate any differences. Ironically, and perhaps just as importantly, Gokhale greatly influenced the direction of Gandhi's life by his untimely death. The picture of Gandhi seeking the political independence of India and attempting to spread his message of 'nonviolence of the brave' as head of the Servants of India takes some conjuring with.

H. S. L. POLAK, HERMANN KALLENBACH, MAGANLAL GANDHI AND JAMNALAL BAJAJ

The choices for the substantive chapters in this section on those influencing Gandhi may come as something of a surprise. The individuals involved are not as well known as perhaps they should be, and, except for Polak and Kallenbach who feature prominently in Gandhi's own writings about his South Africa days and in those by others who cover that era (generally using Gandhi's writings as the source), do not come across as significant influences on the Mahatma. Further, of course, they are younger than Gandhi and joined him because of what he had to offer them. In short they are more disciples than teachers, and seemingly far more influenced than influencing.

---

[143] As is at least hinted at by Erikson, *Gandhi's Truth*, p. 286.

However, they are part of dialectical processes in Gandhi's life. At times of internal questing and turmoil they were very involved in the eventual direction Gandhi's life was to take. And often the spiritual, intellectual and emotional movement also had a very obvious geographical manifestation.

Gandhi physically relocated himself several times during his long life and I had decided to see if there were any persons intricately involved in these relocations. The young Gandhi's move to London to study law was to a large degree outside his control. His shift to South Africa seems to have come from something of a sense of failure and a chance opportunity to find work rather than someone pushing or pulling him there. However, in South Africa his semi-move from his middle-class suburban home to a life of simplified rural, communal, manual labouring existence at Phoenix Settlement seems to be strongly tied up with his relationship to Henry Polak (and the trigger event of reading the book Polak lent him). In the same way, his later move to Tolstoy Farm can only be understood in terms of his relationship with Hermann Kallenbach.

He was destined to go back to India – after all, even though it lasted for almost twenty years, the original trip to South Africa was only seen as a temporary job assignment as nothing else was on the horizon in his native land. While the desire to go home grew in Gandhi, the way it happened is linked to his relationship to Gopal Krishna Gokhale. Gokhale was not, however, the cause of the move. Once established in Ahmedabad it seemed that Gandhi would direct his own social and spiritual experiments, as well as the national campaigns he periodically led, from his base at the Sabarmati Satyagraha Ashram. To understand how he could come to leave what was both his home and the home of his ashram family, it is instructive to view his relationship with Maganlal Gandhi. Of all the places that he could have settled in following this abandonment of the ashram, he chose, admittedly centrally located in the subcontinent but hot, dusty and far from the centres of power, to live near the town of Wardha. As Patel was Gandhi's chief organiser in Gujarat and Prasad in Bihar, Jamnalal Bajaj was Gandhi's lieutenant in the Central Provinces. While all three were immersed in the totality of Gandhi's programme, the first two placed more emphasis on political work while Bajaj concentrated more on Gandhi's constructive activities and headed up many work organisations that were based in Wardha. This may be part of the reason for Gandhi's relocation to there, but it can only fully be understood through an understanding of his deeper relationship with Bajaj.

The influence of these four persons may not have changed his fundamental world views in the way that his involvement with various religious

thinkers and the writings of Ruskin and Tolstoy did, but they were instrumental in the process and paved the way for some of those changes that were large enough to induce him to uproot himself and physically relocate. Of course these influences, as we shall see, were deeper than merely pointing to more choice real estate. The geographical moves were in all cases enmeshed with deeper inward progress also.

CHAPTER 3

Henry Polak and the setting up of Phoenix Settlement

INTRODUCTION

Of course Gandhi's technique of satyagraha as a method of nonviolent struggle against oppression had its genesis in South Africa. However it was not until 1906, that is twelve years after Gandhi had arrived in the country that satyagraha was commenced – until then the grievances of the Indian community were 'dealt with in the usual orthodox ways of petitions, memoranda, addresses, questions in Parliament, public speeches, and so on'.[1] By this time Gandhi had built a successful legal career and lived a middle-class life. From 1903 he lived in a well-to-do suburb of Johannesburg, and between 1906 and 1908 in a house shared with the Polaks when they were not living on the communal property at Phoenix which was set up after much internal turmoil and soul-searching that was moving him in the direction of a more simplified life of public service, a movement that was facilitated by his relationship with Henry Polak. Here I am not so interested in telling of the 'working' relationship between Polak and Gandhi the political campaigners. I am more interested in their early relationship, one that brought about the changes in Gandhi (and Polak) that enabled them to be non-orthodox political activists and Gandhi to go on and become the head of several religiously based ashrams.

POLAK JOINS GANDHI

In early 1904 Gandhi was showing concern about the insanitary and over-crowded conditions of Indians in the Indian Location in Johannesburg. He wrote to the Medical Officer of Health foreshadowing an outbreak of an epidemic[2] and two-and-a-half weeks later he informed the Medical

---

[1] H. S. L. Polak, 'Satyagraha and its Origin in South Africa', in Kshitis Roy (ed.), *Gandhi Memorial Peace Number* (Shantiniketan: The Visva-Bharati Quarterly, 1949), p. III.
[2] See Letter to Dr Porter, 11 February 1904.

Officer that indeed pneumonic plague had broken out.[3] Gandhi worked tirelessly in the anti-plague campaign and wrote critical letters to the press and articles in the paper *Indian Opinion* for which, although not the formal editor, he was chief financial backer and ultimately responsible.[4]

The short, stocky, luxuriantly dark wavy-haired and bespectacled twenty-two-year-old Polak met the thirty-five-year-old Gandhi in Johannesburg in March 1904, soon after he joined the editorial staff of *The Transvaal Critic*. As a newspaperman he read *Indian Opinion*. From it he learned about the position of Indians in the country. He read the comments in the papers about Gandhi's views of the relationship between the Indian community and how its lack of the vote led to municipal neglect in its overcrowded section of the city and hence the outbreak of plague, and 'as a faithful journalist'[5] decided to talk to Gandhi. He had a glimpse of Gandhi at Ziegler's vegetarian restaurant and although he saw nothing remarkable about the black turbaned lawyer, this desire was increased on the discovery that Gandhi was a fellow Tolstoyan vegetarian.

A few days later the opportunity came. Miss Ada Bissicks, the proprietor of a vegetarian restaurant that Gandhi frequented (and partially financed), told Polak that Gandhi would be attending an 'At Home' at her house the following evening and invited him to come as well. 'So we met, and the meeting changed the current of both our lives',[6] recalled Polak. It was clear from the start that the meeting would not be merely one of journalist and subject. The 'real card of introduction' was the fact that Polak was the only other person Gandhi had met who had read a certain book on nature cure for disease. Gandhi invited Polak to his office so that the latter could peruse the shelf full of Tolstoy books that Gandhi kept there. A lengthy conversation in Gandhi's chambers followed. They discussed books and Polak's deep interest in India. It very soon became apparent that Polak was a lover of justice who harboured no racial prejudice and that besides vegetarianism and nature cure the two of them had many other things in common, including a pull towards a more simple life, an interest in the Hindu texts and the writings of Tolstoy and Ruskin. Green notes that 'theirs was a New Age union, cemented in the presence of the New Age icons in Gandhi's office'.[7]

---

[3] See reference in Letter to Dr Porter, 18 March 1904.
[4] See Gandhi, *An Autobiography*, pp. 210–11; but note that the paper had been coming out since mid-1903 rather than the 1904 of Gandhi's recollection.
[5] Polak, 'Some South African Reminiscences', p. 230.
[6] *Ibid.*, p. 231.   [7] Green, *Gandhi*, p. 153.

Polak also informed Gandhi that he had differences with his own conservative paper on the 'Indian Question' but his editor had allowed him to write about the issue in a way that did not necessarily support the arch-conservative paper's policy on racial and colour issues. Polak offered Gandhi his own services, free of charge, as a writer for *Indian Opinion* and they were soon close friends. The association with Gandhi's paper lasted until Polak left South Africa twelve years later.[8]

Gandhi remembered the meeting somewhat differently: the meeting occurring in the restaurant where Polak sent Gandhi his card with a desire to talk and was invited to join Gandhi at his table. The young journalist had wanted to talk to the Indian community leader about the plague. In a later recollection Gandhi notes that he was quick to sum up his young soon-to-be soulmate and lieutenant:

Mr. Polak's candour drew me to him. The same evening we got to know each other. We seemed to hold closely similar views on the essential things of life. He liked simple life. He had a wonderful faculty of translating into practice anything that appealed to his intellect. Some of the changes that he had made in his life were as prompt as they were radical.[9]

A little more than a dozen years after the Johannesburg meeting, Gandhi related the event to his secretary and explained how he managed to 'capture' Polak:

I judged Polak within five hours. He read my letter published in a newspaper and wrote me a letter. He then came to see me and I at once saw what he was, and since then he became my man. He married and started his practice as a pleader only after he joined me. He told me before marriage that he must earn a little for his children. I told him plainly, 'You are mine and the responsibility to provide for you and your children is mine, not yours. I am getting you married, as I see no objection to your marrying.' His marriage was celebrated at my residence.[10]

While his family was in India, Gandhi was living in a modest room behind his chambers. When Gandhi took larger premises in Troyville in anticipation of the return of his family, Polak took over the Rissik Street room and this 'helped to bring me into closer contact with him'.[11] After hearing the news of the financial plight of *Indian Opinion* from Albert West, Gandhi was worried that it would be forced to close 'with the consequent

[8] Polak, 'Some South African Reminiscences', p. 235.   [9] Gandhi, *An Autobiography*, p. 219.
[10] 'Talk with Mahadev Desai', 31 August 1917.
[11] Polak, 'Some South African Reminiscences', p. 232.

loss of public service which this would entail'.[12] To set things straight, in September 1904, he had to undertake a hurried trip to Durban, from where the paper was being published. For the journey, Polak lent Gandhi a book that he had just finished reading. That book was Ruskin's *Unto This Last*.[13]

THE FOUNDING OF PHOENIX SETTLEMENT

During the trip Gandhi made a flying visit to see his cousin Abhaychand who owned a store in Tongaat. He was greatly attracted by the gardens and wondered why his relatives were 'wasting their time in the store when so much work and so much beauty lay around them'. They could cultivate the rich ground and do it far better than the paid labourers who were doing the gardening. 'I had been reading Ruskin's "Unto This Last" on my way down, and the influence of the book clung to me. Surely such a dream might be realised.'[14] In Durban, Gandhi told West of the impact the book had had on him 'and proposed that *Indian Opinion* should be removed to a farm, on which everyone should labour, drawing the same living wage of three pounds, and attending to the press work in spare time'.[15] The agrarian commune would see Indians and Europeans living together in Gandhi's first intentional community in a simple and healthy environment, and in mutual support learning from each other. Gandhi knew of no other non-religious organisation that had managed to operate on these principles and noted that if it succeeded 'we cannot but think that it would be worthy of imitation'.[16]

However, most of the press workers were not interested in leaving the city for an out-of-the-way communal farm, and many supporters ridiculed the idea, but his nephew Chhaganlal Gandhi, West and some others agreed to make the move, being 'blind to possible difficulties'.[17] Gandhi immediately advertised for appropriate land 'near a railway station in the vicinity of Durban'. An offer came from Phoenix, halfway between Durban and Tongaat. Gandhi and West inspected the land and within a week twenty acres had been purchased: 'It had a nice little spring and a few orange and mango trees. Adjoining it was a piece of eighty acres which had many more

---

[12] *Ibid.*, p. 233; and Albert West, 'In the Early Days with Gandhi', *The Illustrated Weekly of India*, 3 October 1965, p. 31.
[13] Polak, 'Some South African Reminiscences', p. 239.　　[14] Quoted in Doke, *M. K. Gandhi*, p. 108.
[15] Gandhi, *An Autobiography*, p. 221; West 'In the Early Days with Gandhi', p. 33.
[16] 'Ourselves', *Indian Opinion*, 24 December 1904.
[17] West, 'In the Early Days with Gandhi', p. 33.

fruit trees and a dilapidated cottage. We purchased this too, the total cost being a thousand pounds.'[18]

The land was in the valley of the Peizang river fourteen miles from Durban and two-and-a-half miles from Phoenix station. The property had been owned by Thomas Watkins whose first crop of sugar cane had been destroyed by fire and because he replanted the crop in the ashes, he called his farm Phoenix.[19] The farm was surrounded by cane fields, overgrown, infested with snakes and uninhabited, yet within a month a shed had been erected to house the press and during October and November the transfer of the press from Durban to Phoenix, in 'four large farm wagons with spans of sixteen bullocks each', had been completed. The workers slept on the floor of the newly erected press building or in tents, but owing to 'the prevalence of snakes and mosquitos, the press floor was generally preferred'.[20] On Christmas Eve, without any interruption to the publication schedule, the first number of *Indian Opinion* was issued from Phoenix.

Gandhi, preoccupied with his legal practice in Johannesburg, could not resettle to Phoenix, however he stayed and worked there whenever he could.[21] Although he was away far more than he was in residence, Gandhi housed his wife and children on the settlement for lengthy periods. According to Thomson, the chronicler of Gandhi's ashrams, Gandhi led something of a schizophrenic lifestyle at this time, trying to reconcile his value system as embodied in the life of poverty of Phoenix and his own career of successful lawyer, earning between £4,000 and £5,000 annually, and public activist and spokesperson for the Indian community.[22] Gandhi himself talked with regret about not being able to spend enough time at Phoenix because his 'original idea had been gradually to retire from practice, go and live at the Settlement, earn my livelihood by manual work there, and find the joy of service in the fulfilment of Phoenix'.[23] When he could tear himself away from his outside work and was present, the life at Phoenix 'was always much enriched'.[24] In summing up the history of Phoenix during Gandhi's day, Thomson concludes:

The early hopes that Phoenix would develop into a health, agricultural and educational centre *par excellence* were thwarted by a number of factors. Among these were

[18] Gandhi, *An Autobiography*, p. 222.
[19] Gillian Berning, *Gandhi Letters: From Upper House to Lower House* (n. p.: Local History Museum, 1994), p. 41.
[20] West, 'In the Early Days with Gandhi', p. 33.
[21] Mark Thomson, *Gandhi and His Ashrams* (Bombay: Popular, 1993), p. 49.
[22] *Ibid.*, p. 54.   [23] Gandhi, *An Autobiography*, p. 224.
[24] Thomson, *Gandhi and His Ashrams*, p. 63.

the demands of running the paper, the severe disruptions caused by the political struggle, during which many settlers served terms of imprisonment, and ultimately the departure of Gandhi from South Africa in 1914.[25]

The buildings at the commune were barely ready and they 'had hardly settled down' when Gandhi had to leave the 'newly constructed nest' to return to his pressing engagements in Johannesburg. On his return, he told Polak of the changes and noted that 'His joy knew no bounds when he learned that the loan of his book had been so fruitful.' Polak quickly volunteered to join the community, gave a month's notice to his chief at *The Critic*, leaving a potentially secure career, and was soon sharing quarters with West at Phoenix running *Indian Opinion*. According to Gandhi, Polak took to life at Phoenix 'like a duck takes to water', however Gandhi needed a legal assistant and asked Polak to become his clerk and to qualify as an attorney so that they could more quickly finish their work and 'more quickly realise their ideals' of communal life.[26]

In May 1905, Polak left Phoenix not to return until a year later when Gandhi relocated his entire household there. He became articled to Gandhi and two years later was admitted as an attorney of the Supreme Court of Transvaal, where his practice 'consisted almost entirely of defending passive resisters in court, free of charge', his expenses being covered by the Transvaal-based British Indian Association.[27] Polak had long been impressed with Gandhi's approach to legal ethics[28] but when he left the settlement to throw himself into the work involved he became entangled not only in Gandhi's public life, but again also in his inner quest.

THE RELATIONSHIP BETWEEN GANDHI AND POLAK

After Gandhi had sent Polak to India to represent the cause of the Transvaal Indians, he decided to introduce his lieutenant to the readers of *Indian Opinion*. We learn from Gandhi that Henry Salomon (*sic*) Leon Polak was born in 1882 at Dover, England. He was an undergraduate at London University, had obtained many certificates in literary and economic subjects, issued by the London Chamber of Commerce and other educational bodies. He completed his education at the Ecole de Commerce, Neuchatel, Switzerland (where he had studied the works of Tolstoy), and was

---

[25] *Ibid.*, pp. 60–1.   [26] Gandhi, *An Autobiography*, p. 225.   [27] Swan, *Gandhi*, p. 139.
[28] For Gandhi's approach to legal ethics, see Thomas Weber, 'Legal Ethics/Gandhian Ethics', *Gandhi Marg* 7 (1986), pp. 692–706.

subsequently appointed Assistant Secretary of the Society of Chemical Industry, in London. As a youth, 'ethics had a fascinating attraction for him' to the point where for Henry 'religion and ethics are convertible terms'. He joined the South Place Ethical Society in London, 'and it was from an ethical standpoint that he felt himself called upon to take up Indian work'. For reasons of health, Polak came to South Africa in the early part of 1903 where he took the job of a journalist.

We further learn that since 1906 Polak had held the position of Assistant Honorary Secretary of the Transvaal British Indian Association and that

during the last three years, Mr. Polak has known no rest. He has, besides using his able pen freely for the cause, travelled throughout South Africa, either making collections in aid of the passive resistance struggle, or addressing public meetings and enlightening Indians in different parts of the sub-continent as to the nature of the struggle. His knowledge of the different questions affecting British Indian settlers and Asiatic legislation in South Africa is almost unrivalled.[29]

Polak was engaged to Millie Graham Downs, whom he had met at the London Ethical Society, before he ventured to South Africa. It appears that not long after his meeting with Gandhi he had been invited to shift in to the Troyville residence and the two friends rapidly 'began to live like blood brothers'.[30] When Gandhi's family arrived from India to join him towards the close of 1905, Polak wrote to Millie in England that Gandhi (who had not yet settled on celibacy as an ideal) wanted her there also and that they should be married. She accepted the idea and in a few months was in Johannesburg where she and Henry were married at the very end of 1905 without even the necessity of 'a special dress' or religious rites – their 'common religion' being 'the religion of ethics'. Having a 'coloured' person as best man, and Polak's habit of referring to himself and friends as 'we Indians'[31] meant that the ceremony at the registry office had to be put off 'pending inquires' to ensure that it was not a mixed marriage. Gandhi had to intervene and obtain a note from the Chief Magistrate to clear up the 'amusing incident'.[32]

Millie shifted into a joint family household that was a mix of European and Indian styles, customs and people and one in which Gandhi had 'introduced as much simplicity as was possible in a barrister's house'.[33] As there was a houseboy and cook, there was no housework to do, and,

---

[29] 'Mr. Polak and His Work', *Indian Opinion*, 3 July 1909.   [30] Gandhi, *An Autobiography*, p. 227.
[31] At Phoenix Settlement, Polak was known by the Indian name 'Keshavlal' (Keshav is a name for the Hindu gods Vishnu or Krishna meaning 'long-haired' or 'having much hair.') Prabhudas Gandhi, *My Childhood With Gandhi* (Ahmedabad: Navajivan, 1957), p. 56.
[32] Gandhi, *An Autobiography*, p. 227.   [33] *Ibid.*, p. 228.

although not a trained teacher, Millie took on the work of educating the Gandhi children and also teaching Kasturba Gandhi a few words of English. From her account, Gandhi came to rely on her advice on the furnishing of the household.[34]

In June 1906 the suburban household was abandoned and all the members of Gandhi's household went to Phoenix. Millie did not greatly like the life there and after about a month and a half, because of her isolated life and 'a native rebellion',[35] she left the settlement for Durban before the Polaks returned to Johannesburg in August with Gandhi. When Polak took over editorship of *Indian Opinion* they continued to live in Gandhi's Johannesburg household with Henry spending several days a week at Phoenix to complete the editorial work on the paper.[36] Gandhi's wife and children remained at the settlement and it would be more than six years before Gandhi himself resided there on a permanent basis.

A quarter of a century later Millie wrote a book on Gandhi giving an insight into life in the Johannesburg household. Although this book is about Gandhi and Millie Polak's relationship with him, it is perhaps surprising how little light it sheds on the relationship between Polak and Gandhi. Nevertheless, from her account, although Polak was articled to Gandhi, the relationship does not appear to be one of a senior lawyer and his apprentice. There appears to be common purpose and an equality here – they lived together, took their meals together in a 'busy little household' where often guests joined them and generally around a dozen sat down to dinner every night and Gandhi even assisted in the process of weaning the Polaks' child.[37] When the political struggle for Indians' rights meant that representations had to be made to India, it was Polak that Gandhi sent. Polak comes across as being Gandhi's right-hand man and confidant in his New Age experiments – although Millie decided that it was not for her, Gandhi and Polak undertook their dietary experiments, which could last 'for weeks or months at a time'.[38] Polak certainly was not an uncritical disciple. At one stage he did not speak to Gandhi for four days when he thought that Gandhi was letting down the India cause by not responding to a distorted, malicious and damaging newspaper article. When he did

[34] See, John C. Vine, 'Interview with Mrs. Millie Graham Polak', 2 May 1960, in S. Durai Raja Singam, 'They Were Ready to Talk About Gandhi', unpublished manuscript, (n.d.), pp. 16–20.

[35] This was the so-called 'Zulu Rebellion'. Although Gandhi's sympathies may have been with the Zulus, he felt that as a subject of the Empire he had to assist the British. He formed an Indian Ambulance corps which was in active service for six weeks, tending the, mostly Zulu, wounded.

[36] Thomson, *Gandhi and His Ashrams*, p. 62.

[37] Millie Graham Polak, *Mr. Gandhi: The Man* (London: Allen and Unwin, 1931), pp. 31, 97.

[38] *Ibid.*, p. 82.

break his silence he argued angrily with the Mahatma-to-be. The impasse (although we are never told why Gandhi did not take up the pen) ended when Gandhi suggested that Henry could write the rejoinder.[39]

At 6.30 every morning the male members took to the task of grinding wheat for the home-baked bread, both as a practical necessity and as a form of exercise which was supplemented by skipping (at which Gandhi was adept).[40] The Johannesburg house, in a 'fairly good middle class neighbourhood, on the outskirts of town', was a free-standing, two-storied, eight-roomed modern villa surrounded by a garden and facing the open space of the hilly countryside. In the hot weather the residents often slept on the upstairs veranda.[41] From here they went to Phoenix with its unlined huts of corrugated iron and rough wooden supports, where the bathrooms were lean-tos with holes in the roof under suspended watering cans, operated by lengths of cord, to serve as showers.[42] Millie notes that the ideas they had had when discussing the simple life and reading about it in the study, ideas that sounded so right and reasonable, 'were often found impracticable when applied to the hard facts of life'.[43] When Gandhi had to move residence to be nearer to his political activities, he went with the Polaks rather than his own immediate family.

Although in his early correspondences Gandhi uses formal addresses, for example referring to Polak as 'Dear Mr. Polak', when Gandhi had to go to England on a deputation in 1906 his description of Polak's parents and sisters, who received him so warmly, tell of his very informal relationship with Henry.[44] Gandhi jokingly wrote to Polak that his two sisters were so lovable that if he were 'unmarried, or young or believed in mixed marriage, you know what I would have done!'[45] Almost fifteen years later, in a letter to Mahadev Desai, Gandhi recalls that 'I used to tell Polak that he had two wives, Mrs. Polak and I, for he would pour himself out only before us two and likewise be angry only with us.'[46]

In short, the shared Gandhi/Polak household was a hotbed of experimentation in health, dietary and educational matters.[47] In this laboratory

[39] *Ibid.*, pp. 24–7.   [40] *Ibid.*, p. 23.   [41] *Ibid.*, pp. 18–19.   [42] *Ibid.*, p. 49.   [43] *Ibid.*, p. 55.

[44] As time went on, Gandhi shed formality in his writings to friends, not just the Polaks. Within two years of this letter his correspondence was always addressed to 'My Dear Henry' or 'My Dear Polak', and where for others in his orbit he would soon begin signing letters as 'Bapu' [father], to the Polaks he for ever remained 'Bhai' [brother].

[45] Letter to H. S. L. Polak, 26 October 1906. And Maud, one of the sisters, seems quite clearly to be infatuated with him. See Letters to Millie Graham Polak, 14 November 1909 and to H. S. L. Polak, 15 November 1909.

[46] Letter to Mahadev Desai, 15 May 1920.

[47] See Millie Graham Polak, 'In the South African Days', in Chandrashanker Shukla (ed.), *Incidents of Gandhiji's Life* (Bombay: Vora, 1949), pp. 247–51.

life ideologies were being forged, and probably the supportive atmosphere of fellow cranks, in particular Henry Polak, ensured that the experiments were conducted with much enthusiasm. It seems that experiments with Truth are easier if done in the company of fellow-seekers and soulmates.

POLAK AS INSTRUMENTAL IN GANDHI'S PROGRESS

Perhaps Polak was a friend along for the ride in a very creatively evolving time in Gandhi's life and perhaps, to at least some degree, he was instrumental in bringing about the changes we see in Gandhi. In an important and early biography of Gandhi, written in three sections by those who knew him at the relevant time, the small biographical sketch of Polak, who covered Gandhi's early life until he left South Africa, informs us that, 'In 1904 he launched Gandhi on the "simple-life" practice which he maintained till his death.' We are further informed that, 'From 1904–14 he was Gandhi's closest colleague and confidant, and his lieutenant in his long Passive Resistance struggle in South Africa. He was a pioneer of Gandhi's movement to end indentured-labour emigration from India.'[48] Elsewhere, Polak notes that in giving Gandhi Ruskin's *Unto This Last* a 'deep and fundamental change' in Gandhi's thinking, that had been 'developing quietly for some time' finally crystallized with his intervention.[49] Of course self-claims do not always stand up to more objective scrutiny, after all who would not want to be credited with, if it was not an entirely preposterous proposition, something of the order of launching the Mahatma on the life practice that became synonymous with his saintly persona? Nevertheless, in this case they should not be discounted too easily.

In the early, most creative time in their relationship, Polak and Gandhi were so close physically that there is no available correspondence to shed further light on other forms of closeness. Diary extracts of the time when they were engaged in their most creative experimentation, had they existed, would have been most illuminating. However some later letters, especially those between Gandhi and Millie, do throw some light on their interactions.

Gandhi wrote to Millie in London welcoming her to South Africa and Millie later was to remember that the letter 'set the tone to the whole of my relationship with him, establishing him in my life as a loving and understanding elder brother and showed the human tenderness of the

[48] H. S. L. Polak, H. N. Brailsord and Lord Pethick-Lawrence, *Mahatma Gandhi* (London: Odhams Press, 1949), p. 9.
[49] Polak, 'Some South African Reminiscences', p. 238.

man'.[50] Their closeness became such that when Gandhi's wife Kasturba wanted something for herself or her children, she would ask Millie to intercede with Gandhi on her behalf. Although she often disagreed with Gandhi, and, although it did not dent their relationship, did so fearlessly, she was a fellow traveller with Gandhi who could enjoy good-naturedly having a laugh at Gandhi's expense.[51] He addressed her in his letters as 'My Dear Millie', and ended them 'With love', signing them as 'Brother', and the letters themselves were quite personal in content, touching on the deepest of feelings.[52]

In their 'bachelor' days, before the return of his family to South Africa from India and the arrival of Millie, Henry and Gandhi used to eat salads and uncooked vegetables regularly at vegetarian restaurants. With some friends, in a state of high amusement, they formed the 'Amalgamated Society of Onion Eaters' with Gandhi as President and Polak as Treasurer of a non-existent treasury.[53] In some of their dietary experiments, Henry was ahead of Gandhi: for example when Polak decided to go on a cleansing and will-power affirming fast, Gandhi and the other friends tried to dissuade him, least it do him harm.[54] Polak lived with Gandhi before the latter's experiments with asceticism – this was sometime before Gandhi's own first fast. Perhaps the new relationship with Polak was already bearing fruit.

There are, however, concrete examples where in these early days Polak did have an influence on Gandhi. Soon he was coaching the attorney on his speaking style. In rapid speech, Gandhi had a habit of hesitation and a drawing of breath when seeking the appropriate word. He brought this to Gandhi's attention and suggested that it would be beneficial to correct the habit so that it would not distract from his argument in public speech. Gandhi took the suggestion on board and eliminated the habit. Gandhi gave Polak his badge from the London Vegetarian Society when he joined Gandhi's household in Johannesburg. This was a period of intellectual and spiritual ferment. Polak describes their relationship as one of bhai (brother) and chhotabhai (younger brother).[55] Polak's later letters to Gandhi seem to back this up – they do not show a worshipful acolyte but someone who was quite capable of expressing difference and more often someone who could

---

[50] M. G. Polak, *Mr. Gandhi*, p. 11. See Gandhi's letter to Millie Graham Polak, 3 July 1905, awaiting her arrival.

[51] See for example her description of life at Phoenix, Letter to H. S. L. Polak, 15 November 1909.

[52] See for example, Letter to Millie Graham Polak, 31 December 1909.

[53] Polak, 'Some South African Reminiscences', p. 240.

[54] *Ibid.*   [55] *Ibid.*, pp. 233, 241, 244.

poke gentle fun at his friend's more immoderate habits.[56] Back in India, Gandhi would recall that Polak 'would fight every inch of ground before conceding any of my points, compel me to think deeply and draw me out to a firm decision'.[57]

Until his first intense encounter with his new young English friend, Gandhi was still something of an armchair New Ager. Now, living together, they could put their shared ideals into practice. They read books on nature cure and healthy and ethical diets and followed the various mud and water therapies (steam baths, cold plunge and hip baths, enemas) they espoused, used their recipes and experimented with their diets. There was no one before Henry with whom Gandhi could do these things. Green perceptively notes that 'This rebellion against scientific medicine was profoundly important for its symbolic rejection of elements of Western culture of which most people were most proud.'[58] This rebellion was facilitated by Polak's wholehearted participation.

Even though he was rarely able to stay there for longer than a few weeks at a time, often with very lengthy periods in between, the settlement at Phoenix was crucial in the development of Gandhi's ideas and future domestic and political modus operandi. Probably at some time Gandhi would have come to the idea of setting up a rural self-sufficient community even if Polak had not given him a copy of Ruskin's book to read. After all, that book was just the final nudge in a steady groping towards the idea, but one that was greatly accelerated by the participation of Polak in the time between their meeting at Mrs Bissiks' home and Gandhi's trip to Durban to investigate the financial position of *Indian Opinion*. And while the establishment of the settlement was important in itself,[59] it was only the most visible symbol of changes that Gandhi was undergoing at this time. To understand these changes adequately, one must also understand the relationship between Gandhi and Henry Polak.

Polak was not a mere disciple of Gandhi. They debated, argued (Polak thought Gandhi was doing the wrong thing and hampering the life chances of his children by teaching them only in Gujarati and neglecting English[60]), and bounced ideas off each other. In fact, the relationship appears to have

---

[56] See Green, *Gandhi*, p. 178.

[57] Mahadev Desai, *Day to Day with Gandhi: Secretary's Diary* (Rajghat, Varanasi: Sarva Seva Sangh, 1968), vol. I, p. 181.

[58] Green, *Gandhi*, p. 154.

[59] 'In South Africa, my best creation was Phoenix. Without it, there would have been no satyagraha in that country. Without the Ashram here [at Sabarmati], satyagraha will be impossible in India.' 'Address to Ashram Inmates', 17 February 1919.

[60] Gandhi, *Autobiography*, p. 230.

been so close that Kasturba 'out of jealousy' used to call Polak Gandhi's 'first-born'.[61]

With his family at Phoenix, Gandhi was in Johannesburg with the Polaks continuing his legal work until about 1908 when it was gradually suspended so that he could devote himself full-time to the satyagraha struggle. As the campaign became more heated, he was badly beaten up and stayed with the Dokes to recuperate until, soon after, he started living with Kallenback, his next soulmate.

THE END OF RELATIONSHIP

After Polak had been registered as an Attorney of the Supreme Court of the Transvaal, he earned a reputation in the Indian community for defending those charged with offenses that arose from Gandhi's 'passive resistance'. He remained a tireless co-worker in the campaigns led by Gandhi for the equality of the Indian community. When the 'Great March' of satyagrahis into the Transvaal under Gandhi's leadership took place in November 1913, Gandhi wanted to keep Polak out of the battle so that he could go to India and do propaganda work there. However, when Gandhi was arrested, Polak had to step into his place and soon both he and Kallenbach were in prison with Gandhi. Polak served a sentence of three months simple imprisonment.

Gandhi and Polak had an agreement that when the South African campaign came to an end Polak should return to England so that his children could be 'brought up in an atmosphere free from racial and colour prejudice'.[62] But now Gandhi felt 'the call to return to India' and knew that one of them had to stay in South Africa to 'see the Agreement through'. He asked if Polak would stay 'to serve the Indian community in his place' as he had often done during Gandhi's imprisonments and trips to England. They referred the matter to Millie, 'who told him that, in all the circumstances, though it was a terrible disappointment, she felt that I must free him for his great mission. Who can say what might have been the course of political events in India, had the decision been otherwise and he had been obliged to remain in South Africa?'[63]

Gandhi left South Africa for India via London in July 1914. The Phoenix ashramites left for India under the leadership of Maganlal Gandhi two

---

[61] Letter to Millie Graham Polak, 14 November 1909; and letter to Henry on the following day.
[62] Polak, 'Some South African Reminiscences', p. 246.
[63] *Ibid.*, pp. 246–47; see also Polak, Brailsford and Pethick-Lawrence, *Mahatma Gandhi*, p. 94.

weeks later. The Polaks and their two young children stayed on to ensure the implementation of the agreement to remove the poll-tax on indentured Indian labourers and accept the legality of non-Christian marriages with the South African government following the conclusion of the campaign. In 1916 they went to India and stayed until 1917 to help end the practice of indentured Indians being sent to South Africa.[64] Henry spent time with Gandhi at Champaran. Even after the Polaks settled back in England, they maintained an active interest in Indian affairs and in particular the issue of Indians overseas.

Gandhi the person was not neglected either. As an appendix to a collection of speeches and writings of Gandhi originally published in 1918, Polak provided an appreciation of Gandhi in which his friend is a saint, nothing less. Polak explains that Gandhi's extraordinary love of truth is a characteristic that marks him out from others, that 'his self-suppression and courtesy are universally recognised and appreciated', that his 'generosity is proverbial', that his 'sense of public duty is profound' (after all, he was willing to leave ailing and possibly dying children and wife to God rather than interrupt his public duty), that 'his chivalry is at once the admiration of his friends and followers and the confusion of enemies', and that 'his simplicity is extreme'. The hagiographical sketch informs us that for Gandhi religion was everything (religious men are often politicians in disguise while Gandhi is a religious man in the guise of a politician) and that the self-suffering involved in his self-denial and attempts to purify his physical nature are, for him, a 'daily joy and delight'.[65]

Eventually, however, Henry's politics diverged from Gandhi's. He could not understand Gandhi's policies of recruitment of Indian troops to fight for the British in the Great War and did not agree with the Quit India movement during the Second World War. At the time of the Khilafat movement, Polak thought that Gandhi had become too narrow in his views 'because he was cooped up in India and not knowing anything of the new life in Europe'. From the other side, Gandhi came to see the new life in Europe, which Polak could not appreciate because, 'being in the thick of it', he could not 'feel the foul stench that modern Europe is filling the world with', as a place of dishonesty and 'idolatrous worship of brute force and money'.[66] Polak came to see Gandhi as 'too extravagant in his

[64] Homer A. Jack, 'Henry S. L. Polak', *Gandhi Marg* 3 (1959), p. 291.
[65] H. S. L. Polak, 'Appendix II' in M. K. Gandhi, *Speeches and Writings of M. K. Gandhi* (Madras: G. A. Natesan, 1922), Appendices, pp. 38–44.
[66] Letter to H. S. L. Polak, 27 March 1920.

methods and too religious in his principles'.[67] According to Pyarelal, 'He even conducted active propaganda against us in the USA, which at the time hurt Gandhiji deeply and for some time he and Polak were almost on non-speaking terms.'[68] In Gandhi's biography of the South African struggle, where he gives a description of his European supporters, the space devoted to Henry Polak is surprisingly small – one paragraph as opposed to the four-and-a-half pages for Albert West, and over a page for Kallenbach (who also gets extensive coverage in the chapters dealing with Tolstoy Farm). The paragraph finishes with the observation that 'The Polaks did not see eye to eye with us in the Non-cooperation movement, but they are still serving India to the best of their ability.'[69]

Regardless of these periods of active disagreement, to the end of Gandhi's life they kept up a friendly correspondence. Any late divergence in views, or downplaying of the connection, cannot detract from the supportive and productive relationship they shared during the period of Gandhi's adoption of a more simple life around the time of his reading of Ruskin and his relocation, incomplete as it was, to the rural settlement at Phoenix from the household of a busy lawyer in Johannesburg. The relatively short period when the two single men were in the middle of their most intense relationship was a life-changing one for Gandhi, turning him from city lawyer to constructive worker and spiritual seeker ashramite.

---

[67] Martin Green, *The Origins of Nonviolence: Tolstoy and Gandhi in their Historical Settings* (University Park: Pennsylvania State University Press, 1986), p. 151.
[68] Pyarelal and Sushila Nayar, *In Gandhiji's Mirror* (Delhi: Oxford University Press, 1991), p. 299.
[69] Gandhi, *Satyagraha in South Africa*, p. 273.

CHAPTER 4

Hermann Kallenbach and the move to Tolstoy Farm

INTRODUCTION

After the rush of creativity in 1904 and 1905 with his Jewish soulmate Polak, Gandhi had another close Jewish friend who also took on the position of soulmate and was influential in another burst of inner questing in the Mahatma-in-making, and was involved with Gandhi in another geographical relocation.

Kallenbach was perhaps less challenging to Gandhi than Polak, partly because he became deeply involved in Gandhi's life later, but he was also less resistant to Gandhi, possibly because at the stage of their greatest closeness Gandhi was more sure of himself, and because Kallenbach was less assertive of his own temperament.[1] When he came into contact with Gandhi, he threw his lot in with his mentor, turning his back on his former profligate life with the type of zeal displayed by late-in-life converts. When he was separated from Gandhi he readily fell back into his old ways, only to give them up once more when later in life he again spent time with the Mahatma. Regardless of his changes of direction and the power Gandhi held over him, he also had a large influence on Gandhi. Tolstoy Farm became the prototype Gandhian ashram and the forging of the institution as a spiritual laboratory, rather than merely as an experiment in communal living, was done together with Hermann Kallenbach. In fact Tolstoy Farm owes its very existence to Kallenbach. Gandhi's life may have been significantly different without Tolstoy Farm, and without Kallenbach there may have been no equivalent of Tolstoy Farm to help mould the Mahatma we know.

HERMANN KALLENBACH BEFORE GANDHI

Hermann Kallenbach was born in 1871 to a Jewish family in Neustadt in East Prussia. One of seven children, he was raised in a small village near the

---

[1] Green, *The Origins of Nonviolence*, p. 151.

Baltic coast but his upbringing was not one of the Jewish shtetl. His father was a timber merchant and education was taken seriously in the family. Hermann was educated in German schools and in 1890 became apprenticed to a master carpenter in Königsberg, and a year later to a master mason in Stuttgart. During the apprenticeships he was also a student at the Royal School for Architects in Stuttgart. In 1893/94 he worked as a draftsman in an architect's office following which he served a year in the Royal Engineers Battalion in the German army. The studies were complemented by an avid interest in body building, ice-skating, swimming and cycling. He graduated in May 1896 with qualifications as a mason, carpenter, building technician and architect.[2] Three months later the twenty-five-year-old Kallenbach left for South Africa to join his uncles Henry and Simon Sacke in Johannesburg, a boom town with a need for those in the building trade.

From 1896 and 1906, with a break to further his architectural studies in Europe during the Boer War between 1899 and 1901, Kallenbach practised as an architect in Durban and Johannesburg as Senior Partner of the firm Kallenbach & Reynolds. In 1906 he was registered as a member of the Transvaal Institute of Architects in Johannesburg.[3]

Sometime in 1903 Kallenbach met Gandhi through Gandhi's barrister friend and co-secretary of the Natal Indian Congress, R. K. Khan, who 'had discovered a deep vein of otherworldliness' in Kallenbach and decided to introduce him to Gandhi. At the first meeting, Gandhi was 'startled by his love of luxury and extravagance', however they discussed deep matters of religion such as those concerning the Buddha's renunciation. As was the case with Polak, he ate with the barrister Gandhi at vegetarian restaurants and eventually their acquaintance grew 'into very close friendship, so much so that we thought alike, and he was convinced that he must carry out in his life the changes I was making in mine'.[4] But the influences were not all one way, and even if again in this important relationship Kallenbach was the junior partner (with the exception of Gokhale, this was usual with Gandhi's close relationships after about this time), his own progress was facilitated by the company of someone who agreed with him, supported him and made suggestions about possible further life changes.

In May 1907, Gandhi wrote to *The Star* about the degrading effects of the racist *Asiatic Registration Act*. A short time later Kallenbach who, while 'not taking part in political matters' had been 'following with interest

---

[2] Isa Sarid and Christian Bartolf, *Hermann Kallenbach: Mahatma Gandhi's Friend in South Africa* (Berlin: Gandhi Informations Zentrum, 1997), pp. 10–12.
[3] *Ibid.*, pp. 115–16.   [4] Gandhi, *An Autobiography*, p. 242.

the various stages of action among the Transvaal Indians in their struggle to defend their legitimate rights', also wrote to the paper criticising the legislation and backing the Indian opposition. He finished the letter by declaring that he would 'consider it a privilege to visit my Indian friends in the gaol and to do my utmost to redress the hardships of prison life which they are prepared to undergo'.[5] In print Gandhi complimented Kallenbach on his 'noble letter' hoping that it would herald the beginning of further support from outside the community. It must have been a huge political risk for a successful businessman to write to the daily press a letter that could see him branded a race-traitor.

Of course by this time Kallenbach was a firm friend of Gandhi's and understood the debates about race competition in South Africa, however the friendship was not yet so close that he was prepared to give up his lifestyle and throw his lot in with Gandhi. A year later he wrote to his brother Simon about Gandhi and the settlement at Phoenix. He noted that the 'system of this colony is to educate and show [the inmates] a way of life in which they can live as an example to their fellow Indians, a tremendously modest and yet a lovable way of life'. However, he quickly added: 'I do *not* intend to join the community of this colony.'[6]

FROM UPPER HOUSE TO LOWER HOUSE

In his account of the South Africa days, Gandhi remembered his friend Kallenbach as

a man of strong feelings, wide sympathies and child-like simplicity. He is an architect by profession, but there is no work, however lowly, which he would consider to be beneath his dignity. When I broke up my Johannesburg establishment, I lived with him, but he would be hurt if I offered to pay him my share of the household expenses, and would plead that I was responsible for considerable savings in his domestic economy. This was indeed true.[7]

Gandhi's influence on Kallenbach grew stronger the longer they knew each other. Gandhi induced Kallenbach to become a vegetarian, give up alcohol and tobacco and, under Gandhi's influence, he managed to reduce his personal expenditure by 90 per cent. Gandhi's compromise with the government over registration certificates in early 1908 saw him labelled as

---

[5] See Gandhi's 'Johannesburg Letter', *Indian Opinion*, 8 May 1907.
[6] Kallenbach to Simon Kallenbach, 10 June 1908; quoted in Sarid and Bartolf, *Hermann Kallenbach*, pp. 14–15.
[7] Gandhi, *Satyagraha in South Africa*, pp. 273–4.

a traitor by some in the Indian community. Kallenbach, with revolver in pocket, started acting as his personal bodyguard. When Gandhi discovered this he shamed his friend into getting rid of the weapon by asking whether 'Ruskin or Tolstoy in any of their books suggested that one should carry a revolver in one's pocket'.[8] A short time after this, on 10 February in the well-known incident, Gandhi was severely beaten up by the enraged Pathan Mir Alam. Following his convalescence at the home of his old friend Reverend Doke, Gandhi took up temporary residence in Kallenbach's home while his family remained at Phoenix.

Although in 1908 Kallenbach was not yet ready to live communally at Phoenix, Gandhi's impact on him was great. In his letter to Simon Kallenbach he recounted how he had not eaten meat for two years, fish for one year, and 'for the last 18 months I have given up my sex life'. He added: 'I believe that I have gained in character – strength – mental vitality and physical development; my bodily well-being has become better and bigger . . . I have changed my daily life in order to simplify it and I found out that, in every direction, this change has helped me; and I hope that I shall be able to continue my life accordingly.'[9] Kallenbach also had the privilege of sharing Gandhi's first penitential fast at Phoenix in 1913 over the 'moral lapse' of two inmates and of being arrested with Gandhi and Polak in November 1913.

On Gandhi's release from prison in December 1908, following the serving of a two-month sentence for not having a registration card and refusing to be finger printed, Kallenbach turned up to the prison with a new car to fetch his friend. Gandhi was far from impressed at the unnecessary expense, and directed his hapless companion to 'Put a match to it at once.' Kallenbach protested that he could not afford to do that and for the following year the car remained in the garage unused until Kallenbach sold it. It took another eleven years before he would have another car.[10]

In July 1914 on the voyage to meet Gokhale in London after the final departure from South Africa, Gandhi again brutally demonstrated to his friend his disdain for worldly goods. Before sailing, Kallenbach purchased a pair of binoculars to help out one of his uncles who was strapped for cash. Although he did not need them, as a face-saving gesture to help out a relative, he explained that they would be useful on the voyage. Another pair was given to him as a parting present by friends. He had no time to consult

---

[8] Prabhudas Gandhi, *My Childhood with Gandhi*, p. 69.
[9] Kallenbach to Simon Kallenbach, 10 June 1908; quoted in Sarid and Bartolf, *Hermann Kallenbach*, pp. 16–17.
[10] Desai, 'Weekly Letter: Hermann Kallenbach', *Harijan*, 29 May 1937.

Gandhi on these matters. On the ship, coming to know that Kallenbach had two pairs of binoculars, someone offered to buy one pair from him. This Kallenbach reported to Gandhi who became 'very much annoyed when he found that I had purchased a costly pair of binoculars without his permission'.[11] In Gandhi's version of what followed there were daily discussions about the objects. He recalled that he tried to impress on his friend 'that this possession was not in keeping with the ideal of simplicity that we aspired to reach'. Their discussions came to a head one day, as they were standing near the porthole of their cabin. 'Rather than allow these to be a bone of contention between us, why not throw them into the sea and be done with them?' Gandhi asked. Kallenbach reportedly instructed Gandhi to 'throw the wretched things away', whereupon Gandhi 'flung them into the sea. They were worth some £7, but their value lay less in their price than in Mr Kallenbach's infatuation for them. However, having got rid of them, he never regretted it.'[12] In Kallenbach's version, as told to Mahadev Desai many years later, there does not seem to be much discussion at all. Gandhi 'asked' Kallenbach to throw them into the sea and when he did not have the heart to do it, 'without the slightest twitch of conscience' Gandhi threw both pairs into the ocean. Desai was shocked by the story and asked why Gandhi would have disposed of the other pair, the pair that was a gift from friends. Poor Kallenbach still could not quite understand the logic of Gandhi's actions and added that he 'could not help crying that day'. Kallenbach was wealthy and liked buying small expensive items (such as silver serviette rings) without seeing the need to consult Gandhi, who would promptly 'throw them on the rubbish heap', 'shouting in distress' the question 'Don't you still understand me?' Looking back at Gandhi's treatment of him, Kallenbach insisted that Gandhi 'lavished his affection on me and therefore dealt with me more severely than he would have done with others. That was the tyranny of his affection, but that affection is my proudest possession.'[13]

The letters between Gandhi and Kallenbach before the move to Tolstoy Farm, besides the reports of the satyagraha struggle, contain much discussion about diet experiments and bowel movements and about Kallenbach's, perhaps excessive, almost disciple-like devotion to his mentor.[14] And during Gandhi's trip to London to further the cause of South African Indians, he wrote to Kallenbach informing him that his portrait is the only one on the mantelpiece opposite his bed,[15] and compared Kallenbach's friendship with

---

[11] *Ibid.*   [12] Gandhi, *An Autobiography*, p. 254.   [13] Desai, 'Weekly Letter'.
[14] See, for example, Letter to Kallenbach, 30 August 1909.
[15] Letter to Kallenbach, 24 September 1909.

those one reads about in history books and novels, praying that he would never forfeit his friend's superhuman love.[16] When Gandhi had shifted to Tolstoy Farm and Kallenbach was in Europe visiting family, Gandhi kept him informed of happenings on the community and also of his own internal struggles and insights, as well as reminding him not to fall back into ways of luxury but to keep poverty and suffering as the goal. Later correspondences are partly newsletters, partly love letters (with Kallenbach complaining when Gandhi's letters are too short or there is too long a time between them), a vehicle for Gandhi to complain about his 'venomous' wife (with whom Kallenbach had a close relationship) in a way that he would only do with the closest confidant, and partly descriptions of their various diets.[17]

From 1909 Gandhi and Kallenbach addressed each other as Upper House and Lower House respectively.[18] Gandhi terms Kallenbach's letters 'charming love notes', and Kallenbach refers to Kasturba as 'Mother'. After 1910 Gandhi signs his letters to Kallenbach 'with love' and at times refers to themselves as being 'one soul in two bodies'.[19] Hunt asserts that the relationship was 'clearly homoerotic' while certainly not homosexual.[20] The love relationship also contained a lot of humour while, in keeping with the addresses used by Gandhi and Kallenbach for each other, demonstrating who was the senior and who the junior partner.[21] This is best illustrated by an 'agreement' struck between the two at the end of July 1911 before Kallenbach went to England and Scotland to visit various New Agers and Tolstoyans, and to East Prussia to visit his family:

Articles of Agreement between Lower House and Upper House. Lower House is to proceed to Europe on a sacred pilgrimage to the members of his family during the month of August next. Lower House is not to spend any money beyond necessaries befitting the position of a simple-living poor farmer. Lower House is not to contract any marriage tie during his absence. Lower House shall not look lustfully upon any woman. Lower House is to travel 3rd-class whether by sea or land. Lower House may, if the exigencies of his business in Johannesburg permit it, visit India with Dr. Mehta. In the event of his so doing he will travel the same class as Dr. Mehta.

[16] Letter to Kallenbach, 30 August 1909. [17] See for example Letter to Kallenbach, 12 April 1914.

[18] In English parliamentary practice of the time, the Upper House (or House of Lords) was the highest appeal court and without its consent no laws could be made. The Lower House (or House of Commons) had control of the Treasury. The titles were wonderfully apt.

[19] See, for example, Letters to Kallenbach, 15 March 1914 and 17 April 1914.

[20] James D. Hunt, 'The Kallenbach Papers and Tolstoy Farm', unpublished working paper presented to the Association for Asian Studies meeting in Washington, DC, 6–9 April 1995, p. 4.

[21] Green states that sceptics characterised Kallenbach as Gandhi's puppet and that both Gandhi and Kallenbach 'worried about whether he was'. See Green, *Gandhi*, p. 181.

Lower House will not tarry long in London or any other place, save the homes of the members of the family. The consideration for all the above tasks imposed by Lower House on himself is more love and yet more love between the two Houses such love as, they hope, the world has not seen. In witness whereof the parties hereto solemnly affix their signatures in the presence of the Maker of all this 29th day of July at Tolstoy Farm.

Signed by Upper House and Lower House in their own hands.

FROM LOWER HOUSE TO UPPER HOUSE

Gandhi's struggle with the government over the unfair treatment of Indian indentured labourers lasted for eight years. He later admitted that he was unsure whether they could have managed this and whether the people could have borne the hardships had there been no Tolstoy Farm.[22] As the campaigners were becoming dispirited at the length of the struggle and as the more wealthy merchants drifted away leaving a greater number of poorer resisters, Gandhi realised that they needed to be properly trained in the resolve necessary to prosecute an effective satyagraha campaign and somehow that campaign had to be put on a sounder financial footing. For this a 'central place where a corporate sense of purpose might be instilled' became necessary.[23] The struggle had shifted to the Transvaal after 1906 and this meant that Gandhi could not spend the time he may have wanted at Phoenix, instead he had to operate from his Johannesburg headquarters. During the intensification of the satyagraha campaign in 1908–9, Gandhi cut back on his practice of law for lack of time, abandoned his Johannesburg home and moved in permanently with Kallenbach.[24] And, in the following year, when it became time for the establishment of a settlement for the dependants of the satyagrahis who had been imprisoned, where they could do some valuable work to help defray the costs of the campaign and even earn something of a living, it was clear that it had to be near Johannesburg. Gandhi had money and was also being funded by the Indian community

---

[22] Gandhi, *Satyagraha in South Africa*, p. 393.

[23] Surendra Bhana, 'The Tolstoy Farm: Gandhi's Experiment in 'Cooperative Commonwealth'', *South African Historical Journal* 7 (1975), available at www.anc.org.za/andocs/history/people/gandhi/bhana.htm

[24] The chronology is a little unclear here. James Hunt notes that 'For about two years [before the establishing of Tolstoy Farm] Gandhi has been sharing a house with the bachelor architect, Hermann Kallenbach, six miles from Johannesburg.' This would put the move to Kallenbach's house to 1908. James D. Hunt, 'Experiments in Forming a Community of Service: The Evolution of Gandhi's First Ashrams, Phoenix and Tolstoy Farm', in K. L. Seshagiri Rao and Henry O. Thompson (eds.) *World Problems and Human Responsibility: Gandhian Perspectives* (Barrytown, NY: Unification Theological Seminary, 1988), p. 187. Kallenbach says that Gandhi had lived with him since 1907 (see below).

in whose name he was leading the struggle, however the legal position in the Transvaal was different to the one in Natal. Here Indians could only legally own land in certain urban locations, and, for Gandhi's plan to come to fruition, European ownership was required.[25] Kallenbach came to the rescue.

While Kallenbach spoke on the Indian cause at various meetings, it was not until early in 1910 that he decided to take a more active part in the movement. At this stage Gandhi was looking to purchase a property from public funds to concentrate the dependent families. Kallenbach continues the story:

At this time, I offered to purchase a farm at my own expense, in order to be able to extend a refuge to the families and their dependants. My offer was accepted. I purchased a farm approximately 20 miles south of Johannesburg, in May 1910. I named the farm 'Tolstoy Farm'. . . . Mr. Gandhi, and from time to time his sons or friends, lived with me from the beginning of 1907. In June 1910 we all moved to Tolstoy Farm. We lived the life of simple farmers, and had only one vegetarian kitchen for all settlers.[26]

On 30 May 1910, Kallenbach formally offered Gandhi the use of his farm in writing:

In accordance with our conversation, I offer to you the use of my farm near Lawley for passive resisters and their indigent families; the families and passive resisters to live on the farm free of any rent or charge, as long as the struggle with the Transvaal Government lasts. They may also use, free of charge, all the buildings not at present used by me.

Any structural alterations, additions or improvements made by you may be removed at your pleasure on the termination of occupation, or they will be paid for by me at a valuation in the usual manner, the terms of payment to be mutually agreed upon by us.

I propose to pay, at a valuation in the usual manner, [for] all the agricultural improvements that may have been made by the settlers. The settlers to withdraw from the farm on the termination of the struggle.[27]

In one of his letters to Tolstoy, Gandhi told the Count that Kallenbach was deeply touched by his writings and that he had gone through most of the experiences described in Tolstoy's book *My Confessions*. As a spur to 'further effort in living up to the ideals held before the world by you', after consultation with Gandhi, he named the property 'Tolstoy Farm'.[28] Two

---

[25] Hunt, 'The Kallenbach Papers and Tolstoy Farm', p. 2.
[26] From Kallenbach's letter diary to his sister Jeanette from Krugersdorp Jail, 21 November 1913, quoted in Sarid and Bartolf, *Hermann Kallenbach*, p. 34.
[27] See Letter to Kallenbach, 30 May 1910.   [28] Letter to Tolstoy, 15 August 1910.

years later Kallenbach threw his lot in completely with the Indian struggle and placed his Johannesburg mansion 'Mountain View' at the disposal of Indian families, gave up his architectural work and moved to Tolstoy Farm where Hermann became known as 'Hanuman'.[29]

The 1,100-acre farm was far enough from Johannesburg to free it from the 'varied distractions of a city'[30] but only one mile from the local station of Lawley. The soil at the property was fertile. The farm contained almost 1,000 orange, apricot, plum, fig, almond and walnut trees, which would provide income, meaningful labour and food, as well as two wells and a spring for water. The small house built by the previous owner, while somewhat dilapidated, could accommodate six people.

The farm was to be self-sufficient, totally dispensing with the use of servants. It was also to be more communal than Phoenix where each resident family had their own house and plot of land. Here inmates were to live in shared accommodation, eat from a common kitchen and cultivate the land jointly. The village model of Phoenix Settlement was replaced by a joint family model of Tolstoy Farm. For two months the residents lived in tents while permanent buildings were constructed under the guidance of Kallenbach (who also paid for the building materials), a European mason and a Gujarati carpenter. The first two blocks erected were the dormitories where the men and women were housed separately, and other buildings soon followed: a house for Kallenbach, a school house and a workshop for carpentry and shoemaking. When the initial buildings were up, Kasturba joined her husband at the farm. Gandhi persuaded the Christian and Muslim members of the community to give up meat and it goes without saying that the drinking of alcohol and smoking were totally prohibited.

In 1912 Gandhi and Kallenbach were heavily back into dietetic experimentation and Kallenbach suggested that they give up milk because they constantly discussed its harmful effects and unnaturalness after infancy. Both of them gave up milk 'there and then'. Soon the two Tolstoyans had come to live on a diet of fruit, nuts and olive oil, enabling them to abandon cooking almost entirely. The ingredients were the cheapest available because their 'ambition was to live the life of the poorest people'.[31]

It was made a rule that train travel to Johannesburg could only be undertaken for public business and then only by third class. Those who wanted to go on pleasure trips had to walk and carry all their provisions with them so as not to have to spend money on food in the city. The journey by foot

[29] Prabhudas Gandhi, *My Childhood with Gandhi*, p. 135.
[30] Gandhi, *Satyagraha in South Africa*, p. 357.   [31] Gandhi, *An Autobiography*, pp. 242–3.

was done in a day with the traveller rising at 2 a.m. and setting out half an hour later. Johannesburg would be reached in six or seven hours (the record time being four hours and eighteen minutes set by Kallenbach). This saved a great deal of money and benefited the walkers but increased the money spent on shoes.

Gandhi wanted every young person at Tolstoy Farm to be trained in some useful manual vocation and for this reason, soon after the farm had been settled, in July 1910 Kallenbach went to the Mariann Hill German Trappist monastery near Durban to learn sandal-making. He taught Gandhi the craft and soon Gandhi was passing this knowledge on to others as Kallenbach was teaching carpentry.[32] In a short time Gandhi was able to claim that he was 'mostly busy making sandals these days'. Not only did he like the work but could brag in a letter to Maganlal at Phoenix that 'I have already made about fifteen pairs. When you need new ones now, please send me the measurements. And when you do so, mark the places where the strap is to be fixed – that is, on the outer side of the big toe and the little toe.'[33]

The burden of teaching at the farm school was largely borne by Gandhi and Kallenbach. The children learned tolerance for each other's religions and customs and Gandhi termed the schooling experiment, imperfect though it might have been due to 'mischievous and lazy' youngsters, fatigue on the part of students and teachers after a heavy morning of physical labour, and because of all too frequently absent teachers, 'a thoughtful and religious experiment' and one of the sweetest reminiscences of his time at Tolstoy Farm.[34]

At the farm Gandhi allowed the children of both sexes a great deal of freedom to mix naturally even at the swimming place (something later he came to see as a mistake with his increasing abhorrence of sexuality and diminished belief in the innocence of children[35]) and with the inmates he experimented with diets, health cures, fasting and the non-separation of private from public morality. His chief co-seeker, however, was always Kallenbach.

Kallenbach, the ex-lover of luxury who previously 'never hesitated to secure for his comfort everything that money could buy' lived and worked

[32] *Ibid.*, p. 246.   [33] Letter to Maganlal Gandhi, 14 February 1911.
[34] Gandhi, *Satyagraha in South Africa*, p. 369.
[35] See the disturbing passage where Gandhi tells of young men making fun of two girls and his cutting the long hair off the two victims as a 'warning to every young man that no evil eye might be cast upon them, and as a lesson to every girl that no one dare assail their purity'. Gandhi, *Satyagraha in South Africa*, p. 373.

at Tolstoy Farm as a simple member of the Indian community. He became the chief orchardist, teacher and financial backer of the farm and also was a regular walker to Johannesburg. For his life at the farm he earned the sobriquet of fool or lunatic from some Europeans, while others 'honoured him for his renunciation'.[36]

Gandhi and Kallenbach indulged at length in spiritual discussions and if either was convinced intellectually of a new truth, attempts to put it into practical application were made immediately. This is best illustrated when Gandhi convinced Kallenbach that it was as wrong to 'kill snakes and other such animals'. Once the logic of the position was clear, it had to be pushed to its inevitable conclusion: if it was wrong to kill snakes, their friendship should be cultivated. Kallenbach purchased books on snakes in order to be able to identify the species, taught the inmates of the farm the ability to distinguish the poisonous ones from those that protected field crops and even caught and tamed a large cobra which he hand fed. He and Gandhi had discussions on fear and love in respect to the relationship between snakes and humans. However, Gandhi had not achieved the spiritual equanimity that Raychand had written to him about more than fifteen years before, and he gave permission for a snake to be killed when no other way was found to remove if from Kallenbach's room.[37]

There were no plans to continue the farm after the struggle was over, however, when it seemed that an accommodation was at hand in early 1911, Gandhi decided to stay on at Tolstoy Farm with Kallenbach. At the beginning of 1913 the settlement was abandoned. Kallenbach was torn over the prospect of leaving his beloved farm and the start of a 'rift emerged between the two friends'.[38] The remaining inmates joined the Phoenix Settlement which now 'was no longer meant for the workers of *Indian Opinion* only; it was a satyagraha institution'. This greatly changed the earlier community:

The even tenor of the lives of the settlers at Phoenix was disturbed, and they had now to discern certainty in the midst of uncertainty like the satyagrahis. But they were equal to the new demands made upon them. As at Tolstoy Farm, so also at Phoenix I established a common kitchen which some joined while others had private kitchens of their own. The congregational prayer in the evening played a large part in our lives. And the final satyagraha campaign was started by the inmates of Phoenix Settlement in 1913.[39]

---

[36] *Ibid.*, p. 381. [37] *Ibid.*, pp. 382–5.
[38] Hunt, 'Experiments in Forming a Community', p. 193.
[39] M. K. Gandhi, *Ashram Observances in Action* (Ahmedabad: Navajivan, 1955), p. 6.

THE MEANING OF TOLSTOY FARM

Less than seven months after he had written the Gujarati document *Hind Swaraj* (for which Kallenbach had just helped Gandhi prepare an English translation[40]), Tolstoy Farm provided Gandhi with a way to put his arguments in his political and social manifesto into practice. Here was a real chance to experiment in a rural setting with the dignity of human labour in a community without doctors, lawyers or the oppressive hand of the state. He could, in fact had to, implement his ideas of communal harmony as the residents were from different races and linguistic groups as well as from different religions. It contained men, women and children with residents staying for varying periods of time. In Bhana's assessment, this provided Gandhi with a 'heterogeneous microcosm in which his leadership would prepare him for his role in the macrocosm of his battles in India later'.[41] Here the motivation in the first instance was not about running a printing press but as a venue for training in a satyagrahi lifestyle through spiritual, mental and physical exercise.[42] In short, it served the purpose of a training ground for spiritual matters that would also give the residents the strength needed for the political campaign that was unfolding in much the same way as later the Sabarmati Ashram would for the Salt Satyagraha.

James Hunt points out that while Gandhi was little more than an irregular visitor to Phoenix Settlement, at Tolstoy Farm

he was for the first time the physical as well as the moral center of a community. It was his first taste of the full experience of community life. Here he was able to go further into creating the true family of colleagues and disciples he sought. He introduced changes in the conditions of membership, the economic base, diet and eating patterns, housing arrangements, property rights, and religious practices (especially vows and fasting.)[43]

In short, Tolstoy Farm not only formed the prototype for his future ashrams, it also contributed to his political methodology. According to Gandhi, the shared experiments in diet and physical labour yielded excellent spiritual results. These 'dangerous' experiments were only possible 'in a struggle of which self-purification was the very essence'.[44] And Gandhi and Kallenbach

---

[40] Berning, *Gandhi Letters*, p. 50.   [41] Bhana, 'The Tolstoy Farm'.

[42] The practically based and spiritually oriented education system he established at Tolstoy Farm became the prototype for Gandhi's later 'Nai Talim', or new education system evolved at Sevagram from 1937 onwards. For the South African antecedents of the scheme see Marjorie Sykes, *The Story of Nai Talim: Fifty Years of Education at Sevagram 1937–1987* (Wardha: Nai Talim Samiti, 1988), pp. 8–15.

[43] Hunt, 'The Kallenbach Papers and Tolstoy Farm', p. 10.

[44] Gandhi, *Satyagraha in South Africa*, pp. 392–3.

'set the example of renunciation and discipline' that permeated Tolstoy Farm.[45] For Gandhi the political struggle was closely linked with the inner struggle, and Tolstoy Farm was a crucible of both. Later in life, as he was preparing the Sabarmati Ashram for the Civil Disobedience campaign against the government, Gandhi could look back on his time in South Africa and say that 'My faith and courage were at their highest in Tolstoy Farm. I have been praying to God to permit me to re-attain that height, but the prayer has not yet been heard.'[46]

HERMANN KALLENBACH AFTER GANDHI

In July 1914, the South Africa phase of his life behind him, Gandhi, with Kasturba and Kallenbach, sailed to England to meet Gokhale before the final return to the land of his birth. The rest of the Phoenix group, under the charge of Maganlal Gandhi, went directly to India. In London, as part of their contribution to the war effort, Gandhi and Kallenbach offered their services as non-combatants for an 'Indian Field Ambulance Corps'. The Gandhis and Kallenbach lived together in London but they could not leave together for India as planned. For all the years he had lived in South Africa, Kallenbach had not taken out British citizenship and did not receive entry permission for India during the war years. Regardless of Gandhi's attempted intercession,[47] Gandhi and his wife had to leave without him. In 1915 Hermann Kallenbach was interned as an enemy alien in a detention camp on the Isle of Man.

Both Gandhi and Kallenbach were saddened by their forced parting. In his autobiography, written in serial form from late 1925 until early 1929, Gandhi looked back on the repercussions of leaving Kallenbach and noted that, 'It was a great wrench for me to part from Mr. Kallenbach, but I could see that his pang was greater. Could he have come to India, he would have been leading today the simple happy life of a farmer and weaver. Now he is in South Africa, leading his old life and doing brisk business as an architect.'[48] Without the influence of the Mahatma, Kallenbach fell back into his old ways, nevertheless Kallenbach's influence on Gandhi had been an important part of the linear development of Mahatmaship and the Gandhian ashram.

---

[45] Thomson, *Gandhi and His Ashrams*, p. 74.   [46] Gandhi, *Satyagraha in South Africa*, p. 371.
[47] See Gandhi's letter to Under Secretary for Colonies, 10 August 1914; and Gandhi's letter to C. Roberts, 24 August 1914.
[48] Gandhi, *An Autobiography*, p. 265.

Less than two weeks after Gandhi and his group had established themselves at the Kochrab Ashram in Ahmedabad, the Mahatma wrote to Kallenbach complaining about overwork, Kasturba's illness, and loneliness. He
added, 'I feel like crying out to you "Do come and help me!"'[49] Mahadev
Desai records Gandhi as often saying: 'If Kallenbach were here, he would
be in charge of the plans of the Ashram and he would build it after his own
heart,' and Maganlal Gandhi, who ended up running the ashram, 'would
say: "How I wish Kallenbach was here. He would have been a thorough
good task-master to all of us."'[50] Of course it was not to be. Kallenbach
remained in internment until 1917 when he was released to Germany in a
prisoners exchange.[51] Following this, Gandhi wrote several letters to Kallenbach, but received no reply. Finally, a mutual friend reported to Gandhi
on his erstwhile companion. Gandhi responded: 'Pray tell him that we
all think of him and miss him so often. I miss him most of all.' While
Gandhi was busy with his inquiry into the conditions of the workers on
the Champaran indigo farms, he added:

It is here I miss our friend's presence. I cannot imagine myself doing this class of
work without him. I know he would have been delighted to be in the thick of it.
He would have walked with me to the villages and lived with me among the simple
folk. He would have seen the planters. He would have made friends with them
and would have played an important part in bringing about a settlement. But that
was not to be.[52]

Over half a year later Gandhi wrote to Kallenbach from Champaran:

How often do I not want to hug you. Daily do I have novel experiences here
which I should like you to share with me. But this monstrous War never seems to
be ending. All the peace talk only enhances the agony. However, like all human
institutions it must have an end, and our friendship must be a poor affair if it
cannot bide its time and be all the stronger and purer for the weary waiting.[53]

However much they may have missed each other, they were not to
meet for twenty-three years after their London parting. In the meantime
Kallenbach went back to South Africa, helped more of his family migrate
from Germany, and also returned to his old ways as a wealthy architect being involved in the construction of many significant buildings in
Johannesburg.

Even though 'For years after Gandhiji's return to India from South
Africa his name was a kind of legend to those of us who gathered around

---

[49] Letter to Kallenbach, 4 June 1915.   [50] Desai, 'Weekly Letter'.
[51] Sarid and Bartolf, *Hermann Kallenbach*, pp. 62–4.   [52] Letter to Turner, 30 April 1917.
[53] Letter to Kallenbach, 21 December 1917.

Gandhiji',[54] one can't help wondering how Kallenbach would have fitted in to Gandhi's India life. Would he have become the manager of the Sabarmati Ashram instead of Maganlal, or would he eventually have become disillusioned as Gandhi stepped up his public life and the until then privileged relationship could not be maintained at a level that would have satisfied him? As it was, after the war Kallenbach returned to Johannesburg and his former profession. Finally in 1937, and again in 1939, Kallenbach made it to India to be with his old friend. During his last visit he tried to enlist Gandhi into the Zionist cause. Gandhi's call to the Jews to offer nonviolent resistance to Hitler did not impress Kallenbach and they had several talks on the issue of Hitler, the war and Palestine without being able to convince each other. Their abiding affection, however, remained and Kallenbach seemed to have 'come home' when he was again in physical proximity with Gandhi. Although Gandhi wanted him to settle in India, during the 1939 visit he developed malaria. He left to recuperate and never returned. Being again out of Gandhi's orbit he felt the responsibility for the welfare of his family, including those who were still behind in Germany and saw a need to keep up his source of income to assist them. His architectural work in South Africa prospered and he was responsible for the development of the most elegant suburbs of Johannesburg. While his prosperity grew, his health waned and he 'felt weak, most unhappy, lonely and forlorn'.[55]

Kallenbach never married and in his post-Gandhi years he became somewhat depressed. His niece Hanna Lazar noted that although he never needed recognition or acknowledgement for his achievements, a 'measure of appreciation, be it ever so small, might have raised his spirits in difficult times'.[56] Hanna and her daughter Isa Sarid knew of his inner turmoil but could not comfort him and he ended his days as a disappointed man, worst of all a man disappointed in himself. He died on 25 March 1945 in Johannesburg. He left the major share of his assets for Jewish settlements in Palestine and his library to the Hebrew University in Jerusalem. Seven years later, in accordance with his will, his ashes were transported to Kibbutz Degania in Israel.

---

[54] Desai, 'Weekly Letter'.   [55] Sarid and Bartolf, *Hermann Kallenbach*, p. 81.
[56] Quoted in *ibid.*, p. 8.

CHAPTER 5

Maganlal Gandhi and the decision to leave Sabarmati

INTRODUCTION

The original buildings of Gandhi's Harijan Ashram at Sabarmati in Ahmedabad are striking in their simple aesthetics. Here beauty, a sense of peace and feeling of functionality are combined. Gandhi and Kasturba's home, Hriday Kunj, with its courtyard and large veranda and the small hut, used at different times by Vinoba Bhave and Mirabehn, along with the nearby prayer ground are at the heart of the complex. It is to here that tourists wander after they have been through the more recently erected picture galleries. But there is much more to the ashram. There are workshops, guest quarters and, now over busy Ashram Road, the living quarters of many of the families who once resided there. Possibly, however, the most imposing single household building, in a corner of the main complex near a small temple, one that until recently was locked up and rarely visited, is Magan Niwas, the once home of Gandhi's second cousin, the ashram's manager, Maganlal Gandhi.

I was at the ashram for a long period in 1982–3. I walked the grounds daily, often meditated in the prayer grounds in the early mornings, sat on the veranda of Gandhi's house while trying to learn to spin with diminutive ashram resident Mangaldasbhai, leaned over the wall in the evenings watching the buffalos being taken along the generally almost dry river-bed of the Sabarmati between the ashram and the textile mills on the opposite bank, and watched the bright green parrots as they flitted around. Although I never went inside, Maganlal's home intrigued me, and the sheer beauty of the settlement, especially imagining how it must have looked before Ahmedabad crept up to it and then engulfed it, had me pondering how Gandhi could ever have left such an idyllic setting. And more, how he could have left his devoted ashram colleagues.

MAGANLAL GANDHI JOINS HIS 'UNCLE'

After eight years in South Africa where he had moved from being a legal assistant to successful barrister to a champion of the rights of indentured Indians, Gandhi had sailed to his native India in early 1902 with the promise to return within a year if the community he had been working with again needed him. Eight months later he was on the way back. Although he left his wife and children behind, believing that the need for his work would take no more than a year, he was accompanied by some young members of his family. One of them was Maganlal Gandhi. Although Gandhi referred to Maganlal and his elder brother Chhaganlal as nephews, they were in fact the sons of his older cousin Kushalbhai Gandhi, the orphaned son of Gandhi's father's sister, who was raised by Gandhi's own parents as one of Gandhi's elder brothers.[1] He had just sat his matriculation examinations and while awaiting the results and trying to find work had visited Gandhi in Bombay. Gandhi invited him to go to South Africa and, after his father's permission had been obtained, Maganlal's life was to take a dramatic turn. He went to South Africa in search of a living but ended up in a life of service, not least in service to his uncle. The twenty-year-old joined another Gandhi nephew who had gone to Natal in 1896 with Gandhi following a visit to India by the Mahatma-to-be. This thirty-year-old cousin, Abhaychand, was the storekeeper in the township of Tongaat near Durban who Gandhi would later visit as he was formulating the idea of establishing an intentional rural community. Maganlal joined Abhaychand as a partner. Here Maganlal became acquainted with Zulus and a number of other Indian storekeepers for whom he undertook part-time jobs and he was soon the manager of a branch store in the dense forest near the township of Stanger.[2]

Although it seems that Maganlal was diligent and successful in his work, he was not happy. The youth was conservatively religious with an other-worldly bent and his strange and multi-faith and morally lax surroundings made his religious practices difficult to implement. In June, 1903, he wrote about his inner turmoil to his religious mentor Nathuram Sharma:

I am writing this to relieve my soul of the anguish caused by my inability to observe the rules of caste or even to perform the daily morning ritual of purification, prayer

[1] Arun and Sunanda Gandhi, *The Forgotten Woman: The Untold Story of Kastur Gandhi, Wife of Mahatma Gandhi* (Huntsville: Ozark Mountain Publishers, 1998), p. 110; and Pyarelal, *Mahatma Gandhi, volume II: Discovery of Satyagraha – On the Threshold* (Bombay: Sevak Prakashan, 1980), p. 399.

[2] See Prabhudas Gandhi, 'Magankaka', Navajivan Trust (ed.), *Ashram No Pran* (Ahmedabad: Navajivan, 1993), pp. 14–17; Prabhudas Gandhi, *My Childhood with Gandhi* (Ahmedabad: Navajivan, 1957), p. 34; and Pyarelal, *Mahatma Gandhi, volume III: The Birth of Satyagraha: From Petitioning to Passive Resistance* (Ahmedabad: Navajivan, 1986), p. 429.

and worship . . . All I can do, whenever possible, is to close my eyes morning and evening, concentrate on an image of Shiva and after repeating the sacred five-lettered prayer prostrate myself mentally before you . . . I am . . . caught in the coils of perplexity . . . (the heart within me burns) and I do not know where and to whom to look for refuge . . . I am in an evil place . . . reeking of violence and sinful ways. The very idea of being sucked into the whirlpool of sin takes the life out of me . . . On the ocean of the world my frail bark is tossed by the stormy gusts of desire. There are dangerous reefs and rocks ahead, and . . . all around . . . and the inexperienced pilot of my discrimination within is scarcely able to hold the helm to its course.[3]

While Maganlal was determined to work hard to help out his parents who had financially overcommitted themselves in arranging his marriage, the direction of his life came from Gandhi, under whose guidance he claims to have 'put myself wholly'.[4] His letters about his uncle portray a 'starry-eyed admiration'.[5] When Gandhi was setting up his Phoenix Settlement in 1904, he invited friends and relatives to join and help him. Maganlal and others volunteered, but as Gandhi noted: 'The others went back to business. Maganlal Gandhi left his business for good to cast his lot with me, and by ability, sacrifice and devotion stands foremost among my original co-workers in my ethical experiments.'[6] And Gandhi was not wrong, as he moved to simplify his own life, Maganlal followed suit. He gave up spicy food and, following deep inner turmoil, though young with his young wife now at his side, and although Gandhi's own son Manilal refused, he took a vow of celibacy.

Soon Maganlal, along with Chhaganlal who had remained to head up Gandhi's household in India but had joined him in South Africa in 1904, were looking after Gandhi's new Phoenix Settlement. And in 1907, at least in some sense of the word, Maganlal invented satyagraha.

Gandhi at this time was leading a mass movement to counter laws which discriminated against Indians in South Africa. He originally used the term 'passive-resistance', but soon came to realise that this could lead to misunderstandings and was searching for an Indian word. On 27 December, in a competition announced in his paper *Indian Opinion*, Gandhi offered a £2 prize to the person who came up with a suitable name. Maganlal sent

[3] Pyarelal, *Mahatma Gandhi, volume III: The Birth of Satyagraha*, pp. 430–1.
[4] In a letter to his youngest daughter, written in 1925, Maganlal records how Gandhi had asked him to write weekly from Tongaat to Johannesburg detailing his inner thoughts. Gandhi's return letters guided not just his reading and study programme, but also his life. See the letters section of Navajivan Trust, *Ashram No Pran*, pp. 94–7, at p. 95.
[5] Pyarelal, *Mahatma Gandhi, volume III: The Birth of Satyagraha*, p. 431.
[6] Gandhi, *An Autobiography*, p. 222.

in the best entry. He had suggested 'sadagraha' (sad = good, agraha = firmness in). Gandhi modified it slightly to 'satyagraha' (sat = truth, agraha = firmness in).[7]

As more and more leaders of Gandhi's movement offered themselves for imprisonment, Maganlal became the mainstay of the movement from the outside. He wrote, printed, published and mailed *Indian Opinion*, looked after the children and their education, and when hundreds of strikers flowed into Phoenix, he had to care for them as well. Maganlal was denied the honour of going to jail with the others in order to take on the heavy burden of continuing all of the necessary work on the outside. The routine was punishing and his health suffered but he proved his dedication and managerial skills. Eventually Gandhi's reliance on Maganlal and Maganlal's place in Gandhi's estimation led to resentment on the part of Gandhi's sons, particularly his eldest Harilal, who reportedly felt marginalised by his cousin,[8] and even on the part of Gandhi's wife, who felt that 'usurpers . . . had displaced her sons'.[9]

When Gandhi finally left South Africa, he returned to India via England. Maganlal meanwhile led most of the residents of Phoenix directly to India, where he took charge of the Phoenix group when they stayed, before settling in Ahmedabad, with the poet Rabindranath Tagore in his school called Shantiniketan in Bengal. Again showing his high regard for Maganlal, Gandhi wrote that it was his nephew's task to 'see that all the rules of the Phoenix Ashram should be scrupulously observed. I saw that, by dint of his love, knowledge and perseverance, he made his fragrance felt in the whole of Shantiniketan.'[10] Maganlal was not just a gifted organiser and tireless worker, he was also the embodiment of Gandhi's spiritual and moral quest, in the Mahatma's words, 'a living example of the saying: "Practise as you preach."'[11]

MAGANLAL AND THE SABARMATI ASHRAM

At Gandhi's first Ahmedabad ashram, at Kochrab, there was widespread dissent when he decided to admit an 'untouchable' family. Kasturba and

---

[7] Sushila Nayar, *Mahatma Gandhi, volume IV: Satyagraha at Work* (Ahmedabad: Navajivan, 1989), p. 119; Gandhi, *An Autobiography*, p. 235.

[8] Green, *Gandhi*, p. 183.

[9] *Ibid.*, p. 263. Not only was Gandhi favouring Maganlal over Harilal, but at the very time that he was denying formal education to his eldest son, he sent Chhaganlal Gandhi to England to study law. See Nayar, *Mahatma Gandhi, volume IV: Satyagraha at Work*, p. 44.

[10] Gandhi, *An Autobiography*, pp. 280–1.   [11] 'Magankaka', *Navajivan*, 5 August 1928

Maganlal (or at least Maganlal's wife Santok[12]) opposed the admission. Santok fasted over the decision, Gandhi fasted over Santok's attitude.[13] While Kasturba gave in, Maganlal and Santok packed to leave the ashram only to be talked out of it by the Mahatma who could not afford to lose his chief lieutenant. He sent Maganlal and his family to Madras to learn weaving (a craft traditionally practised only by 'untouchables'[14]) 'and to ponder the situation that had developed'. They lived in Madras for six months before returning to the ashram. In the meantime they had 'mastered the art of weaving and after mature consideration also washed their hearts clean of untouchability'.[15] This seems to be true for Maganlal, but not for Santok[16] about whom Gandhi could say almost fifteen years later that she 'never liked the common kitchen, nor the inmates of the Ashram'.[17] It is perhaps interesting that this incident is not recounted in Gandhi's *Autobiography*. There is mention of neighbours and outside supporters being unhappy with the inclusion of the 'untouchable' Dudabhai and his family in the ashram, but no mention of the views of Maganlal and his wife. This chapter of the *Autobiography* was penned and originally published in Gandhi's various newspapers just a few months after Maganlal's untimely death. Gandhi often wrote about his colleagues 'seeing the light', but in this case he seems to have been preserving the untarnished memory of his recently departed 'nephew and chosen son',[18] one who, in the memory of C. F. Andrews, had a love for untouchables that 'was nothing less than a passion'.[19]

While Gandhi was busy being the Mahatma, Maganlal took care of business. At the religious festival, the Kumbh Mela, in Haridwar in 1915, while Gandhi was constantly preoccupied by darshan-seekers, his trusted lieutenant had to fulfil his master's pledge to take care of the covering of excreta in the latrines,[20] and when Gandhi decided to take his group of over forty souls who shared a common kitchen from Kochrab to a plot of land at Sabarmati, where 'there was no building . . . and no tree' and house them under canvas, he admitted that 'the whole conception

---

[12] See Letter to Hermann Kallenbach, 24 September 1915.

[13] See the September 11 entry in Gandhi's diary for 1915.

[14] Prabhudas Gandhi, 'Magankaka', p. 29.   [15] Gandhi, *Ashram Observances in Action*, p. 78.

[16] A year later, after a period of absence, when the 'untouchable' family returned to the ashram, Santok again 'suddenly decided to leave'. Maganlal was torn between love for his wife and love for Gandhi, putting him 'through the most terrible times of his life'. See Gandhi's Letter to Hermann Kallenbach, 10 September 1916.

[17] Letter to Narandas Gandhi, a brother of Maganlal and Chhaganlal, 16 January 1929.

[18] Erikson, *Gandhi's Truth*, p. 317.   [19] 'Andrews Tribute', *Young India*, 24 May 1928.

[20] Gandhi, *An Autobiography*, p. 286.

about the removal was mine, the execution was as usual left to Maganlal'.[21]
Under Maganlal's leadership the prickly shrubs, rocks, sand and cacti were
removed from the river bank and vegetables and neem trees were planted,
and 'in a very short time the barren land became green with vegetables'.[22]
Maganlal designed and supervised the construction of all the buildings,
he systematised the management of the ashram, introduced discipline and
took control of ashram craft work. Maganlal Gandhi was not just another
ashramite who happened to be in charge. It is not an exaggeration to say that
the ashram at Sabarmati was Maganlal's creation and that to a large degree
he was the 'soul' of the ashram.[23] Further, Gandhi's later secretary and
biographer, Sabarmati Ashram resident Pyarelal records that the Mahatma
was grooming Maganlal 'as his heir'.[24] Gandhi himself made this explicit
in his letter to his wife when he requested her to be a mother to the one
who had trained himself to carry on his work.[25]

The year before Maganlal's death, writing about the Phoenix Settlement
in his *Autobiography*, Gandhi spoke highly of his young nephew who 'left
his business for good and cast in his lot with me, and by ability, sacrifice
and devotion stands foremost among my original co-workers in my ethical
experiments'.[26] He praised the abilities of his young charge in learning
compositing and 'all the other branches of press work' that were necessary
for the functioning of Gandhi's paper, adding that 'I have always thought
that he was not conscious of his own capacity.'[27] Further, when they had
settled at Sabarmati, Gandhi decided that the inmates should weave their
own cloth. However, as the ashramites 'all belonged either to the liberal
professions or to business' rather than being artisans, they did not know how
to operate the loom. Again Maganlal came to the rescue: 'Maganlal Gandhi
was not to be easily baffled. Possessed of a natural talent for mechanics, he
was able fully to master the art before long, and one after another several new
weavers were trained up in the Ashram.'[28] This process seems to have been
repeated in the spinning of thread: 'Maganlal Gandhi, by bringing to bear

---

[21] *Ibid.*, p. 316.
[22] Narayan Desai, *The Fire and the Rose [Biography of Mahadevbhai]* (Ahmedabad: Navajivan, 1995),
p. 85.
[23] A Gujarati book of essays and reflections on Maganlal is titled 'Soul of the Ashram'. See Navajivan
Trust, *Ashram No Pran*.
[24] Sushila Nayar, *Mahatma Gandhi, volume VI: Salt Satyagraha: The Watershed* (Ahmedabad: Navajivan,
1995), p. 96.
[25] Gandhi wrote to his wife telling her to be 'mother to Maganlal. He has parted from his parents and
made my work his own. At present it is Maganlal, if anyone, who has so trained himself that he can
carry on my work after me. Who will give him the needed strength? It is for you to show concern
for his suffering, to be solicitous on his meals, to save him from all manner of worries.' Letter to
Kasturba Gandhi, 23 April 1918.
[26] Gandhi, *An Autobiography*, p. 222.   [27] *Ibid.*, p. 225.   [28] *Ibid.*, p. 360.

all his splendid mechanical talent on the wheel, made many improvements in it, and wheels and their accessories began to be manufactured at the Ashram.'[29] At this time, Gandhi compares his later secretary and future favourite 'son', Mahadev Desai, unfavourably with Maganlal (not enough initiative or originality while Maganlal's self-surrender is 'of the highest order, but he has never . . . surrendered his judgement'[30]). There was nothing in Maganlal's Gandhism that was half-hearted. This made him a hard taskmaster and it seems that this was often resented by other inmates.

Maganlal's nephew, (Chhaganlal's son) Prabhudas Gandhi, in his life sketch of his uncle, notes that Maganlal was a strict disciplinarian who was prone to anger and would beat him if he told lies. Later he was to realise how hard Maganlal fought to tame his outbursts (by, for example, working to control his palate and giving up his favourite foods) and the pain he felt at his recourse to anger.[31] Maganlal was also something of a loner who did not make close friendships and tended to keep his thoughts to himself. When there were complaints about him to Gandhi, he clearly realised his limitations and felt humbled, redoubling his praying and scripture reading. In his final years he struggled to purify himself by seeking non-attachment and to overcome his angry outbursts.[32]

When unrest among the ashramites over Maganlal's leadership came to a head, Gandhi called a meeting and backed his 'nephew':

The inmates are satisfied with nothing in the Ashram. The reason? Dissatisfaction over Maganlal's ideas and conduct, over his manner of speaking and over a certain partiality in his actions . . . One of my creations here in the Ashram is Maganlal. If I have found from experience five million shortcomings in Maganlal, I have found ten million virtues in him. Beside him, Polak is a mere child; the blows that Maganlal has endured, Polak has not. Maganlal has offered all his work as sacrifice, not for my sake but for the sake of an ideal. . . .

It boils down to this, that I cannot run the Ashram after sending away Maganlal. If I send him away, I would be the only one left in the Ashram. For the tasks we have undertaken, Maganlal, too, is fully needed. I have yet to see a better man than he. To be sure, he is short-tempered, has his imperfections, but on the whole he is a fine man. As for his honesty, I have no doubt. You must take it as proved that I am bad to the extent that Maganlal is bad. . . .

You may persuade me to give up either the Ashram or Maganlal. I shall not send him away so long as I have not come to feel that he goes about setting one against another. To measure a man's worth, the world has no other yardstick than his work. As the work, so the man. . . . However, the fine, systematic work which Maganlal has done, none else has.[33]

---

[29] *Ibid.*, p. 362.   [30] Letter to Mahadev Desai, 13 August 1921.
[31] Prabhudas Gandhi, 'Magankaka', pp. 18, 22–4.   [32] *Ibid.*, pp. 31–2.
[33] 'Address to Ashram inmates', 17 February 1919.

GANDHI WIDOWED

Maganlal was in Bihar on Gandhi's instructions to see how the constructive work involving the uplift of women in Champaran, under the directions of his daughter Radha, was progressing when he succumbed to a bout of pneumonia following a chill and died in Patna on 23 April 1928. News of Maganlal's sudden death reached Gandhi on his day of silence. Although ordering that daily work must not cease, Gandhi forsook his practice of weekly silence for the first time[34] 'to express his own grief and to console those around him'.[35] At the time, Gandhi stated that 'Maganlal was the life of the Ashram,[36] I am not it, it was his light that illuminated me . . . I could drink the cup of poison like Mirabai . . . But this separation from Maganlal is more unbearable. But I must harden my heart.'[37] Gandhi's secretary commented that Gandhi's 'loss at this moment is far greater than I can imagine'.[38] Three days later, Gandhi published a loving obituary in his paper under the title 'My Best Comrade Gone':

He whom I had singled out as heir to my all is no more. Maganlal K. Gandhi, a grandson of an uncle of mine had been with me in my work since 1904 . . . Maganlal Gandhi went with me to South Africa in 1903 in the hope of making a bit of fortune. But hardly had he been store-keeping for one year, when he responded to my sudden call to self-imposed poverty, joined the Phoenix settlement and never once faltered or failed after so joining me. If he had not dedicated himself to the country's service, his undoubted abilities and indefatigable industry would have made him a merchant prince . . .

He closely studied and followed my spiritual career and when I presented to my co-workers *brahmacharya* as a rule of life even for married men in search of Truth, he was the first to perceive the beauty and the necessity of the practice and, though it cost him to my knowledge a terrific struggle, he carried it through to success, taking his wife along with him by patient argument instead of imposing his views on her.

When satyagraha was born, he was in the forefront . . .

On our return to India, it was he again who made it possible to found the Ashram in the austere manner in which it was founded. Here he was called to a newer and more difficult task. He proved equal to it. Untouchability was a very severe trial for him. Just for one brief moment his heart seemed to give way. But it was only for a second. He saw that love had no bounds and that it was necessary

---

[34] Kalelkar, *Stray Glimpses of Bapu*, p. 130.

[35] Nayar, *Mahatma Gandhi, volume VI: Salt Satyagraha*, p. 97.

[36] Mahadev Desai concurred in this. In his 'agitated and bewildered' state, he wrote that 'Maganlal was the Ashram and Ashram was Maganlal', Desai, *The Fire and the Rose*, p. 417.

[37] From Mahadev Desai's Gujarati diary, vol. XII : 84–7, quoted in Nayar, *Mahatma Gandhi, volume VI: Salt Satyagraha*, p. 97.

[38] Desai, *The Fire and the Rose*, p. 417.

to live down the ways of 'untouchables', if only because the so-called higher castes were responsible for them.

The mechanical department of the Ashram was not a continuation of the Phoenix activity. Here we had to learn weaving, spinning, carding, and ginning. Again I turned to Maganlal. Though the conception was mine, his were the hands to reduce it to execution. He learnt weaving and all the other processes that cotton had to go through before it became khadi. He was a born mechanic . . .

Let not the reader imagine that he knew nothing of politics. He did, but he chose the path of silent, selfless constructive service. He was my hands, my feet and my eyes. The world knows so little of how much my so-called greatness depends upon the incessant toil and drudgery of silent, devoted, able and pure workers, men as well as women. And among them all Maganlal was to me the greatest, the best and the purest.

As I am penning these lines, I hear the sobs of the widow bewailing the death of her dear husband. Little does she realize that I am more widowed than she. And but for a living faith in God, I should become a raving maniac for the loss of one who was dearer to me than my own sons, who never once deceived me or failed me, who was a personification of industry, who was the watchdog of the Ashram in all its aspects – material, moral and spiritual. His life is an inspiration for me, a standing demonstration of the efficacy and the supremacy of the moral law. In his own life he proved visibly for me not for a few days, not for a few months, but for twenty-four long years – now alas all too short – that service of the country, service of humanity and self-realization or knowledge of God are synonymous terms.

Maganlal is dead, but he lives in his work whose imprints he who runs may read on every particle of dust in the Ashram.[39]

Another three days later in his Gujarati paper, *Navajivan*, Gandhi expressed similar sentiments in an article entitled 'Soul of the Ashram':

When Shri Vallabhbhai received the news of Maganlal Gandhi's death, he wired: 'The soul of the Ashram has departed.' There was no exaggeration in this. I cannot imagine the existence of Satyagraha Ashram without Maganlal. Many of my activities were started because I knew that he was there. If ever there was a person with whom I identified myself, it was Maganlal. We often have to consider whether certain matters will hurt another person, even if that person be one's own son or wife. I never had to entertain such fear with regard to Maganlal. I never hesitated to set him the most difficult tasks. I very often put him in embarrassing situations and he silently bore with them. He regarded no work as too mean.

If I were fit to be anyone's guru, I would have proclaimed him my first disciple . . . But if Maganlal was not a disciple, he was certainly a servant. I am convinced that no master could possibly find a servant better or more loyal than Maganlal. This may be a conjecture, but I can assert from my experience that I have not found another servant like him. It has been my good fortune always

[39] 'My Best Comrade Gone', *Young India*, 26 April 1928.

to have found co-workers, or servants if you like, who were faithful, virtuous, intelligent and industrious. Still, Maganlal was the best of all these co-workers and servants.

The three streams of knowledge, devotion and action continuously flowed within Maganlal and, by offering his knowledge and his devotion in the *yajna* [religious sacrifice] of action, he demonstrated before everyone their true form. And because in this way each action of his was full of awareness, knowledge and faith, his life attained the very summit of sannyasa [renunciation]. Maganlal had renounced his all. I never saw an iota of self-interest in any of his actions. He showed – not once, not for a short time but time after time for twenty-four years incessantly – that true sannyasa lay in selfless action or action without desire for reward . . . With each day I realize more and more that my mahatmaship, which is a mere adornment, depends on others. I have shone with the glory borrowed from my innumerable co-workers. However, no one has done more to add to this glory than Maganlal. He co-operated with me fully and with intelligence in all my activities – physical or spiritual. I see no better instance than Maganlal of one who made a tremendous effort to act as he believed. Maganlal was awake all the twenty-four hours establishing unity of thought and action. He used up all his energy in this.

On the day of Maganlal's death, Gandhi wrote to Jawaharlal Nehru that 'Of course you know already the calamity that has befallen me on the death of Maganlal. It is well-nigh unbearable. However I am putting on a brave front.'[40] And his account of his work in South Africa, *Satyagraha in South Africa*, which appeared only days after Maganlal's death was dedicated to his disciple.

A year later, on noting that he had forgotten the anniversary of Maganlal's death, Gandhi remarked that in fact he observes it every day.[41] And when Jamnalal Bajaj, a disciple so close that he was known as Gandhi's fifth son, passed away in early 1942, Gandhi lamented that this was the biggest personal blow that he had suffered since Maganlal's death.[42]

THE SABARMATI ASHRAM

The importance of Maganlal for Gandhi and the ashram at Sabarmati, although it tends to disappear from Gandhi biographies, cannot be overestimated. He planned every building, planted every tree, lived Gandhi's philosophy the way others could not and maintained ashram discipline.

---

[40] Letter to Jawaharlal Nehru, 28 April 1928.   [41] Letter to Chhaganlal Joshi, 17 May 1929.
[42] 'Fiery Ordeal', in *Harijan Sevak*, 22 February 1942.

Kaka Kalelkar, a close associate of Gandhi's at the time, claimed that the light of idealism and sincerity that shone in the ashram was that of Maganlal and even that the richness of the living atmosphere of the community was due to Maganlal rather than to Gandhi himself.[43]

The ashram was situated on the banks of the river Sabarmati, not far from Ahmedabad, a busy industrial city of 300,000 inhabitants. Soon after Gandhi had returned to India, his South African days behind him, he was invited by several cities, and promised various forms of assistance, to set up an ashram – a community of religious people – in their neighbourhood. The Mahatma had chosen Ahmedabad, the main city of the Gujarat portion of the British-ruled Bombay Presidency.

The ashram was originally established in a large rented house at Kochrab, a village across the river on the outskirts of the city, on 25 May 1915. The finance for the venture came from his supporters. There were about twenty inmates, most of them from South Africa, and most of them speaking South Indian languages. Gandhi himself was a Gujarati and so the choice of Ahmedabad, as a place from where he could re-acquaint himself with India after a twenty-year absence, was understandable. According to Gillion, however, 'It was not only because he and they were Gujaratis that Gandhi found a congenial home among the Ahmedabadis and a place in their hearts unrivalled elsewhere in India; it was also because Ahmedabad was a city which had not lost its corporate identity and been swept overboard by the West but which valued traditional culture, social responsibility and harmony.'[44]

The community aimed at self-sufficiency, and discipline was a by-word. The principal occupations were the teaching of Sanskrit, weaving and carpentry. There were no servants, caste distinctions were not observed and the emancipation of women through the setting aside of customary restrictions was insisted upon. This defiance of conservative tradition, especially as one of the principal objectives of the ashram was the eradication of untouchability, was often to get the small community into trouble in its early years.

Soon the ashram boasted sixty inmates, men, women and children and the suitability of a building which was designed for a well-to-do family became glaringly inadequate. A plague outbreak in Kochrab during the middle of 1917 was the final signal to move to a new site.

---

[43] Kaka Kalelkar, 'Tapasvi Jivan', Navajivan Trust, *Ashram No Pran*, p. 80.
[44] K. L. Gillion, *Ahmedabad: A Study in Indian Urban History* (Canberra: Australian National University Press, 1969), p. 157.

During 1916 negotiations were under way for a larger block away from the city and the purchase of thirty-six acres at Sabarmati, a riverside junction station several miles from the city centre, was completed during the plague. Gandhi happily wrote later that 'there was one defect in the Ashram at Kochrab which was remedied after we had removed to Sabarmati. An Ashram without orchard, farm or cattle would not be a complete unit. At Sabarmati we had cultivable land and therefore went in for agriculture at once.'[45] Perhaps, even more happily, the site was near a temple dedicated to the sage Dadheechi, who was known for his self-sacrificing renunciation. It was also near an ever-present reminder of mortality, the cremation grounds of Dudheswar, and further, in Gandhi's words, 'Its vicinity to the Sabarmati Central Jail was for me a special attraction. As jail-going was understood to be the normal lot of *Satyagrahis*, I liked this position. And I knew that the sites selected for jails have generally clean surroundings.'[46] Could any Mahatma have desired more?

By 1930 there were close to 200 inmates at the Satyagraha Ashram. Madeleine Slade, a British admiral's daughter, renamed Mirabehn by Gandhi when she took up residence in late 1925, wrote that at this time 'The Ashram reached its zenith in physical energy and moral strength. Every morning and evening Bapu spoke in the prayers, and an atmosphere of uplifting inspiration filled the air.'[47]

This seemingly idealistic picture of a disciplined utopian community ready to do battle in the nationalist cause does not, however, tell the whole story. There were also dark undercurrents. Gandhi's political programme meant that he was away from the ashram for lengthy periods of time. His spirit and letters were not always enough to keep his followers on the straight and narrow.[48] Maganlal, and later his successor Chhaganlal Joshi, could not be expected to provide 'the level of inspiration and guidance so essential to the smooth functioning of the diverse community'.[49] As early as 1918, Gandhi had been informed by the son of nephew Chhaganlal Gandhi that in the Mahatma's absence the ashram appeared lifeless.[50] Nevertheless, Maganlal tried tirelessly to keep the ashram functioning in Gandhi's spirit. He was not only the manager of the Sabarmati Ashram or even, as the Gujarati sources so often say, its soul, but he was also Gandhi's first real disciple, one who did not only conform to the discipline of the ashram but

---

[45] Gandhi, *Ashram Observances in Action*, p. 12.   [46] Gandhi, *An Autobiography*, p. 357.
[47] M. K. Gandhi, *Bapu's Letters to Mira [1924–1948]* (Ahmedabad: Navajivan, 1949), p. 98. For the daily routine of the Ashram, see Gandhi, *Ashram Observances in Action*, pp. 123–4.
[48] See Thomson, *Gandhi and His Ashrams*, p. 114.   [49] *Ibid.*, p. 115.
[50] See Letter to Prabhudas Gandhi, 2 February 1918.

fully internalised and tried to live by the vows.[51] Although Maganlal was unhappy when Gandhi was absent from the ashram and Gandhi made it clear that action in the wider political sphere was occasionally inevitable,[52] it was Gandhi's very confidence in Maganlal's ability to run the ashram according to his wishes that enabled the Mahatma to travel around the country the way he did.[53]

Mark Thomson notes that Maganlal's death 'was a crushing blow to Gandhi and seemed to hasten the decline of standards within the Ashram'.[54] And, in turn, these declining standards seem to have made it easier for the Mahatma to turn his back on his community. The absence of the soul of the ashram and Gandhi's 'noblest representative', was deeply felt in terms of the functioning of the community and in terms of Gandhi's feeling of connectedness with it.

The ashram attracted its share of unsuitable applicants, rules were violated and petty bickering became the norm.[55] A few months after Maganlal's passing, it was decided not to admit new members for a year except in special circumstances 'since a lot of changes are made and are still being made at the Ashram', and then only after careful vetting.[56] The use of the communal kitchen was more strongly enforced, the rules of celibacy tightened and, because of unworthiness, the name was changed from Satyagraha Ashram to Udyog Mandir ('Temple of Crafts')[57] with the hope that it will 'one day justify its existence and reconvert itself into the Satyagraha Ashram'.[58]

Gandhi's efforts to reinvigorate the ashram seemed to come to little and a series of shocks to the Mahatma and scandals to outside observers in the following year perhaps doomed the fate of the establishment. It was discovered that Chhaganlal, Maganlal's older brother, had been guilty of petty money thefts from the ashram over many years, that a widow at the ashram had been seduced by another ashramite, and that Kasturba had retained some cash gifts to her for her personal use rather than place them into the ashram's consolidated revenue. Rumours about the changes and scandals were circulating and, against the advice of the ashram's management, Gandhi, eschewing any secrecy, aired them in public.[59]

---

[51] See Chhaganlal Joshi, *Satyagraha Ashram ane Gandhi Parivar* (Ahmedabad: Sabarmati Ashram Suraksha ane Smarak Trust, 1975), pp. 14–15.
[52] Balvantsinha, *Bapuka Ashram Parivar* (Ahmedabad: Navajivan, 1972), p. 30.
[53] Mahadev Desai, 'Apartim Sadhak', Navajivan Trust, *Ashram No Pran*, p. 57.
[54] Thomson, *Gandhi and His Ashrams*, p. 117.   [55] *Ibid.*, p. 120.
[56] Letter to Bechar Parmar, 23 June 1928.
[57] 'Handicap of Mahatmaship', *Young India*, 8 November 1928.
[58] 'My Shame and Sorrow', *Bombay Chronicle*, 8 April 1929.   [59] *Ibid.*

Ashramites began to leave in the wake of the scandals and although, according to Thomson, Gandhi 'persevered, but in spite of his claim that the Ashram was purer for these revelations, he gradually distanced himself from its operation and appeared to prepare for its ultimate closure'.[60]

THE DECISION TO LEAVE

Gandhi spent most of the year in which Maganlal died in Magan Niwas, consoling Santok (and probably himself) and did not return to live in his own house for the remainder of his stay at the ashram.[61] During the following year he was there only for short visits. In 1930 he was more or less a permanent resident up until the start of the Salt March in March, building the discipline among the marchers-to-be. However when he left for Dandi, Gandhi promised not to return to the ashram until India had gained her independence. Thomson notes that at the time he was probably 'relieved to have an opportunity of dissociating himself from the Ashram. However, during the struggle the ashramites performed creditably, and renewed his faith in the worthiness of the Sabarmati experiment. But now he was unable to settle there without attracting the attention of a host of critics.'[62]

After his release from prison, following what became known as the Salt Satyagraha, and the pact with Viceroy Lord Irwin, Gandhi re-entered Ahmedabad city on 7 April 1931, for the first time since his departure for the Salt March. Although he spent over three weeks in total in the city, staying with friends or at the Gujarat Vidyapith, the educational institute he had founded nearby, his visits to the ashram consisted of only two very brief stops.

Immediately on his return from the Round Table Conference in London, the bitterly disappointed leader announced the commencement of the Civil Disobedience campaign which was a continuation of the Salt Satyagraha. The repression was even greater than that of before the Gandhi/Irwin Pact. On 4 January 1932 Gandhi was again arrested and on the 20th the Government raided the Sabarmati Satyagraha Ashram. During the Mahatma's absence things had deteriorated further with the community, and one family had even been requested to leave. The ashram's internal problems made its closure inevitable, but even in this act political mileage could be gained.

---

[60] Thomson, *Gandhi and His Ashrams*, p. 128; see also Letter to Chhaganlal Joshi, 6 May 1929.
[61] Kalelkar, *Stray Glimpses of Bapu*, p. 130.   [62] Thomson, *Gandhi and His Ashrams*, p. 132.

On 8 May 1933, after having served one year and four months, Gandhi was released from prison and within a few weeks, spent mostly at Poona and then staying with friends in Ahmedabad, Gandhi started discussions with Mahadev Desai on the future management of the ashram. On the last day of May, Gandhi received a suggestion to rename the ashram as the Harijan Ashram. On 22 July, after several lengthy visits to his former headquarters and following a discussion with a deputation of Harijans, Gandhi decided to sacrifice the ashram. That same day he wrote to Jamnalal Bajaj explaining that 'The reason for handing over the control of the Ashram is that it is better to hand over ourselves what the Government is sure to take by force in due course. Instead of carrying away our belongings one after another against land revenue, let them take the entire land.'[63]

The ashram authorities had refused to pay land revenues to the Government for the previous two years, and had therefore suffered the confiscation of goods of considerable value. Gandhi decided that the ashram, which had been in existence for eighteen years, sixteen at its present site, should be turned over to the Government – the ultimate sacrifice.

On 26 July, in a long letter to the Home Secretary to the Government of Bombay, Gandhi made his strange request. He wrote:

My first constructive act on return to India in 1915 was to found the Satyagraha Ashram for the purpose of serving Truth. The inmates are under the vows of truth, ahimsa, celibacy, control of palate, poverty, fearlessness, removal of untouchability, swadeshi with respect for religions and bread labour. The present site for the Ashram was bought in 1916. It conducts today certain activities mostly through the labour of inmates. But it does need to supplement that labour with ordinary paid labour. Its principal activities are: Khadi production as a village industry without the aid of power driven machinery, dairy, agriculture, scientific scavenging and literary education. The Ashram has 107 inmates at present (men 42, women 31, boys 12 and girls 22). This number excludes those who are in prison and those who are otherwise engaged outside. Up to now it has trained nearly 1,000 persons in the manufacture of khadi. Most of these, so far as my knowledge goes, are doing useful constructive work and earning an honest livelihood . . .

The Ashram owns immovable property estimated at about Rs. 3,60,000 and movables including cash estimated at over Rs. 3,00,000. The Ashram takes no part in politics so-called. But it does believe in non-co-operation and civil disobedience as indispensable, under certain circumstances, for the observance of truth and non-violence. Hence, the civil disobedience campaign of 1930 was started by the march to Dandi of nearly eighty inmates of the Ashram.

---

[63] Letter to Jamnalal Bajaj, 22 July 1933.

Time has now arrived for the Ashram to make a greater sacrifice in the face of the existing situation – on the one hand the growing terrorism by the Government and on the other the equally growing demoralization among the people . . .

Hence, mere incarceration can bring little satisfaction. Moreover, I quite clearly see that the vast constructive programme of the Ashram cannot be carried on with safety, unless the Ashram ceases entirely to have anything to do with the campaign. To accept such a position will be to deny the creed. Up to now I had hoped that the existence of the Ashram side by side with the civil resistance of its individual members was possible and that there was bound to be an honourable peace between Government and the Congress in the near future even though the Congress goal might not be immediately realized. The unfortunate rejection by His Excellency the Viceroy of the honest advance of the Congress through me, in the interest of peace, shows clearly that the Government do not seek or desire peace, they want an abject surrender by the largest and the admittedly most, if not the only, popular political organization in the country. This is impossible so long as the Congress continues to repose confidence in its present advisers. The struggle therefore is bound to be prolonged and calls for much greater sacrifice than the people have hitherto undergone. It follows that the greatest measure of sacrifice is to be expected of me as the author of the movement. I can therefore only offer that which is nearest and dearest to me and for the building of which I and many other members of the Ashram have laboured with infinite patience and care all these eighteen years. Every head of cattle and every tree has its history and sacred associations. They are all members of a big family. What was once a barren plot of land has been turned by human endeavour into a fair-sized model garden colony. It will not be without a tear that we shall break up the family and its activities. I have had many and prayerful conversations with the inmates and they have, men and women, unanimously approved of the proposal to give up the present activities. Those who are at all able have decided to offer individual civil disobedience after the suspension period is over.[64]

In a press interview, Gandhi added that 'The disbandment of the Ashram would mean that every inmate would constitute a walking ashram, carrying with him or her the responsibility for realising the Ashram ideal, no matter where situated, whether in prison or outside.'[65] On the 27th Gandhi told a special correspondent of *The Daily Herald*:

The members of the Ashram and I came to the conclusion that we should no longer enjoy these things when others have been deprived of what was just as precious as the things of the Ashram to the Ashram people. Moreover, many members of the Ashram having decided to offer individual civil disobedience, it would be wrong to expect the Government to treat the Ashram differently from other properties

---

[64] Letter to the Home Secretary to the Government of Bombay, 26 July 1933; see also Letter to Home Secretary, 26 July 1933.
[65] 'Interview to *The Hindu*', *The Hindu*, 27 July 1933.

similarly affected. Of course, there is a fundamental difference. The Ashram is a public trust, with well defined objects; and if the members of such a public institution adopt an attitude which brings upon them the heavy hand of the law, good or bad, the property which is the subject-matter of the trust might not be easily affected. It is for this reason that we have decided that we should voluntarily give up possession of the properties to the Government. Hence this step to be taken of disbanding the Ashram.[66]

On 30 July, Gandhi offered the ashram library to the municipality and informed the Government that on 1 August the ashram would be completely vacated. Gandhi intended to march to the village of Ras with twenty-three companions as the first leg of a search for a new home. Before he could set off, along with Kasturba, Mahadev Desai and thirty other inmates, Gandhi was again arrested. The following day the Government formally refused to take possession of the ashram. On 30 September, five weeks after his release, Gandhi donated the ashram to the Harijan Sevak Sangh and by November the institution was becoming known as the Harijan Ashram. On 5 September 1939, the property of the ex-Satyagraha Ashram/Udyog Mandir was vested in trust for the uplift of Harijans and officially became the Harijan Ashram.

Maganlal Gandhi did not influence the Mahatma the way that Raychand, Tolstoy or Ruskin did, or even the way his early colleagues Polak and Kallenbach did. He was, after all, much younger and a disciple. In their relationship it was Gandhi who was quite obviously the major source of influence, not the other way around. However, Gandhi relied on Maganlal far more than at least the English-language record shows and his death seems to have been a watershed event in Gandhi's life. It would probably be an exaggeration to say that Gandhi could leave the ashram merely because Maganlal had died almost two years before. But it does seem that with the departure of the ashram's creator and his right hand person and chief fellow-seeker there, the soul of the establishment had, as he claimed, to a large extent departed. The ashram was now little more than a collection of buildings with all too frequently squabbling inmates. It seems that this made it far easier to leave, and the time had come to set up new headquarters in a place where the void left by Maganlal's passing was not as evident. Although Maganlal's tireless work allowed Gandhi to be the Mahatma, in his death Maganlal asserted an influence over his master in a way that he could not even have conceived of in life.

---

[66] 'Interview to *The Daily Herald*', *The Hindu*, 28 July 1933.

Maganlal's death may have had one other very significant consequence. By this time Mahadev Desai was already, as some have said, Gandhi's alter-ego and Boswell, but he was not the heir to Gandhi's political movement or necessarily his most committed spiritual disciple. Gandhi's world had become enlarged and one person could no longer be heir to all of the Mahatma's programme. Ashe points out that the search for a substitute was natural and although he sees Gandhi as primarily a political actor, he correctly observes that 'instead of looking for a non-political heir, as Maganlal would have been, he reached out. He realized – an impressive fact in anyone nearing sixty – that to go further he would have to extend himself, through alliance with a younger leader.'[67] That political leader was to be Jawaharlal Nehru. Following the passing of Maganlal, the roles of secretaries and political, religious and social heirs were largely separated. To the degree that they were still together in one person, that person was Jamnalal Bajaj.

[67] Ashe, *Gandhi*, p. 277.

CHAPTER 6

Jamnalal Bajaj and the move to Sevagram

INTRODUCTION

After having left Sabarmati, the political campaign of the Civil Disobedience movement launched by the Salt March behind him, it was not by
accident that Gandhi set up his next and last ashram in a small village not
far from the town of Wardha, in the geographical centre of India. Before
settling (as much as the Mahatma was ever able to settle anywhere) by the
side of Segaon village, Gandhi lived for a while with some of his erstwhile
ashramites in Wardha at the branch Satyagraha Ashram which had been set
up by his spiritual heir Vinoba Bhave, and then with a group of followers
at a large house with extensive orange orchards which had been donated to
him by Jamnalal Bajaj. The property was named Maganwadi in memory
of Maganlal Gandhi. But why is it that Vinoba had gone to Wardha in the
first place? And why did Gandhi also end up there – was it as simple as
Vinoba's presence? Was it the gift of property from Bajaj when presumably
Gandhi could have chosen any part of India and received as much property
as he needed? Was there something special about Wardha which attracted
both Vinoba and Gandhi? Surely it was not the healthy climate, as the
malaria-ridden Wardha district is one of the hottest areas of India.[1] The
influence of Jamnalal Bajaj, the constructive worker, spiritual seeker and
Gandhi's adopted son, is the key.

FROM SABARMATI TO WARDHA

Vinoba biographers inform us that 'Sri Jamnalal Bajaj, a wealthy person and
another adopted son of Gandhiji, had opened a branch of the Satyagraha

---

[1] Gandhi's disciple Mirabehn describes the 118° F plus May and June temperatures in which metal
objects, even inside buildings, could not be touched, and where wet cloths had to be perpetually
wrapped around heads as a matter of survival. She added that the prospect of settling in a place
with such a climate 'needed all one's courage'. Mira Behn [Madeleine Slade], *The Spirit's Pilgrimage*
(London: Longmans, 1960), p. 193.

ashram of Sabarmati at Wardha in the Central Provinces',[2] or that at 'the importunity of Jamnalal Bajaj'[3] Gandhi had started this branch of the Satyagraha Ashram at Wardha on 14 January 1921. Baja had long wanted Gandhi to relocate to Wardha, but, as a Gujarati, Gandhi felt that he could work better from his own district. A branch of the Sabarmati Ashram was the next best way 'to provide a constant standing temptation for the Mahatma to visit Wardha'.[4] Bajaj's choice to head up the new ashram was Vinoba, but Maganlal Gandhi decided he could not spare him from Sabarmati. Ramniklal Modi, a senior member of the Sabarmati Ashram, was then appointed the first director. However, as his health was not good and the climate did not suit him, Modi did not stay long. To replace him, in spite of further protests by Maganlal, Gandhi then sent Vinoba to take on all the responsibilities for the ashram in the place that is now known as Maganwadi. Along with an old childhood friend from his Baroda days and four students, Vinoba arrived in Wardha on 8 April 1921. Soon he moved the ashram to the simpler surroundings of a smaller house with a thatched roof about two miles away, near Bajaj's residence of Bajajwadi, where it operated until the end of 1923. In early 1924, Vinoba moved his headquarters to a new building constructed by Bajaj at what later became known as the Mahila Ashram, then, at the end of 1932, he shifted to the 'untouchable' locality in the village of Nalwadi, a few miles from Wardha, to support himself by spinning and working alone.[5] In 1938, following a serious illness, to get away from the noise and dust of the busy nearby Nagpur road, he moved to Bajaj's holiday bungalow at Paunar, four miles from Wardha. This became the site of his final ashram. In all, from 1921 until the end of his life in mid-November 1982, Vinoba shifted his headquarters five times but remained within five miles of Wardha.

Following the Salt Satyagraha and Civil Disobedience movement and several rounds of imprisonment in the early 1930s, Gandhi was finally set free, homeless, in August 1934. Two months later he officially retired from Congress and spent a year touring India for the cause of the removal of 'untouchability.' Bajaj again started urging Gandhi to settle in Wardha (as Vallabhbhai Patel had been pushing for Bardoli in Gujarat) where he had dreams of setting up a fully fledged Gandhian centre. Already the ashram

[2] Vasant Nargolkar, *The Creed of Saint Vinoba* (Bombay: Bharatiya Vidya Bhavan, 1963), p. 26.
[3] Kanti Shah, *Vinoba: Life and Mission [An Introductory Study]* (Rajghat, Varanasi: Sarva Seva Sangh, 1979), p. 22
[4] B. R. Nanda, *In Gandhiji's Footsteps: The Life and Times of Jamnalal Bajaj* (Delhi: Oxford University Press, 1990), p. 90.
[5] Suresh Ram, *Vinoba and His Mission [Being an Account of the Rise and Growth of the Bhoodan Yajna Movement]* (Rajghat, Varanasi: Akhil Bharat Sarva Seva Sangh, 1962), pp. 19–20.

under the leadership of Vinoba was there, as was the Mahila Seva Mandal, for the shelter and education of women and girls who came from families of workers where the men had gone to jail in the independence struggle. To placate Bajaj, Gandhi had committed himself to spending around one month a year there, staying with Vinoba, before attending the annual Congress session. He did this more or less regularly in December from 1925 onwards. However, following his abandonment of the ashram at Sabarmati and final release from prison, Wardha increasingly became Gandhi's base. In December 1934 Gandhi decided to set up the All India Village Industries Association (AIVIA) and, while considering where it should be located, Bajaj reiterated the offer he made to Gandhi eighteen years earlier. Bajaj argued strongly for Wardha, pointing out that not only was it in a central position in India, but also that he would provide the land, building and furniture to get the project established.[6] When Gandhi accepted the offer, Bajaj placed his spacious two-storied garden house on the outskirts of the town, with its twenty acres of orange orchards, at the Mahatma's disposal. It was this place that Gandhi named Maganwadi. Along with fifteen to twenty followers, Gandhi moved into the large house which also came to serve the dual purposes of Gandhi's new home and as headquarters of the AIVIA under the management of the economist J. C. Kumarappa. Gandhi noted that his moving to Wardha was done while 'ignoring Sardar's anger born out of his love', adding that Patel 'could have easily secured for me ten orchards against one here, but he could not find for me a Jamnalal there and, therefore, I let the ten orchards go'.[7] Although some of his critics saw Gandhi's increasing emphasis on constructive work as being irrelevant to the political struggle, the divergence had led to Gandhi announcing his retirement from politics at the previous October Congress session. This, and the formation of the AIVIA, 'offered an opportunity that Jamnalal seized with both hands'.[8] Soon Wardha became the de facto nationalist capital of India and Bajajwadi, Bajaj's house, came to serve as a guest house to accommodate nationalist workers who were visiting Wardha.

JAMNALAL BAJAJ — THE FIFTH SON

Jamnalal Bajaj was born into a family of modest means in 1889 in the village of Kashi-ka-bas in Jaipur state.[9] How, from these humble beginnings,

6 Balvantsinha, *Under the Shelter of Bapu* (Ahmedabad: Navajivan, 1962), p. 33.
7 Letter to Kamalnayan Bajaj, 22 November 1945.
8 B. R. Nanda, *In Search of Gandhi: Essays and Reflections* (New Delhi: Oxford University Press, 2002), p. 207.
9 This biographical account is largely based on Nanda, *In Gandhiji's Footsteps*; Shriman Narayan, *Jamnalal Bajaj: Gandhiji's Fifth Son* (New Delhi: Publications Division, Ministry of Information and

he became a leading millionaire industrialist and intimate of the Mahatma is a story that is hard to understand for those who come from a time and place where the sacredness of the nuclear family is a given. Bajaj's village was also the home village of Marwari Seth Bachharaj Bajaj, a well-to-do Wardha businessman. The childless Seth had earlier adopted a son who died soon after his marriage, before the birth of any children. Now he, his wife Saidibai, and bereaved daughter-in-law Basanti Devi, returned to their home district seeking a child for adoption by the young widow so that the family line could continue. In 1894, on their way to the Kashi-ka-bas village temple they saw an appealing young boy of about four or five years in age playing in front of a house. The Seth's wife took a liking to the lad, and, following some enquiries, discovered that he was the son of Birdibai, an old acquaintance of hers. She looked up Birdibai, and, as the two women were talking, in rushed young Jamnalal. Then, 'Saidibai asked whose child he was, Birdibai in her innocence said, "Ap ka hi hai" ("He is yours") as is often said in courtesy in Indian villages. Saidibai took these words literally and when she rose to leave, she asked for the boy in adoption, much to Birdibai's surprise.' The parents did not want to part with their son and 'only with considerable difficulty were they persuaded to do so'.[10] In gratitude Bachharaj had a well sunk in the village where, up till then, water had to be carted from some four miles away.

Jamnalal was taken to Wardha where he was given a modest education and was trained in the ways of business from an early age. At ten he was betrothed and at the age thirteen he was married to Janakidevi, a young girl of around nine years in age, from a wealthy Indore family. By the time of his marriage, Jamnalal was fully absorbed in the family business and circumstances forced him into a closer relationship with Bachharaj because Saidibai had died in the year of his betrothal and Basanti Devi did not live long after his marriage.

There is a story of Jamnalal angering Bachharaj by preferring to dress in simple clothes even when the circumstances seemed to require much finery. One of these occasions caused such anger in his adoptive grandfather that he reminded Jamnalal that he had come to a position of wealth without ever having had to work for it and that he did not pay due regard to the wishes of his guardian. In response, the deeply hurt seventeen-year-old wrote to the

Broadcasting, Government of India, 1974); Kaka Kalelkar, 'Jamnalalji as I Knew Him', in Kalelkar (ed.), *To a Gandhian Capitalist* (Bombay: Sevak Prakashan, 1979), pp. 13–20; U. S. Mohan Rao, 'Introduction', in Kalelkar, *To a Gandhian Capitalist*, pp. 23–64; M. V. Kamath, *Gandhi's Coolie: Life and Times of Ramakrishna Bajaj* (Ahmedabad: Allied Publishers, 1988), pp. 1–9; and the chapter about Bajaj in Pyarelal and Nayar, *In Gandhiji's Mirror*, pp. 247–69.

[10] Pyarelal and Nayar, *In Gandhiji's Mirror*, p. 250.

old man that he was renouncing his wealth and leaving the house, taking nothing more than the clothes that he was wearing.[11] Bachharaj tracked Jamnalal down before he could board a train for Hardwar or Rishikesh to become a sannyasi and, after much difficulty, persuaded him to return home. It is reported that this episode left a 'deep mark' on the young man's mind: 'He always felt that he had no right to enjoy the wealth he had come by, thanks to his adoption by Bachharaj; wealth which he had once renounced. Even before he met Gandhiji he believed in the simple life, travelled third class, and considered his wealth a trust.'[12]

Six months after this incident, when Jamnalal was eighteen, Bachharaj died and Jamnalal inherited the family fortune, which, with his acute business acumen, he managed to increase further, but without ever doing anything unfair or unethical.

Unfortunately, no psycho-biography of Bajaj has been written, but the circumstances of his childhood provide a rich mine for the understanding of his relationship with Gandhi who he so badly needed to fulfil the role of surrogate parent. While he had always possessed a spiritual bent, from the time of Bachharaj's death in particular, Bajaj was in search of a father figure and mentor. He sought out association with holy men, scholars and scientists in his quest for a guru who could guide him through his inner struggles but settled on Gandhi at a time when no one could have predicted the heights to which the Mahatma would rise. For Bajaj, Gandhi's deeds seemed to match his words and his asceticism matched a similar streak in Bajaj himself. In later life, Bajaj confessed that he had felt 'almost uncontrollable rage against his father' who had abandoned him. 'It seemed monstrous that a child should be deprived of the love of his own parents', and he retained a 'strong revulsion against the practice of adopting children.'[13] But not of adopting fathers.

While Gandhi was still in South Africa, Bajaj had heard of his work and was impressed. He was in Bombay to greet Gandhi on his return to India and he visited him at Kochrab as soon as he could. By the end of 1915 he was completely under the Mahatma's spell. Quickly, Bajaj became one of his chief financial backers and soon the acquaintanceship grew into a deep affection on both sides. Bajaj insisted that his family wear khadi and attempted to reorganise his life along the lines of Gandhi's idea of trusteeship, where the wealthy person sees his money as being held in trust

---

[11] For the letter, see Desai's article in Gujarati *Navajivan*, 11 July 1926, titled 'Jamnalalji – A Pilgrim'. After Bajaj's death, Mahadev Desai translated and published this letter in *Harijan*, 22 February 1942.
[12] Pyarelal and Nayar, *In Gandhiji's Mirror*, p. 252.   [13] Nanda, *In Gandhiji's Footsteps*, p. 27.

for the poor. Bajaj visited Gandhi regularly and sent Janakidevi and their five children to stay at the Sabarmati Ashram from time to time. One of the reasons occasionally cited for his wanting a branch ashram to be set up at Wardha was so that an appropriate ashram atmosphere could be provided for the education of his own children. His eldest daughter was married at Sabarmati Ashram and his eldest son was partially educated there and later, along with one of his younger daughters, was placed in Vinoba's ashram for a few years. In fact the relationships were so close that Bajaj came to consider Vinoba his guru – but a guru was not enough. After the Nagpur Congress of 1920, where at Gandhi's urging he had served as chairman of the reception committee and where Gandhi assumed supreme leadership of the organisation, the adopted son Bajaj consciously adopted Gandhi as his father by asking the Mahatma to adopt him as a son. Following Bajaj's death, Gandhi recounted how this came about:

Twenty-two years ago a young man of thirty came to me and said, 'I want to ask something of you.'

'Ask, and it shall be given, if it is at all within my power to give,' I replied with some surprise.

'Regard me as your son Devdas,' the young man said.

'Agreed,' I replied. 'But what have you asked of me? You are the giver, I am the gainer.'

The young man was no other than Jamnalal Bajaj. People know something of what this sacrament meant. But few know the extent of the part played by the self-adopted son. Never before, I can say, was a mortal blessed with a 'son' like him. Of course I have many sons and daughters in the sense that they do some of my work. But Jamnalalji surrendered himself and his without reservation. There is hardly any activity of mine in which I did not receive his full-hearted co-operation and in which it did not prove to be of the greatest value. He was gifted with a quick intelligence. He was a merchant prince. He placed at my disposal his ample possessions. He was constantly on the vigil and looked after my work, my comforts, my health and my finances. He would also bring up the workers to me. Where am I to get another son like him now? The day he died he and Janakidevi were to come to me. We had to decide a number of things. But God willed it otherwise and he died almost at the very hour he should have been with me. The death of such a son is a stunning blow to the father. Never before have I felt so forlorn except when Maganlal was snatched from me fourteen years ago.[14]

In 1922, in response to a letter from Bajaj, Gandhi wrote: 'You have indeed, made yourself my fifth son. But I am striving to be a worthy father to you. It is no ordinary responsibility which a man who adopts a son

---

[14] 'Fiery Ordeal', *Harijan Sevak*, 22 February 1942.

undertakes. May God help me, and may I be worthy of the responsibility in this very life.'[15] A later exchange of letters between them in early May 1924 makes this relationship clear. Gandhi addressed a letter to Bajaj as 'Bhai [brother] Jamnalal' instead of as 'Chiranjiv Jamnalal', the usual form of address by a father (and one which Gandhi would later use more freely for his followers). The upset Jamnalal wrote to Gandhi asking if he was no longer fit to be a son. Gandhi replied:

Chi. Jamnalal,
Your being unhappy has made me also unhappy. I avoided the use of *Chi.* in the letter to you, because I sent it unsealed, and because I could not decide just then as to the propriety or otherwise of the prefix *Chi.* as applied to you being read by all those who happened to see the letter. I therefore used *Bhai.* How are we to decide whether you are fit to be a *Chi.* or whether I deserve to take the place of father to you? As you have doubts about yourself, so do I have about myself. If you are imperfect, so am I. I had to take thought about my own fitness before agreeing to be a father to you. In agreeing to be that, I yielded to your love. May God make me worthy of that position. If any deficiencies remain in you, they will be evidence of the failure of my touch. I am confident that, if we try, both of us will succeed. Even if we fail, God who is hungry only for our devotion and can look into the innermost recesses of our heart, will deal with us according to our deserts. I will, therefore, continue to look upon you as *Chi.* as long as I do not consciously harbour impurity in myself.
Blessings from
Bapu

Some thirty years after her husband's death, Janakidevi remembered that it was said that Gandhi 'was a storm that blew my husband hither and thither'.[16] The description may not be far from the mark. At one stage, Bajaj, the promoter of khadi, wanted to purchase a textile mill to show that such enterprises could be run along Gandhian lines and done so economically without exploiting the workers. The incongruence of a khadi propagandist producing mill cloth displeased Gandhi who more or less told him to give up the idea,[17] and Jamnalal dutifully obeyed. Another example came in 1921 when Gandhi called for a boycott of British goods. Bajaj did not only eschew British cloth but made a bonfire of everything in his house that was British made, including carpets and upholstered furniture. Towards the end of his life, Bajaj, looking back on his twenty-four-year association with the Mahatma, could say: 'My faith in him went on increasing. I went

[15] Letter to Jamnalal Bajaj, 16 March 1922.   [16] Mehta, *Mahatma Gandhi and His Apostles*, p. 59.
[17] See Letter to Jamnalal Bajaj, 27 September 1934.

on identifying myself with him more and more. Today he is my ideal and my guiding star whose command I obey. His affection is my life.'[18]

In 1924 Bajaj founded the Mahila Seva Mandal to uplift the status of women in India. A year earlier he had founded and served as the first president of the Gandhi Seva Sangh, an organisation of those who believed in truth and nonviolence and had pledged themselves to carrying on Gandhi's constructive programme (centred around the promotion of khadi and village industries, a national language, basic education, the removal of untouchability, village sanitation and Hindu–Muslim unity), and had been sentenced to eighteen months imprisonment for his role in the Nagpur Flag Satyagraha. In 1925 he became treasurer of the Charkha Sangh (Spinners' Association) with Gandhi as president. Bajaj was excommunicated from his caste for his anti-untouchability activities and in 1928, when anti-untouchability work was still in its infancy, he opposed the temple trustees and threw open the family financed Laxminarayan Temple in Wardha to 'untouchables', making it one of the, if not *the* first temples to be opened to all castes in the country.[19] Later he became secretary of the Congress Anti-Untouchability Committee. He was also president of the All India Hindi Sahitya Sammelan (an association for promoting Hindustani as the national language) and, although far more interested in constructive activities than politics, served a lengthy period as Congress treasurer. In 1934 he resigned the presidentship, and later his membership, of the Gandhi Seva Sangh because he felt that he could not live up to the strict rules laid down by the association. He explained that, because he was aware of his own frailties, he 'did not regard Bapu as my "Guru" nor accept him as such'; however he 'certainly accepted him as my father'.[20] During the Salt Satyagraha, Bajaj was sentenced to two years imprisonment and in 1939 he was again imprisoned when he defied an order prohibiting his entry into Jaipur State to organise famine relief work. He was arrested a further time during the Individual Civil Disobedience movement of 1941.

Although Bajaj did much to establish Gandhian institutions and indeed to bankroll Gandhi's activities in and around Wardha, and to work at being a trustee zamindar, he was lacking in spiritual solace. He often battled with depression, with feelings of spiritual unworthiness, with his adherence to

---

[18] Quoted in Pyarelal and Nayar, *In Gandhiji's Mirror*, p. 257.

[19] Earlier he had thrown open his wells, ginning factories and gardens but the temple trustees thwarted the opening of the temple. For an account of the protests at the opening and consequent boycott by caste Hindus, see T. V. Parvate, *Jamnalal Bajaj [A Brief Study of his Life and Character]* (Ahmedabad, Navajivan, 1962), pp. 54–8; and Mahadev Desai, *Day to Day with Gandhi: Secretary's Diary* (Rajghat, Varanasi: Sarva Seva Sangh, 1974), vol. IX, p. 19.

[20] Jamnalal Bajaj, 'In Search of a Guru', in Kalelkar (ed.), *To a Gandhian Capitalist*, pp. 9–12, at p. 12.

celibacy, and even thoughts of suicide. In his times of greatest mental disturbance he sought Gandhi's guidance.[21] Eventually, Gandhi directed him to see Ananadamayi Ma, the guru of Jawaharlal Nehru's wife Kamala.[22] He visited her on several occasions towards the end of his life. On his insistence on knowing the time of his death, she would only inform him that he needed to take precautions for six months. Bajaj was leading Gandhi's campaign of service to cows at this stage and, following the instructions from his spiritual teacher, shifted into a simple unfurnished hut at Gopuri[23] (as the northern part of Nalwadi was named at this time) to devote himself to cow service work and to undertake spiritual practice. While the emphasis on work with cows may have appeared anachronistic to Gandhi's English-speaking co-workers, it was close to the Mahatma's heart and he was delighted when Bajaj took up the cause.[24] Jamnalal renounced travel outside Wardha and gave up the use of all vehicles. By his own insistence he lived alone until, in the last week of his life, he relented and let Janakidevi join him. Apparently as his six-month period of caution and preparation was coming to an end, following the five-kilometre walk to the house of one of his sons, the fifty-two-year-old Bajaj collapsed and died of a cerebral haemorrhage on 11 February 1942.[25] Janakidevi wanted to end her own life on her husband's funeral pyre by committing sati. Gandhi instructed her to complete Jamnalal's unfinished work instead.[26] She gave all her private wealth to the cause of cow protection and later spent years walking with Vinoba on his Bhoodan yatra.

Three days after Jamnalal's death, Mahadev Desai wrote to leading Gandhian worker Rajagopalachari about the event and it's impact on Gandhi:

You are right. Bapu is in greatest need of consolation. He is bearing himself up bravely, trying to console all – Janakibehn and the children – and incessantly thinks of plans to carry on with redoubled zeal his great work, but as he was speaking to these members of the family yesterday he broke down. I think his grief is as deep and profound as it was on Maganlal Gandhi's death. Everything here – even Sevagram with Bapu – seems empty without him.[27]

---

[21] See for example his letter to Gandhi on 4 November 1938, in Kalelkar (ed.), *To a Gandhian Capitalist*, pp. 128–31.

[22] See Letter to Jamnalal Bajaj, 30 July 1941.

[23] While the hut no longer exists, being replace by Shanti Kuti a building with picture exhibits of Bajaj, a photograph of the thatched hut can be found in Mulk Raj Anand, *Homage to Jamnalal Bajaj: A Pictorial Biography* (Ahmedabad: Allied Publishers, 1988), p. 98.

[24] Nanda, *In Gandhiji's Footsteps*, p. 353.

[25] For Bajaj's death, see Savitri Bajaj, *I Write as I Feel* (Bombay: Sevak, 1977), pp. 40–1; and Kamath, *Gandhi's Coolie*, p 73.

[26] See 'Speech at Prayer Meeting', *Harijanbandhu*, 22 February 1942.

[27] Mahadev Desai to C. Rajagopalachari, 14 February 1942, Appendix IV in *CWMG*, LXXV, pp. 454–5.

Mahadev Desai, in his summation of Bajaj's life work, added:

Never since the death of Maganlal Gandhi in 1928 had any bereavement dealt such a staggering blow to Gandhiji as the sudden and premature death of Jamnalalji. Words fail me when I attempt to describe the feeling of desolation. For two days he bore up bravely consoling the bereaved widow and the aged mother, but on the third day he broke down as he was saying: 'Childless people adopt sons. But Jamnalalji adopted me as father. He should have been an heir to my all, instead he has left me an heir to his all!'[28]

Just six months after Jamnalal's death, Mahadev Desai also passed away. Although in some senses Jawaharlal Nehru became something akin to his next adopted son, never again would Gandhi have relationships like the ones he had with Hermann Kallenbach, or Maganlal Gandhi, or Jamnalal Bajaj, or Mahadev Desai, and never again would he officially move his headquarters to another site.

FROM WARDHA TO SEVAGRAM

Mirabehn was staying with Gandhi at Maganwadi but found the conditions too confining. Besides some ex-Sabarmati Ashram residents, the group around Gandhi consisted of 'a strange medley of various kinds of cranky people', including a sleep walker and a sufferer of St.Vitus' dance. This ensured 'that in the dead of night blood-curdling shrieks would rend the air'.[29] She tried to find relief by going for long solitary walks in the early mornings. To reach the open countryside she had to pass through the small nearby village of Sindi. The insanitary conditions of the village appalled her and so, with the help of Mahadev Desai and other Maganwadi inmates and Gandhi's strong encouragement, she began a sanitation programme in the village. The success of efforts to discourage the villagers from defiling their environment, however, was minimal. Gandhi therefore instructed Mirabehn to take a contingent of Maganwadi residents and visitors who had come to see Gandhi to the village every morning to clean its roads.[30] Sushila Nayar, Pyarelal's sister and later Gandhi's physician, recalls how on a summer vacation in 1935 she joined the sanitation workers in Sindi but 'the villagers merely pointed out to us where the excreta was, but never joined us in removing it!'[31] One day Gandhi also joined the group of sanitation workers, which often included Jamnalal Bajaj among its ranks, and encouraged the villagers to join in. He instructed them on the techniques

[28] *Harijan*, 22 February 1942.   [29] Mira Behn, *The Spirit's Pilgrimage*, p. 191.
[30] Gandhi, *Bapu's Letters to Mira*, 1949, p. 273.   [31] Pyarelal and Nayar, *In Gandhiji's Mirror*, p. 262.

of building simple earth latrines so that the waste could be used as manure for fodder and vegetable crops and that would leave the village clean.[32]

Towards the end of the year Gandhi's high blood pressure was troubling him and the cramped conditions at Maganwadi, along with the lack of progress in sanitation efforts in Sindi and other nearby villages visited, left him, in the words of a biographer, 'frustrated and contributed to his poor health'.[33] Mirabehn noted that 'his nerves were becoming severely strained'.[34] He wrote to a friend who had requested a message for his paper that he was 'really and literally drained dry' and that he should stop all his writing 'and simply bury myself in a village and there work away for all I am worth, and that I should love to do in perfect silence'.[35] Gandhi decided to move to Sindi alone and work for and with the villagers while he was regaining his health. His associates at Maganwadi were shocked by the idea and he only agreed to remain where he could get adequate medical attention when Mirabehn offered to take his place in the village.[36]

A small, one-roomed cottage was built for Mirabehn in Sindi. Although the village was peopled by low castes, even they had their strict hierarchy. When, on the her first day there, Mirabehn accepted water from a man of the lowest caste in order to wash her hands, she was henceforth refused permission to take water from wells belonging to those of slightly higher castes.[37] Although she made some progress in the village, it was extremely slow and meagre. In reality Sindi was little more than an outlying urban slum of Wardha and Mirabehn decided that she needed to experiment in a more typical Indian village. After the services of Gajanan Naik were secured as a replacement for her in Sindi, she began the quest for a more suitable village within an five mile radius. She walked day after day in all directions but was not very impressed with what she found. The villagers were indifferent when they were not openly hostile to her. Eventually she settled on Segaon, about five miles to the east of Wardha as the least unsatisfactory of a poor lot. Although there was no connecting road and the village was built in a low-lying area between two water channels, and hence prone to malaria outbreaks, the advantage of Segaon was that the people 'were a little more responsive' and that it contained an orchard and farm belonging to Bajaj. Soon a hut had been built for her at the edge of the village and she had relocated there from Sindi. The population of the village stood at around 600 residents, two-thirds of whom were 'untouchables'.

---

[32] See 'Advice to Villagers', *Harijan*, 15 March 1935.   [33] Thomson, *Gandhi and His Ashrams*, p. 187.
[34] Mira Behn, *The Spirit's Pilgrimage*, p. 194.   [35] Letter to C. R. Srinivasan, 26 August 1935.
[36] Mira Behn, *The Spirit's Pilgrimage*, p. 194; and Gandhi, *Bapu's Letters to Mira*, p. 275.
[37] Mira Behn, *The Spirit's Pilgrimage*, p. 194.

At this stage, Gandhi's health took a turn for the worse and he left Maganwadi for a new and as yet unoccupied school building at the Mahila Ashram which was on the Segaon side of Wardha, only about four miles away. After an improvement in his health, Gandhi went to Ahmedabad to continue his recuperation. Against the advice of friends, it became increasingly clear to him that he had to settle in a village and work alone because village co-workers should be cultivated from within the village itself rather than imposed upon it from the outside. As Mirabehn had already made a start there, that village was to be Segaon as soon as he could convince Bajaj of the idea. In April 1936, after he had returned to Maganwadi, Gandhi wrote to Mirabehn that 'Jamnalalji has given full authority to commence building operations.'[38]

In the early morning of 30 April, Gandhi walked from Wardha to Segaon to select a site for his hut[39] and Bajaj organised a meeting of the villagers so that Gandhi could put his plans to them.[40] The village headman welcomed the Mahatma but also warned him that he personally could not co-operate in Gandhi's anti-untouchability programme[41] and on that very first trip to the village a serious assault occurred among the villagers.[42] While Gandhi went to the cool climate of the Nandi Hills in the south near Bangalore to complete his convalescence, Mirabehn and a small group from Maganwadi supervised the construction of Gandhi's future abode, known as Adi Niwas. Gandhi arrived in mid-June to take up residence, but very quickly, against his wishes, he had gathered a group of followers around himself. He wrote in some sadness that 'This has become a confused household instead of a hermitage it was expected to be. Such has been my fate! I must find my hermitage from within.'[43] As the number of cows increased, the need for extra grazing land and an additional well became apparent, and Bajaj provided them. Later Bajaj was asked for his whole estate and he acceded to the request and handed his entire land over to the enterprise[44] and soon a complete ashram had again established itself around the Mahatma.

In March 1940, after gaining the approval of the villagers, Gandhi changed the name of Segaon to Sevagram (village of service) because there was another larger village of a similar name (Shegaon) that had a post office and railway station 132 miles to the west of Wardha. This meant that there

---

[38] Letter to Mirabehn, 21 April 1936.
[39] Gandhi spent the next few nights in a shelter under some guava trees, a place that is now known as the 'first abode'.
[40] See Nanda, *In Search of Gandhi*, p. 210.   [41] Mira Behn, *The Spirit's Pilgrimage*, p. 203.
[42] Balvantsinha, *Under the Shelter of Bapu*, pp. 80–1.   [43] Letter to Mirabehn, 20 July 1936.
[44] Balvantsinha, *Under the Shelter of Bapu*, pp. 96–7.

was often confusion in the post.[45] The government formally gazetted the change of name and the postal authorities opened a cottage post office with telegraph facilities in the village.[46] This sickness-inducing, snake, scorpion and tick-infested summer inferno and winter swamp without road, railway station, shop or post office became Gandhi's final ashram.

JAMNALAL BAJAJ AND SEGAON

Not only was Bajaj a wealthy businessman of the area who had long been willing to finance Gandhi's activities in the Wardha district, but he was also the main zamindar of Segaon village. In the nineteenth century, the British government had organised a system of land management that included the vesting of land ownership in indigenous revenue collectors known as zamindars (or malguzars in the Central Provinces). The zamindars became a new landlord class with obligations to their colonial patrons by way of taxes. In the case of villages such as Segaon where there were joint proprietors, 'each had a defined share, most commonly a legal fractional share, on which the profits and burdens, though not the land itself, were divided'. Jamnalal Bajaj held a 75 per cent share of Segaon and Babasaheb Deshmukh, another malguzar, the other 25 per cent. Of the total 1,550 acres of village land, 220 were owned by the malguzars with the rest being divided among sixty small landholders.[47]

While it may have been Mirabehn's work in the villages, which was at least partly undertaken as a way of escaping the chaos of Maganwadi, that inspired Gandhi to consider village work as his own destiny, ironically it was Bajaj, who made village work in the area possible, who was initially most opposed to the idea. Bajaj feared for Gandhi's health in the harsh environment of solitary life in the village. Because of Bajaj's legal rights in the village, his approval of the scheme was essential and, once it had been received, Gandhi's theories of trusteeship were to be extended from capitalist/worker to zamindar/villager with Bajaj as the chief experimental subject.

In March, Gandhi sent a note to Bajaj answering questions about the proposed move. He informed his benefactor that he would live with his wife if she desired it, otherwise alone in a hut that should be built as cheaply as possible. He noted that a select number from his secretariat could stay in

---

[45] See 'Segaon, Not Shegaon', *Harijan*, 5 December 1936; and 'Segaon Becomes Sevagram', *Harijan* 9 March 1940.
[46] Narayan, *Jamnalal Bajaj*, p. 122; and Mira Behn, *The Spirit's Pilgrimage*, p. 215.
[47] Thomson, *Gandhi and His Ashrams*, p. 189.

a simple hut in the village, but that other than them and Mirabehn, people 'from the outside' should not come to see him in Segaon but 'may see me only at Maganwadi on the days fixed for my going there'. He added that his experiment would give momentum to village industries and that whatever 'defects there may be' in his way of thinking would come to the surface if he lived in the village, and others would be encouraged to take up similar work.[48] Eventually Bajaj acquiesced to Gandhi's wishes and financed much of the village programme, instructing his farm manager and workers to give their complete co-operation to Gandhi.[49]

Needless to say, Gandhi never achieved his goal of living even relatively alone in Segaon. In the words of Thomson, the experiment 'revealed the extent to which he had become a victim of his own charisma'.[50] He was unable to seclude himself from those who were desperate for physical proximity to him, and most of these people had little interest in village work. Although Gandhi had no intention of establishing an ashram at Sevagram, soon his hut was crowded, necessitating the construction of further buildings: Bajaj organised for a small hut to be built for Kasturba, followed by one for Bajaj's own use, houses for Mahadev Desai and Kishorelal Mashruwala (who was with Gandhi at the Sabarmati Ashram and was now President of the Gandhi Seva Sangh), a hut for a leper nursed by Gandhi, a guest house, and a kitchen to provide for all the inmates and visitors. Bajaj even financed a road to be built, connecting the Ashram with Wardha.[51] What was to be Gandhi's hut in a village that would slowly become his model village, became a separate ashram at the side of Segaon, eventually having little connection with it.

At times Gandhi seems disillusioned with the calls on his time, the often dysfunctional nature of the community at Sevagram[52] and the inability to carry on his proposed village work the way he envisaged, and eventually the lengths of time he spent there became progressively shorter, and with the coming of the new political struggle in the 1940s, his village programme had to be abandoned by him.

Gandhi had hoped that if he could turn Segaon into a model village by his example it could lay the foundations for the fulfillment of his vision of a sarvodaya social order. The villagers, however, remained suspicious

---

[48] 'My Idea of Living in a Village', 19 March 1936.
[49] Thomson, *Gandhi and His Ashrams*, p. 194.   [50] *Ibid.*, p. 196.
[51] Although the absence of a road made it inconvenient for the national leaders who came to visit him in Segaon, Gandhi was not enthusiastic about having a road built because he wanted them to understand the plight of those who lived in India's villages. Nanda, *In Gandhiji's Footsteps*, p. 220.
[52] See the assessment by Thomson, *Gandhi and His Ashrams*, pp. 198–200; and 'To Gujaratis', *Harijanbandhu*, 28 January 1940.

of the ashram and its mostly middle-class members and the way that they flaunted traditional caste distinctions and rules. They failed to copy the agricultural and dietary practices of Sevagram, to at least some degree because, all the good intentions aside, 'the expenditure of the Ashram was far in excess of the collective means of the village'.[53] Jamnalal Bajaj subsidised the Ashram budget by placing all the malguzari and farm profits that accrued to him from Segaon at Gandhi's disposal, and Sevagram never managed to be completely self-supporting. 'The crowd of people drawn to Sevagram clearly benefited from this support more than the villagers, who resented the presence of the somewhat parasitic community.'[54]

THE END OF COMMUNAL EXPERIMENTS

On the day that he moved to Segaon, Gandhi was asked by one of his workers whether it might not have been better to undertake a tour throughout the country with the message of rural reconstruction 'rather than bury yourself in this village?' From November 1933 until August 1934, Gandhi had undertaken a Harijan Tour which proved to be a 'godsend' that had 'worked a silent revolution in people's minds' in a way that 'nothing else could have achieved it'. The worker asked Gandhi if he couldn't again undertake such a tour: Gandhi was quite clear in his answer:

Oh, no. There is no similarity between the two cases. In Harijan work the practical and the theoretical aspects were combined. Here I cannot combine the two. I have been talking theory all these days, talking and giving advice on village work, without having personally come to grips with the difficulties of village work. If I undertook the tour, say, after passing three seasons in a village and among the villagers, a year hence I should be able to talk with knowledge and experience which I have not got today. Yesterday I went to Sindi to see how Gajanan Naik was working. The condition of things there is scarcely better but he is carrying on his work, patiently and perseveringly. The moment I saw him last morning I said to myself: 'If I had been working with Gajanan, I should certainly have had intimate experience of the difficulties he is meeting with.' No. It is clearer to me than ever before that my place is in the village.[55]

Gandhi clearly understood the symbolic importance of his decision to work alone in a village in a way that would focus the 'public gaze on village work rather than his press image'.[56] He wanted to experiment with what

[53] Thomson, *Gandhi and His Ashrams*, p. 208.   [54] *Ibid.*, pp. 208–9.
[55] 'Discussion with a Worker', *Harijan*, 9 May 1936.   [56] Thomson, *Gandhi and His Ashrams*, p. 196.

he saw as the 'triple malady' afflicting India's villages: the lack of sanitation, a deficient diet and a general feeling of inertia:

In Segaon where Mirabehn is working, all the outside circumstances are more favourable than anywhere else. The zamindars there are Jamnalalji and Babasaheb Deshmukh. They place no obstacles; they, on the contrary, help her. And yet, do you think she gets much co-operation from the people? Not that they are wilfully obstructive. They are not interested in their own welfare. They don't appreciate modern sanitary methods. They don't want to exert themselves beyond scratching their farms or doing such labour as they are used to. These difficulties are real and serious. But they must not baffle us. We must have an unquenchable faith in our mission. We must be patient with the people. We are ourselves novices in village work. We have to deal with a chronic disease. Patience and perseverance, if we have them, overcome mountains of difficulties. We are like nurses who may not leave their patients because they are reported to have an incurable disease.

The only way is to sit down in their midst and work away in steadfast faith, as their scavengers, their nurses, their servants, not as their patrons, and to forget all our prejudices are prepossessions. Let us for a moment forget even swaraj, and certainly forget the 'haves' whose presence oppresses us at every step. They are there. There are many who are dealing with these big problems. Let us tackle the humbler work of the village which is necessary now and would be even after we have reached our goal. Indeed, the village work when it becomes successful will itself bring us nearer the goal.[57]

Sevagram was to be the final laboratory in Gandhi's quest for both a free India and a free self. In August 1936, Gandhi had a discussion with the Polish engineer Maurice Frydman, whom he had met at Nandi and who wanted to design a better spinning wheel. When Frydman asked if his settling in Segaon was 'just humanitarian', Gandhi explained that he was there to serve no one but himself by finding self-realisation through service to the villagers. He continued:

Man's ultimate aim is the realization of God, and all his activities, social, political, religious, have to be guided by the ultimate aim of the vision of God. The immediate service of all human beings becomes a necessary part of the endeavour simply because the only way to find God is to see Him in His creation and be one with it. This can only be done by service of all. And this cannot be done except through one's country. I am part and parcel of the whole, and I cannot find Him apart from the rest of humanity. My countrymen are my nearest neighbours. They have become so helpless, so resourceless, so inert that I must concentrate on serving them. If I could persuade myself that I should find Him in a Himalayan cave, I would proceed there immediately. But I know that I cannot find Him apart from humanity.

[57] 'Speech at AIVIA Meeting', *Harijan*, 16 May 1936.

Frydman then asked Gandhi what the 'secret of his concentration on the village' was. Gandhi answered:

I have been saying that if untouchability stays, Hinduism goes; even so I would say that if the village perishes, India will perish too. It will be no more India, Her own mission in the world will get lost. The revival of the village is possible only when it is no more exploited. Industrialization on a mass scale will necessarily lead to passive or active exploitation of the villagers as the problems of competition and marketing come in. Therefore we have to concentrate on the village being self-contained, manufacturing mainly for use. Provided this character of the village industry is maintained, there would be no objection to villagers using even the modern machines and tools that they can make and can afford to use. Only they should not be used as a means of exploitation of others.[58]

A little later, he answered his own question 'Why am I at Segaon?' by claiming that 'I believe that my message will have a better chance of penetrating the masses of India, and maybe through them to the world.'[59]

Whatever can be said about the success or otherwise of the Sevagram experiment, it served as a laboratory for the investigation of the plight of villages and for attempts at instituting a constructive programme aimed at helping to usher in a sarvodaya social order, and even for Gandhi's larger quest in trying to find his own self-realisation through identification with his fellow humans. Gandhi provided the foundations that could have been, and may still be, built upon by way of a more equitable social order, and provided an example, that has been picked up by others, of where to seek the meaning of life. Without the hold of Jamnalal Bajaj, his 'fifth son', on him, Gandhi would not have been in Wardha to initiate at least the more prosaic of these experiments, and, without the financial backing of Bajaj, neither Sevagram nor the many Gandhian hospitals, dairies or educational institutions would have come into existence.

However, Jamnalal Bajaj was important to Gandhi not just because he had the money to finance various Gandhian projects, but also, in essence, because he could be part of a larger Gandhian experiment and, if it succeeded, provide a model of trusteeship for other capitalists.[60] Bajaj's background made him crave a father and with Gandhi he found one. As a 'son' he wanted his ageing 'parent' near him, where he could relieve Gandhi of some of the burdens of his work. Once at the feet of the Mahatma, it is

---

[58] 'A Discussion with Maurice Frydman', *Harijan*, 29 August 1936.
[59] 'Answer to Questions', *Harijan*, 12 December 1936.
[60] After Bajaj's death Gandhi proclaimed that, 'Whenever I wrote of wealthy men becoming trustees of their wealth for the common good I had always this merchant prince principally in mind.' See 'Seth Jamnalal Bajaj', *Harijan*, 15 February 1942.

quite obvious that Bajaj, who was as happy in a hut as in a mansion, would gladly have given up all his wealth. Gandhi, however, encouraged him to earn more – but to do it ethically and spend it in the service of the down-trodden people of India. Gandhi wanted to awaken the 'potentialities of his character by helping him to understand the spirituality and universality of satyagraha'.[61] Bajaj was politically active but it was not his main connection with Gandhi. He was more deeply involved in the Mahatma's constructive work and took his spiritual experiments and strictures to heart and struggled with them the way Maganlal had. This is possibly the most important point of connection. Gandhi may have been the greatest influence in Bajaj's life, but Jamnalal Bajaj, in turn, greatly influenced the Mahatma not only in where he lived, but also in the formation of his central philosophy of trusteeship and the way a son influences a father.

[61] Kalelkar, 'Jamnalalji as I Knew Him', p. 15.

CHAPTER 7

The top of the hourglass: Gandhi influenced

THE POLITICAL GANDHI AND THE WHOLE GANDHI

The biographies of Gandhi tend to be political biographies. The central story of the India phase of his life focuses on the three main political campaigns for Indian freedom that he led: the 1921–2 Non-cooperation movement, the 1930–33 Civil Disobedience movement and the 1942–3 Quit India movement. The lengthy periods between these campaigns are glossed over, seen as lulls in Gandhi's life. This however gives a very limited view of the Mahatma. Gandhi's talk of Swaraj, that is independence or freedom, is generally interpreted merely as independence for the Indian nation from British rule. However, for Gandhi political activism had a more fundamental role. It was to a large degree educative, helping to train the soul and develop character so as to aid the quest for individual perfection. Swaraj means self-rule and to limit this to political self-rule is to largely miss the point. The three campaigns are not three isolated bursts of political activity, but examples of a lifelong quest for swaraj temporarily focusing at the macro level.

Narayan Desai, one of the few remaining Gandhians who knew the Mahatma intimately (his father was Mahadev Desai, Gandhi's chief personal secretary, and he grew up in Gandhi's ashrams), who was a leading figure in the post-Gandhi Gandhian movement and who is the most recent Gandhi biographer, notes that Gandhi gave three great gifts to humanity[1] and that satyagraha, Gandhi's nonviolent activism, representing the political Gandhi, is only one of them. This however is the one that English language books about Gandhi focus on. With this focus, Gandhi's co-workers, the ones who take on starring roles in the biographies, are Nehru and Patel. The political Gandhi, however, is a very truncated one and a more complete

---

[1] For a detailed discussion of the 'three gifts' see Narayan Desai, *My Gandhi* (Ahmedabad: Navajivan, 1999), pp. 51–90.

analysis of the Mahatma would include comprehensive reference to other influencing co-workers.

Gandhi held before himself, and attempted to place before the masses, a picture of an ideal society that was to be the goal of collective endeavour, as the approach towards Truth was to be the goal for the individual. This vision was summed up in the word 'Ramrajya', the 'Kingdom of God', where there were equal rights for princes and paupers,[2] where even the lowliest person could get swift justice without elaborate and costly procedures,[3] where inequalities that allowed some to roll in riches while the masses did not have enough to eat were abolished,[4] and where sovereignty of the people was based on pure moral authority rather than coercive power.[5] Political independence for the country may have been a step towards Ramrajya, but was certainly no guarantee of it.

Gandhi firmly believed that all forms of exploitation and oppression to a large degree rested on the acquiescence of the victims. With this in mind he noted that 'exploitation of the poor can be extinguished not by effecting the destruction of a few millionaires, but by removing the ignorance of the poor and teaching them to non-cooperate with the exploiters'.[6] It was again partly for the educative purpose of pointing this out to the oppressed that he instituted what he called the 'constructive programme'. Although this programme was tied to India's independence struggle, it was not merely a tactical manoeuvre to assist in achieving that seemingly larger and more important goal. The constructive programme involved future leaders in the struggle and put them in contact with the masses (working not just *for* the people, but *with* them), helping to bring about the society Gandhi envisaged in a future free India, and indeed a future just world. In fact, Gandhi claimed that the wholesale fulfilment of the constructive programme '*is* complete independence' because if the nation was involved in the very process of rebuilding itself in the image of its dreams 'from the very bottom upwards', it would by definition be free.[7]

The programme, in its original context, dealt mainly with the problems of communal unity and the uplift of the rural masses. This approach aimed to produce 'something beneficial to the community, especially to the poor

[2] 'Answers to Zamindars', *The Pioneer*, 3 August 1934.
[3] 'Speech at Public Meeting, Bhopal', *Young India*, 19 September 1929.
[4] 'Question Box', *Harijan*, 1 June 1947.
[5] 'Speech at Exhibition Ground, Faizpur', *Harijan*, 2 January 1937.
[6] 'Question Box', *Harijan*, 28 July 1940.
[7] See M. K. Gandhi, *Constructive Programme: Its Meaning and Place* (Ahmedabad: Navajivan, 1941), p. 3.

and unemployed' and provided 'the kind of work, which the poor and unemployed can themselves do and thus self-respectingly help themselves'.[8]

In situations of social conflict and mass satyagraha campaigns, Gandhi made it a point to couple constructive work to civil disobedience, sometimes seeming to say that constructive work was an aid to the civil disobedience campaign and at other times putting the formula around the other way. In fact civil disobedience 'without the constructive programme will be like a paralysed hand attempting to lift a spoon'.[9] Perhaps it could even be said that large oppositional satyagraha campaigns cannot be fully nonviolent if they are not accompanied by some form of positive constructive programme. The constructive programme, in Desai's scheme, is another of Gandhi's great gifts, and Gandhi's first ashrams were its early laboratories[10] and it was the *raison d'etre* of Sevagram.

For Gandhi this constructive work offered replacement for what satyagrahis were opposing at the very time they were opposing it. Without it, because fundamental changes would not have been made, civil disobedience, if it succeeded in overthrowing a set of oppressors, would merely exchange one group of leaders with another similar group.[11] Contrasting himself with the 'born politician' Sardar Patel, Gandhi claimed that 'I was born for the constructive programme. It is part of my soul. Politics is a kind of botheration for me.'[12] Further, during one of his major political campaigns, Gandhi remarked that 'the work of social reform or self-purification . . . is a hundred times dearer to me than what is called purely political work',[13] and during another, following pressure to launch civil disobedience, Mahadev Desai records Gandhi as having said that 'in placing civil disobedience before constructive work I was wrong . . . I feared that I should estrange co-workers and so carried on with imperfect Ahimsa'.[14] Gandhi was well aware that political freedom was easier to achieve than economic, social and moral freedom in part because they are 'less exciting and not spectacular'.[15] Political biographies also seem to be more exciting and spectacular than those focussing on the social and moral aspects of Gandhi's life. The main co-workers he had in his constructive work, who, like Bajaj, are at least as important to him as his political co-workers, tend to disappear from the record.

---

[8] See Richard B. Gregg, *A Discipline for Non-Violence* (Ahmedabad: Navajivan, 1941), p. 5.
[9] Gandhi, *Constructive Programme*, p. 36.   [10] Desai, *My Gandhi*, p. 56.
[11] See Gandhi, *Hind Swaraj*, p. 30.
[12] 'Speech at Gandhi Seva Sangh Meeting – II', Malikanda, 21 February 1940.
[13] 'Speech at Ahmedabad', *Young India*, 6 August 1931.
[14] 'Before the Gandhi Seva Sangh', *Harijan*, 21 July 1940.
[15] Gandhi, *Constructive Programme*, p. 37.

If we look at Gandhi's relationship with Maganlal and Vinoba we realise that there is even more to the Mahatma, something obvious to Desai but that most biographies make far too little of. Although Maganlal is generally reduced to the person who helped to coin the term 'satyagraha', the relationship Gandhi had with him was one of the most important of his life. How come he disappears from the (at least non-Gujarati) record almost completely? Desai points out that there was a third gift from Gandhi: his eleven vows, a set of rules which established the code of conduct for his ashram inmates and which are key to understanding Gandhi's religious quest.

Gandhi firmly believed that life could not be compartmentalised, that actions and the reasons on which they are based, whether they be political, economic, social or spiritual, are interrelated, and that these actions have a direct bearing upon the achievement of the ultimate aim of life. Gandhi himself named this aim as 'moksha', a liberation of the self, and claimed that his life, including his 'ventures in the political field are directed to this same end'.[16] Again, although the spiritual Gandhi does not fit too comfortably in primarily political biographies except to set up the Mahatma as the conscience of humanity, without understanding Gandhi's spiritual quest, we do not understand Gandhi. If the spiritual Gandhi is relegated to a very secondary position, important relationships and influencers such as Maganlal also disappear from the record.[17]

For Gandhi the vow was a powerful tool in the spiritual quest because vows enable acts which are not possible by ordinary self-denial to become possible through extraordinary self-denial.[18] Through his eleven ashram vows, Gandhi turned personal virtues into public values. The vows were to adhere to truth, nonviolence, celibacy, non-possession, non-stealing, control of the palate, fearlessness, equal respect for all religions, bread labour (the dignity of manual work), the removal of untouchability (as an institution and from one's own heart), and swadeshi (the favouring of locally produced goods, neighbourliness).[19]

---

[16] Gandhi, *An Autobiography*, p. xiv.

[17] This is not to say that Maganlal was little more than one of the close associates of the spiritual Gandhi. He was also one of Gandhi's chief lieutenants in the constructive programme, being the chief architect of the Mahatma's khadi scheme. See C. Shambu Prasad, 'Gandhi and Maganlal: Khadi Science and the Gandhian Scientist', in Bindu Puri (ed.), *Mahatma Gandhi and His Contemporaries* (Shimla: Indian Institute of Advanced Study, 2001), pp. 228–51.

[18] See Thomas Weber, *Conflict Resolution and Gandhian Ethics* (New Delhi: Gandhi Peace Foundation, 1991), pp. 131–2.

[19] See Gandhi's 'Introduction' to *Ashram Observances in Action*, pp. 3–12.

Gandhi spent a lifetime struggling with these vows. And how could he have done otherwise? They constituted the road map of the spiritual quest that was the great endeavour of his life of which even his political activities were in reality only a sub-branch. For Gandhi, applying a set of techniques may have meant that nonviolent political activism was more likely to achieve its immediate political goals. However, living within the rules required for a successful satyagraha campaign as Gandhi understood it, also constituted the type of life that is worth living. As we shall see later, Gene Sharp may have attempted to secularise Gandhi's political activism to make it more palatable to the western mind, but in doing so he repeats the work of the English language biographers who tend to secularise Gandhi's life when they write their stories about the father of Indian independence. But the political Gandhi is no substitute for the whole Gandhi.

GANDHI'S NON-POLITICAL RELATIONSHIPS

While the most commonly focused upon relationships in Gandhi's later life are those with his colleagues in the independence struggle, for the childhood, London-based and South African Gandhi many of those who influenced him are not political in the narrow sense. While it could be argued that to a large degree this is because the young Gandhi is not yet a major political activist, clearly a spiritual hunger played a more important part in the formation of his character than a raised political consciousness and commitment.

We all have schoolhood friends, and Gandhi was no different. Sheikh Mehtab pushed the young Gandhi beyond his comfort zone into acts of rebellion against parents and culture, and put strains on his marriage with pressure to be more macho. Although Mehtab was the cause of great problems, Gandhi could not abandon his friend; he stayed in what resembled an abusive relationship with the hope (forlorn as it may have been) of bringing about a reformation. This seems to have had an impact on the shape of his future relationships. Although others may have wanted to have exclusive relationships with him, Gandhi never again allowed such relationships to emerge or at least carry on into the long term – an example is how he struggled to keep Mirabehn at something of an arm's length when she became too dependent.

In London the shy student achieved some modicum of self-respect as the vegetarian and spiritual circles in which he moved took him seriously. Through them he took an interest in his own religious traditions and heritage, started reading some of the great philosophical and ethical writers, made his first public speeches and wrote his first articles. His spiritual quest was awakened and areas in which he demonstrated competence revealed themselves. This process was pushed even further with the Christian missionaries who became his intellectual mentors in South Africa. They not only fuelled his spiritual quest, but the influence was so strong that it appears that the Hindu Mahatma-to-be came close to converting to Christianity. These religious patrons also showed Gandhi the flaws in their faith and, out of the torment of the soul this led to, had him seek solace in his own faith through the guidance of his next spiritual mentor Raychandbhai. Raychand helped clarify for Gandhi the meaning of Hinduism and gave him a large degree of spiritual certainty that was to stay with him for the rest of his life. Nevertheless Gandhi's Hinduism remained tinged with Christian ethics that included charity and a refusal to blame past lives for present conditions, and had no truck with untouchability.

Along with these spiritual fellow travellers, Tolstoy helped to influence Gandhi onto the path that created the spiritual seeker, the Gandhi of the eleven vows. Of course Tolstoy, together with Ruskin, also had a large impact on the formation of Gandhi the constructive actionist and even the political Gandhi through his lesson of passive resistance. The early political activist Gandhi took inspiration from the selfless example of Gokhale and found vindication of what he was doing in the writings of Thoreau.

During much of Gandhi's life, although not necessarily reflected in the literature, his closest relationships were with those who 'surrendered' themselves fully to his wider quest, including his social work and spiritual experiments, not merely to his political campaigns. They were the ones who helped determine his way of life and even its geographical setting. There seems to be something of a pattern here among Gandhi's disciples, especially the European ones. He totally takes over their lives when there is physical proximity, but when that ends their lives tend to revert to a pattern that is, literally, more normal. Perhaps, Gandhi's best-known western disciple, Madeleine Slade (Mirabehn) is the classic example. She needed to be physically close to her master and when she was away from him she would become ill and would need to be brought back so he could nurse her. After Gandhi's death she eventually returned to Europe and her first obsession, Beethoven. Gandhi had the tendency to attract obsessive lovelorn followers who wanted exclusive relationships with him. Initially he seems to relish the close relationship of a new soulmate, uses it as an aid to a burst of spiritual growth before the next plateau period. Eventually, after the initial flush of love and mutual experimentation, Gandhi moved on, leaving the forlorn friend as just one of many other friends, criticising them for their attachment. This pattern is clear with Kallenbach and Mirabehn, although less clear with Polak who had a stronger sense of self than the other two and a supportive and loving spouse. Jamnalal Bajaj, the adopted son who so desperately wanted to be Gandhi's, was upset when Gandhi addressed him as 'bhai', brother, the term he used for his co-workers, instead of using the usual form of address a father uses for his son. Although not neglected by Gandhi, the close relationship was not an exclusive one and possibly because of this Bajaj struggled with his attempt at living up to his self-proclaimed status as the Mahatma's son and disciple. In his final months he felt the need to go elsewhere to seek spiritual solace.

GANDHI INFLUENCED AND HIS ASHRAMS

Reading popular life and times books about Gandhi we get a strong sense of the circumstances of the setting up of Tolstoy Farm and the Satyagraha Ashram at Kochrab and Sabarmati, but the reasons for the setting up of Phoenix Settlement (that he read a book the day before!), the leaving of Sabarmati and the choice of Wardha as the next headquarters are far less clear. While the setting up of Tolstoy Farm can be understood by reading about the political Gandhi, only an understanding of the whole Gandhi and the spiritual and constructive work relationships that were part of this, give us worthwhile clues to his comings and goings from the other ashrams.

Polak had the power to influence Gandhi's life, but when the intensity of the early relationship abated, although perhaps the most important one, he became 'just' another political co-worker. It was the relatively short full-tilt soulmate relationship between them, in 1904, that led to the formation of Phoenix Settlement and changed the course of Gandhi's life. Out of the dialectical relationship with chhotabhai Henry, Gandhi started his simple life experiments, and that relationship made Gandhi receptive to Ruskin's message in *Unto This Last*, a book that helped set the tone for the constructive programme and Gandhi's economic philosophy.

The second intentional community was Tolstoy Farm. It was to be run on the principles of simple living, bread labour and spiritual practice in keeping with what Gandhi and Kallenbach saw as the teachings of the sage of Russia. Kallenbach not only allowed the setting up of the farm through his financial support (in fact, legally, he was the owner of Tolstoy Farm), but the bond of love between him and Gandhi and the experimental ferment of their relationship set the climate for the move to the property and its communal living arrangements.

Phoenix Settlement and Tolstoy Farm, and underplayed accounts of the relationships with Polak and Kallenbach, are commented upon at reasonable length in Gandhi biographies – because they are discussed in Gandhi's *Autobiography* and *Satyagraha in South Africa*, the main sources of information on Gandhi's South Africa years. The founding of the Sabarmati Ashram is also well covered for the same reason. However, the abandonment of Sabarmati and the relocation to Wardha came after the period covered in Gandhi's writings and are, consequently, far less well documented.

There is some fairly often cited but poorly thought through rhetoric about why Gandhi left Sabarmati and why he settled in Sevagram. Most books tell us that he left Sabarmati when he embarked on the historic Salt March vowing not to return until he had achieved independence for India. Gandhi was not politically naive. He knew that he would not achieve independence in a month or a year. In fact it took another seventeen years after the dramatic march to Dandi. He also knew that the campaign he was launching would result in serious sacrifice for many, and he certainly did not want his sacrifice to be any less than that of his followers. They would possibly be stripped of their lands and homes, could he do any less than give up his? On the night before he set out for the seaside to make illegal salt, the Mahatma informed a crowd of 10,000 which had gathered on the sandy expanse of the Sabarmati river bank below the ashram that he would not return 'till Swaraj is established in India . . . We are as good as parting from the Ashram and from our homes. Only with complete victory can we return to this place.'[20]

However, at this stage property had not been confiscated and Gandhi could have vowed to make any number of other sacrifices that would cause less distress to those he was leaving behind. It seemed that he was ready to leave the ashram. This readiness is not understandable without understanding Gandhi's relationship with Maganlal. With Maganlal's death, the decision to leave his home and ashram family became much less difficult for Gandhi than it seems possible from reading the sections dealing with this in the English sources. And this in turn is because English sources generally do not mention Maganlal in any detail except to point out his prize-winning entry in Gandhi's newspaper competition to coin an appropriate word for the Mahatma's developing form of nonviolent activism, and certainly make nothing of the intense relationship between the two, nothing of the degree to which Maganlal's creation was the embodiment of Gandhi's ideal of what

---

[20] Speech at Prayer Meeting, Sabarmati Ashram, 11 March 1930. See also Thomas Weber, *On the Salt March: The Historiography of Gandhi's March to Dandi* (New Delhi: HarperCollins, 1997), p. 132.

the ashram should be, and nothing of the way his death influenced Gandhi's attitude towards his headquarters.[21]

The same is true for Jamnalal Bajaj. When Gandhi left Ahmedabad he could have gone anywhere. We are informed that he chose Wardha because it was the geographical centre of India, implying his own symbolic identification with the country, that the location made it easier for followers and fellow workers from all over the subcontinent to be able to reach him, and because it could provide the stepping stone to settling in an out-of-the-way village. In terms of sacrifice Wardha is ideal, providing a thoroughly unpleasant environment for much of the year. The thought of settling in a village did not come to Gandhi until one and a half years after he had made Wardha his headquarters. And the symbolic explanation does not seem to be quite adequate to the task. The move is intricately tied up with Gandhi's relationship with Bajaj. It was because of Bajaj that Vinoba was in the area and because of Bajaj, the 'son' who wanted his 'father' near him, that Gandhi ended up in this geographical centre. The popular English Gandhi biographies make even less of Bajaj than they do of Maganlal.

At Maganwadi, as at Sabarmati a few years before, Gandhi became frustrated with the demands made on him, not least by the squabbling, eccentric and dependent people he managed to attract to himself. His nerves were affected and he wanted space, to be alone. The poverty and filth he saw around himself at Sindi, perhaps exacerbated by the constant demands on his time for articles and interviews, forced him to realise that his political and literary activities were not going to achieve the social changes he so desired. He had been preaching his social message for a long time with precious few indications that he was being listened to. The answer was to live alone in a village, to be an example of the changes he wanted to see adopted by the masses, by doing scavenging work, working directly with the downtrodden. In this way he could get away from the constraints that had taken over his life, and live the simple life of service he craved. Bajaj, by the gift of village land, held out the hope that this could be achieved. However, by this time Gandhi had become a victim of circumstances and the actions of his followers in effect conspired to thwart his plans.

The physical appearance of all of Gandhi's ashrams reveal something of the personal development of the Mahatma. Phoenix Settlement was a communally run farm, of the type that became common among the

---

[21] For example the popular biographies by Louis Fischer (*The Life of Mahatma Gandhi* (New York: Collier, 1962)), B. R. Nanda (*Mahatma Gandhi: A Biography* (London: Oxford University Press, 1981)) and Payne (*The Life and Death of Mahatma Gandhi*), only mention Maganlal in passing.

'alternative' community in the West in the late 1960s and early 1970s. The
land was worked together but individual houses for the various nuclear
families were retained. Tolstoy Farm more closely resembled a kibbutz where
meals were taken in a common kitchen and the community attempted to
function as a family unit in itself. Kallenbach, his chief supporter in this
venture, was to become a champion of the kibbutz idea in his later life.

While little is left of the South African ashrams, the two Indian ones have
been preserved reasonably intact. The buildings at Sabarmati are those of a
planned institution, with workshops and industrial units developed as integral components. It was an intentional community rather than the almost
accidental and *ad hoc* one at Sevagram. The buildings are very substantial
and built to last, the houses are far bigger and more formal than the carefully
constructed but nevertheless village huts of Sevagram. Sabarmati was to be
a training ground for ashramites, not the home of a villager undertaking
scavenging work and hoping to influence his neighbours. However, by the
mid-1930s Gandhi wanted to be a simple villager, a simple villager who
ended up being followed by his retinue. Gandhi had earlier claimed that
ashram life was part of his nature, later he craved solitude and the life of
simple service. In Ahmedabad he was consciously founding an ashram, in
Segaon he was trying to escape from one.

Phoenix Settlement and Tolstoy Farm had been early experiments in
communal living and stepping stones on the path to building a viable fully
fledged ashram around the Mahatma. In South Africa, Gandhi wanted to
finish the political struggle quickly so that he could return to the spiritual
life of the commune. In India, Maganlal built such a communal institution
as a centre of political, social and spiritual experimentation. Here Gandhi
could train his co-workers to be the nonviolent fighters in the cause of
the freedom struggle. Maganwadi, as a continuation of the Satyagraha
Ashram at Sabarmati, may have had a similar aim to the degree that any
was articulated, but gradually Gandhi wanted to leave institutions behind
to live a spiritual life of example. At the time of his relocation to Segaon,
Gandhi distanced himself from power politics and had become preoccupied
with the question of village work. He wanted to go it alone, to show by his
own example how a dedicated village worker should operate and do it in a
way that he could put some of the theory that he had been preaching for
many years into practise. Bajaj, who made Sevagram possible, built himself
a hut near Gandhi's so that he could be close to his master. However,
near his end he settled alone in a simple hut at Gopuri doing socially useful
work and carrying out his sadhana (spiritual penance). He did what Gandhi
wanted to do but no longer could.

CONCLUSION

Of course influence is a complex matter. The webs are intricate. So, while I have concentrated on one specific relationship as being particularly important in the development of a certain aspect of Gandhi's philosophy (or concentrated on Gandhi as being particularly important in the development of a certain aspect of philosophy of one of the people discussed in the second half of this book) this is not to be taken as implying that this particular influencer of Gandhi, or on the other side Gandhi himself, was solely responsible for this development – only that it strikes me as important and telling. It should also be noted that Gandhi managed to gather a group of incredibly talented individuals around him. They dedicated their lives and, indeed, destinies to him and his movements. However, influence does not always flow only in one direction. Although it may be more lopsided than equally mutual, influence, where there is direct contact, always flows both ways where individuals are concerned (and could it have been otherwise give the caliber of many of these co-workers and disciples). Polak, Kallenbach, Maganlal Gandhi and Bajaj are clear examples of the influenced also being strong influencers.

The selection of who to include among the list of influencers – the top of the hourglass – is of course a subjective one. A political biography of Gandhi would include or at least emphasise different characters than, for example, a spiritual biography. The introductory chapter included those that Gandhi himself saw as influences, such as Tolstoy, Ruskin and Raychandbhai, and these clearly are not only political ones, but also, and primarily, social and spiritual. The others, although Gandhi may not expressly mention them as great influences, nevertheless, from his writings and later actions, seem to me to be of large significance. And again, beyond doubt, they are not merely influencers of the political Gandhi.

From the time he left for London, until approximately the turn of the twentieth century, Gandhi was remaking himself spiritually and philosophically. For the next decade he was also remaking himself as a political leader. Later he tried to recast himself as social worker and again attempted to spend more time in his spiritual quest. These different phases had different influencers and different close relationships, which in turn tell us about Gandhi himself. Without understanding these relationships as being more than those of the influenced we cannot fully understand the whole Gandhi – Gandhi the constructive worker and spiritual seeker, as well as Gandhi the political actor.

PART III

Gandhi's influence

CHAPTER 8

The influential Gandhi

INTRODUCTION

Actions and movements stem from ideas. Philosophies live beyond the philosophers who conceive them, influencing others who integrate the ideas into new philosophies that may form the basis of new ways of knowing and praxis.

Is there anyone who grew up in the first half of the twentieth century who was not in some way influenced by Mahatma Gandhi? In India, perhaps most of the major political figures were influenced by Gandhi in a substantial way – and how many of the non-political social activists? How is one to decide who to include in a list of those influenced by the Mahatma?

The few direct disciples of Gandhi who are left are becoming increasingly aged and marginalised in today's India. The mass movements led by Vinoba and Jayaprakash Narayan are fading into distant memory and the realisation is dawning that there is no one else of their stature on the horizon to revitalise the movement, and that there is no groundswell for Gandhian values that would again put the elderly Gandhians into the forefront of a major campaign. It is also becoming clear that they have not been able to impress the youth of the country and build the next generation of Gandhian leadership. The influence of Gandhi seems to be fading.

Of course this is only partly true. Gandhi's legacy is not confined to the 'Gandhian movement' and his influence has spread widely, and other movements that have grown out of this influence attest to its relevance. The question to me here is a counterfactual one: who would not have become the important figure they did become without the profound influence of Gandhi?

In the case of Indians, Jawaharlal Nehru was groomed for political leadership and he would probably have become an Indian Prime Minister regardless of his close relationship with the Mahatma. He came from one of the top political families in the country. The influence of his illustrious father, his Harrow and Cambridge schooling and English legal training seemed to almost preordain him for the lofty position he came to hold. And besides, as close as he was to Gandhi, it is problematic to call him a Gandhian in any real sense. He did not share Gandhi's pacifism or economic principles and his policies in government were not founded on any particularly Gandhian vision.

Perhaps even Jayaprakash Narayan, more truly Gandhi's political heir than Nehru, would have been JP without Gandhi. JP was a political activist by nature. He spent seven years in the 1920s studying in the United States where he wrote a Masters dissertation on Marx. On his return to India he became a leading political figure, but a Socialist rather than Gandhian one. Although he remained on friendly terms with Gandhi, and indeed his wife had stayed at Gandhi's ashrams, as a believer in class struggle he was also a critic of Gandhi. Unlike the Mahatma, he did not welcome British imprisonment but escaped to organise sabotage and armed resistance. With the coming of Independence and the scramble for political power, JP started questioning his beliefs and with the advent of Vinoba's Bhoodan 'land gift' movement, he gave up party politics and joined the walking saint. But even here he remained his own person, eventually causing a rift within the Gandhian movement as he split from his mentor to clash head-on with the power of Indira Gandhi with his call to 'Total Revolution', which in turn led to the imposition of a 'state of emergency' in 1975. Of course Gandhi, directly and through Vinoba, had a large influence on JP. However, it seems fair to say that he would have reached the political heights he did reach without this influence. In older age many of the more reflective of those political figures who are committed to working with the downtrodden have a time of crisis when they realise how little their political activities have achieved in changing the world and JP appears to have been no different. He was a person searching for the best avenue for his mission all his life and with his intellect and organisational talents he would undoubtably have been a major Indian political figure without the Gandhian connections.

But would Rajendra Prasad have become India's first President, or Vallabhbhai Patel become the indomitable Sardar, without Gandhi? Quite probably not. It is a fair assessment that they may simply have remained successful, public-spirited provincial lawyers and eventually High Court judges without the intervention of Gandhi in their lives. When, on Gandhi's birthday in 1950, at a public speech, Patel said: 'I only know this much that

I am where Bapu has put me"[1] it was not mere hyperbole. And he could also have been speaking for Prasad.

Many of Gandhi's other closest colleagues remained trusted assistants or disciples. Of course Gandhi influenced them – but in the larger scheme of things they did not have any particular impact on their country or the world except to the degree that they helped Gandhi. Vinoba Bhave is a notable exception here. What he would have become had Gandhi not come into his life we will never know; but it is safe to say that without Gandhi he would not have led the world's largest non-coercive land redistribution campaign and found himself praised worldwide as a saint. It is more than conceivable that he may have ended his days as an obscure holy man and Sanskrit scholar.[2] Even being with Gandhi, if the Mahatma had not pushed him, almost reluctantly, into political activity, Vinoba may have remained an isolated, scholarly confidant hidden in Gandhi's shadow. The famed 'tree-hugging' Chipko movement of the Indian Himalayas to a large degree grew out of the constructive work in the mountains by the long-term Gandhian activist Sunderlal Bahuguna. At roughly the time Arne Næss was evolving the idea of a 'deep ecology' in the West, Bahuguna was instrumental in setting the groundwork for the establishment of a rural women-centred Gandhian environmental movement in the land where Gandhi's closest western disciple had lived. The work of Bahuguna the environmental activist grew out of his vocation as a Gandhian constructive worker.

Many who are not Indians have also commented on their debt to Gandhi. Catherine Ingram, in her book *In the Footsteps of Gandhi,* records her conversations with many of them. Marjorie Hope and James Young did something similar a dozen years before.[3] These people are nonviolent activists, often in the Gandhian mould, but this does not mean that they owe their activism or even their techniques directly to Gandhi. For example, Danilo Dolci, the 'Gandhi of Sicily' who struggled for the rights of the poor and against the Mafia, often using fasts as a tactic, was, in the words of his biographer, 'influenced by Gandhi much as the latter was influenced by

[1] Quoted in G. M. Nanurkar (ed.), *Sardar Patel – In Tune with the Millions–II* (Ahmedabad: Sardar Vallabhbhai Patel Smarak Bhavan, 1976), p. 263.
[2] Vinoba follower and biographer, Nirmala Deshpande answers her own hypothetical question of what would have become of Vinoba had he gone to the Himalayas as he planned instead of to Gandhi in Ahmedabad, by noting that 'In that case, perhaps, an unknown spiritual seeker would have sat in some cave of the Himalayas engaged in his rigorous religious routine. And the world would not have found "Vinoba".' Nirmala Deshpande, *Vinoba* (New Delhi: National Book Trust, 2001), p. 15.
[3] Marjorie Hope and James Young, *The Struggle for Humanity: Agents of Nonviolent Change in a Violent World* (Maryknoll, NY: Orbis, 1977).

Thoreau'[4] in that he received backing for what he was already doing when he read Gandhi.

Gandhi, the anti-imperialist fighter, helped start the process of decolonisation. Others, particularly those from Africa, followed his example and several named the Mahatma as a source of inspiration. Albert Luthuli, the former president of the African National Congress and the first Nobel peace laureate who did not hail from the ranks of western civilisation, received the 1960 award for engaging in nonviolent struggle against apartheid. Julius Nyerere, the former president of Tanzania, was awarded the inaugural Gandhi Peace Prize for those who have worked for peace, nonviolence and 'the amelioration of human suffering particularly on the less privileged sections of the society contributing towards social justice and harmony' in 1995. Kwame Nkrumah, the Gold Coast/Ghanaian statesman and anti-white domination leader and pan-African spokesperson, because of his use of Gandhian methods (which he called positive action) in his country's independence struggle, was known as the 'Gandhi of Africa.' While they tended to use nonviolence pragmatically, rather than out of a deep principled conviction, all three of them acknowledged their debt to Gandhi.[5] When *Time* magazine named Albert Einstein as its Person of the Century and Franklin Delano Roosevelt and Mohandas Gandhi as runners-up, Nelson Mandela, the most highly revered anti-apartheid hero and the 1993 Nobel Peace Prize recipient, was asked to write an appreciation of the Mahatma. Before Mandela turned to sabotage against the racist South African regime, he claimed that he was a follower of the Gandhian strategy, at least until 'there came a point in our struggle when the brute force of the oppressor could no longer be countered through passive resistance alone'.[6] While they could all be classified as Gandhi-inspired to at least some degree, probably the African leader who owes the most to Gandhi as an influence on principles rather than merely tactics, and who most readily recognises this debt, is Kenneth Kaunda, the father of independent Zambia.

Of the other major non-Indian figures that I have selected as Gandhi-influenced, probably already far too much has been written on Martin

[4] James McNeish, *Fire Under the Ashes: The Life of Danilo Dolci* (London: Hodder and Stoughton, 1965), p. 132.
[5] See Bill Sutherland and Matt Meyer, *Guns and Gandhi in Africa: Pan African Insights on Nonviolence, Armed Struggle and Liberation in Africa* (Trenton, NJ: Africa World Press, 2000).
[6] Nelson Mandela, 'The Sacred Warrior: The Liberator of South Africa Looks at the Seminal Work of the Liberator of India', *Time*, 31 December 1999 (special issue on the Person of the Century), p. 88. But see also Stephen Zunes, 'The Role of Nonviolent Action in the Collapse of Apartheid', *Gandhi Marg*, 20 (1999), pp. 398–429, where it is argued that nonviolence was instrumental in bringing down the apartheid regime and that where violence was resorted to it in fact set back the struggle.

Luther King Jr. He was not just a brilliant orator and organiser, and fearless fighter for black civil rights, he was also a nonviolent fighter, and probably this is at least partly a result of the influence of Gandhi – yet this aspect can sustain some further examination. On the other hand, not enough has been written about Lanza del Vasto – at least not in English. He was a true Gandhian Christian and his founding of 'ashrams' in France and the anti-nuclear and anti-colonialist actions of his community have come directly from his understanding of Gandhi, with whom he had spent time in the late 1930s.

By selecting Prasad, Patel, Bhave, Kaunda, King, Lanza del Vasto, and Bahuguna as the brief case studies of those who were deeply touched by Gandhi and went on to do important things in political, peace and non-violence movements, I am deeply conscious that in this list I have not included any women while the studies on latter-day Gandhi followers by Mark Shepard,[7] Ishwar Harris[8] and Ingram do. I do not want to artificially add Gandhi-influenced figures who had little lasting impact, or in whose life or work it is necessary to inflate the Gandhi influence to make them fit simply for the sake of some sort of symmetry. For much of Gandhi's life and the decades immediately thereafter, the public sphere was still largely a masculine domain. Nevertheless, there is one woman who clearly could be in this list, but I chose to leave out: Maude Royden. Gandhi's concept of placing a 'living-wall' of unarmed men, women and children in the path of an invading army as a defence measure has become the starting point for many of those advocating the use of nonviolent interpositionary peace brigades as buffers between warring parties in order to halt hostilities. Maude Royden, a friend of Gandhi's, was not only instrumental in the attempt to deploy a 'Peace Army' in China in 1932 as part of the earliest major endeavour at putting the proposal into action, she was also a long-standing and influential preacher and pacifist. The reason I have not, in the end, included Royden is because since I wrote about her in the late 1980s,[9] I have begun to suspect that, contrary to the suggestion in my earlier paper that she probably got her idea for a 'peace army' from Gandhi's thinking about a 'living-wall', she may in fact have been instrumental in shaping Gandhi's ideas about defence and peace brigades – rather than

---

[7] Mark Shepard, *Gandhi Today: A Report on Mahatma Gandhi's Successors* (Arcata, CA: Simple Productions, 1987).

[8] Ishwar C. Harris, *Gandhians in Contemporary India: The Vision and the Visionaries* (Lewiston, NY: The Edwin Mellen Press, 1998).

[9] See Thomas Weber, 'Gandhi's "Living Wall" and Maude Royden's "Peace Army"', *Gandhi Marg* 10 (1988), pp. 199–212.

Gandhi having a major influence in her life, she becomes a minor one in Gandhi's.

Geoffrey Ostergaard, in his classic history of the post-Gandhi Gandhian movement in India, describes three distinct types of 'Gandhism.' Many leading Congress stalwarts went on to become politicians ('political Gandhism'), others headed up Gandhian institutions and voluntary organisations to promote various aspects of Gandhi's 'constructive programme' ('institutional Gandhism'), still others carried on Gandhi's work in the villages, excepting nonviolent revolution as a goal ('revolutionary Gandhism').[10] Jayaprakash Narayan and Vinoba Bhave are the leading representatives of the third group. Of the first group, best represented by Gandhian lieutenants Jawaharlal Nehru, Vallabhbhai Patel, Chakravarti Rajagopalachari and Rajendra Prasad, it was Prasad who most closely merged his beliefs with those of the Mahatma. If there was a hint of difference between him and Gandhi he almost invariably concluded that the problem was with him and lined up unquestioningly behind his mentor.

Rajendra Prasad was a statesman and a scholar. He studied law at Presidency College in Calcutta but finally gave up his legal practice to join the Non-cooperation movement in 1920. He became a journalist in the nationalist cause and a lifelong worker to establish Hindi as the national language and to remove the blot of 'untouchability' from India. Prasad was imprisoned several times by the British for his nationalist activities, including for a period of almost three years in 1942–5. He went on to become chairman of the Indian National Congress in 1934, 1939 and 1947, and chairman of the Constituent Assembly of India between 1946 and 1949, helping to shape the Constitution and as Minister in charge of the Department of Food and Agriculture at a time of serious food crisis in the country. During the period leading up to Partition and Independence, Prasad and Vallabhbhai Patel served as Congress representatives on the government appointed Partition Committee, chaired by Lord Mountbatten, which oversaw the division of the assets of the Raj. Later, following Partition, he served as chairman of a committee set up in Delhi to restore order following the rioting in the capital. Rajendra Prasad was elected the first President of independent India, holding the position from 1950 until 1962. His health, which had caused

[10] Geoffrey Ostergaard, *Nonviolent Revolution in India* (New Delhi: Gandhi Peace Foundation, 1985), pp. 4–5.

him problems throughout his life, deteriorated rapidly after his retirement from office and the death of his wife shortly after. He passed away at the end of February 1963. He had achieved a great deal as a Gandhian and nationalist leader, however, unlike Nehru, he did not seem to be destined to such lofty positions. The turning point in his life came with his work with Gandhi during the 1917 Champaran campaign, Gandhi's first major public initiative following his return to India from South Africa.

Prasad was born in December 1884, in a small village in north Bihar, to a once prosperous orthodox (believing in purdah, strict caste separation, child marriage and no widow remarriage) Hindu landed family. At the age of thirteen he was married to Rajbanshi Devi who was to become the mother of his two sons, born in 1906 and 1909. As a teenager he was introduced to the idea of swadeshi by his older brother who was studying in Calcutta. From the age of about twenty-five he wore 'Swadeshi cloth only till Gandhiji started the khadi movement'.[11] He had a distinguished academic career in Calcutta, receiving several very welcome scholarships and obtaining firsts in his degrees of Master of Arts and Master of Laws. He had hankered after public service from a young age and falling under the spell of Gokhale wanted to join the Servants of India Society. By this time his father was dead and the family had fallen on harder times. He revered his older brother Mahendra as head of the family and his own guardian. It was clear that his brother could not cope with bearing the entire financial burden of the family alone and could not support Rajendra's decision to engage in a life of humble service because the anticipated brilliant career of the younger brother seemed to be their financial lifeline. In 1910 the disappointed Rajendra acceded to family wishes, and soon after this his mother died. While Mahendra looked after the extended family, including his brother's wife and children, Rajendra's own work and political activities meant that he only saw those closest to him on holidays. In his *Autobiography*, noting that he had been married for forty-five years, he wondered if he and his wife 'have lived together for as many months. Even when I was practising as a lawyer in Calcutta, I had to live by myself.'[12] Later his immediate family was to spend long periods in Gandhi's Sabarmati Ashram.

As a student he had formed a Bihari students club in Calcutta, took part in the College Union and helped run its monthly magazine. After the completion of his law degree in 1910, he commenced legal practice

[11] Rajendra Prasad, *Rajendra Prasad: Autobiography* (New Delhi: National Book Trust, 1994), p. 28.
[12] *Ibid.*, p. 23.

in the city and took up a professorship at the Law College the following year. He also joined the Congress and, because he was well known
through his student politics activities and academic achievements, was
immediately elected a Member of the All-India Congress Committee in
1911. When, following the separation of Bihar from Bengal, the Patna High
court commenced functioning in March 1916, he shifted to Patna where he
became one of the leading advocates and built up a flourishing and lucrative
practice.

Peasant representatives had met Gandhi at the Lucknow Congress session in December 1916 and informed him of the suffering of poor labourers
on the farms of British indigo planters in the Champaran district of Bihar.
They urged Gandhi to sponsor a resolution concerning their plight but
Gandhi refused to do so until he could verify the facts they were presenting him – and this, he felt, he could only achieve through his own
personal investigation. In April 1917, Gandhi had found the time for his
inquiries.

At this time Rajendra Prasad was a prosperous Patna lawyer who,
although involved with the nationalist cause, knew very little about Gandhi.
He had gone to a reception in Gandhi's honour in Calcutta in 1915, had
seen him at the Lucknow Congress, and attended the All-India Congress
Committee meeting in Calcutta from where Gandhi had decided to find
out about the conditions of the indigo labourers, but it seems that Gandhi
had made very little impression on him. At this stage Gandhi's knowledge
of Hindi was not sufficient to conduct the work of interviewing peasants
about their lives and the Champaran dialect further increased the need
for local interpreters and assistants. Prasad was one of the lawyers who
answered Gandhi's call, assuming that he would be needed for his legal
expertise. Very soon he realised that this was to be no ordinary legal action,
that Gandhi the lawyer was not interested in what the volunteers thought
he must have had in mind. Instead he asked them if they were prepared
to go to jail.[13] This was Prasad's first meeting with the Mahatma. In his
recollections of the meeting he seems puzzled by his own behaviour: he still
did not feel that Gandhi had made any great impact or that the meeting
would 'lead to a complete change in my outlook and my life'. Prasad was a
cautious person and he notes that, 'I do not know, therefore, how it came
to pass that I accepted, without thought, Gandhiji's suggestion and decided

[13] For Prasad's recollections of the Champaran campaign, see Rajendra Prasad, *Satyagraha in
Champaran* (Ahmedabad: Navajivan, 1949); and Rajendra Prasad, *At the Feet of Mahatma Gandhi*
(Westport, CT: Greenwood, 1971), pp. 24–72.

to go to jail.'At this time there was no suggestion in the minds of any of the volunteers that they would be devoting their lives to the service of the country, although most of them consequently did: 'Perhaps it was some magnetic quality of Gandhiji's which, without any awareness on our part at that time, exercised a kind of irresistible fascination on us and impelled us to follow him unquestioningly.'[14]

During the campaign, Gandhi taught his young volunteers, without whose help he felt it was impossible to 'take a single step' in the campaign,[15] to do away with their servants and assume manual work themselves and abandon their caste restrictions on inter-dining. This was to be the first time that the caste-conscious lawyer, in his mid-thirties, 'partook of the food prepared by a man belonging to a different caste'.[16] For Prasad, his time with Gandhi in Champaran was a training camp in Gandhian techniques and thought. From the work of recording the statements of the peasants, he learned of the problems and hopes of the poor villagers of India and to put aside fear.[17] The year he spent with Gandhi changed the successful lawyer: 'Our living together became simpler. We washed our own clothes, carried water from the well, washed our utensils and helped the cook. Any short journey to nearby villages we did on foot. We travelled by third class in trains. We gave up ease and comfort without demur.'[18]

Prasad developed a great affection for Gandhi and also confidence in his technique of nonviolence: 'By the time the agitation ended, we all had become his ardent devotees and zealous advocates of his method.' Gandhi had fought the injustices committed by the planters without bearing any ill will against them personally. Prasad concluded that 'The results were quick and satisfactory because it was Satyagraha truly conducted.'[19] He summed up the changes to the lives of the volunteers succinctly:

Most of us who joined Gandhiji in Champaran were lawyers and not one had joined him with the idea of giving up the profession. But when we started working in Champaran, our whole outlook changed. We found it impossible, once we had undertaken it, to go back to our avocations without completing the task at hand. Thus people who went there for a few days remained for months. When we had finished the work in Champaran, we returned home with new ideas, a new courage and a new programme.[20]

Later he toured with the Mahatma, visiting the recently occupied Sabarmati Ashram site, and met and became friends with Vallabhbhai Patel.

[14] Prasad, *At the Feet of Mahatma Gandhi*, pp. 18–19.   [15] Gandhi, *An Autobiography*, p. 309.
[16] Prasad, *At the Feet of Mahatma Gandhi*, p. 37.   [17] Prasad, *Rajendra Prasad*, p. 93.
[18] *Ibid.*, p. 98.   [19] *Ibid.*, pp. 86, 97.   [20] *Ibid.*, p. 100.

He accompanied Gandhi to Kaira district in Gujarat where the Mahatma was organising a campaign of civil disobedience over excessive land taxes. When, later, Gandhi started his largely unsuccessful recruitment campaign for Gujaratis of the district to enlist in the army to help in the British war effort, the by-nature pacifist Prasad did the same (also unsuccessfully) in Bihar at the request of the government.

As Gandhian campaigns came and went, he mirrored them in his home state but he would maintain contact through visits to Gandhi and always spent time with the Mahatma during the latter's illnesses. At Gandhi's request he started a national educational college in Patna. During his ceaseless touring in Bihar as the local spokesperson for Gandhi, he became an experienced and fluent public speaker who could talk 'for hours on end'.[21] In order to help spread the Congress message, he also commenced editing a new Hindi weekly called *Desh*, and wrote for the English bi-weekly *Searchlight*.

Although he was not at first convinced that Gandhi was completely correct in calling off the Non-cooperation movement following the killing of police at Chauri Chaura in February 1922 because of the demoralising effect it would have on the nationalist movement, after some thought, going against the opinion of most leading nationalists, he decided that Gandhi's action had been the correct one. He attended Gandhi's trial and sentencing which resulted from the movement and when his leader was taken from the Ahmedabad court to commence his six years of imprisonment, 'people like me could not control themselves and burst into tears. From there we returned home feeling as if we had been orphaned.'[22]

During the 1930 Salt Satyagraha, he demonstrated his immersion in Gandhian principles when he called off agitation on Good Friday so that the British Christian officers could attend Church and the Muslim mounted police could attend Friday prayers.[23] Eventually he was arrested, providing him with his first experience of jail life. In prison he occupied himself with reading and spinning and learned weaving in the prison workshop. In Gandhian fashion, he seems to have relished his time in Hazaribagh jail noting that he suffered no inconvenience at all but cherished the many contacts he made there.[24] Due to his ill health, he was released in early 1934 before the completion of his sentence, and soon he was leading the relief effort in earthquake-devastated Bihar where, at his request, Gandhi joined him.

[21] Prasad, *At the Feet of Mahatma Gandhi*, p. 101.   [22] *Ibid.*, p. 116.
[23] Prasad, *Rajendra Prasad*, pp. 309–10.   [24] *Ibid.*, p. 324.

Following his brother's death a few months later, Prasad was to endure the worst period in his life. The financial difficulties of the family now descended on his shoulders and it seemed that the extent of family debt would end his high-level nationalist political career. Gandhi requested Jamnalal Bajaj, a close friend of Prasad's as well as being one of the main creditors of the Prasad family, to help in the matter. He organised for the ancestral family lands to be sold and debts to be cleared and 'During the trying years immediately after my brothers's death, for all practical purposes, Jamnalal stepped into my brother's place. As ever before, I became free from the cares of the family.'[25] This allowed him to serve his first tenure as President of the Congress.

Gandhi regularly spent a part of the winter at the Swaraj Ashram he had established in Bardoli in Gujarat during the Non-cooperation campaign and which served as Patel's principal residence. Prasad accompanied him on one of these trips and pointed out that Gandhi's writings on the 'constructive programme' were not easy to find if one did not have the time to leaf through the pages of Gandhi's paper *Harijan*. He asked the Mahatma to produce a pamphlet on the subject. Gandhi completed the task on the train journey to the ashram and Prasad wrote a complimentary pamphlet. He became primary backer of the programme in Bihar.

Most of Prasad's autobiography was penned in prison between 1942 and 1945. There this leading Congressman clearly shows his ideological, and not merely tactical, commitment to nonviolence and Gandhian principles. He laments the fact that 'many of my countrymen, even Congress workers, who have been maintaining non-violence throughout in their service to the country, are now losing faith in the sacred creed of nonviolence'.[26] In 1946 he was invited into the pre-independence Interim Government. Following twenty-six years of Congress work, except for a very brief time after his brother's death, Rajendra Prasad had never had to look after his own domestic affairs. He visited his family only during his illnesses, yet now he had to set up a household in Delhi and run it on a steady monthly salary, and for the first time work from an office. Soon he was the first citizen of a free republic and it must have pained him to see his country turn its back on some of his most cherished Gandhian beliefs.

During the Constituent Assembly debates on the draft of the Indian Constitution, the differences between the conservative Gandhian Prasad and the other more pragmatic politicians became evident. There was hot

---

[25] *Ibid.*, p. 388. [26] *Ibid.*, p. 146.

debate over proposed Clause 1 of Article 253 that, harking back to the Salt Satyagraha of 1930, declared that 'no duties on salt shall be levied by the Union'. Some members of the Assembly saw the attempt to remove the clause as an outrage on the history of the freedom movement, one that could only have been committed after the Mahatma's death, and one that could open the door for levying future taxes on salt. While Rajendra Prasad argued strongly that the clause should remain in the Constitution, 'as a memento of the glorious struggle which we had', the clause was defeated. Opponents of its retention, including Nehru, thought that the hands of future governments should not be tied in matters of taxation.[27]

Not only was he the first and longest serving President of the Republic, but also the most unassuming. Even in his high office, Prasad led a modest life doing his sacrificial spinning daily and occasionally arguing with Nehru when he wanted to simplify protocol.[28] He declared that his salary and allowances were too high and had them reduced by 80 per cent.[29] He saw the irony of being a pacifist and devoted believer in nonviolence and, as President, being the Supreme Commander of the country's military might. He knew that nonviolence could not be established in a state that did not renounce armies and war but saw India as lacking the courage to show the way, declaring that, 'When Gandhiji was alive, his courage infected others, today we have not shed our fear as he would like us to do and so we maintain our armed forces in spite of their incongruity.'[30]

As India moved ever more rapidly to becoming a modern industrial state, he appeared to be fighting a rearguard action, attempting to keep it tied to its Gandhian roots. As an optimistic Gandhian himself, he overestimated the lasting deep influence of the Mahatma on his beloved country. When unveiling a portrait of the 'Father of the Nation' in the Constituent Assembly in 1947, he declared that Gandhi's influence had

permeated our life to an extent which probably we do not ourselves quite appreciate and fully realise, and the greatness of the Mahatma lies in this, that as time passes, as ages pass, the influence which he has exercised not only on our lives but on the current of world history will be more and more appreciated and more and more realised.[31]

---

[27] Weber, *On the Salt March*, pp. 500–1.

[28] R. L. Handa, *Rajendra Prasad: Twelve Years of Triumph and Despair* (New Delhi: Sterling, 1978), pp. 13–14.

[29] Kewal L. Punjabi, *Rajendra Prasad: First President of India* (London: Macmillan, 1960), pp. 167–8.

[30] Handa, *Rajendra Prasad*, p. 12.

[31] Lok Sabha Secretariate, *Eminent Parliamentarians Monograph Series: Dr. Rajendra Prasad* (New Delhi: Lok Sabha Secretariate, 1990), p. 145.

Several years later, speaking of India, he was far more pessimistic when he asked: 'I wonder if we murdered him only once some eleven years ago or rather if we are not murdering him day-to-day.'[32] Prasad asked his countrymen to put certain questions to themselves on each anniversary of Gandhi's death which seem to be best summarised by one of them: 'Are we ready to be weighed in Gandhihji's scale of values?' He concluded his book on his reminiscences of Gandhi, written while he was President of India, with the words: 'We can make our life purposeful only if we look deep into every corner of our heart to see if there is anything within us which is secretly working against the teachings of Gandhiji.'[33]

VALLABHBHAI PATEL – FROM LAWYER TO SARDAR

The Gujarat Club was the central meeting place of the prominent citizens of Ahmedabad. At the time of Patel's first encounter with Gandhi, he had been in Ahmedabad for almost two years and was quickly on the municipal council. Being the leading barrister in the city, he socialised at the club where he was soon the bridge-playing champion. At this time Gandhi had been in Ahmedabad for about a year at the ashram in Kochrab and was becoming noticed by the leading lights in the city.

There are several versions of Patel's first encounter with Gandhi. In one, the dapper, westernised, sardonic, chain-smoking lawyer was playing a game of bridge at the Gujarat Club with G. V. Mavalankar (who was to become the first Speaker of the Lok Sabha of independent India) when Mahatma Gandhi came to make a speech and collect funds for a nationalist school in the club's hall. Mavalankar asked Vallabhbhai Patel if they should go over and hear what he had to say. Patel answered: 'Who wants to listen to speeches? Let us have another round.'[34] In a newspaper article on the occasion of Patel's seventieth birthday, Mavalankar notes that as an observer to a card game being played by Patel, he decided to go and listen to Gandhi. At this Patel 'passed very sarcastic remarks, discouraging me from going . . . was very sceptical and critical about Gandhi's ideas and plans . . . brutally blunt in expressing his view'.[35] In another version, in June 1916, Patel was playing cards with his friend Chimanlal Thakore when somebody invited them to listen to Gandhi talk about a national school.

[32] Handa, *Rajendra Prasad*, p. 12. [33] Prasad, *At the Feet of Mahatma Gandhi*, p. 329.
[34] R. K. Murthi, *Sardar Patel: The Man and His Contemporaries* (New Delhi: Sterling, 1976), p. 110.
[35] Quoted in B. Krishna, *Sardar Vallabhbhai Patel: India's Iron Man* (New Delhi: HarperCollins, 1996), p. 47. See also Mavlankar's (*sic*) comments in Francis Watson and Hallam Tennyson, *Talking of Gandhi* (New Delhi: Sangam, 1976), p. 12.

He continued his game, remarking that 'I have been told he comes from South Africa. Honestly I think he is a crank and, as you know, I have no use for such people.'[36]

Rajmohan Gandhi, perhaps the most painstaking of Patel's biographers, gives the most detailed version of this story. He notes that within a month of his return to India, Gandhi was being hailed as a Mahatma and to this Patel allegedly responded that 'We already have too many Mahatmas.' When some members of the club visited Gandhi's recently formed ashram, they brought back word of Gandhi's faith in nonviolence which would secure freedom for the country, and also news that the Mahatma wanted educated Indians to grind their own grain and to clean latrines. Patel's response was to ridicule 'the crank' and pass sarcastic comments about Gandhi's 'brilliant ideas'.[37] When Gandhi was invited to visit the club, Patel resented the movement of people past his bridge table on the veranda as they gravitated towards the lawn where the Mahatma was speaking. When he saw Gandhi coming, Mavalankar, who was watching the bridge game, got up to go. Patel asked where his friend was off to and was informed that it was to see Gandhi. Patel answered: 'So what. You'll learn more if you watch our game. I can tell you what he'll say. He will ask you if you know how to sift pebbles from wheat. And that is supposed to bring independence.'[38] Regardless of the laughter, Mavalankar went to hear Gandhi.

How did the cynical Patel, who was not at that time interested in nationalist politics, become one of Gandhi's chief lieutenants and eventually the Deputy Prime Minister, Minister for Home affairs, Minister of Information, Minister of States in the newly independent India, and the person whose crowning achievement was the peaceful integration of the princely states into India and the political unification of the country? Mavalankar believed that Patel's language aside, by the time of the Gujarat Club non-encounter, he already had a sneaking respect for Gandhi. Later Patel himself was to admit that, as a forty-year-old, he was impressed by the quality of the young men that Gandhi had managed to gather around him.

Vallabhbhai Jhaverbhai Patel was born in October 1875 to a reasonably well-off landowning farming family in the fertile charotar area of the Khaira district of Gujarat. He was brought up in an atmosphere of traditional

---

[36] B. K. Ahluwalia, *Sardar Patel: A Life* (New Delhi: Sagar, 1974), p. 32.
[37] Rajmohan Gandhi, *Patel: A Life* (Ahmedabad: Navajivan, 1991), pp. 36–7.
[38] Quoted in Gandhi, *Patel*, p. 37. Tahmankar has several visits by Gandhi to the Club with Patel's reaction softening on each occasion until finally he undergoes an internal conversion. See D. V. Tahmankar, *Sardar Patel* (London: Allen and Unwin, 1970), pp. 15–16.

Hinduism and married at around the age of seventeen. Through the inadequacy of the schools in his area he was, to a large degree, self-educated and did not matriculate until the age of twenty-two after which he passed his pleader's examination which enabled him to practise law in the lower courts. He soon distinguished himself as someone who was meticulous in preparing arguments and brilliant in cross-examination. His wife died in 1908, leaving him from age thirty-three a lifelong widower with a not-quite five-year-old daughter and three-year-old son. Leaving his children in the care of Miss Wilson, a teacher at Queen Mary's School in Bombay from whom they could learn English, in 1910 he went to London to study law in order to further his legal career. Rather than stumbling across vegetarian restaurants and New-Age groups, he went the way of most Indians abroad. He studied conscientiously and passed his final examinations with the highest of honours and returned a westernised gentleman. In 1913 he settled in Ahmedabad and was soon the leading criminal barrister at the Ahmedabad bar, accepting few cases but charging high fees. The understanding in the family was that his brother Vithalbhai would do the public-spirited work while he put his energy into making money. With the entry of Gandhi into his life the lucrative, elitist legal lifestyle would soon vanish.

In the year following Gandhi's visit to the Gujarat Club, Patel's life was to take a revolutionary turn. Gandhi had been invited to preside over a session of the Gujarat Sabha where, independently, Patel was elected secretary. The Sabha (association) was established in 1884 for the economic, political and social advancement of the people of Gujarat and was also functioning as a Congress committee. The organisation was rejuvenated and started to work directly for the welfare of the masses rather than through petitions to the government. When plague broke out in Ahmedabad, Patel headed up the anti-plague campaign. While Gandhi was in Champaran, the crops of Kheda district were washed away by floods and the government would not relent on the payment of land taxes. Patel visited the affected villages on a fact-finding mission. Exchanging his flashy European dress for dhoti and kurta, and, quitting the Gujarat Club, he toured the villages with Gandhi's message of non-cooperation with the authorities. The government confiscated land and animals. The repression was intense and it seemed that the peasants would cave in. However Gandhi, the hero of Champaran, arrived in time and engineered a compromise so that the tax was only levied on those who could afford to pay it, and the no-tax campaign was called off.[39]

---

[39] For a description of the Kheda Satyagraha see Narhari D. Parikh, *Sardar Vallabhbhai Patel* (Ahmedabad: Navajivan, 1953), vol. I, pp. 48–92.

Following Champaran, the Kheda struggle again demonstrated the efficacy of satyagraha and it also propelled Patel into a leadership position in Gujarat. Although perhaps not in results, but certainly in the principles involved,[40] Kheda became for Gujarat what Champaran was for Bihar, and Patel became in his own region what Prasad had became in his. The struggle cemented the relationship between Gandhi and Patel, and under the Mahatma's spell the pompous lawyer became a pre-eminent fighter for the people in Gandhi's causes. The cigarettes and cigars had been replaced by the spinning wheel.

Following the release of prisoners at the end of the campaign, meetings were held in their honour at several towns with Gandhi and Patel present. At one of these meetings Gandhi gave his estimation of his new political right-hand man:

> The sagacity of a general lies in his choice of lieutenants. Certain objectives having been decided upon and rules framed, results will be achieved only if the army goes ahead with its work guided by these. If it fails to do so, the general by himself cannot accomplish anything great . . . I wondered who the deputy general should be. My eye fell upon Shri Vallabhbhai. I must admit that the first time I saw him I wondered who that stiff man could be. What could he do! But, as I came in contact with him, I knew that I must have him. Vallabhbhai saw that this work was far more important than his practice and his work in the municipality, of much account though they were . . . With these thoughts in his mind, he took a plunge. Had I not chanced on Vallabhbhai, what has been achieved would not have been achieved, so happy has been my experience of him.[41]

With the declaration of the Non-cooperation movement in 1920, Patel gave up his legal practice and devoted himself entirely to nationalist work. From this time on he referred to himself as a soldier of his commander-in-chief. Up until Gandhi's arrest in March 1922, Patel 'was saved the anxieties of full leadership', now he had to shoulder the task of guiding the Gandhian movement in Gujarat, however, since the Kheda campaign, for the people he was already *the* leader.[42] In 1923 he commenced a satyagraha campaign in the Borsad area where a punitive tax has been levied on the people who were charged with harbouring criminals.[43] When the government withdrew the tax claim, he came to be known as the 'Commander of Borsad.' Up till 1924 he served as the first Indian municipal commissioner of the city of

---

[40] While the Kheda struggle did not achieve the decisive outcome of Champaran, it must be kept in mind that the campaign in Bihar was merely against white indigo planters, in Gujarat, for the first time, Gandhi and his workers were up against the might of the British Raj.
[41] Speech at Nadiad, 29 June 1918.   [42] Parikh, *Sardar Vallabhbai Patel*, vol. I, pp. 170–1.
[43] For a detailed description of the Borsad Satyagraha see *ibid.*, pp. 221–56.

Ahmedabad, and after was elected municipal president, a post he held until 1928. This was his training ground in public administration.

The campaigns in which he had been involved were successful. However, it was the Bardoli campaign that propelled Patel to national prominence and earned him the title of 'Sardar' – leader – from the people he had worked with, but soon it was a title by which he was known nationally. Vallabhbhai Patel became Sardar Patel the way Mohandas Gandhi had become Mahatma Gandhi. The campaign was defining not only in terms of Patel's life but also in terms of Gandhian satyagraha. In 1928 he led the peasants in the Bardoli district of Gujarat in a campaign to resist the seemingly excessive upward revision of the land tax. He travelled among the people, ate with them and slept in their huts and maintained their resolve as their lands, crops and animals were confiscated. When the confiscations did not force an end to opposition, the government resorted to mass arrests. Almost 90,000 peasants in ninety-two villages resisted the tax. As the stand-off entered its sixth month, the administration agreed to a judicial enquiry and restored confiscated lands. The outcome was that the desired concessions were won and Patel gained a leading place in the national consciousness.[44]

A year and a half later, following his mapping out of the route of Gandhi's historic Salt March, Patel was arrested before the march actually got under-way while he was arousing public consciousness for the coming event. Gandhi knew the high regard in which the Sardar was held along the route and used the arrest to invoke nationalist feelings through an article in his paper.[45]

Patel was to spend most of the following four years in jail, and in the period of early 1932 to mid-1933 he was together with Gandhi in Yeravda prison in Poona. This was the first time that the two of them had actually lived together (Gandhi had invited Patel to live with him at his Ashram, but Patel showed no interest), and it gave them the opportunity to learn more about each other at the deepest level. Patel spent much of their time together 'mothering' the six-years older Gandhi, poking fun at his fads and making him laugh.[46]

As India neared independence and for the few years he lived after-wards, for many of those on the left of the Congress Party, regardless of his organisational efficiency and thoroughness, and indeed power in

---

[44] For accounts of the campaign, see Mahadev Desai, *The Story of Bardoli: Being a History of the Bardoli Satyagraha of 1928 and Its Sequel* (Ahmedabad: Navajivan, 1929); and Parikh, *Sardar Vallabhbhai Patel*, vol. 1, pp. 306–91.

[45] 'Sardar Vallabhbhai Patel', *Young India*, 12 March 1930.

[46] See 'Statement Suspending Civil Disobedience Movement', 8 May 1933.

the party, Patel was seen as a capitalist reactionary. He did not champion Nehru's socialism, but rather favoured free enterprise, gaining him the trust of wealthy conservatives and the donations needed to sustain the Congress. On one occasion the wealthy Gandhi-supporting industrialist G. D. Birla informed Patel that Gandhi had told him that he did not approve of Patel 'collecting money from businessmen'. The characteristic reply was 'This is not his concern. Gandhi is a Mahatma. I am not. I have to do the job.'[47]

Patel's belief in Gandhi's nonviolence was probably always more tactical than Prasad's commitment and he certainly did not hold Gandhi's view that the means were more important than the ends. Towards the latter part of his life he could no longer surrender his individuality to his mentor to the degree that he had earlier, nevertheless throughout he was a faithful supporter and invaluable deputy to Gandhi. As the country was nearing independence, Patel the realist on occasions was to have major differences with Gandhi the idealist. Their ideas and ideals at the time of the coming Partition saw differences emerge between them on first the inevitability of the vivisection of India and then on the question of how far to accede to Muslim interests. In short, although a junior partner who had often been characterised as Gandhi's 'yes-man', Sardar Patel proved in the end to be a co-worker and realist politician rather than disciple: 'When he was my "yes-man," he permitted himself to be so named, because whatever I said instinctively appealed to him . . . When power descended on him, he saw that he could no longer successfully apply the method of non-violence which he used to wield with signal success.'[48]

The differences towards the end of Gandhi's life aside, although Gandhi leaned on Patel because of his organisational abilities, on several occasions during their long association he asked Patel to step aside in favour of Nehru on the issue of Congress leadership. Patel was the leading candidate for the Presidentship at the time of the formation of the Interim Government. Gandhi again intervened in favour of Nehru and this ensured that he, rather than Patel, became the first Prime Minister of India. Nehru was philosophically further from Gandhi than Patel was, but there was a generational gap between the two nationalist politicians and, regardless of their differences, it seemed that Gandhi loved Nehru like a father. Patel was the faithful soldier, but not a son.[49]

[47] Quoted in Tahmankar, *Sardar Patel*, p. 18.
[48] 'Speech at Prayer Meeting', *The Hindustan Times*, 16 January 1948.
[49] Gandhi's colleague Kishorlal Mashruwala summed up the relationship thus: 'I would describe the Gandhi-Patel relationship as that of brothers, Gandhi being the senior brother, and Gandhi-Nehru

Pyarelal, who knew the Sardar well, summed up the relationship on Patel's death:

He was the principal pillar of the edifice of which Gandhiji was the architect and Pandit Nehru the corner stone. I do not know of another instance of such complete surrender of judgement and will on the part of a lieutenant to his general as of the Sardar's to Gandhiji during the days of India's struggle for freedom. 'When I am there, the Sardar's thinking is paralysed', Gandhiji used to say. Things changed in later years, but the basic loyalty and the bond of personal affection that united him and Gandhiji continued unimpaired to the last.[50]

VINOBA BHAVE — FROM SCHOLAR TO WALKING SAINT

Following Gandhi, Vinoba Bhave is generally considered the greatest Gandhian. He has become variously known as Gandhi's moral or spiritual heir, someone who has taken Gandhi's political philosophy in action into new areas and even to new heights, and he is universally acknowledged as a saint. In India his photograph adorns the walls of Gandhian institutions along with that of Gandhi and that other great Gandhian, and eventual Vinoba rival, Jayaprakash Narayan. In the West, Vinoba has made it onto the cover of *Time* magazine.[51]

Vinoba was born to a Chitpavan Brahmin family in the tiny village of Gagode in Baroda State (now Maharashtra) in 1895.[52] His mother and grandfather with whom he lived when the stern, methodical and secularist father was away in government service in the town of Baroda, were deeply religious. At the age of ten, Vinoba took a lifelong vow of celibacy. Until the age of twelve, when he entered high school in Baroda, Vinoba studied at home. At school, with a group of friends, he founded a students' society dedicated to the study of religious and nationalist literature. In 1913, after matriculating, Vinoba went to college. Two-and-a-half years later, as a twenty-year-old, he left home for Bombay to sit his college Intermediate examinations. He never arrived, instead he went to the holy city of Benares (now Varanasi) on a spiritual quest. For the months he stayed there, he lived as a religious mendicant studying the holy texts. Vinoba had a desire

---

as that of father and son.' Kishorlal G. Mashruwala, *In Quest of Truth* (Ahmedabad: Shravana, 1983), p. 148.

[50] Pyarelal and Nayar, *In Gandhiji's Mirror*, p. 122.

[51] See the cover story, 'A Man on Foot', *Time*, 11 May 1953.

[52] For Vinoba's recollections of his early life see Vinoba Bhave, *Moved by Love: The Memoirs of Vinoba Bhave*, trans. Marjorie Sykes from a Hindi text prepared by Kalindi (Dartington, Totnes: Resurgence, 1994), pp. 25–119.

to go to the Himalayas and to Bengal, but instead, as he was to recall later, 'Providence took me to Gandhiji and I found in him not only the peace of the Himalayas but also the burning fervour of revolution typical of Bengal. I said to myself that both of my desires had been fulfilled.'[53]

While he was still in Baroda he had read about Gandhi and decided to write to the Mahatma and, on the strength of Gandhi's answers, resolved to go to Gandhi's Kochrab Ashram in Ahmedabad. He instantly fell under Gandhi's spell and a bond of love that was to last throughout their lives quickly developed. According to one source it was as the result of Vinoba's early efforts at helping the sweeper in latrine cleaning work – a Brahmin doing scavenging work was almost unheard of – that Gandhi insisted that all such work had to be done as part of the daily routine. Some ashramites left as a result of this rule.[54] Gandhi hailed Vinoba as 'one of the rare jewels of the Ashram', adding that 'he has come to purify the Ashram with his own religious merit: he has come not to receive but to give.'[55]

Ill health forced Vinoba to a different climate in 1917. He went to Wai, about forty miles south of Pune, where he spent his year away from the ashram in deep religious study and teaching as well as undertaking a programme of walking to build up his strength and take religious instruction to the villages. On his return, when a school was started at the ashram, now at Sabarmati, Vinoba was appointed religious instructor.

When, at the insistence of Jamnalal Bajaj, a branch of the ashram was set up at Wardha Gandhi sent Vinoba to oversee the institution. For over a quarter of a century at different locations around Wardha, Vinoba undertook a life of religious discipline. Although he mostly worked outside the political arena, he was arrested in 1923 and 1932 during various satyagraha campaigns and at Gandhi's request he became the first to be offered up in the Individual Satyagraha of 1940–1. His final arrest came during the 1942 Quit India movement. In all he was arrested six times and served five and a half years in jail.

When Gandhi selected Vinoba ahead of luminaries like Nehru as the first individual satyagrahi in 1940, the little known ashramite was thrust into the national spotlight. Gandhi felt the need to introduce his disciple to the country through his newspaper. After lauding Vinoba's abilities as a scholar, teacher and, above all, master spinner, Gandhi explained that, 'He has never been in the limelight on the political platform. With many co-workers he believes that silent constructive work with civil disobedience

---

[53] Quoted in Ram, *Vinoba and His Mission*, pp. 15–16.
[54] Shriman Narayan, *Vinoba: His Life and Work* (Bombay: Popular Prakashan, 1970), p. 38.
[55] Quoted in Shah, *Vinoba*, p. 32.

in the background is far more effective than the already heavily crowded political platform. And he thoroughly believes that non-violent resistance is impossible without a heart-belief in and practice of constructive work.'[56]

Vinoba used his prison time to learn about the thoughts of Marx from a communist friend and to translate the Gita and other religious texts. He also spelled out the principles of a nonviolent political order in a booklet titled *Swaraj Sastra*. There Vinoba proclaimed that 'man's happiness lies in giving, but the idea of the right of ownership acts as an obstacle', that villages should be self-sufficient and that collective responsibility is a better incentive to encourage skill, honesty, enthusiasm and a sense of responsibility than the mere payment of wages, and that 'in a non-violent order there will be no police but only a band of public-spirited workers'.[57]

On his release from prison in 1945 his aim was to spend the next twenty years in scavenging work. With Gandhi's assassination all was to change. Vinoba spent a few years searching for a path while many of the Gandhian fraternity looked to him for leadership. Vinoba came to the realisation that, although independence for India had been achieved, Gandhi's mission was still incomplete because the ordinary people had not achieved self-sufficiency and were neither economically free from exploitation nor politically free. During this time, Vinoba formed close bonds with Nehru and JP and, at the insistence of Gandhian friends, he was persuaded to attend a Gandhian conference at Shivarampalli near Hyderabad.

When Vinoba set out from his ashram at Paunar for this third annual conference of Sarvodaya workers, almost 250 miles distant, he resolved to do so on foot. He had already decided to make the return journey by way of Telengana, a Communist-dominated district where the wealthy were being driven from the land which in turn was redistributed to the landless. As the military sought to re-establish control, the hapless peasants were caught in the middle of a deadly power struggle and a cycle of retribution and counter retribution.

Following the conference, on 15 April 1951, Vinoba commenced his walking tour of the district. Three days after leaving Shivarampalli, Vinoba arrived at the village of Pochampalli where a landowner offered to donate some land to the landless and the Bhoodan movement was born.[58] The next twelve years Vinoba, 'the walking saint', spent 'continuously on the march throughout the length and breadth of India', as he said, 'looting with love'.

[56] 'Civil Disobedience', *Harijan*, 20 October 1940.
[57] Vinoba Bhave, *Swaraj Sastra [The Principles of a Non-Violent Political Order]* (Varanasi: Sarva Seva Sangh, 1973), pp. 44, 46, 64, 79.
[58] See Roderick Church, 'Vinoba and the Origins of Bhoodan', *Gandhi Marg* 5 (1983), pp. 469–91.

He covered tens of thousands of miles and begged and received pledges for more than four million acres of land (of which one-and-a-quarter million were found suitable and were redistributed[59]). Eventually Vinoba was to admit that the collection of only 4,000,000 acres of Bhoodan land, instead of the target 50,000,000 was a 'poor achievement indeed'. However he still termed Bhoodan a success in bringing about a change in attitudes through feelings of guilt: 'The pride of ownership has gone away altogether. When I go to a village I often find that the big landholders have left their homes for the day. . . . I have got a hold on their heart.'[60]

Now the undisputed leader in the Gandhian fraternity, in early 1958 Vinoba laid down what he saw as the four principles of satyagraha. They were that satyagraha is positive not negative, it should proceed from gentle to gentler to gentlest, there should be happiness on the mere hearing of the word 'satyagraha', and, finally, that there should be no insistence on the part of the satyagrahi, insistence should come from truth itself.[61] In the maintenance of consistency, this meant that satyagraha had to remain non-coercive and had to respect the sovereignty of the opponent by relying solely on conversion.[62] In order to achieve this, satyagraha had to be spiritualised by conforming to the precepts laid down by Vinoba.

Satyagraha had to progress as the political situation progressed (from imperialist domination to 'democracy' in India) and as science progressed. Consequently, Vinoba declared that Jesus' concept of 'resist not evil' and Gandhi's 'nonviolent resistance' were no longer adequate and what now had to take their place was 'nonviolent assistance' in right thinking.[63] Without this all that could be achieved was legislative reform, and that could never lead to the ideal nonviolent society. Although the British had gone, according to Vinoba the strength of village India was being sapped by a centralized authority that was slowly creating a welfare state. What he wanted was a move away from the current forms of government, 'the rule by one' and 'the rule by more than one' to a form where 'all the people may combine and equally share in the responsibility of carrying on their own administration' – in other words, 'rule by all'.[64] The way to achieve this was to arouse people's

---

[59] See Vishwanath Tandon, 'The Bhoodan-Gramdan Movement (1951–74)–A Review', *Gandhi Marg* 5 (1983), p. 496.

[60] Vinoba Bhave, 'Wherein Lies Real Revolution,' *Sarvodaya* 13 (1963), p. 129.

[61] *Bhoodan Yajna*, 7 February 1958, quoted in Vishwanath Tandon 'Vinoba and Satyagraha,' *Gandhi Marg* 2 (1980), p. 387.

[62] See Geoffrey Ostergaard, 'Vinoba's "Gradualist" Versus Western "Immediatist" Anarchism', *Gandhi Marg* 5 (1983), p. 517.

[63] Kanti Shah (ed.), *Vinoba on Gandhi* (Varanasi: Sarva Seva Sangh, 1985), p. 52.

[64] Bhave, *Swaraj Sastra*, p. 19.

power and create a system of self-sufficient village republics free from the coercive power of the state.[65]

Bhoodan, an example of nonviolent assistance, was a stepping stone on the way to this 'rule by all' ideal, which it was hoped would be ushered in by the Gramdan, or 'village gift' movement. In the realized state of gram swaraj the village collectively owned the land and an assembly consisting of all adult village members, through a process of consensual grassroots democracy, decided on the governing of the village without outside interference. By 1974 there were more than 100,000 Gramdan villages in India – unfortunately it was later to transpire that a majority of them were only so on paper, in the villages themselves nothing had changed.

Vinoba's aim was to create conditions which would 'do away with the need to use even the power of the State'.[66] The achievement of this anarchist polity was to come about gradually – he was not actively anti-state; he hoped to bypass the structures on which the state rested (including the police and military) and thus allow it to whither away.

In the early days of the ostensibly land redistributing Bhoodan movement, Vinoba claimed that his aim was to bring about a threefold revolution. First, he wanted to change people's hearts, then to bring about a change in their lives, and thirdly, to change the social structure.[67] Vinoba went so far as to say *this* was the important aspect of Gramdan, the solving of the land problem being 'a very minor matter'.[68]

Bhoodan was a social movement clearly in the Gandhian mould, but Vinoba also brought another cherished directly Gandhian idea into existence. Gandhi had tried, with only limited and temporary success, to establish a Shanti Sena (peace army) during his lifetime and after his death there were some further fleeting attempts at forming an organisation of nonviolent peacekeepers. However, the actual establishment of the Shanti Sena had to wait until Vinoba's Bhoodan movement was astonishing the world with its novel Gandhian approach to the pressing problem of landlessness among India's rural poor.[69]

In the early 1940s while in Nagpur jail, Vinoba conceived the outlines of the principles of a nonviolent social order. The ideal of 'public-spirited

---

[65] *Ibid.*, p. 14.   [66] Vinoba Bhave, *Bhoodan Yagna* (Ahmedabad: Navajivan, 1957), p. 87.
[67] *Harijan*, 8 December 1951; see also Vinoba Bhave, *Third Power* (Varanasi: Sarva Seva Sangh, 1972), p. 68.
[68] Bhave, *Third Power*, p. 71.
[69] See Thomas Weber, 'A Brief History of the Shanti Sena as Seen through the Changing Pledges of the Shanti Sainik', *Gandhi Marg* 13 (1991), pp. 316–26; and Thomas Weber, *Gandhi's Peace Army: The Shanti Sena and Unarmed Peacekeeping* (Syracuse University Press, 1996), pp. 43–52, 69–103.

workers' replacing the police was still with him as he marched throughout the length and breadth of the country, obtaining pledges of land for redistribution. Bhoodan was relatively successful for six years but then, in a utopian move, Vinoba shifted the emphasis from land gifts to 'village gift' or Gramdan. Vinoba realised that if Gramdan proved to be a success, he would have to consider the next step in the creation of a nonviolent social order – the step he had foreshadowed fifteen years before in *Swaraj Sastra*.

On 23 August 1957, the last day of Vinoba's Bhoodan march through the state of Kerala, eight prominent Keralan sarvodaya workers took a pledge in his presence to lay down their lives for the maintenance of peace through nonviolence, becoming the first Shanti Sainiks. Vinoba soon realised that if anything was to become of his now cherished peace brigade idea, he would have to take positive organisational steps, so he declared himself the supreme commander and started work to spread the organisation throughout the country. In 1958 he established a committee under the leadership of women to oversee the Sena and in 1962 it was reorganised and professionalised under JP, who was now Vinoba's chief lieutenant, and JP's chief assistant and son of Gandhi's secretary, Narayan Desai. Here followed the Sena's heyday – as the 1968 Gandhi birth centenary approached, Desai was able to announce that the number of sainiks had exceeded 15,000 and that there were branches in all regions. Sainiks were helping to negotiate peace in Nagaland between the government and rebels; were persuading dacoits (bandits) of the Chambal valley, first under Vinoba then under JP, to surrender to authorities; had done excellent work restoring peace in severe communal disturbances; worked with refugees following the war in Bangladesh; had undertaken peace work in India's sensitive border areas; established training camps to instil the ethos of service and nonviolence in the youth of the country; and had even sent a contingent to troubled Cyprus.[70]

Eventually the differences between the gentle satyagraha-advocating Vinoba and the aggressive satyagrahi JP, following JP's political campaigns in the state of Bihar and his 'Total Revolution' campaign against the increasingly dictatorial government of Prime Minister Mrs Gandhi, led to a split in the Gandhian movement between the Vinobans and JPites. Following the split, the Shanti Sena ceased to exist in 1974. Although there were efforts to resuscitate the organisation, and at one stage there were two rival Senas

[70] See Weber, *Gandhi's Peace Army*, pp. 104–37.

operating, for all intents and purposes Gandhi's dream and Vinoba and JP's achievement was no more.[71]

Before coming to national and world prominence, when he was not being pushed to do otherwise by Gandhi, Vinoba had spent much of his life as a semi-recluse in the quest of spiritual fulfilment and the study of sacred texts. Vinoba again retired to his ashram in 1970 but from the sidelines directed the Gandhian movement. During the constitutional crisis in India following JP's agitation, Vinoba took a vow of silence and spent a year in prayer and meditation. Some took this as tacit support for the government and an abandonment of JP. When the year was up, he devoted his waning energies for outside work to issues such as cow protection. Weak and unwell, in November 1982 at the age of eighty-seven, he declined to take food or liquids for ten days until he passed away in the mode of an ancient Hindu sage. Some Gandhians have claimed that the failure to achieve a nonviolent revolution of the type that JP (and indeed Gandhi) was aiming for is at least partly the fault of Vinoba who refused to sanction the use of assertive satyagraha. Nargolkar makes the point that 'The nonviolent struggle for Indian independence was led by a Mahatma who happened to be a political activist, while the post-independence movement for the establishment of a more egalitarian social order through Bhoodan, Gramdan and Gram-swarajya was conceived and guided by a saint, who, apart from being deeply spiritual, was . . . by temperament a teacher disinclined to action.'[72] Vinoba's campaigns re-energised a somewhat dispirited Gandhian movement in India and again provided faith for the idea of a nonviolent alternative. While he certainly furthered Gandhi's project and may also have diminished it,[73] he was convinced throughout that what he was doing was nothing but Gandhi's work:

My Inner Self bears witness that I have tried my utmost to follow the course of Ahimsa and of Love, as shown by Gandhiji: I have put in maximum effort. I cannot remember being remiss in these even for a moment. After Bapu's departure, I kept on doing Bapu's work. I have not an iota of doubt on this account. Bapu has been constantly with me. I believe my thinking contains the essence of Bapu's. Nothing else helps me more in personally reflecting on what Bapu has said.[74]

[71] See generally Ostergaard, *Nonviolent Revolution in India*; Roderick Church, 'Vinoba Bhave, Jayaprakash Narayan and Indian Democracy', *Gandhian Perspectives* 2 (1980). pp. 89–129; and Weber, *Gandhi's Peace Army*, pp. 92–103.

[72] See Vasant Nargolkar, 'Vinoba and Satyagraha,' *Gandhi Marg* 2 (1981), p. 667.

[73] See Devdutt, 'Vinoba and the Gandhian Tradition', *Gandhi Marg* 5 (1983), pp. 600–15.

[74] Quoted in Shah, *Vinoba*, p. 99.

KENNETH KAUNDA — AND NONVIOLENCE IN AFRICA

Kenneth David Kaunda was born in 1924 to school teacher parents on a Presbyterian mission in Northern Rhodesia. His father was the first African Christian missionary to his people, and his mother was the first African woman to hold a teaching post in the country. His father, who ran the home according to strict Christian principles and held daily prayer services for his children, died when Kaunda was eight years old so he and his four siblings had to help out with the physical work to keep the household functioning. In 1941 he was selected to go to Munali, a new elite African secondary school in Lusaka. Here the shy stammering youth excelled in his academic studies and at the age of nineteen, although he had not completed his school certificate, was called home by the missionaries to become boarding master of his old primary school. In 1946 Kaunda was married to Betty Banda, another school teacher, with whom he was to have nine children. He travelled to Southern Rhodesia to teach but the racism in the white-dominated state forced him to return home. Gradually it dawned on him that even in his native Northern Rhodesia the best land was taken by whites and to be served in shops he had to stand in line in 'kaffirs only' queues while whites used the main entrance.[75] Although his political awakening was a gradual one, as early as 1947 he had remarked to his missionary friend and biographer Fergus Macpherson that racial oppression was a 'great burden of evil' that had to be removed.[76]

In 1949 Kaunda started working for the Northern Rhodesia African Congress. Soon he was the organising secretary for the Northern Province. This put him in close contact with the grassroots of the movement. In 1953 the British government federated Southern (Zimbabwe) and Northern (Zambia) Rhodesia and Nyasaland (Malawi). The move was resented by black Africans who believed that power would reside with the whites of Southern Rhodesia and gave strength to the call for national independence based on majority rule. In that year Kaunda helped to organise the party's newspaper and became its editor. Boycotts against Zambian butchers and other enterprises which were engaged in discriminatory practices were successfully conducted in the following year – and at this time Kaunda became a vegetarian. Soon he and the Congress leadership were in prison. In 1957 Kaunda was proclaiming the power of boycotts. A clause spelling out the

---

[75] For biographical material on Kaunda's early life see Kenneth Kaunda, *Zambia Shall be Free: An Autobiography* (London: Heinemann, 1962).

[76] Fergus Macpherson, *Kenneth Kaunda of Zambia: The Times and the Man* (Lusaka: Oxford University Press, 1974), p. 70.

Northern Rhodesia African Congress' affirmation of nonviolence was written into its constitution and Hope and Young point out that during the boycott of discriminating businesses, Congress leaders 'always sent letters to the local Chamber of Commerce, describing their complaints and asking for a conference to discuss the issues – a demand that was rarely met'.[77]

During a period in England in the latter half of 1957 to study the workings of British politics, Kaunda came to the conclusion that British governments and political establishments 'only recognised power in the colonies when it emanated from well-organised, mass groups, led with dedicated discipline'.[78] And this he believed necessitated Gandhi's nonviolent approach, one which was being used successfully in neighbouring Tanganyika by Julius Nyerere.

The following year Kaunda split with the Congress leadership and formed the Zambian African National Congress, with himself as president. The support base that he had built up as a party organiser allowed him to take the major part of the old Congress operating structure into the new ZANC which he used to promote his plan of 'positive nonviolent action' – his campaign of civil disobedience against the imposition of federation. A few months later, when the new militant organisation was banned, rioting broke out in Lusaka and Kaunda was arrested. His imprisonment made him a national hero. Shortly after his release, in early 1960, Kaunda was elected president of the newly formed United National Independence Party which showed spectacular growth in support. This in turn meant that party discipline became more difficult to maintain and Kaunda was forced to emphasise nonviolence continuously – it became the central point of every speech he made and was continually reinforced in his numerous articles.[79]

In December he and other UNIP leaders were invited to London by the British authorities to discuss the future of the colonies. However, as no action seemed to be forthcoming, in 1962 he threatened a general strike and backed the Gandhi-inspired World Peace Brigade that planned a march of hundreds of international activists into Northern Rhodesia to dramatise the situation in the country.[80] Before the WPB action or general strike

---

[77] Hope and Young, *The Struggle for Humanity*, p. 232.

[78] John Hatch, *Two African Statesmen: Kaunda of Zambia and Nyerere of Tanzania* (London: Secker and Warburg, 1976), p. 147.

[79] *Ibid.*, p. 161.

[80] For the World Peace Brigade Northern Rhodesia action, see Charles C. Walker, 'Nonviolence in Eastern Africa 1962–4: The World Peace Brigade and Zambian Independence', in A. Paul Hare and Herbert H. Blumberg (eds.), *Liberation Without Violence: A Third Party Approach* (Totowa, NJ: Rowman and Littlefield, 1977), pp. 157–77.

took place, the British stepped in and proposed a new constitution that was acceptable to the UNIP. Kaunda's party won the 1964 elections and following complete independence, he became the first president of the Republic of Zambia at the youthful age of thirty-nine.

Kaunda had long advocated the use of nonviolent direct action, but he felt that he had to review his political choices when Zambia gained its freedom. As head of the party that was obviously going to win the first elections, he had the choice of remaining outside the political fray and exercising his influence from the sidelines the way Gandhi did; or going into government. Although long committed to principled nonviolence and counselled by Jayaprakash Narayan, one of the co-chairs of the World Peace Brigade, not to take the presidential position,[81] he decided to 'be a politician, and go into government'.[82] Like Prasad before him, he was faced with a dilemma. He struggled with the problem of how, as a believer in nonviolence and a head of state, he could defend his country against aggression from South Africa and Rhodesia. He noted the philosophical principle that 'he who affirms the state affirms violence' and considered it unfair and unrealistic that everyone should become a saint.[83] This, however, did not mean that he was discarding his beliefs in nonviolence or suggesting that violence or nonviolence were morally equivalent. He pointed out that 'I have found that the demands of political realism have led me to modify my pacifist convictions', adding by way of question to his critics: 'Have you tried running a country on the basis of pacifist principles without qualification or modification, or do you know anyone who has?'[84]

In keeping with his own personal lifestyle, in power he started to demand in his speeches that other leaders of the country set an example for the people, to live a simple life of service that eschewed personal gain.[85]

When the white minority government of (Southern) Rhodesia uni-laterally declared independence in 1965, Kaunda's Zambia faced severe problems. Most of the country's imports came from Rhodesia and the export of its goods was dependent on the Rhodesian railway, nevertheless Kaunda joined other countries in imposing sanctions on his neighbour while some other leaders of newly independent black countries accepted

[81] See Kenneth David Kaunda, *Kaunda on Violence* (London: Sphere, 1980), pp. 19–23; and Hope and Young, *The Struggle for Humanity*, p. 241.
[82] Sutherland and Meyer, *Guns and Gandhi in Africa*, p. 96.
[83] *Ibid.*, pp. 98–9; and Kaunda, *Kaunda on Violence*, pp. 40–1.
[84] Sutherland and Meyer, *Guns and Gandhi in Africa*, p. 102. This neatly summarises the general argument which is the thrust of *Kaunda on Violence*.
[85] Hatch, *Two African Statesmen*, p. 213.

financial assistance. Economic retribution followed swiftly and as the leading western states did nothing to end the rebellion or to help Zambia
financially, Kaunda was eventually forced to turn to China for economic
aid, and this did not endear him to the anti-communist western powers.

Things were a little improved by the 1970s. Although Kaunda eventually came to rule a one-party state and became increasingly authoritarian
the longer he was in power, it seems that he remained uncorrupted (while
the rulers of many other newly independent states succumbed), his political prisoners were incarcerated for relatively short periods and were not
tortured, and the Zambian army remained one of the smallest in Africa.
Nevertheless, things deteriorated in the 1970s and 1980s and in 1991, Kaunda
was defeated in a landslide at elections following his legalisation of opposition parties. As the price of copper (Zambia's chief export) fell and the
price of oil (Zambia's chief import) rose in the 1980s, the economy had
weakened substantially. By the time of the election, the country was in a
desperate economic condition partially due to the freezing of economic
aid to Zambia following Kaunda's attempts to go against IMF austerity
programmes that were instituted as a condition of earlier borrowing.

In 1980 Kaunda and Morris produced a book on Kaunda's views on
violence. It was a self-justification for Kaunda's move to a far more pragmatic
position on the questions of the use of violence in relation to his early
strongly pacifist stance (after all Gandhi only had the basically decent British
to contend with while he was faced with far more ruthless opponents[86]).
In the foreword, Morris points out that Kaunda faced a large amount of
criticism because of his active support for the violent freedom movements
in Zimbabwe and Namibia, especially from religious quarters. Morris notes
that Kaunda 'had been the darling of the pacifist cause – possibly the only
world leader since Gandhi to preach and practise non-violence from a
position of power. His change of mind and heart was seen more as an act
of apostasy than one of those convenient U-turns politicians make from
time to time to get their policies back in line with reality.'[87]

Politics is of course the art of the possible and once in power political leaders are generally forced to moderate the rhetoric they so readily
employed in opposition or from the margins. Kaunda the national leader
was no different. His early espousal of Gandhian principles and use of
Gandhian tactics may have become diluted as needs of government forced
a different reality onto him. This, however, does not mean that the earlier
stand was necessarily a temporary phase – it may have been instrumental

---

[86] Kaunda, *Kaunda on Violence*, p. 25.   [87] *Ibid.*, p. 11.

in the making of the man, of getting him to the position he came to hold, and may even be one that he is returning to following the lifting of the burdens of leadership.

Kaunda was deeply influenced by his strong Christian upbringing. Although later in life he saw himself as a religious rather than Christian person, much of his early time in power must be seen in light of his deep Christian faith.[88] He was also powerfully influenced by Kwame Nkrumah's largely nonviolent battle for independence for Ghana, and when he was elected president of the UNIP he told his followers that they needed to follow Nkrumah's three Ss – service, sacrifice and suffering, and made great effort to persuade the party's membership that they had to abide by the party's policy of nonviolence in the tense pre-independence situation.[89] A further significant influence came from the Indian independence struggle which had provided inspiration to a whole generation of aspiring African anti-imperialist leaders. And with this came Gandhi and his brand of civil disobedience which appeared to be the best tactic to achieve national independence. Following the attainment of freedom, Kaunda's Zambia was characterised by what was known as the four 'positive negatives': nonviolence, nonracialism, nonpartisanism and nonalignment.

A short introductory primer to Kaunda's life explains that, as the newly installed president of Zambia, he was so busy that he had little time for reading, however 'He is anxious to return to the works of Mahatma Gandhi, who had a most profound influence upon him a decade ago. It was from Gandhi that he acquired his conviction that non-violence is both right and effective.'[90] A close friend, the white liberal Methodist clergyman Collin Morris, has talked of Kaunda's Gandhian streak which could shame people to change their behaviour in a way that coercion never could and how he maintained not only his dedication to nonviolence but also an insistence that his followers do likewise even to the point of endangering his own leadership.[91] Another acquaintance and biographer has labelled Gandhi as Kaunda's hero and mentor.[92] Gandhi's views on the sacredness of each individual human being is closely echoed in Kaunda's philosophy (which he

---

[88] Richard Hall, *The High Price of Principles: Kaunda and the White South* (Harmondsworth: Penguin, 1973), p. 41

[89] Kaunda, *Zambia Shall be Free*, pp. 152–3.

[90] Richard Hall, *Kaunda: Founder of Zambia* (London: Longmans, 1964), p. 3

[91] Collin M. Morris and Kenneth D. Kaunda, *A Humanist in Africa: Letters to Colin M. Morris from Kenneth D. Kaunda President of Zambia* (Nashville: Abingdon, 1966), p. 9. On this point see also Kaunda, *Kaunda on Violence*, p. 55.

[92] Hatch, *Two African Statesmen*, pp. 152, 173.

terms 'Humanism') and his personal life also seems to mirror something of the Mahatma's asceticism: the vegetarian was also a teetotaller, non-smoker and abstainer from coffee and tea.[93]

Where Kaunda does mention Gandhi in his writings, and he does so quite regularly, with the exception of *Kaunda on Violence*, it seems almost to be in passing and often there is more emphasis on the effectiveness than on the rightness of nonviolence. Kaunda's early autobiography makes no explicit mention of Gandhi's influence on him. Even when he specifically talks of nonviolence, it appears to be for pragmatic rather than ideological reasons. In the later work *Kaunda on Violence*, when he talks of tactics becoming self-defeating if used at the wrong time or in the wrong way, he goes so far as to describe nonviolence as a tactic and adds that 'if anyone should deny the term "tactic" and insist on "gospel" or "absolute law" then we must part company with mutual regret'.[94] However, his language (for example when he calls a mistake a 'Himalayan Error'[95]) often betrays a Gandhian heritage and he has noted that his aim was to combine Gandhi's 'policy of non-violence' with Nkrumah's positive action.[96] Given this seemingly watered down version of Gandhi's philosophy and later distancing of himself from the Mahatma, to what degree can Gandhi be said to have been a significant influence on the thinking and political activity of Kenneth Kaunda?

Kaunda's Gandhian heritage is longstanding. Macpherson maintains that it is important to note Gandhi's influence on the young Kaunda. In early 1947, in their discussions, Kaunda talked of Gandhi's nonviolence as the practical political application of Christ's teachings.[97] Two years later, after Gandhi's assassination, Macpherson lent Kaunda a book on the Mahatma which 'he read thoroughly, as evidenced by his thumb-marks on its pages!'[98] The twenty-four-year-old felt a special affinity with the Mahatma who launched his nonviolence campaigns on African soil.

Kaunda claims that he was first introduced to the serious study of Gandhi's ideas by a Lusaka storekeeper Rambhai Patel. Patel had made 'rough and ready' translations of some of Gandhi's writings and Kaunda incorporated the ideas he gleaned from them into his earliest political speeches. Even thirty years later he recalled them shining 'like gems in a river of mud'. He added that 'Gandhi's philosophy deepened and broadened my own thinking which had been based on a rather narrow but enthusiastic mission-station Christianity', and 'If I owe my faith to Jesus,

[93] Hall, *The High Price of Principles*, 46   [94] Kaunda, *Kaunda on Violence*, p. 28
[95] Kaunda, *Zambia Shall be Free*, p. 114.   [96] *Ibid.*, p. 140.
[97] Macpherson, *Kenneth Kaunda of Zambia*, p. 70.   [98] *Ibid.*, p. 105.

Mahatma Gandhi supplied the hope. His teachings flooded my mind with light, brightening those dark corners where I stored perplexing questions I had gnawed on for years without result.'[99] For him, as someone 'inwardly torn by moral dilemmas', Gandhi's satyagraha 'was a lifebelt thrust into the hand of a drowning man'. As a result of this, 'it was according to the principles of non-violence on the Gandhi model that the final stages of the freedom struggle in Zambia were conducted', becoming the official party policy of the UNIP and ensuring that the history of the final days of the freedom struggle were not written in blood.[100]

During the tenth anniversary of Gandhi's death, when Kaunda claims that his interest in nonviolence policies 'was quickened', he wrote about the efficacy of nonviolence in the independence struggle at a time when it was increasingly coming under attack. His public defence of nonviolence was, however, pragmatic – so as not to give the government any excuse for killing protesters.[101] In May 1958 Kaunda was able to realise his dream of visiting India. There he met Nehru and leaders of the Gandhian movement, saw the places associated with Gandhi's life and studied his work. The visit renewed his belief in nonviolence.[102] Although around the time of his 1959 term of imprisonment, in a smuggled letter to his close followers, Kaunda claimed that the British only really respected 'tough guys', and Hall notes that there was little 'of Gandhianism about it', on his release Kaunda adopted a different tone and gave the UNIP the watchwords of discipline, patience, loyalty and nonviolence.[103] In a June 1961 speech, where Kaunda announced his 'master plan' for ending the territory's association with the Federation, he explicitly declared that 'we in the UNIP follow the Mahatma Gandhi way'.[104] Two years later, when he was awarded an honorary Doctor of Laws degree at Fordham University in the United States, his speech started with an observation on Gandhi and concluded with a lengthy discussion of nonviolence. In Gandhian terms Kaunda noted that nonviolence was not merely a religious issue:

It is political, economic, social and spiritual. It brings man, as an individual living in society, back into the centre of things. Nothing is more necessary, for we are now in danger of getting so wrapped up in machines, organizations and plans that man who is the purpose of it all is treated like an instrument. Man must realize his own importance, both as an individual and as a member of society.[105]

---

[99] Kaunda, *Kaunda on Violence*, pp. 15, 16.   [100] *Ibid.*, pp. 18–19.
[101] Kaunda, *Zambia Shall be Free*, pp. 90–1.
[102] Hope and Young, *The Struggle for Humanity*, p. 233.
[103] Hall, *The High Price of Principles*, p. 46.   [104] Macpherson, *Kenneth Kaunda of Zambia*, p. 335.
[105] Quoted in *ibid.*, p. 416.

Following his exit from the formal political arena, Kaunda again seemed to be coming back to his earlier uncompromised view of nonviolence.[106] Sutherland and Meyer conclude that Kaunda was the

only African leader to become a head of state who adopted Gandhian nonviolence in principle . . . The young freedom fighter was able to lead his people to
independence through essentially nonviolent means. The statesman Kaunda felt
compelled to modify his position on nonviolence in order to govern a nation-state
and to help fellow Africans achieve freedom, especially in apartheid South Africa.
In our dialogue with 'the lion' in his winter of discontent, we found him seeking to become relevant once again through the marriage of his original religious
nonviolent beliefs to all aspects of society.[107]

MARTIN LUTHER KING, JR. — AND SATYAGRAHA IN AMERICA

In the United States, Martin Luther King, Jr. is often put on a par with Gandhi and is far better known than the Mahatma. In 1964 he became the youngest Nobel Peace Prize recipient for his nonviolent leadership of the black civil rights campaigns and was *Time* magazine's 'Man of the Year'. Stamps have been issued in his honour and the Monday nearest his birthday (the third in January) is a national holiday. It has even been argued that King is the 'greatest American who ever lived',[108] and his charisma and oratorical brilliance, as well as what he stood for and accomplished, ensured international fame.

King was born in 1929, into a middle-class family of Baptist preachers. At the age of fifteen he was accepted into a programme for gifted students at Morehouse College in Atlanta, and at eighteen he was ordained and licenced to preach at the Ebenezer Baptist Church in Atlanta, where his father was pastor. He completed his theological studies at Crozer Theological Seminary in Pennsylvania in 1951, graduating at the head of his class. While at the University of Boston he met the music graduate student from a peace activist background, Coretta Scott. They married in 1953. In 1955 he received his Ph.D. for a doctoral dissertation titled 'A Comparison of the Concepts of God in the thinking of Paul Tillich and Henry Nelson Wiesman'. Before he had completed his dissertation, he was invited to become pastor of the historic Dexter Avenue Baptist Church in Montgomery in Alabama and soon found himself as leader of the black boycott of segregated buses in the

---

[106] Sutherland and Meyer, *Guns and Gandhi in Africa*, p. 109.   [107] *Ibid.*, p. 112.
[108] Michael Eric Dyson, *I May Not Get There With You: The True Martin Luther King, Jr.* (New York: The Free Press, 2000), p. ix.

city following Rosa Parks' law-breaking action of sitting in the whites only front of a bus. The boycott lasted 381 days during which he was arrested and his house bombed.[109] In 1956 a Federal court judge issued an injunction ending segregation and King emerged as a national hero of the civil rights movement.

The following year, he went on to found the Southern Christian Leadership Conference to support civil disobedience in the form of pickets, sit-ins and court challenges to secure full citizenship rights for blacks. In 1960 he moved to Atlanta where he was arrested in the campaign to desegregate lunch counters. He was again arrested in 1963 during the Birmingham lunch counter desegregating campaign. From prison he wrote his famous Gandhi-flavoured 'Letter from Birmingham Jail' explaining the need for direct action. Following his release, he helped to organise the historic march on Washington where, during the rally attended by 200,000 people in the shadow of the Lincoln Memorial, he delivered his iconic 'I Have a Dream' speech.

In the mid-1960s he took his campaigns to the north of the United States to highlight housing segregation and more subtle racism than the blatant version of the South. To the distress of some, who saw it as either traitorous or taking the focus off the civil rights campaign, he also became an active opponent of the US involvement in Vietnam.

In his last few years he became more radical and seemingly less hopeful that love would conquer white racism, nevertheless he never approved of slogans such as 'Black Power' or endorsed retaliatory violence. His attempt to unite black moderates and the ever more popular active radicals was not successful and his influence seemed to be waning as his nonviolent approach was increasingly rejected by younger and more militant black leaders. The lack of greater progress in civil rights and seeming cautiousness of his nonviolence led to a questioning of his leadership and even effectiveness. From the left, critics such as Malcolm X came to see King as a lackey of the whites and claimed that his insistence on love and nonviolence scarred the black psyche as much as the oppression that he fought against.[110] Gandhian analysts have claimed that, as with other western activists, King did not make the crucial link that Gandhi had made between satyagraha and a 'constructive programme' (positive work to build the future better society while the present unsatisfactory one is being dismantled) and that

---

[109] The bombing of the King residence occurred, presumably coincidentally, on 30 January – the date of the assassination of Gandhi.
[110] See Dyson, *I May Not Get There With You*, pp. 102–20.

his 'gradual loss of influence within the American civil rights movement was largely due to this oversight'.[111] He was assassinated at the young age of thirty-nine on 4 April 1968 outside a Memphis hotel where he was staying prior to leading a march by striking city sanitation workers. He had been arrested fourteen times in his short life of activism. This was truly a life in the mould of the Mahatma.

Naturally any 'outside' influence on King must be seen in light of his experiences of oppression as a black person in a white-dominated society and in light of the traditions of the black Baptist Protestantism which nurtured him.[112] Sudarshan Kapur argues that African Americans were paying attention to Gandhi's struggles in India and having fruitful exchanges with Gandhians for four decades before King emerged onto the scene and that because of this the King-inspired movement should not be seen as emerging out of a historical vacuum – in fact, the community's long encounter with Gandhi, Gandhians and Gandhian philosophy went some of the way to raising up King the prophet.[113] Eventually the church provided the avenue for the spreading of the idea of Gandhian nonviolence, but, according to Baldwin, it also made him receptive to Gandhi's philosophy and methods in the first place.[114] Nevertheless, the question remains: to what extent did King become what he was, or at least his nonviolent activism become what it did become, because of this 'outside' influence of Gandhi?

Hanigan states that while it is very easy to draw parallels between the two men, given King's actions and the Gandhian rhetoric he employed, and to retrospectively fit King into Gandhi's prophecy that eventually it could be through the American Negroes 'That the unadulterated message of nonviolence will be delivered to the world',[115] there is little evidence to support the claim that King was acting under the influence of Gandhi's techniques at Montgomery.[116] In short, the grounds for comparison are greater than those which demonstrate influence. Hanigan further notes that while Gandhi

---

[111] H. J. N. Horsburgh 'Nonviolence and Impatience', *Gandhi Marg* 12 (1968), pp. 359–61. On this, see also John J. Ansbro, *Martin Luther King, Jr.: The Making of a Mind* (Maryknoll, NY: Orbis, 1983), pp. 141–5.

[112] See generally, Lewis V. Baldwin, *There is a Balm in Gilead: The Cultural Roots of Martin Luther King, Jr.* (Minneapolis: Fortune Press 1991).

[113] See Sudarshan Kapur, *Raising Up a Prophet: The African-American Encounter with Gandhi* (Boston: Beacon Press, 1992).

[114] Baldwin, *There is a Balm in Gilead*, pp. 185–6.

[115] This was said in an interview with another of King's mentors, Dr Howard Thurman in 1936. See *Harijan*, 14 March 1936.

[116] James P. Hanigan, *Martin Luther King, Jr. and the Foundations of Nonviolence* (Lanham: University of America Press, 1984), p. 49.

'was undoubtedly something of an inspiration and model for King', the Mahatma's 'influence grew with King's successes and failures and is certainly not by way of intellectual or spiritual content' as was his black experience.[117] Others argue the opposite. Bishop, for instance, states that 'Many of those who now admire Martin Luther King regard his non-violence as a modern example of Christian pacifism', however this is mistaken because 'such an understanding fails to do justice to Gandhianism'.[118] Seshachari, in something of an overstatement, goes so far as to claim that where Lincoln left off, Gandhi set the Negro 'on the road to final victory', taught Negroes the lesson of nonviolent resistance and gave them a weapon of battle.[119]

In an early article, King spells out the five central points of nonviolence 'as a method in bringing about better racial relations'. They are that nonviolence is not a method for cowards because it *does* resist, it seeks to win the friendship and understanding of the opponent rather than their defeat or humiliation, that it is directed against the forces of evil rather than at persons who are caught in those forces, the guiding principle is love and therefore not only external physical violence must be avoided but also 'internal violence of the spirit', that is one should refuse to hate the opponent, and, finally, 'the method of nonviolence is based on the conviction that the universe is on the side of justice'.[120] This list could have been compiled by anyone who had undertaken a careful reading of Gandhi.

In his history of the Montgomery bus boycott campaign, King talks of disliking the term 'passive resistance' preferring 'active non-violent resistance to evil'. He also provides a slightly different version of the five 'basic aspects' of the philosophy of nonviolence: gone is talk of the universe and justice, instead he explains that suffering should be accepted without retaliation.[121] Further, in an article titled 'Our Struggle', King talks about the black loss of self-respect, of the need for the use of nonviolence rather than retaliatory violence so that 'we can all live together in peace and equality', and of having no desire for victory which only transfers those from the bottom to the top without achieving freedom for all.[122] This language appears to be straight from Gandhi – but did he merely adopt Gandhian rhetoric for something he was already feeling (in the way Gandhi adopted Thoreau's

---

[117] *Ibid.*, p. 134.

[118] Peter D. Bishop, *A Technique for Loving: Non-violence in Indian and Christian Traditions* (London: SMC Press, 1981), p. 93.

[119] See Seshachari, *Gandhi and the American Scene*, pp. 138–59.

[120] Martin Luther King, Jr., 'Nonviolence and Racial Justice', *Christian Century* 74 (6 February 1957), pp. 165–7, reproduced in James Melvin Washington (ed.) *A Testament of Hope: The Essential Writings of Martin Luther King, Jr.* (San Francisco: HarperCollins, 1986), pp. 5–9.

[121] Martin Luther King, Jr., *Stride Towards Freedom* (New York: Harper and Row, 1958), pp. 102–3.

[122] 'Our Struggle', *Liberation*, April 1956, reproduced in *A Testament of Hope*, pp. 75–81, at p. 81.

terminology for something he was already doing), or can Gandhi be seen as a genuinely formative influence?

Close friends of King's, like the Atlanta Quaker June Yungblut, have stated that King was 'deeply influenced by Gandhi's powerful work',[123] and scholars have also often made the same point. For example, Smith points out that there 'was much in Gandhi that appealed to King', including love, nonviolence, humility, self-sacrifice, the relationship of means to ends, and the obligation to act against evil, and consequently much of 'Gandhism would go into the formulation of the philosophy and technique of King's social protest movement'.[124] King himself said as much and so did his wife. King has claimed that 'The spirit of passive resistance came to me from the Bible and the teachings of Jesus. The techniques of execution came from Gandhi.'[125] When asked which books have influenced his thinking very strongly, King listed five, and three of those were about Gandhi: Louis Fischer's *The Life of Mahatma Gandhi*, Gandhi's own *Autobiography* and Richard B. Gregg's *The Power of Nonviolence*. The other two were Thoreau's *Civil Disobedience* and Walter Rauschenbusch's *Christianity and the Social Crisis*.[126] Prior to coming to Montgomery, he had stated that 'I had read most of the major works on Gandhi and also Thoreau's *Essay on Civil Disobedience*. Both of these strains of thought had profound influence on my thinking. I firmly believe that the Gandhian philosophy of non-violent resistance is the only logical and moral approach to the solution of the race problem in the United States.'[127]

The main source where the relationship between King and Gandhi is spelled out by King himself is in his book *Stride Towards Freedom*. Here he relates how, as a college freshman, before being introduced to Gandhi, he read Thoreau's 'Essay on Civil Disobedience' and was 'fascinated by the idea of refusing to cooperate with an evil system. I was so deeply moved that I reread the book several times. This was my first intellectual contact with the theory of non-violent resistance.'[128]

---

[123] See June J. Yungblut's essay in G. Ramachandran and T. K. Mahadevan (eds.), *Nonviolence After Gandhi: A Study of Martin Luther King Jr* (New Delhi: Gandhi Peace Foundation, 1968), p. 52.

[124] Donald H. Smith, 'An Exegesis of Martin Luther King, Jr.'s Social Philosophy', in David J. Garrow (ed.), *Martin Luther King, Jr.: Civil Rights Leader, Theologian, Orator* (Brooklyn: Carlson, 1989), vol. III, p. 835.

[125] *Reporter*, 8 March 1956, quoted in George Hendrick, 'Gandhi and Dr Martin Luther King', *Gandhi Marg* 3 (1959), p. 19. In a later restatement this becomes 'Christ furnished the spirit and motivation while Gandhi furnished the method', King, *Stride Towards Freedom*, p. 85

[126] Letter to Lawrence M. Byrd, 25 April 1957, quoted in Martin Luther King, Jr., *The Papers of Martin Luther King, Jr.: Volume IV: Symbol of the Movement, January 1957–December 1958* (Berkeley: University of California Press, 2000), pp. 183–4.

[127] Quoted in Hendrick, 'Gandhi and Dr Martin Luther King', p. 21.

[128] King, *Stride Towards Freedom*, p. 91.

In her autobiographical account of her life with King, his wife Coretta notes that he told her that the turning point of his thinking about how to reconcile Christian pacifism with activism came when he heard a lecture on Gandhi by one of his mentors, Dr Mordecai Johnson, the black president of Howard University, at Friendship Hall in Philadelphia in the spring of 1950.[129] King found the message of the lecture to be 'so profound and electrifying' that he left the meeting and 'brought a half-dozen books on Gandhi's life and works'.[130] And at this point he 'became deeply influenced by Gandhi, never realizing that I would live in a situation where it would be useful and meaningful'.[131] A little while later he took a course at Crozer on the psychology of religion and for his research paper and oral presentation he chose to work on Gandhi.[132] While Coretta King did not think that at this stage, in the late 1940s and early 1950s, 'he as yet consciously considered applying the Gandhian technique of nonviolence to the Negro Movement, the idea began germinating in his mind'.[133] King records that as a result of this study of Gandhi,

The whole concept of 'Satyagraha' was profoundly significant to me. As I delved deeper into the philosophy of Gandhi my skepticism concerning the power of love gradually diminished, and I came to see for the first time its potency in the area of social reform. Prior to reading Gandhi, I had about concluded that the ethics of Jesus were only effective in individual relationship. The 'turn the other cheek' philosophy and the 'love your enemies' philosophy were only valid, I felt, when individuals were in conflict with other individuals; when racial groups and nations were in conflict a more realistic approach seemed necessary. But after reading Gandhi, I saw how utterly mistaken I was . . . I came to feel that this was the only morally and practically sound method open to oppressed people in their struggle for freedom.[134]

He added that,

My study of Gandhi convinced me that true pacifism is not nonresistance to evil, but nonviolent resistance to evil. Between the two positions, there is a world of difference. Gandhi resisted evil with as much vigor and power as the violent resister, but he resisted with love instead of hate. True pacifism is not unrealistic submission

[129] Coretta Scott King, *My Life with Martin Luther King, Jr.* (London: Hodder and Stoughton, 1969), p. 71.
[130] King, *Stride Towards Freedom*, p. 96.
[131] Interview with Martin Agronsky for 'Look Here', in King, *The Papers of Martin Luther King, Jr.*, pp. 292–9, at p. 297.
[132] Kenneth L. Smith and G. Zepp Jr., *Search for the Beloved Community: The Thinking of Martin Luther King, Jr.* (Valley Forge: Judson Press, 1974), pp. 47–8.
[133] Coretta King, *My Life with Martin Luther King, Jr.*, p. 72.
[134] King, *Stride Towards Freedom*, pp. 96–7.

to evil power, as Niebuhr contends. It is rather a courageous confrontation of evil by the power of love, in the faith that it is better to be the recipient of violence than the inflicter of it, since the latter only multiplies the existence of violence and bitterness in the universe, while the former may develop a sense of shame in the opponent, and thereby bring about a transformation of the heart.[135]

By the time of the Montgomery bus boycott, the Congress of Racial Equality (CORE) had already been using Gandhian nonviolent action in desegregation campaigns for a decade, with the book *War Without Violence: A Study of Gandhi's Method and its Accomplishment* by the ex-Gandhi activist Krishnalal Shridharani serving as their 'semiofficial bible'.[136] A leading light in these campaigns was Bayard Rustin, a disciple of influential American pacifist A. J. Muste and Gandhi. He went to Montgomery to assist in the protest and became an advisor to King, who he attempted to push further along the Gandhian path.[137] As the movement unfolded, 'the inspiration of Mahatma Gandhi began to exert its influence'.[138] Not long after the start of the struggle, a sympathetic white woman, Juliette Morgan, wrote to the local paper comparing the bus boycott with Gandhi's Salt March. She was vilified by the white community for making the comparison, and indeed lost her job as a city librarian because of her public stand against segregation, but as a result soon the 'name of Mahatma Gandhi was well-known in Montgomery'.[139] During the bus boycott King started consciously emulating the Gandhian technique, noting that 'Gandhi was the guiding light of our technique of nonviolent social change'.[140] Further, he was becoming firmly convinced that the black leadership had to suffer as Gandhi had – and this, although King was daunted by the prospect, meant being prepared to go to jail.[141] As the struggle unfolded and King could 'see the power of nonviolence more and more', not only did he give intellectual assent to it as a method, but 'it became a commitment to a way of life'.[142]

In March 1959, King visited India, 'as a pilgrim' rather than as a tourist, at the invitation of the Gandhian movement.[143] While there, King 'made

---

[135] *Ibid.*, pp. 98–9.
[136] Taylor Branch, *Parting the Waters: America in the King Years 1954–63* (New York: Simon and Schuster, 1988), p. 171.
[137] See David J. Garrow, *Bearing the Cross: Martin Luther King, Jr., and the Southern Christian Leadership Conference* (New York: William Morrow, 1986), pp. 72–3.
[138] King, *Stride Towards Freedom*, pp. 84–5.   [139] *Ibid.*, p. 85.
[140] Clayborne Carson (ed.), *The Autobiography of Martin Luther King, Jr.* (London: Little Brown and Company, 1999), p. 121; and Coretta King, *My Life with Martin Luther King, Jr.*, p. 135.
[141] Coretta King, *My Life with Martin Luther King, Jr.*, p. 177.
[142] King, *Stride Towards Freedom*, p. 101.
[143] Coretta King, *My Life with Martin Luther King, Jr.*, p. 188. For King's trip to India, see Branch, *Parting the Waters*, pp. 250–4.

speeches all over India, always emphasising his debt to Gandhian think-ing'.[144] Following the trip he noted that in India he saw none of the hatred that usually follows a violent struggle, and for achieving this victory for love he judged Gandhi to be 'by all standards of measurement . . . one of the half-dozen greatest men in world-history'.[145] In India he even spent a little time walking and talking with Vinoba Bhave who was on his Bhoodan march at the time.

It appears that the trip had a great impact on King's mind. He learned that nonviolence required great patience and that the American expectation of rapid gains might have been unrealistic. He returned from India 'more devoted than ever to Gandhian ideals of nonviolence and simplicity of living. He constantly pondered how to apply them in America', and he 'was more determined than ever to live as simply as possible'.[146] The India trip allegedly caused a Gandhian self-searching in King, but in the end he decided that in 'the conditions prevailing in America, we had to have certain things, and that he must strive to be more like Gandhi spiritually'.[147]

Although America was engulfed in rioting, at the end of his life King still held firm to nonviolence. In an article that appeared posthumously, he reiterated his absolute commitment. Even if nonviolent protest was to fail, he declared that he would go on preaching it. He claimed that he planned 'to stand by nonviolence because I have found it to be a philosophy of life that regulates not only my dealings in the struggle for racial justice but also my dealings with people, with my own self'.[148]

The above discussion is not sufficient for the assertions that the 'impact of Gandhism on the life of Martin Luther King, Jr. . . . was enormous . . . Gandhi furnished King with the essential tactics of non-violence in a movement'[149] and that King was the 'greatest Gandhian that ever lived'.[150] Although King's speeches in India proclaiming his debt to Gandhi are simply what could be expected in the circumstances, and an alliance of his movement with the name of Gandhi could be seen as having positive political pay-offs among the many white Americans who greatly admired Gandhi and had supported the Indian independence struggle, it would appear that King *was* influenced by Gandhi. However, whether it was a

[144] Coretta King, *My Life with Martin Luther King, Jr.*, p. 191.

[145] Quoted in Ansboro, *Martin Luther King, Jr.*, p. 6.

[146] Coretta King, *My Life with Martin Luther King Jr.*, p. 192.   [147] *Ibid.*, p. 133.

[148] Martin Luther King, Jr., 'Showdown for Nonviolence', *Look*, 16 April 1968, pp. 23–5; quoted in *A Testament of Hope*, pp. 64–72, at p. 69

[149] Upendra Kumar Baruah, *Portrait of a Gandhian: Biography of Dr. Martin Luther King, Jr.* (Gauhati: the author), 1985, p. i.

[150] Baruah, *Portrait of a Gandhian*, p. 25.

decisive influence or merely one of inspiration will probably never be deter-mined. Without Gandhi he surely would still have been a great civil rights activist, but possibly his methods of activism may have evolved differently. Perhaps King was a faithful disciple of the Mahatma and the Montgomery bus boycott was the first major successful Gandhian campaign in America, but then again perhaps Adam Roberts is correct when he claims that 'For King and his movement, Montgomery crystallized the idea of nonvio-lence, not *vice versa*.'[151] Autobiography may subjectively be an experiment in truth, but objectively it is often wanting in this regard. Nevertheless, in this instance, until there is any evidence to the contrary, we can do worse than take King's own words at face value.

SHANTIDAS — AND GANDHIAN ASHRAMS IN FRANCE

Joseph Jean Lanza del Vasto is something of a French icon, but, although he has been described as the man who 'keeps Gandhi alive in the west', he is little known outside the French-speaking world. He was a writer, acquaintance of Gandhi and Vinoba, pioneer of European nonviolence and the founder of the Community of the Ark.

Lanza del Vasto was a French-speaking Italian born in San Vito dei Normanni on the heel of the boot of Italy in September 1901.[152] His mother was from a prominent Belgian family and his father a Sicilian nobleman whose ancient and illustrious forebears counted emperors and kings among their members. He had a privileged childhood, travelling widely in Europe with a retinue of servants. Along with his two younger brothers, he spoke English with the governess, French with his parents and Italian with the servants. He attended high school in Paris but found the lessons dull and was a mediocre student because he 'had quickly realized that to all the things I questioned, they did not want to give an answer'.[153] He studied philosophy at the universities of Florence and Pisa and wrote a dissertation for his Doctorate of Philosophy on the question of the Trinity. While reading Thomas Aquinas' work on the Trinity in the Saint's *Summa Theologica*,

---

[151] Adam Roberts in Ramachandran and Mahadevan, *Nonviolence After Gandhi*, p. 68.
[152] His autobiography, *Les Enfances d'une Pensée* (Paris: Denoël, 1970), has not been translated into English. The biographical information presented here has come from the 'Publisher's Introduction' to his most widely read book, *Return to the Source* (London: Rider, 1971), pp. 7–15; the chapter on him, 'Gandhi's Disciple in the West: Shantidas', in Hope and Young, *The Struggle for Humanity*, pp. 41–70; and Jacques Semelin, 'Lanza del Vasto, Joseph Jean (1901–1981)', in Roger Powers and William Vogele (eds.), *Protest, Power, and Change: An Encyclopedia of Nonviolent Action from ACT-UP to Women's Suffrage* (New York and London: Garland, 1997), p. 300.
[153] Quoted in Hope and Young, *The Struggle for Humanity*, p. 43.

he experienced what he has called his 'conversion' to Catholicism. The academic life, however, could not satisfy him in his quest for existential understanding because 'philosophy and all the sciences put together cannot account for the existence of a fly'.[154] He turned his back on his high society lifestyle for one of voluntary poverty, becoming a vagabond. He travelled widely in Europe, rejecting profits, comforts or sense of belonging. With his trust in God as his security, he took odd jobs such as washing dishes and teaching Latin or selling his own art and craft work as the need arose. In this way, he experienced 'poverty, hunger and, at times, ridicule. But ever observant, ever curious, he sought in every situation and every trade a fresh meaning of truth and a more genuine contact with human beings.'[155]

During his student days at Florence, a girl had given him a copy of Romain Rolland's biography of Gandhi and now the desire to learn from the Mahatma came to the fore. At the age of thirty-five, as part of a spiritual quest in search of 'that distance that sharpens sight and makes one see clearly . . . this clarity whose name is Detachment',[156] he travelled to Asia in the closing days of 1936. That journey, lyrically detailed in his classic book *Return to the Source*, began with him being 'delivered' of his trousers, jacket and shirt in Madurai. He donned a loincloth and 'stepped into the field of human relations unimpeded' as people for whom a foreigner was little more than easy prey 'vanished into space' and he found himself invited into the confidences and homes of many Indians.[157] The pilgrimage culminated in this meeting with Gandhi in 1937. Following an audience with Ramana Maharishi (who did not overly impress him), Lanza del Vasto came to the conclusion that the serenity of the East could not satisfy his roving western mind because he believed that 'charity is greater than wisdom', and so he set out for Wardha 'to learn how to become a better Christian'.[158] That encounter was to prove to be the turning point of his life. Gandhi gave him the name 'Shantidas' (Servant of Peace) and introduced him to nonviolence, convincing him that it was the central truth of Christianity.

Arriving at Gandhi's hut at Segaon village, Lanza del Vasto encountered the half-naked Mahatma sitting on the ground:

He waves to me – yes, to me! – makes me sit down beside him and smiles to me. He speaks – and speaks of nothing else but me – asking me who I am, what I do and what I want. And no sooner has he asked than I discover that I am nothing, have never done anything and want nothing except to stay like this in his shadow.[159]

---

[154] 'Publisher's Introduction', *Return to the Source*, p. 8.   [155] *Ibid.*
[156] Lanza del Vasto, *Return to the Source*, p. 18.   [157] *Ibid.*, pp. 35–6.
[158] *Ibid.*, p. 97.   [159] *Ibid.*, p. 101.

He stayed with Gandhi for three months doing manual work and learning from his master. It was during this period that he 'received instructions to found a Gandhian Order in Europe' and it was also there 'that the request and offer were made to me to "stay another five years with us, in order to prepare yourself properly"'. However, Shantidas recalled that 'I was driven mad with haste within me, I felt the war coming and wanted to have made a start in order to face the event. And so I left in all haste, shedding tears. And five years later I had done nothing and did not know what to do. And the war had come . . .'[160]

The stay at Gandhi's ashram had convinced him of the evils of western time-saving and abundance-producing mechanisation that left people pressed for time, without contentment and surrounded by slums.[161] Lanza del Vasto came to the realisation that the system of salaried workers, constantly looking for better pay and conditions was nothing more than 'slavery in a modern form'.[162] He concluded that if a machine is useful, then it should be used, 'but if it becomes necessary, then it is your urgent duty to throw it away, for it will inevitably catch you up in its wheels and enslave you . . . The machine enslaves, the hand sets free.'[163] He also learned the fundamentals of Gandhian nonviolence: the 'enemy' was not evil only mistaken in the thought that he had an enemy[164] and nonviolence was not merely to be a technique of action but also 'a personal rule for reaching inner self-unity, which required a communal way of life to be achieved'.[165] Later, as an outgrowth of what he had learned from the Mahatma, Vasto was to formulate his 'axioms of nonviolence' which held that (1) You do not have the right to return evil for evil. (2) The end does not justify the means. (3) Fear, constraint, and force will never establish justice. (4) It is not true that violence is justified in the use of self-defense. (5) It is not true that murder is justified when the 'common good' demands it. (6) It is false that technology, economy and politics are morally neutral. And, (7) It is completely false that the established order represents justice.[166]

After his pilgrimage into the Himalayas following the sacred river Ganges to its source, it dawned on him that 'by virtue of the very principle of Swadeshi, the place of a Western disciple of Gandhi was in the West and

---

[160] Lanza del Vasto, *Gandhi to Vinoba: The New Pilgrimage* (London: Rider, 1956), p. 74.
[161] Lanza del Vasto, *Return to the Source*, pp. 107–8.
[162] T. K. Mahadevan (ed.), *Truth and Nonviolence: A UNESCO Symposium on Gandhi* (New Delhi: Gandhi Peace Foundation, 1970), p. 285.
[163] Lanza del Vasto, *Return to the Source*, p. 111.   [164] *Ibid.*, p. 118.
[165] Semelin, 'Lanza del Vasto', p. 300.
[166] Lanza del Vasto, *Warriors of Peace: Writings on the Technique of Nonviolence* (New York: Knopf, 1974), pp. 53–7.

his task to sow the seed on the most thankless of all ground – at home. For nowhere was the need for his teaching greater.'[167] He wrote to Gandhi with his intention. The reply instructed him to follow his inner voice. On a final visit to Gandhi's ashram in September 1937, the Mahatma again asked him to examine whether it was God's or his own will to attempt to implant Gandhi's doctrine in the west.[168] At their final meeting at the Haripura session of the Indian National Congress in February, the Mahatma gave his blessings: '[I]t is right that you should go, that you should be put to the trial you are looking for, away from me. You will see if non-violence is strong enough in you to impose itself on those you live with. A lukewarm thing loses its heat when it touches something else, a burning thing sets fire to everything it touches.'[169]

Following travels on foot through the Middle East in 1938 and 1939, he returned to Paris just before the war broke out with the intention of founding a community based on the example of Gandhi's ashrams. During the German occupation, he left the French capital for unoccupied southern France where life was more normal and in Marseilles he met a woman who shared his love of music. She was to become his constant companion and most devoted disciple. In 1943 he published his best-selling account of his Indian pilgrimage and in 1944, as the war was drawing to a close, during his regular 'Commentary on the Gospels' sessions in Paris he was asked to form a group that centred around handicrafts. It was, however, not until 1948, following the shocking news of his master's assassination and his marriage to Simone Gebelin (Chanterelle), whom he found he loved more than his own solitude,[170] that he founded the original rural 'Community of the Ark' in a wing of his wife's family's country home in Tournier in the southwest of France.

The community was open to all and eventually proved dysfunctional and so in 1953 Lanza del Vasto left and, following some months in India marching with Vinoba on his Bhoodan yatra in early 1954,[171] returned to found a much larger community near Bollène in the Rhone valley in the south of France. This community had far stricter entry procedures – to be a member one had to be a novice for three years and then be admitted by unanimous vote, nevertheless many wanted to join.[172] The problem of

---

[167] Lanza del Vasto, *Return to the Source*, p. 243.   [168] *Ibid.*, pp. 259–60.   [169] *Ibid.*, p. 290.

[170] Hope and Young, *The Struggle for Humanity*, p. 50. He named his wife Chanterelle because of her singing. Her music has left an indelible mark on the Community of the Ark.

[171] See Lanza del Vasto, *Gandhi to Vinoba*.

[172] This rule even applies to children who were born in the community. When they had finished their studies they were asked to live in the outside world for long enough to see if they were truly 'called', and then they had to undergo the three year training period like everyone else.

increasing numbers and limited living space was solved by the acquisition of La Borie Noble, a property of 2,000 acres near Montpellier. The group moved there in 1963 and since has built up a village of several impressive stone buildings on the site, and eventually two further communities on the land (Nogaret and La Flayssière).

The Ark, which was dedicated to achieving self-sufficiency in food, clothing and energy, was created as 'a patriarchal,'[173] nonviolent, hard-working, and ecumenical order'.[174] The community did not represent a withdrawal from the world, maintaining good relations with the nearby villages and the older children attended the local high school. The community became a centre for nonviolent activism against the French use of torture during the Algerian war of independence, against the interment camps for Algerians living in France and classed as 'suspected persons', in aid of those refusing to undertake military service in Algeria and for the recognition of the right of conscientious objection, and against the French production of nuclear weapons. Lanza del Vasto and the community were also instrumental in the ten-year-long, and ultimately successful, nonviolent struggle by Larzac peasants against the expansion of a local military base that threatened to take their lands.

There are now several communities of the Ark (branches have been established in Italy, Spain, Morocco, Belgium, Argentina and Canada), each ideally of between thirty and fifty adults and children under the authority of a patriarch designated by Shantidas as the head of the entire Order.[175] An attempt is made to apply the precepts of nonviolence at all levels, to work towards the achievement of a unity in life, and to provide inner preparation to outside nonviolent activism. The Ark's constitution proclaims that the 'aim of manual labour is not only to obtain one's daily bread by pure means, but to bring about an inner harmonisation between body and soul'. In fact in the Gandhian ashrams of the Ark, the first kind of work that needs to be done is 'the work on oneself'.[176] The communities are unmechanised with all work done by hand or horsedrawn plough. Members take vows of service (which begins with manual work so as not to be a burden on others), obedience to the rules of the Ark, responsibility and co-responsibility,

---

[173] A pamphlet produced by the community titled *The Ark: Elements of a Non-Violent World* (n.p., n.d.), states that 'The Order is called Patriarchal in that it is more a tribe than a monastery'. Lanza del Vasto believed that although the community was founded on principles of nonviolence and consensus it is nevertheless patriarchal because 'only communities with strong leadership endure.' See Hope and Young, *The Struggle for Humanity*, pp. 67–68.
[174] Semelin, 'Lanza del Vasto', p. 300.
[175] Since the death of Shantidas, women have taken more leadership roles.
[176] Mahadevan, *Truth and Nonviolence*, p. 286.

purification (from personal acrimony, gain or domination, from attachments, and aversions and prejudices), poverty (to attain detachment and charity and to live lives that are simple, sober and proper), truth, and nonviolence (to humans, and as far as possible to all other living creatures, in order to defend justice, resolve conflicts and redress wrongs).[177] All is not work however, and prayer, meditation, festivals, music and dance play a significant part in the life of the Ark, which also has as another of its rules 'a respect for beauty and refusal to tolerate things ugly even if convenient, practical and expedient'.[178]

In keeping with nonviolence principles, decisions affecting the life of the community are taken by the members by consensus because there is 'no reason why a larger number should be more right against a smaller number or even against one man'. Of course consensus is difficult to achieve and it may need a time of reflection in silence and then fasting; 'nevertheless, the time that is taken up in achieving unanimity is not time lost'.[179]

If a member falls short of their own self-expectation, they must do penance. If they observe a shortcoming in another member who is not prepared to atone for it, they must again take the penance, perhaps in the form of a fast or the doing of the work the other refused to do, upon themself instead.[180] This self-imposed sanction is the only one permitted because 'No one has the right to inflict on anyone else the slightest retribution or punishment; no one is pure enough for that.' In short, nonviolent justice 'is justice without punishment'.[181] As totally anarchistic communities do not survive, this does not mean a free for all, rather it means that punishment is replaced by penance. According to Shantidas it is the 'gem' of 'a rule which lays down a rhythm of life, the manner of dress, the hours of work, the times of prayer'.[182] The vows of the Order are repeated annually and after seven years a member may be permitted by the council to make a lifelong vow. The Order divests itself of all its money each summer, least it becomes rich and proclaims that the 'only revolution from which good can result, is the Gandhian revolution'.

In 1960 the Ark opened sites that conscientious objectors refusing to serve in Algeria could come to and do community service and be supported in the

[177] Oliver and Cris Popenoe, *Seeds of Tomorrow: New Age Communities that Work* (San Francisco: Harper and Rowe, 1984), p. 142.
[178] 'Publisher's Introduction', *Return to the Source*, p. 14.
[179] Mahadevan, *Truth and Nonviolence*, pp. 287–288.
[180] On 'coresponsibility' see Mark Shepard, *The Community of the Ark* (Arcata, CA.: Simple Productions, 1990), pp. 29–30.
[181] Mahadevan, *Truth and Nonviolence*, p. 289.
[182] 'Publisher's Introduction', *Return to the Source*, p. 10.

event of arrest by volunteers all claiming to be the wanted person, so that rather than arresting the offender, police were forced to arrest half a dozen people.[183] Lanza del Vasto himself has undertaken several fasts as part of his nonviolent protests – both as a means of self-purification in preparation for action and as a way of forcing an opponent to 'think more deeply'.[184] He fasted with Danilo Dolci in 1956, for twenty-one days against French torture in Algeria; in 1957 for forty days in Rome in personal penance for the sake of assisting the Second Vatican Council;[185] and in 1971 his fast inspired the protest by French peasant farmers against the expansion of a military base. That protest, which used a wide variety of nonviolent actions and linked the farmers' struggle to the causes of antimilitarism, labour and the Third World, has been lauded as 'the first large, sustained, intentional campaign of nonviolent struggle in France'.[186] Early tactics included dumping manure in front of the house of the pro-extension mayor, but following a two week fast by Vasto the local farmers were convinced to choose nonviolent action over violent or constitutional methods. From 1972 protests included the grazing of sheep under the Eiffel Tower, a rally by 100,000 people harvesting wheat for the starving in Africa, sit-ins and blockades. Unused farms that had been purchased by the military were occupied, town halls were invaded, a military camp raided and its files destroyed. Military manoeuvres were disrupted, meetings with government representatives were boycotted, 'reverse strikes' of illegal constructive and cultivation work were carried out, army lands were illegally ploughed, and after ten years of struggle the Save Larzac movement won a total victory with the abandonment of the military expansion project.

Regardless of the nonviolent activism conducted by members of the Ark, its primary function is to be an ashram in the Gandhian mould. According to Shantidas:

Much more than going into the streets, distributing tracts, speaking to crowds, knocking on doors, leading walks and campaigns, invading bomb factories, undertaking public fasts, braving the police, being beaten and jailed . . . the most efficient action and the most significant testimony in favor of nonviolence and truth is living:

---

[183] *Ibid.*, p. 13.   [184] Hope and Young, *The Struggle for Humanity*, p. 59.

[185] Lanza del Vasto, *Warriors of Peace*, pp 165–73. A staunch Catholic, Lanza del Vasto wrote to the Pope during Vatican II about the threat of nuclear war and in longing for 'the message of peace the world needs today, the bold, absolute, in short, the evangelical word' and fasted prayerfully. His hopes were answered when, through his wife, he was sent an advance copy of the Papal encyclical *Pacem in Terris*, which contained statements that 'have never been said, pages that might have been signed by your husband', p. 170.

[186] See Brad Bennet, 'Larzac (France), 1971–1981', Powers and Vogele, *Protest, Power, and Change*, p. 301; and Roger Rawlinson, *Larzac–A Victory for Nonviolence* (London: Quaker Peace and Service, 1983).

living a life that is one,[187] where everything goes in the same sense, from prayer and meditation to laboring for our daily bread, from teaching of the doctrine to the making of manure, from cooking to singing and dancing around the fire; living a life in which there is no violence or unfairness, neither hidden violence nor brutal violence; neither legal and permitted unfairness, nor illegal unfairness. What matters is to show that such a life is possible and even not more difficult than a life of gain, nor more unpleasant than a life of pleasure, nor less natural than an 'ordinary' life. What matters is to find the nonviolent answer to all the questions man is faced with today, as at all epochs, to formulate the answer clearly and do our utmost to carry it into effect. What matters is to discover whether there is such a thing as a nonviolent economy, free of all forms of pressure and closed to all forms of unfairness; whether there is such a thing as nonviolent authority, independent of force and carrying no privileges; whether there is such a thing as nonviolent justice, justice without punishment, and punishment without violence; such things as nonviolent farming, nonviolent medicine, nonviolent psychiatry, nonviolent diet.[188]

Shantidas, Gandhi's first 'heir in the West', died on 5 January 1981 while visiting a branch community of the Ark in Murcia in southern Spain. He is buried at La Borie Noble.

SUNDERLAL BAHUGUNA — AND SAVING THE HIMALAYAS

In the 1980s and 1990s much was published on women's movements, people's movements and environmental movements and often in this literature there was mention of the Indian women-dominated environmental tree-hugging Chipko movement. This movement had a long and intricate genesis that involved colonial practices, hardship in the Himalayan villages of the headwaters of the Ganges, particularly for women, and communist agitation. However, to a large degree the celebrated movement grew out of years of work by dedicated Gandhian workers, and in particular by Sunderlal Bahuguna.

In the early 1970s India experienced the large-scale emergence of 'action groups', usually led by radicalised, often JP inspired, middle-class youth or urban intellectuals. Primarily non-political in the narrow sense, these groups were concerned with local injustices and they engaged in direct

---

[187] Elsewhere he notes that the great lesson Gandhi gave him was essentially 'the unity of life'. He clarifies this by pointing out the western habit of seeing things in terms of opposing concepts, as dualities, had to be eliminated. 'To reach unity, one must start from inward unity', and therefore the definition of truth should be 'The outside as the inside . . . to live and be in truth means that our appearances and our actions should correspond to what we have within us.' Mahadevan, *Truth and Nonviolence*, pp. 284, 184, 60.

[188] Lanza del Vasto, *Warriors of Peace*, pp. 48–9.

action to protest against the social evils that occurred around them. The Chipko movement is perhaps India's most celebrated action group. The BBC has made a documentary about Chipko,[189] and India's *The Illustrated Weekly* has included the advent of the movement in its list of 'The Ten Most Momentous Events Since India Won Freedom' (along with the assassination of Gandhi, the liberation of Bangladesh, the lifting of Mrs Gandhi's Emergency) and its two leading lights, Sunderlal Bahuguna and Chandi Prasad Bhatt, in its list of 'Fifty Indians Who Matter.'[190]

The term 'Chipko', loosely translated, is Hindi for 'hug', and the movement that originated in the Uttarkhand Himalayas was dedicated to saving trees, by hugging them if necessary, upon the arrival of axemen. The movement was a decentralised reaction to threatening circumstances, sometimes guided by Gandhian sarvodaya workers and sometimes arising spontaneously. To a large degree the movement was one by illiterate hill women who were protesting the only way they knew against the fact that, as forests disappear, they had to go ever further to collect fuel for cooking fires and fodder leaves for their animals.

Of course the emergence of Chipko is not without context. There had been a long history of forest activism in the Garhwal hills stemming from the curtailment of established local rights after the start of commercial logging in the middle of the nineteenth century.[191] Gandhi's Civil Disobedience campaign of 1930 manifested itself as the Forest Satyagraha in the area, and the Chipko leadership, rather than being composed of youthful urban radicals, was made up of local middle-aged Gandhians who came from a long history of struggle against the forest laws. They could inspire the impoverished locals who had little employment opportunities, yet saw their only immediately available exploitable resource – the forests – being utilised exclusively by outsiders. And beside the forest actions of the independence struggle, there was also a strong Gandhian heritage in the area in the guise of two of the Mahatma's most renowned European women followers, Mirabehn and Sarala Devi (Catherine Mary Heilman) who had made their homes there.[192] They saw what was happening to the locals and to the environment. Young sarvodaya workers, inspired by Gandhi to work with the people and *among* the people, were also active in the region. The

---

[189] *Axing the Himalayas*, made by Richard Taylor for the BBC *The World Around Us* series in 1981.
[190] *The Illustrated Weekly*, 26 May 1985.
[191] See Ramachandra Guha, *The Unquiet Woods: Ecological Change and Peasant Resistance in the Himalaya* (Berkeley: University of California Press, 1989).
[192] See Mira Behn, 'Something Wrong in the Himalaya', Chipko Information Centre, *Save Himalaya*, pamphlet (Silyara, n.d)., pp. 5–10; and Sunderlal Bahuguna, 'Gandhi's Betis', Chipko Information Centre, *Save Himalaya*, pp. 1–4.

Gandhian matriarchs further inspired them. These workers at first strove to achieve economic self-sufficiency for the local people and eventually, after extensively touring the area and appraising the overall situation first-hand, made the connection between deforestation and poverty, between environmental despoliation and the floods and landslides that threatened not only the hill villages but which also wreaked havoc on the plains below. When these various threads came together, the call to hug trees was given and Chipko was born.

While to some Chipko is primarily a peasant resistance movement that has had communist and Gandhian influence[193] for others it is primarily a Gandhian movement.[194] To the degree that the movement has had leaders, there is debate about who the 'father' of the Chipko movement is. For some it is Chandi Prasad Bhatt and his Dashauli Gram Swarajya Sangh (Daushauli district village Self-Rule Society around the town of Gopeshwar),[195] while for others it is Sunderlal Bahuguna.[196] Chandi Prasad Bhatt was the leading figure in the most celebrated early Chipko actions: the one that first gave the call to hug the trees during the protest against the granting of trees from the Mandal forest to the Simon Company to make sporting goods in mid 1973; and the one to save thousands of trees in the Reni forest in early 1974. Sunderlal Bahuguna was the leading sarvodaya worker in the region, he was the inspiration for Bhatt and assumed the role of the messenger of Chipko, walking from village to village spreading the message of conservation and nonviolence. While Bhatt was a tireless local worker, Bahuguna assumed the position of overall leadership. Shiva and Bandhyopadhyay sum up the relationship by pointing out that Bahuguna 'has not been a "grass-roots activist" in the narrow sense of the term though he has created grass-roots activists in all parts of the country. Bhatt, who himself is the best example of such activists generated by Bahuguna, on the other hand, believes in concentrating on his region of influence and working towards consolidation.'[197]

[193] See Guha, *The Unquiet Woods*.

[194] See Thomas Weber, *Hugging the Trees The Story of the Chipko Movement* (New Delhi: Penguin, 1989); and J. Bandyopadhyay and Vandana Shiva, 'Chipko', *Seminar* (February 1987), pp. 33–8.

[195] See Shepard, *Gandhi Today*, pp. 63–80; and Anupam Mishra and Satyendra Tripathi, *Chipko Movement: Uttarkhand Women's bid to save forest wealth* (New Delhi: People's Action for Development with Justice, 1978).

[196] See Weber, *Hugging the Trees*; and Jayanta Bandyopadhyay and Vandana Shiva, 'Chipko: Rekindling India's Forest Culture', *The Ecologist* 17 (1987), pp. 26–34.

[197] Vandana Shiva and Jayanto Bandhyopadhyay, *Chipko: India's Civilisational Response to the Forest Crisis*, pamphlet (New Delhi: The Indian National Trust for Art and Cultural Heritage, 1986), pp. 9–20. For a detailed account of the battle for 'ownership' of Chipko by the leading figures and partisan academics and supporters, see Manisha Aryal, 'Axing Chipko', *Himal* 7 (1994), pp. 8–23.

In 1915, soon after his return to India from South Africa, Gandhi visited Rishikesh, where the Ganges flows from the mountains to the plains. He remarked that he was 'charmed with the natural scenery' and 'bowed my head in reverence to our ancestors for their sense of the beautiful in Nature, and for their foresight in investing beautiful manifestations of nature with a religious significance'.[198] As many devout Hindus do, he also often referred to the Himalayas as a possible place for retirement if he was ever to turn his back on the hurly-burly of political life or become convinced that he could find self-realisation apart from the masses. However, he never actually penetrated into the Himalayas proper. His disciples Mirabehn and Sarala Devi did.

Mirabehn, the British admiral's daughter who became Gandhi's most famous western disciple, experienced physical symptoms when she was away from Gandhi. Nevertheless, following her release from her imprisonment with her master during the Quit India campaign, she found that the 'Himalayas were calling'.[199] She lived in various places in sight of the great mountains doing khadi and cattle development work until, in 1950, she finally moved into the mountains proper, twenty-five miles beyond the town of Tehri, where she set up an ashram in the midst of a pine forest and commenced her investigation of the forest problem. Before her return to Europe in 1959, she wrote an insightful article under the title 'Something Wrong in the Himalaya', on the connection between the decline in forest health and floods on the plains, for the *Hindustan Times*. She was to be an inspiration for the youthful Sunderlal Bahuguna.

Sarala Devi was born to German parents in London in 1901. She went to India to teach in a school in Udaipur in 1928 and in 1936 she joined Gandhi at Sevagram to assist with his experiments in basic education. The climate was excessively hot and so, in 1941, Gandhi sent her into the Kumaon hills. During the Quit India campaign, both before and after her imprisonment, she went from village to village working with the families of political prisoners. As a result of these experiences she came to admire the strength of the hill women and after Independence she decided to settle among them. She established the Lakshmi Ashram in Kausani for the education of hill girls along Gandhian lines and soon she had collected a band of dedicated young women social workers around her. Her disciples brought a new awakening to the hill people, especially the women, through their campaigning for prohibition. One of these disciples was Vimla Nautial who, after working in Vinoba's Bhoodan movement in Bihar, later married

[198] Gandhi, *An Autobiography*, p. 328.   [199] Mira Behn, *The Spirit's Pilgrimage*, p. 259.

Sunderlal Bahuguna. Saralabehn strove to create environmental awareness by publishing numerous articles and books on ecological problems, and founded societies for the uplift of the local population and environmental protection.

Bahuguna was born in the village of Marava in the princely state of Tehri Garhwal in 1927.[200] His father was a forest officer and he grew up surrounded by the beauty of the mountains and the river Ganges which flowed close to his childhood home. His father died young and his mother had to work hard to provide for the family. This helped him see difficulties experienced by mountain women. In 1940, at the age of thirteen, he came into contact with the well-known local Gandhian freedom fighter Sri Dev Suman. Through Suman he became familiar with Gandhian literature and Gandhi's campaigns and philosophy. Suman led movements against the British and the oppressive regime in Tehri Garhwal. He was imprisoned in 1944 and died in jail following a lengthy fast. Against the wishes of his family, the association with Suman led Bahuguna and other like-minded friends to participate in activities relating to the nationalist movement. At age seventeen it put Bahuguna in prison for almost five months. On his release for medical reasons, he was placed on a police watch list. At age eighteen, he decided to go to Lahore where, in a colourful period that included poverty, excellent grades, police harassment, tutoring a wealthy landlord's children in a village, and the serious study of Gandhi's writings, he completed his Bachelor of Arts degree.

In 1947 Bahuguna returned to his mountain home but the authorities refused the known troublemaker entry to Tehri, so, in protest, he commenced the first of several fasts he would conduct during his life. He entered politics on a full-time basis and soon he was general secretary of the Tehri branch of the Congress party. He was sent to Delhi to publicise the freedom struggle in Garhwal and during this time he made invaluable media contacts. For the rest of his life a major source of his income would be provided by his journalism.

When he returned to the hills, Bahuguna often visited Mirabehn and helped with Hindi translation for her autobiography. Under her inspiration, and the inspiration of Thakkar Bapa, one of Gandhi's chief lieutenants in anti-untouchability work, Bahuguna turned his interests towards constructive work. He set up the Thakkar Bapa Hostel for poor students catering

---

[200] The material on Bahuguna's life comes from Weber, *Hugging the Trees*, pp. 33–8; Bharat Dogra, *Living for Others: Vimla and Sunderlal Bahuguna* (New Delhi: Bharat Dogra, 1993); Harris, *Gandhians in Contemporary India*, pp. 266–72; and interviews with Sunderlal Bahuguna and various newspaper articles by him.

especially to the needs of 'untouchables' who were forced to eat separately in college and school hostels. Although high caste, he lived in the hostel and played a leading part in securing entry to important temples for those at the bottom of the Hindu social order. His work for Harijan uplift and rural reconstruction also brought him into close contact with Sarlabehn. His political activities continued until 1956 when he married Vimla Nautial. She persuaded him to heed Gandhi's last wish and leave party politics to work directly with the rural poor. After his marriage, he travelled to Kashmir to seek Mirabehn's advice and the elderly Gandhian sketched the original plan for Bahuguna's Navjivan ('New Life') Ashram which was eventually to double as the Chipko Information Centre. The ashram was sited on a ridge just above the remote Garhwal hill village of Silyara, close to where Mirabehn had lived.

Cultivatable land on the slopes was limited and the hill population was growing rapidly. Under-employment and poverty were rife and most of the villagers were landless or only marginal landholders. In order to achieve economic uplift for the poor, Bahuguna started a school at his ashram and various cooperatives were formed, for example to secure road-building work for the locals. Even though he was now a sarvodaya leader, he retained the skills of a politician and could stir crowds to action and explain complex issues to simple isolated villagers, which he did during his incessant travelling. In 1960, with the Bhoodan movement in full swing, Vinoba asked him to take the message of gram swaraj to the Himalayan communities. Following Vinoba's instructions, Bahuguna and a group of others walked, village to village, from the borders of Himachal Pradesh to those of Nepal. During this period, Bahuguna inspired other idealistic youth, including Bhatt, a booking clerk for a transport company in Joshimath, to take up sarvodaya work and later to establish local industries. Vimla stayed behind in Silyara and continued the work of the ashram and ashram school.

In 1963, after seeing many deforested hills on his tours, Bahuguna penned an article for the *Hindustan* pointing out that the environmental condition of the Himalayas could lead to floods on the plains. In time his activities became more closely tied to the questions concerning the use of the forests. In 1968 a memorial was erected to the seventeen people killed by the army of the ruler of Tehri Garhwal state in 1930 when they protested against the forest policies. The day of the massacre, 30 May, was declared Forest Day. On the following Forest Day, Vinoba's representative, D. K. Gupta, visited the site and during the ceremony Bahuguna and other activists took a pledge to protect the forests. A manifesto was issued and its message was taken by sarvodaya workers from village to village to raise awareness of the local inhabitants. The manifesto read:

Since time immemorial, forests have remained the socio-economic basis of our lives. Protection of trees is our main duty and we solicit our birthright to get our basic needs and employment in forests and forest products. To maintain a loving relationship with forests, the basis of our happiness, it is essential that the treasure of the forests be used primarily for the needs of the inhabitants of the region. For this the material used in village industry and other daily needs should be made available to common-folk and small industries should be set up in the vicinity of forests for the processing of raw materials obtained there. Cooperative societies of forest labourers should be established and the [outside] contractor system should be done away with.[201]

Regardless of this, during the years between 1965 and 1971, Bahuguna, his wife and other Uttarkhand sarvodaya workers dedicated themselves to the uplift of the hill women and to combat drunkenness. By 1971, five out of eight districts in Uttarkhand had been declared 'dry'. The experiences of these years allowed the Bahugunas to see the condition of the people and the environment at first hand. It gave them the necessary background to be able to undertake the work that would soon be required of them and taught them about the power of people to solve their own problems.

In 1964, Bhatt had set up the Daushali Gram Swarajya Sangh to start village industries based on the natural resources of the forests. Vested interests and corrupt officials conspired with the administration to cripple the industries and by 1971 this led to widespread dissatisfaction and demonstrations against discriminatory policies. Bahuguna toured the countryside explaining the injustices while the frustrated Bhatt, with the DGSS resin turpentine plant idle for eight months because of a lack of allocation of raw material, visited the state capital Lucknow and Delhi with the grievances of the people. Bahuguna's many contacts and experience as a publicist and journalist opened doors to the world of mass media. In November 1972, two large daily newspapers carried reports of the work of DGSS and the hardships it faced as a result of vested commercial interests and a discriminatory forest policy.

A campaign of demonstrations was launched. On the site of the 1930 martyrdom, a rally was held on 11 December 1972. Sarvodaya workers explained the exploitative situation with regard to the forest and its produce to the villagers. Demonstrations at Uttarkashi and Gopeshwar followed. The movement was now consciously being taken to the masses in the

---

[201] Quoted in Weber, *Hugging the Trees*, p. 34.

Garhwal region. The organisational base of the future Chipko movement had been established by these actions and its rapid spread was ensured by the grass-roots efforts of the sarvodaya activists led by Bahuguna, and the public awareness that developed as a consequence.

Between 1973 and 1975, Bahuguna walked more than 2,600 miles to observe the problems of deforestation and other related environmental issues. In 1972 and 1979 he undertook lengthy fasts to stop tree felling and force a change in the commercial forest policy. In 1981, to a large degree because of his activities, the government, under the direction of Prime Minister Indira Gandhi, instituted a ban on felling of green trees above 1,000 metres and on slopes greater than thirty degrees. Between 1981 and 1983 Bahuguna walked the length of the Himalayas, from Srinagar in Kashmir to Kohima in Nagaland, over 3,000 miles, to raise ecological awareness among the people. His consciousness-raising foot marches have inspired many in India and as a result Chipko-like movements have commenced in Karnataka (Appiko) and Rajasthan (Save Aravlli).

As the celebrated period of Chipko activism wound down with the cessation of logging in the Ganges headwaters, Bahuguna's growing environmental awareness expanded his environmental and philosophical horizons. Environmental problems were no longer merely local – the entire Himalayan area was under threat, and indeed mountain areas in many places throughout the world. A new conservationist ethic had to be achieved and Bahuguna took up another crusade. He came to the conclusion that it was not enough to fight for trees to be made available to meet the needs of local forest industries, but because the ecological crisis was so great, trees had to be protected from *all* commercial felling. For him the motto changed from 'no trees are to be cut until the needs of locals are met' to 'save trees to save mankind'. Bahuguna found a supportive theoretical framework for his shift in thinking in the Gandhian view of rural self-sufficiency where villagers lived a non-exploitative simple life in harmony with their surroundings.

Perhaps another turning point in Bahuguna's life came with his meeting with Richard St Barbe Baker, the famed 'Man of the Trees' in Delhi during a vegetarian congress in 1977. At this stage, to many Bahuguna was seen as an enemy of science, someone who was blocking progress. St Barbe Baker's uncompromising patronage did much to firm Bahuguna's ecological views, not least by introducing him to the works of E. F. Schumacher, and give them added credibility.[202] Bahuguna went on to become a major

---

[202] St Barbe Baker, one of the founders of the World Forestry Congress, complained to Bahuguna that he was not allowed to screen Schumacher's film *On the Edge of the Forest* at the eighth Congress

environmental figure on the world stage. He has travelled extensively taking his environmental message to forums where he could get a hearing and has been honoured with countless international awards (including the Right Livelihood Award in 1987). He preached a message that states quite simply that the earth can no longer support our desires for luxury. We must learn to do without, to lead simple and dignified lives. The formula he set out to achieve this is what he called the three As – austerity (people cannot go on the way they have been, as so-called development leads to pollution and environmental degradation), alternatives and afforestation. He deliberately places austerity at the head of the list but, because of its unpleasant con- notation for most people, effort, he claims, is put into afforestation, which will never be enough to ensure a permanent economy.

Bahuguna has not been shy in saying that what the Indian cities are doing the Himalayas, the wealthy North is doing to the impoverished South:

Affluence of the industrial world is based on plundering *our* resources. The Third World, which is basically in the tropics, today exports large quantities of hardwood to the three markets of Japan, America and Europe. In 1950, the tropics exported a mere 4.2 million cubic metres. In 1980, we exported 66 million cubic metres. Switzerland has its own forests, but for *coffins* they import wood from Africa! That is impossible. It is also unethical.[203]

After much fame and attention, both national and international, dur- ing the 1990s and early years of the new century, the aging Bahuguna has camped on the banks of the Ganges 'accepting loneliness and even ridicule',[204] as well as imprisonment in his protest against the construction of the massive Tehri dam in an area of high seismic activity. During this, his last major satyagraha campaign, from his camp by the side of the submerg- ing town, he has kept pressure on the government by undertaking several lengthy fasts.

ARNE NÆSS, JOHAN GALTUNG, E. F. SCHUMACHER
AND GENE SHARP

In the 'Gandhi Influenced' part of this book, the main chapters looked at four people who were instrumental in the movement of Gandhi to new

in Jakarta in 1979 because the organisers considered it too one-sided. He commented that 'What I could not say in 45 years, Schumacher has said in 45 minutes.' Bahuguna took to screening the film as part of his programme.
[203] Interview in *The Illustrated Weekly*, 23 June 1985, pp. 42–5 at p. 44.
[204] Dogra, *Living for Others*, p. 22.

physical locations to go with his new understandings. In the four substantive chapters that follow, I will examine movements of a different sort. I will investigate Gandhi's influence on significant bodies of knowledge that, in the relatively recent past, have gained popularity in the West to the point that they changed the directions of thought and have been instrumental in encouraging important social movements. In short, through the chosen examples I am not only looking at Gandhi's influence, but also his relevance. I will survey the new environmentalism in the form of deep ecology, the discipline of peace research that is now concerned with far more than the prevention of war, the branch of people-centered economics that has come to be known as 'Buddhist economics', and the brand of political activism that is known as nonviolent direct action. I will do this by investigating the Mahatma's contribution to the intellectual development of the leading figures in these fields: Arne Næss, Johan Galtung, E. F. Schumacher and Gene Sharp.

While there is no shortage of writings on Gandhi or Gandhian philosophy, attention to his influence on, or relevance to, fields of knowledge or praxis other than nonviolent political activism has been scant. Many environmental activists who claim that 'deep ecology' is their guiding philosophy have barely heard the name of Arne Næss, who coined the term. While Næss readily admits his debt to Gandhi, works about him tend to gloss over this connection or ignore it. For example, the chapter on deep ecology in Merchant's book about 'radical ecology'[205] contains a long list of its supposed sources, including the debt owed to interpreters of eastern philosophy such as Alan Watts, Daisetz Suzuki and Gary Snyder, without even mentioning Gandhi. The deep ecology of Næss not only talks of a personal identification with nature but of self-realization being dependent on it. For those who know Gandhian philosophy well, this line of reasoning is readily recognised. However, Næss' writings on Gandhi are not particularly well known and Gandhi's influence on him has not received due recognition.

Peace research is a diverse field and Gandhi's influence has only touched certain areas of it. While he is generally not mentioned, and potential causal links rarely investigated, the literature on conflict resolution is commonly quite 'Gandhian' in its approach.[206] In much of the international relations, defence, security, ethnic conflict and related peace areas the possible

---

[205] Carolyn Merchant, *Radical Ecology: The Search for a Livable World* (New York: Routledge, 1992), p. 88.

[206] See Thomas Weber, 'Gandhian Philosophy, Conflict Resolution Theory and Practical Approaches to Negotiation', *Journal of Peace Research* 38 (2001), pp. 493–513.

relevance of Gandhian philosophy is generally not even an issue considered worthy of investigation. Nevertheless, as modern peace research is not understandable without Galtung's contribution, so Galtung's work in the area is not understandable without a knowledge of Gandhi's contribution to his thought.

Unlike the works of Næss and Galtung, Schumacher's writings have made it onto popular best-seller lists. The Gandhian connection, at least at a superficial level, was also originally more explicit. However, Schumacher's 'small is beautiful' philosophy eventually came to be known as 'Buddhist economics' and gradually the links with Gandhi took a back seat. His concern for Third World poverty lead to the formation of the Intermediate Technology Group which aims to develop tools and work methods that are appropriate to the people using them. While this practical work can only be lauded, its philosophical underpinning should also be remembered.

Of the Gandhi-influenced thinkers examined in detail here, Galtung and Gene Sharp are the ones who started their life's work by directly studying Gandhi. However, in the case of Sharp, Gandhi did not merely influence his view of the area he was working in, Gandhi was the area. Although Gandhi is acknowledged as the leading figure in nonviolent activism, it must be remembered that what he and Gene Sharp, the current leading theorist of nonviolent direct action, have had to say are quite different although they come from the same root. This difference is interesting because of the four, Sharp, the one initially most steeped in Gandhi, is the one who has deliberately distanced himself from this influence. With Næss, Galtung and Schumacher, the current of Gandhian thought has flowed freely, while in the case of Sharp Gandhi has almost been totally expunged.

In short, those who want to have a better understanding of deep ecology, peace research, Buddhist economics or nonviolent activism, and more particularly, those who are interested in the philosophy of Næss, Galtung, Schumacher or Sharp, need to go back to Gandhi for a fuller picture. And by reading these authors we can get a better view of the whole, not merely the politician, Gandhi – get a glimpse of what it was about his life or thought that others took as being fundamentally important and where his influence been most relevant after his death.

CHAPTER 9

Arne Næss – the ecological movement finds depth

INTRODUCTION

Arne Næss was born in 1912 and at the age of twenty-seven was appointed to the Chair of Philosophy at the University of Oslo as the country's youngest professor, a job he held until 1969 when he retired to devote himself full-time to remedying the environmental problems he perceived. In between, he was part of the Norwegian resistance movement against Nazi occupation and took part in the first ascent of Tirich Mir, the highest peak (at 7,690 metres) in the Hindu Kush, as part of the Norwegian team in July 1950. The American academic philosopher and leading ecological thinker, George Sessions has stated that he is confident that when Næss' philosophical works are finally gathered together, 'he will be recognised as a leading philosopher of the latter half of the twentieth century', and more than this, 'For his work in developing an ecological philosophy and paradigm, and by articulating and helping to launch the long-range deep ecology movement, he may well be recognized as one of the most important philosophers of the 20th century.'[1]

Although a conservation ethic had been around for decades before the publication of books such as Rachel Carson's landmark *Silent Spring* and studies such as the Club of Rome's *Limits to Growth*,[2] Arne Næss took environmental philosophy and activism into new areas with his call for a 'deep ecology'. This concept has provided the framework for a wide variety of ecological movements from those of spiritual New Agers to radical tree spikers.

In 1973 the summary of a lecture given the year before in Bucharest at the World Future Research Conference by the Norwegian philosopher

---

[1] George Sessions, 'Arne Naess and the Union of Theory and Practice', in Alan Drengson and Yuich Inoue (eds.), *The Deep Ecology Movement: An Introductory Anthology* (Berkeley: North Atlantic Books, 1995), pp. 54–63, at p. 63.
[2] See Roderick Nash, *The Rights of Nature: A History of Environmental Ethics* (Madison, WI: University of Wisconsin Press, 1989).

was published in the English language Norwegian philosophical journal *Inquiry*. That short paper, 'The Shallow and the Deep, Long-Range Ecology Movement. A Summary',[3] was to take on paradigm-shifting proportions. It introduced us to a terminology that has since become commonplace. And 'like any genuinely subversive philosophy [it] has inspired a movement and a wide following from politicians to poets'.[4]

This paper points out that a shallow but influential ecological movement and a deep but less influential one compete for our attention. Arne Næss characterises the 'shallow' ecological movement as one that fights pollution and resource depletion in order to preserve human health and affluence while the 'deep' ecological movement operates out of a deep-seated respect and even veneration for ways and forms of life, and accords them an 'equal right to live and blossom'.[5]

In a later elaboration, he puts the contrast between the two in its most stark form: shallow ecology sees that 'natural diversity is valuable as a resource for us', noting that 'it is nonsense to talk about value except as value for mankind', and adds that in this formulation 'plant species should be saved because of their value as genetic reserves for human agriculture and medicine'. On the other hand, deep ecology sees that 'natural diversity has its own (intrinsic) value', and notes that 'equating value with value for humans reveals a racial prejudice', and adds that 'plant species should be saved because of their intrinsic value'.[6]

During a camping trip in California's Death Valley in 1984, Næss and George Sessions jointly formulated a set of eight basic principles[7] which they presented as a minimum description of the general features of the deep ecology movement: the 'well being and flourishing' of human and nonhuman life have intrinsic value;[8] the richness and diversity of life forms contribute to the realisation of these values and are therefore also intrinsic

---

[3] Arne Naess, 'The Shallow and the Deep, Long-Range Ecology Movement. A Summary', *Inquiry* 16 (1973), pp. 95–100.

[4] 'Preface' to Nina Witoszek and Andrew Brennan (eds.), *Philosophical Dialogues: Arne Næss and the Progress of Ecophilosophy* (Lanham, MD: Rowman and Littlefield, 1999), p. xv.

[5] More recently Næss has substituted the term 'same rights' for 'equal rights', explaining that this provides less opportunity for misinterpretation – after all a parent has a duty to protect a child, for example from a poisonous insect, even if he or she risks killing the insect (personal communication, 27 January 1998).

[6] Arne Naess, 'Identification as a Source of Deep Ecological Attitudes', in Michael Tobias (ed.), *Deep Ecology* (San Diego: Avant Books, 1984), p. 257.

[7] Arne Naess and George Sessions, 'Platform Principles of the Deep Ecology Movement', in Bill Devall and George Sessions, *Deep Ecology: Living as if Nature Mattered* (Salt Lake City, UT: Gibbs Smith, 1985), pp. 69–70.

[8] Næss now prefers: 'every living being has intrinsic value; the well being and flourishing of human and nonhuman beings have intrinsic value' (personal communication, 27 January 1998).

values; humans have no right to reduce this richness or diversity except where it is necessary to satisfy vital needs; the flourishing of human life and culture is compatible with a large decrease in human population and a flourishing of nonhuman life requires it;[9] human interference with nature is excessive and increasing; therefore, economic, technological and ideological policies must change, this ideological change will mean an appreciation of the quality of life rather than the standard of living; and those who subscribe to these points 'have an obligation directly or indirectly to try to implement the necessary changes'.

THE INFLUENCE OF GANDHI

Næss' father died when he was only one year old and he never really formed a close bond with his mother and consequently 'Feeling apart in many human relations, I identified with "nature".'[10] While he grew up in Oslo he often holidayed at the family's mountain cottage:

From about the age of eight a definite mountain became for me a symbol of benevolent, equiminded, strong 'father', or of an ideal human nature. These characteristics were there in spite of the obvious fact that the mountain, with its slippery stones, icy fog and dangerous precipices, did not protect me or care for me in any trivial sense. It required me to show respect and take care. The mountain loved me but in a way similar to that of my 10- and 11-years older brothers who were eager to toughen me up.[11]

He tells the story of walking in the highest mountains of Norway at age fifteen. He was stopped by a snow drift with nowhere to sleep. Finally he came across a very old man and stayed with him for a week in a mountaineering cottage. They talked about nature and the old man played the violin. 'The effect of this week established my conviction of an inner relation between mountains and mountain people, a certain greatness, cleanness, a concentration upon what is essential, a self-sufficiency; and consequently a disregard of luxury, of complicated means of all kinds.'[12]

---

[9] Næss now prefers: 'The flourishing of human life and cultures is compatible with a substantially smaller human population. The flourishing of nonhuman life would gain from the presence of a substantially smaller one' Arne Næss 'Comments on Guha's "Radical American Environmentalism and Wilderness Preservation: A Third World Critique"', in Witoszek and Brennan, *Philosophical Dialogues*, footnote 3 on p. 333.

[10] Arne Naess, 'How My Philosophy Seemed to Develop', in Andre Mercier and Maja Svilar (eds.), *Philosophers on their Own Work* (Bern: Peter Lang, 1982), vol. X, p. 210.

[11] Naess, 'How My Philosophy Seemed to Develop', pp. 212–13.

[12] Arne Naess, 'Modesty and the Conquest of Mountains', in Michael Tobias (ed.), *The Mountain Spirit* (New York: Overlook, 1979), p. 14.

When he was twenty-six he built a hut for himself on his favourite mountain. This, the highest private dwelling in the country, he called Tvergastein, after the name used for the quartz crystals found in the area. Throughout his life he has spent as much time as he could, living as simply as possible, in the splendid isolation of his hut.

The rugged Norwegian countryside, with its small population and rural culture, was an early formative factor,[13] and of course he was the product of a long Norwegian nature tradition with its own particular cognitive–ethical fabric.[14] As a philosopher he researched and was influenced by Spinoza[15] who maintained a spiritual vision of the unity and sacredness of nature and believed that the highest level of knowledge was an intuitive and mystical kind of knowing where subject/object distinctions disappeared as the mind united with the whole of nature.[16] However, as important as those inputs were, they are not the only ones.

In a now famous debate, that predated deep ecology, with the English philosopher Alfred Ayer on Dutch television in 1971, Næss spelled out his view of what, for him, it means to be a philosopher: 'I consider myself a philosopher when I am trying to convince people of nonviolence, consistent nonviolence whatever happens.' He continued:

I think I believe in the ultimate unity of all living beings. This is a very vague and ambiguous phrase, but I have to rely on it. It is a task for analytical philosophy to suggest more precise formulations. Because I have such principles, I also have a program of action, the main outline of which is part of my philosophy. So I might suddenly try to win you over to consistent nonviolence and to persuade you to join some kind of movement – and this in spite of my not believing that I possess any guarantee that I have found my truths.[17]

Later on, to push Næss to greater clarity on this, the moderator asked, 'Does your offensive nonviolence . . . imply that you would prefer to be killed by someone else rather than kill someone else?' Næss answered:

It would be more than a preference, actually. It might be that I would prefer to kill the other person, but I value the preference negatively. Norms have to do

---

[13] See the introductory chapter to Peter Reed and David Rothenberg (eds.), *Wisdom in the Open Air: The Norwegian Roots of Deep Ecology* (Minneapolis: University of Minnesota Press, 1993).

[14] See Nina Witoszek, 'Arne Næss and the Norwegian Nature Tradition', in Witoszek and Brennan, *Philosophical Dialogues*, pp. 451–65.

[15] David Rothenberg, *Is it Painful to Think?: Conversations with Arne Naess father of deep ecology* (Sydney: Allen and Unwin, 1993), pp. 91–101.

[16] See Arne Naess, 'Environmental Ethics and Spinoza's Ethics: Comments on Genevieve Lloyd's Article', *Inquiry*, 23 (1980), pp. 313–25; and Peder Anker, 'Ecosophy: An Outline of its Megaethics', *The Trumpeter* 15 (1998), available at http://trumpeter.athabascau.ca/contents/v15.1/anker.html

[17] Arne Næss, Alfred Ayer and Fons Elders, 'The Glass Is on the Table: The Empiricist versus Total View', quoted in Witoszek and Brennan, *Philosophical Dialogues*, p. 14.

with evaluations, with pretensions to objectivity, rather than preferences. Let me formulate it thus: I hope I would prefer to be killed by someone else rather than to kill, and I ought to prefer it.[18]

While the references at this point are implicit, nevertheless here we have the advaitist (non-dualist) philosopher acting in the world.

This attempt to give deep ecology a legitimising lineage by linking it to eastern spiritual traditions is frowned upon by some critics. The Indian environmentalist scholar Ramchandra Guha, for example, objects to the 'persistent invocation of Eastern philosophies' as being the forerunners of deep ecology. Guha points out that philosophies which are 'complex and internally differentiated' are lumped together in a way that makes them spiritual precursors of deep ecology. Further, he complains that the 'intensely political, pragmatic, and Christian influenced thinker . . . Gandhi has been accorded a wholly undeserved place in the deep ecological pantheon'.[19]

Gandhi may not deserve a place in the deep ecological pantheon in terms of Guha's objections, however through Gandhi's strong influence on Arne Næss, the 'father of deep ecology', there is a direct link between the Mahatma and the movement. In fact Næss himself admits in a brief third person account of his philosophy that 'his work on the philosophy of ecology, or *ecosophy*,[20] developed out of his work on Spinoza and Gandhi and his relationship with the mountains of Norway'.[21] When a young child asked Næss to fill in a questionnaire about himself and to list his favourite things, the replies were quite telling. They emphasise simplicity (favourite food: oatmeal, potatoes, meat; favourite clothes: old ones), a love for the Norwegian outdoors (favourite country: Norway, favourite sport: skiing), climbing when young (favourite animal: moose, favourite colour: green, and 'the place you've always wanted to visit': Tvergastein) and his philosophical predecessors (favourite movie: *Gandhi*, favourite book: Spinoza's *Ethics*).[22]

Næss' older brothers' attempts to toughen him up in childhood left him with no doubt that they could be trusted and that they loved him, but it

---

[18] *Ibid.*, p. 22.
[19] Ramchandra Guha, 'Radical American Environmentalism and Wilderness Preservation: A Third World Critique', in Witoszek and Brennan, *Philosophical Dialogues*, p. 317.
[20] Næss calls his philosophy, which is profoundly concerned with ethics and the idea of self-realization, 'Ecosophy T'. The word is a combination of the Greek words *oikos* (household) and *sophia* (wisdom). The 'household' is the planet. The 'T' stands for Tvergastein, where he has done his most productive philosophical thinking and writing, and it implies that it is only one of several possible formulations for an ecological philosophy.
[21] Devall and Sessions, *Deep Ecology*, p. 225.
[22] Personal communication with Hanna Weber, October 1997.

was a tough love devoid of nonsense or sentimentality. This resulted in 'a detestation and fear of being influenced by manifestations of spirituality and high-sounding notions'. However, Gandhi's 'Spartan life-style and non-violent militancy could be admired in spite of its background in spiritual metaphysics'. Spinoza too, while indulging in '"romantic" notions like perfection and love of God', was a 'tough nut'. This allowed Næss to admire both men of wisdom 'without feeling guilt'.[23] Further, he poses the question: 'Placing human societies and myself, as I had, within the framework of an essentially homogeneous all-embracing Nature, and admiring and feeling nearness to the small carnivores along the shore, how was it possible for me to come early under the strong influence of Gandhian ethics of non-violence?' He answers his own question by harking back to the many solitary childhood hours he spent observing nature on the shoreline of the sea: 'The life to be found in shallow waters may be conceived as essentially peaceful, and favourable to a norm of maximum diversity, richness and multiplicity.'[24]

GANDHI'S PHILOSOPHY IN NÆSS' ECOSOPHY

Gandhi experimented with, and wrote a great deal about, simple living in harmony with the environment[25] but he lived before the advent of the articulation of the deep ecological strands of environmental philosophy. His ideas about human connectedness with nature, therefore, rather than being explicit, must be inferred from an overall reading of the Mahatma's writings. Næss explains that 'Gandhi made manifest the internal relation between self-realisation, non-violence and what sometimes has been called biospherical egalitarianism',[26] and points out that he was 'inevitably' influenced by the Mahatma's metaphysics 'which contributed to keeping him (the Mahatma) going until his death'. Moreover, 'Gandhi's utopia is one of the few that shows ecological balance, and today his rejection of the Western World's material abundance and waste is accepted by progressives of the ecological movement.'[27]

---

[23] Naess, 'How My Philosophy Seemed to Develop', pp. 213–14.   [24] *Ibid.*, p. 224.
[25] See Shahed Power, 'Gandhi and Deep Ecology: Experiencing the Nonhuman Environment', unpublished PhD thesis, Environmental Resources Unit, University of Salford (1991), pp. 12–124.
[26] Arne Naess, '*Self*-Realisation: An Ecological Approach to Being in the World', in John Seed, Joanna Macy, Pat Fleming and Arne Naess (eds.), *Thinking Like a Mountain: Towards a Council of All Beings* (Philadelphia: New Society Publishers, 1988), p. 26.
[27] Arne Naess, *Gandhi and Group Conflict: An Exploration of Satyagraha* (Oslo: Universitetsforlaget, 1974), p. 10.

While Gandhi allowed injured animals to be killed humanely to save them from unreasonable pain and at times even because they caused undue nuisance, his nonviolence encompassed a reverence for all life. In his office at the Sevagram Ashram there is a snake transporting cage and a large wooden scissor-like contraption which was used to pick up the reptiles so that they could be taken beyond the perimeter and released as an alternative to killing them. This attitude is mirrored, and indeed pushed further, in Næss when he makes the point that,

It may be of vital interest to a family of poisonous snakes to remain in a small area where small children play, but it is also of vital interest to children of parents that there are no accidents. The priority rule of nearness makes it justifiable for the parents to remove the snakes. But the priority of vital interest of snakes is important when deciding where to establish the playgrounds.[28]

A review of the Gandhian literature (while keeping in mind the time in which it was written as a reason for anthropocentric expression) readily turns up statements such as: 'If our sense of right and wrong had not become blunt, we would recognise that animals had rights, no less than men';[29] 'I do believe that all God's creatures have the right to live as much as we have';[30] and 'We should feel a more living bond between ourselves and the rest of the animate world.'[31] The clearest indication of Gandhi's respect for nature, however, comes through his interpretation of the Hindu worship of the cow. Gandhi saw cow protection as one of the most wonderful phenomena in human evolution. 'It takes the human being beyond his species. The cow to me means the entire sub-human world. Man, through the cow, is enjoined to realise his identity with all that lives.'[32] 'Hinduism believes in the oneness not merely of all human life but in the oneness of all that lives. Its worship of the cow is, in my opinion, its unique contribution to the evolution of humanitarianism. It is a practical application of the belief in the oneness and, therefore, sacredness of all life';[33] and 'my meaning of cow protection . . . includes . . . the protection and service of both man and bird and beast'.[34]

Perhaps a better way to illustrate Gandhi's concerns with the oneness of life is to look at his writings on ahimsa. Usually translated as nonviolence,

---

[28] Naess, 'Identification as a Source of Deep Ecological Attitudes', pp. 266–7.
[29] 'Harijans and Pigs', *Harijan*, 13 April 1935.   [30] 'Right to Live', *Harijan*, 19 January 1937.
[31] 'Our Brethren the Trees' *Young India*, 5 December 1929.
[32] 'Hinduism', *Young India*, 6 October 1921.
[33] 'Why I Am a Hindu', *Young India*, 20 October 1927.
[34] 'Speech at All-India Cow-Protection Conference, Bombay', *Young India*, 7 May 1925.

it can be seen as the fountainhead of Truth – the ultimate goal of life. From his prison cell in 1930 Gandhi wrote to his ashramites that,

without *Ahimsa* it would not be possible to seek and find Truth. *Ahimsa* and Truth are so intertwined that it is practically impossible to distangle and separate them. They are like two sides of a coin or rather a smooth unstamped metallic disk. Who can say, which is the obverse, and which the reverse? Nevertheless, *ahimsa* is the means, Truth is the end. Means to be means must always be within our reach, and so *ahimsa* is our supreme duty. If we take care of the means we are bound to reach the end sooner or later.[35]

For Gandhi, ahimsa meant 'love' in the Pauline sense and was violated by 'holding on to what the world needs'.[36] As a Hindu, Gandhi had a strong sense of the unity of all life. For him nonviolence meant not only the non-injury of human life, but as noted above, of all living things. This was important because it was the way to Truth (with a capital 'T') which he saw as Absolute – as God or an impersonal all-pervading reality, rather than truth (with a lower-case 't') which was relative, the current position on the way to Truth.

THE REALIZATION OF THE SELF

Næss had been an admirer of Gandhi's nonviolent direct action since 1930 and deeply influenced by his metaphysics. When he read Romain Rolland's Gandhi biography as a young philosophy student in Paris in 1931, he came across Gandhi's statements on Truth and the essential oneness of all life (Rolland's book after all is subtitled 'The Man who Became one with the Universal Being'). Rolland, in trying to explain Gandhi's ideas of cow protection to an uncomprehending Occidental audience, points out that by it 'man concludes a pact of alliance with his dumb brethren; it signifies fraternity between man and beast.'[37] In some of his works, Næss notes that 'ecological preservation is nonviolent at its very core'[38] and quotes Gandhi to make the point: 'I believe in *advaita*, I believe in the essential unity of man and, for that matter, of all that lives. Therefore I believe that if one man gains spiritually, the whole world gains with him and, if one man fails, the

[35] Gandhi, *From Yeravda Mandir*, p. 6.   [36] *Ibid.*, p. 5.
[37] Romain Rolland, *Mahatma Gandhi: The Man who Became One with the Universal Being* (London: Allen and Unwin, 1924), p. 22 in the 1968 reprint by the Publications Division, Ministry of Information and Broadcasting, Government of India, New Delhi.
[38] Naess, '*Self*-Realisation', p. 25.

whole world fails to that extent.'[39] Næss adds that 'When the egotism-ego vanishes, something else grows, that ingredient of the person that tends to identify itself with God, with humanity, all that lives.'[40]

As this implies, for Arne Næss deep ecology is not fundamentally about the value of nature per se, it is about who we are in the larger scheme of things. And, as is the case with most philosophers, Næss has always 'emphatically endorsed' the Platonic dictum that the unexamined life is not worth living.[41] He stresses the spiritual orientation of deep ecology by noting the identification of the 'self' with 'Self' in terms that it is used in the *Bhagavad Gita*[42] (that is as the unity which is one) as the source of deep ecological attitudes. In other words, he links the tenets of his approach to ecology with what may be termed self-realisation. And here the influence of the Mahatma is most clearly discernible. Næss notes that while Gandhi may have been concerned about the political liberation of his homeland, 'the liberation of the individual human being was his supreme aim'.[43]

The link between self-realization and Næss' environmental philosophy can be clearly seen in his discussion of the connection between nonviolence and self-realization in his analysis of the context of Gandhian political ethics. Næss starts with the 'one basic proposition of a normative kind' when investigating Gandhi's teachings on group conflict: 'Seek complete self-realisation' (the 'manifestation of one's potential to the greatest possible degree'). He adds that the 'self to be realised is not the ego, but the large Self created when we identify with all living creatures and ultimately with the whole universe'.[44] He then summarises this connection as:

(1) Self-realization presupposes a search for truth.
(2) In the last analysis all living beings are one.
(3) *Himsa* (violence) against oneself makes complete self-realization impossible.
(4) *Himsa* against a living being is *himsa* against oneself.
(5) *Himsa* against a living being makes complete self-realization impossible.[45]

---

[39] See Naess, *Gandhi and Group Conflict*, p. 42. For the original quotation see 'Not Even Half-Mast', *Young India*, 4 December 1924.
[40] Naess, *Gandhi and Group Conflict*, p. 38.
[41] Naess, 'How My Philosophy Seemed to Develop', p. 215.
[42] See chapter 6, verse 29, which states that one disciplined by yoga sees the Self in all beings, and all beings in the Self. See Naess, 'Identification as a Source of Deep Ecological Attitudes', p. 260. See also Knut A. Jacobsen, '*Bhagavadgita*, Ecosophy T, and Deep Ecology', *Inquiry* 39 (1996), pp. 219–38.
[43] Naess, '*Self*-Realisation', p. 24.   [44] Naess, 'How My Philosophy Seemed to Develop', p. 225.
[45] Adapted from Arne Naess, *Gandhi and the Nuclear Age* (Totowa, NJ: The Bedminster Press, 1965), pp. 28–33.

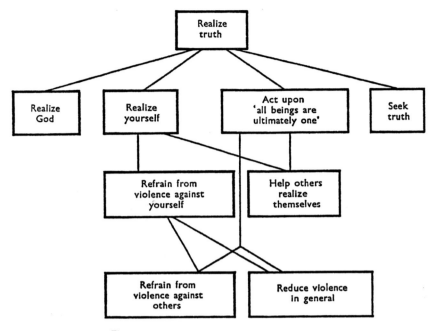

Figure 9.1
Source: Næss, *Gandhi and Group Conflict*, p. 55

This conceptual construction evolved into ever more complex and graphic presentations. In his 1974 work, *Gandhi and Group Conflict* (written about the time of his Bucharest speech), Næss provides various systematisations of Gandhi's teachings on group struggle where self-realization is the top norm and which contains the critical hypothesis that all living beings are ultimately one, such as 'Systematisation *F*', in Figure 9.1.

In a discussion with David Rothenberg over human destruction of the environment without adequate reason (for example where a parent kills the last animal of a species to save his or her child from its attack), Næss is asked whether protection of nature should occur because we should not think only of ourselves or because natural things are part of us also. Næss refuses to separate the two approaches. He answers with another allusion to Gandhi: 'When he was asked, "How do you do these altruistic things all year long?" he said, "I am not doing something altruistic at all. I am trying to improve in Self-realization".'[46] There need be no divide between the intrinsically valuable and the useful. And, in a Gandhian way of feeling

---

[46] Rothenberg, *Is it Painful to Think?*, pp. 141–2.

rather than intellectualising, he adds: 'if you hear a phrase like, "All life is fundamentally one," you should be open to *tasting* this, before asking immediately, "What does this mean?"'[47]

CLARIFYING DEEP ECOLOGY

Næss the deep ecological activist has used his mountaineering skills to further his philosophy in action, acting on his 'obligation to try to implement the necessary changes'. Following ineffectual local protests he defeated a proposal to dam a Norwegian fjord by climbing a vertical cliff at the edge of the fjord and anchoring himself (in a hammock) to the cliff-face and dropping a note informing the authorities that he intended to stay and if the dam was built he would drown. Having close to iconic status in Norway, he was able to prevail and the dam was cancelled.[48]

Næss, the deep ecological theorist, along with others, is attempting to clarify what the deep ecology movement stands for. Ecological philosophies are continually expanding and other writers have also added their analytical skills to the deep ecology literature, and environmental activists of various stripes have experimented with different forms of nonviolent direct action. Recently we have seen the rise of eco-feminism – which combines the insights of ecology and feminism to articulate the premise that the same ideology which authorises class, race, gender, species and other forms of oppression, also sanctions the oppression of nature;[49] Lovelock's Gaia hypothesis – which claims that moral boundaries should not stop with life, but that ecosystems, the planet itself and even the universe are living organisms and could thus have rights superior to those of humans;[50] and aggressively radical movements and philosophies such as Earth First! – the self-proclaimed activist wing of the deep ecology movement, which not only promotes the use of Gandhian nonviolent activism in defense of nature, but more controversially ecotage – the disabling of logging equipment and the illegal spiking of trees so that they cannot be logged economically. After

---

[47] *Ibid.*, p. 151.
[48] Dolores LaChapelle, *Earth Wisdom* (Silverton, CO: International College, 1978), p. 154. For other examples of civil disobedience practiced by Næss, see Reed and Rothenberg, *Wisdom in the Open Air*, pp. 25–6.
[49] See for example Leonie Caldecott and Stephanie Leland (eds.), *Reclaim the Earth: Women Speak out for Life on Earth* (London: Women's Press, 1983); Judith Plant (ed.), *Healing the Wounds: The Promise of Ecofeminism* (Philadelphia: New Society, 1989); Irene Diamond and Gloria Feman Orenstein (eds.), *Reweaving the World: The Emergence of Ecofeminism* (San Fransico: Sierra Club, 1990); and Greta Gaard (ed.), *Ecofeminism: Women, Animals, Nature* (Philadelphia: Temple University Press, 1993).
[50] James Lovelock, *Gaia: A New Look at Life on Earth* (New York: Oxford, 1979).

all, if all living beings are one, then fighting to preserve nature is an act of self-defence.

Næss notes that Gandhi had a rare combination of qualities that included humility towards factual truth, an awareness of human fallibility and the knowledge that at any time he may be proved to be wrong about a factual situation. This never led to inaction, but, in what Næss saw as an 'extremely rare' combination, was balanced by his activism.[51] While Gandhi was an activist rather than merely a contemplative philosopher, he certainly would not have welcomed some of these later developments, and Næss, also an activist, generally does not.[52] Næss reminds Dave Foreman, the leading figure in Earth First! and the editor of *Ecodefense: Field Guide to Monkey-wrenching*,[53] a book that explains how ecotage can best be carried out, that 'the norms of Ecodefense are non-violent but not nonviolent'.[54] For Næss, 'non-violence' is the broader category that does not permit the doing of harm to humans or animals. 'Nonviolence' is the 'technical term for the Gandhian sort of non-violence'. He reminds Foreman, in terms of Gandhi's well-known dictum to hate the sin and not the sinner, that it is not non-violent to call people 'evil,' 'rapers,' 'lazy bastards'. 'It suffices to call their act evil,' and that for the sake of *communication* this should not be done.[55] Arne Næss is a firm believer in revolutionary nonviolence. He reminds us that,

Gandhi supported what he and others called 'nonviolent revolution,' making extensive use of direct actions. But it was a step by step revolution. He insisted that one step at a time 'is enough for me.' If, and only if, the Gandhian terminology is accepted, then I would find it adequate to say that the deep ecology movement is revolutionary. If an action has to be violent in order to be called 'revolutionary,' then the movement is not revolutionary.[56]

This revolutionary nonviolence (without the hyphen) pervades his Ecosophy T, and this in turn provides the philosophical underpinning for much of the other writings on deep ecology.

[51] T. K. Mahadevan (ed.), *Truth and Nonviolence: A UNESCO Symposium on Gandhi* (New Delhi: Gandhi Peace Foundation, 1970), pp. 70, 85–6.

[52] See Arne Næss 'Letter to Dave Foreman, 23 June 1988', in Witoszek and Brennan, *Philosophical Dialogues*, pp. 225–31.

[53] Dave Foreman (ed.), *Ecodefense: A Field Guide to Monkeywrenching* (Tuscon, AZ: A Ned Ludd Book, 1985).

[54] Næss 'Letter to Dave Foreman', p. 227.   [55] *Ibid.*, p. 229.

[56] Arne Næss 'Is the Deep Ecology Vision a Deep Vision or is it Multicolored like the Rainbow? An Answer to Nina Witoszek', in Witoszek and Brennan, *Philosophical Dialogues*, pp. 466–72 at p. 468.

CHAPTER 10

Johan Galtung – peace research moves beyond war

INTRODUCTION

Johan Galtung is one of the great figures in peace research. In 1959 he established the first peace research academy, the International Peace Research Institute in Oslo (PRIO) and served as its director for ten years. In 1964 he also launched the *Journal of Peace Research*, one of the two leading scholarly journals in the field. Although the *Journal of Conflict Resolution* had already been around for over half a dozen years, its empirical agenda did not reflect Galtung's own broader and structural approach to violence in the way the new journal would. PRIO did not hide behind the politically less controversial (and less blatantly normative) category of conflict research,[1] and likewise in the first issue of the *Journal of Peace Research*, where Galtung defined peace as having both negative and positive aspects, he announced the birth of the discipline of peace research. He has written dozens of books and hundreds of published articles, served as a professor or visiting professor of peace studies in countless universities on five continents and acted as a consultant to 'virtually every United Nations agency'.[2] While not without his critics, Galtung has almost single-handedly shifted the focus of peace research, and especially its classroom sibling peace education, to encompass areas such as exploitation and oppression instead of merely the avoidance of war.

After the mass slaughter of the Second World War and fear of nuclear Armageddon in the late 1950s, the budding discipline of peace research concentrated on the elimination of international armed conflict. Researchers, led by those in the USA, attempted to understand war in terms of perceptions that international actors were pursuing incompatible goals and

---

[1] Herbert C. Kelman, 'Reflections on the History and Status of Peace Research', *Conflict Management and Peace Science* 5 (1981), p. 98; and Peter Lawler, *A Question of Values: Johan Galtung's Peace Research* (Boulder, CO: Lynne Reinner, 1995), p. 13.
[2] David P. Barash, *Introduction to Peace Studies* (Belmont, CA: Wadsworth, 1991), p. 8.

they tried to find ways to prevent misconceptions.[3] Peace was interpreted as an absence of war and the discipline of peace research left other social problems to different disciplines.

In some religious traditions, however, 'peace' is understood in the affirmative as wholeness, rather than negatively as absence of war. Thus, threats to peace may come not from those who stir up conflict but from those who acquiesce in the existing state of affairs because 'peace' is too often understood as simply the damping down of conflicts which are aimed at changing the status quo. If peace is construed as an affirmative concept, wholeness and fulfilment must be opened up for all and all must have a share in power which is an essential ingredient in a fully human existence.[4]

GALTUNG'S EXPANDED VIEW OF VIOLENCE

This line of thinking is echoed in the peace research of Johan Galtung which outlined a broader notion of peace than the negative definitions previously favoured by the American school: 'Peace research should liberate itself from a materialistic bias dealing with bodies, dead or alive, healthy or unhealthy – in other words with mortality and morbidity only, and not with the *mental and spiritual dimensions of violence and human growth and development.*'[5]

Primarily as a response to the work of Galtung, the central concern of peace research for many researchers moved from direct violence and its elimination or reduction (negative peace) to the broader agenda that also includes structural violence and its elimination (positive peace).[6] This broader and increasingly popular school of peace research – major peace studies texts now generally start off with discussions about the meaning of peace, strongly influenced by the concepts formulated by Galtung – places great emphasis on the elimination of exploitation and oppression.

'Structural violence' is unintended structure-generated (rather than actor-generated) harm done to human beings. It is an indirect form of violence built into social, political and economic structures that gives rise to unequal power and consequently unequal life chances. It includes exploitation, alienation, marginalisation, poverty, deprivation, misery etc. and exists

---

[3] Ghanshyam Pardesi, 'Editor's Introduction', to Ghanshyam Pardesi (ed.), *Contemporary Peace Research* (Brighton: Harvester, 1982), pp. 1–29.

[4] John Macquarrie, *The Concept of Peace* (London: SCM, 1973), pp. 30, 32–3, 38.

[5] Johan Galtung, 'Twenty-five Years of Peace Research: Ten Challenges and Some Responses', *Journal of Peace Research* 22 (1985), p. 156.

[6] Johan Galtung, 'Violence, Peace and Peace Research', *Journal of Peace Research* 6 (1969), pp. 167–91; and Johan Galtung, 'A Structural Theory of Imperialism', *Journal of Peace Research* 8 (1971), pp. 81–118.

when basic needs for security, freedom, welfare and identity are not being met. In its horizontal version, violent structures keep apart people who want to be together, and keep together people who want to be apart.[7] With its opposite, 'positive peace', words that come to mind are 'harmony', 'cooperation' and 'integration'.[8]

For Galtung, 'Violence can be defined as the cause of the difference between the potential and the actual, between what could have been and what is.'[9] In other words, and to put it into terms that Næss would approve of, this conception of violence is based 'on a distinction between the potential and actual level of self-realization of human beings, particularly on the "avoidable causes of a differential between the two"'.[10]

Extreme structural violence can lead to death by denying even the most basic needs such as those for food and shelter. So negative peace can be insufficient to protect human life. While death can obviously be caused by deliberate direct violence, it can also be caused by the mere neglect of those in need. Positive peace means not only ending wars, but also freedom from want, the attainment of justice, the protection of human rights and an absence of exploitation.[11] In other words the opposite of peace is violence *not* war. These insights were Galtung's major gift to the discipline.

Although Galtung had been edging towards this distinction ten years earlier,[12] it was not made explicit until his 1969 paper, 'Violence, Peace and Peace Research'. While some have suggested that leftist attacks on Galtung as a 'bourgeois social scientist' and his peace research as an ideological discipline which corresponded to 'the interests of the ruling classes in the leading capitalist nations'[13] may have had something to do with this shift in thinking, in explaining its origins Galtung himself points to his desire to link the theories of peace, conflict and development; the emerging distinction between actor-oriented and structure-oriented social cosmologies, and, the one he puts first, 'the exposure to Gandhian thinking', including through his writings on Gandhi's political ethics with Arne Næss.[14]

---

[7] Johan Galtung, *Peace by Peaceful Means: Peace and Conflict, Development and Civilisation* (London and Oslo: Sage, 1996), p. 67.

[8] Galtung, 'Twenty-five Years of Peace Research', p. 145.

[9] Galtung, 'Violence, Peace and Peace Research', p. 169.

[10] Johan Galtung, 'Introduction', in Johan Galtung, *Essays in Peace Research*. vol. I, *Peace: Research – Education – Action* (Copenhagen: Ejlers, 1975), p. 24.

[11] Galtung, 'Twenty-five Years of Peace Research', p. 145.

[12] For example in Johan Galtung, 'Pacifism from a Sociological Point of View', *Journal of Conflict Resolution* 3 (1959), pp. 67–84.

[13] Pekka Korhonen, *The Geometry of Power: Johan Galtung's Conception of Power* (Tampere Peace Research Institute, 1990), p. 106.

[14] Galtung, 'Introduction', vol. I, p. 22.

Galtung explained that development for the poor is frequently championed in order to prevent violence, whereas for him inequalities 'were in and by themselves violence . . . unnecessary evils in their own right – not because they might *lead to* some other type of violence'.[15] He noted that Gandhi was the only author or politician who 'clearly fought against both the sudden, deliberate direct violence engaged in by actors, and the continuous, not necessarily intended, violence built into the social structures'.[16] While some used structural violence to prevent direct violence (in the law and order tradition), some used direct violence to abolish structural violence (in the revolutionary tradition), and still others condoned one or the other while attempting to alleviate the plight of the victims (in the Christian *caritas* tradition), Gandhi 'was equally opposed to all three'. But in fact 'Gandhi's general pattern of action is more tailor-made for structural conflict.'[17]

Galtung's work is not palatable to all. For example Kenneth Boulding, another of the peace research greats and one of the founders of the *Journal of Conflict Resolution*, disagrees with Galtung over the latter's overly normative approach (where his description of reality may suffer), his lack of understanding of the needs for hierarchy in modern complex societies, and the general 'fuzziness' of his terms.[18] Here the debate between the Gandhi-inspired sociologist Galtung and the economic empirical streams of particularly American peace research most clearly comes into focus. Others have pointed out that Galtung's concept of violence seems to be anything that Galtung does not like,[19] and still other 'peace' researchers have advocated direct violence where it can reduce structural violence. Nevertheless, this work set the future agenda for a peace research concerned with more than international relations and Galtung's changed definitions of peace have been paralleled by a change in the political environment of peace research from

---

[15] *Ibid.*, pp. 23–4.   [16] *Ibid.*, p. 24.

[17] Johan Galtung, 'Gandhian Themes', in Ingemund Gullvåg and Jon Wetlesen (eds.), *In Sceptical Wonder: Inquiries into the Philosophy of Arne Naess on the Occasion of his 70th Birthday* (Oslo: Universitetsforlaget, 1982), p. 225. See also Johan Galtung, 'Gandhi and Conflictology', *Papers: A Collection of Works Previously Available Only in Manuscript or Very Limited Circulation Mimeographed or Photocopied Editions*, vol. v, *Papers in English 1968–1972* (Oslo: PRIO, 1980), p. 142; and Johan Galtung, *The Way is the Goal: Gandhi Today* (Ahmedabad: Gujarat Vidyapith Peace Research Centre, 1992), p. 73.

[18] Kenneth E. Boulding, 'Twelve Friendly Quarrels with Johan Galtung', *Journal of Peace Research* 14 (1977), pp. 75–86.

[19] See for example Kjell Eide, 'Note on Galtung's Concept of "Violence"', *Journal of Peace Research* 8 (1971), p. 71. In its kindest formulation, the contention here is that Galtung wants to include every social problem under the rubric of peace research, thus diluting its focus.

'East-West tension and the politics of "brinkmanship", to the North-South confrontation over demands for structural changes'.[20]

Lawler notes that pacifism 'remained the raison d'être of peace research for Galtung' because without it 'what was the point?' This pacifism, however, was in no way to be construed as an apology for inaction in dealing with social conflicts because of a fear of seeming to advocate direct violence. The task was now 'to explore the nature of violence and develop nonviolent strategies for change. With the benefit of hindsight, here can be detected the traces of a Gandhian conception of pacifism as a positive philosophy of action, not simply a moral posture of refusal.'[21] From the time of his analysis of structural violence during a trip to India in 1969, for Galtung, 'the peace researcher would increasingly be cast less in the role of enlightened technocrat and more in the role of political activist – Gandhi's karmayogi'.[22]

For those who have followed Galtung's intellectual career the influence of Gandhi is evident. Twenty years after his formulation of the concept of 'structural violence', Galtung was to introduce a new term to peace research: 'cultural violence' ('any aspect of a culture that can be used to legitimize violence in its direct or structural form'). Its antithesis, cultural peace, is closely linked to Gandhian doctrines of the unity of life and the unity of means and ends.[23] Even more recently he has moved to champion oriental civilisations and in particular a Buddhist world view as the main hope for peace. The introduction to eastern thought generally was through Gandhi, and Galtung's Buddhism is again heavily influenced by his earlier reading of Gandhi.[24] Although Gandhi was not a Buddhist, Galtung claimed that 'his thought and action in rejecting the caste system were so utterly buddhist that I wonder whether this is not an at least equally correct label'.[25] As hinted at, while Galtung moves further into Buddhism, he is taking

---

[20] Hans-Henrik Holm, 'Johan Galtung and the Science of Human Fulfilment: From Petal – Picking to Mega Research', in Nils Petter Gleditsch, Odvar Leine, Hans-Henrik Holm, Tord Høvik, Arne Martin Klausen, Erik Rudeng and Håkan Wiberg (eds.), *Johan Galtung: A Bibliography of his Scholarly and Popular Writings 1951–1980* (Oslo: PRIO, 1980), p. 32.

[21] Lawler, *A Question of Values*, p. 79. This is something of an understatement. Careful observers, who know Galtung's work and Gandhi's philosophy well, may not need too much hindsight to find far more than this.

[22] Lawler, *A Question of Values*, p. 87.

[23] Johan Galtung, 'Cultural Violence', *Journal of Peace Research* 27 (1990), pp. 291–305.

[24] See Lawler, *A Question of Values*, chapter 8 'Peace as Nirvana', pp. 191–222; Johan Galtung, *Buddhism: A Quest for Unity and Peace* (Honolulu: Dae Won Sa Buddhist Temple, 1988), p. vii; and Johan Galtung and Daisaku Ikeda, *Choose Peace: A Dialogue between Johan Galtung and Daisaku Ikeda* (London: Pluto, 1995), p. ix.

[25] Galtung, *Buddhism*, p. viii.

Gandhi with him. He talks of Gandhi's way of 'avoiding false dichotomies' as his Hindu-Buddhist way of approaching the world, and Gandhi's nonviolence which was born from a Hindu-Buddhist unity of life.[26] Further, Gandhi's Buddhist inclinations (even though there is scant evidence that Gandhi actually made any detailed study of Buddhism in his own life, and did not live among Buddhists, a fact conceded by Galtung) and departure from mainstream Hinduism is reflected for Galtung in Gandhi's nonviolence, his rejection of a vertical caste system, and his fascination with small communities (that seem to echo the Buddhist idea of the sangha).[27]

GALTUNG AND GANDHI

Although the connection between Galtung and Gandhi receives scant attention in peace research circles,[28] or is very much implicit,[29] and a recent speech has called for the 'adding of Gandhi to Galtung',[30] the work of Johan Galtung is centrally and obviously influenced by Gandhian philosophy. While Galtung, makes several references to this influence on his thought in the introductory chapters in his *Essays in Peace Research* and elsewhere, even Lawler, the recent chronicler of Galtung's peace research, gives the Gandhian influence less than due regard. For him Galtung seems to have moved from positivism to Buddhism, while, according to Galtung himself, 'it was Gandhi all the time'.[31]

Galtung was born into an elite Norwegian family in 1930. His physician father (hence the frequent employment in his work of a 'medical model' to judge the health of the international system?) was imprisoned by the Nazis for resistance during the German occupation of Norway when the young Johan was only thirteen. These factors must have had a tremendous impact on his development and the charting of his future career, yet, in a sense, Gandhi was Galtung's immediate entrée into the world of peace research. He has acknowledged that as a seventeen-year-old he 'cried bitterly' when

---

[26] Galtung and Ikeda, *Choose Peace*, pp. 7, 19.   [27] *Ibid.*, pp. 64–65.

[28] Korhonen's *The Geometry of Power*, appears to be the only publication that looks systematically at Galtung's influence on the young Galtung, especially on his conception of power. However, even this book claims that by the late 1950s Galtung was 'slowly starting to drift away from Gandhi' (p. 37), although the references to him do not necessarily seem to confirm this.

[29] See Georg Sørensen, 'Utopianism in Peace Research: The Gandhian Heritage', *Journal of Peace Research* 29 (1992), pp. 135–144.

[30] Ted Herman, 'Adding Gandhi to Galtung for Peace Work', *Peace, Environment and Education* 5 (1994), pp. 23–7.

[31] Personal communication, 30 January 1998.

he heard the news of the Mahatma's assassination.[32] In the autumn of 1953, Galtung attended a lecture on Gandhi by Arne Næss and 'it seems that this lecture directed his generally antimilitaristic views into a distinctly Gandhian direction'.[33] One of the first jobs of the young Norwegian mathematics and sociology student was as an assistant to Næss, helping to prepare a series of lectures on Gandhi. This collaboration eventually resulted in a book on Gandhi's political ethics. Much of Galtung's contribution to *Gandhis Politiske Etikk*, his first major publication, was written during 1954–5 while he was serving a five-and-a-half month sentence as a conscientious objector against military service.

In *Gandhis Politiske Etikk*, Galtung and Næss[34] note that there will always be conflict between groups of people and therefore there is a need to act conscientiously while keeping this in mind. For these struggles, special weapons and strong people to use them are needed, the weapon however is not to be a physical thing but rather Gandhi's satyagraha. The book is a call to action, for 'fighters in a dangerous world'.[35] And that book project, Galtung commented later, 'was also the way I got started on peace research.'[36]

The young Galtung's first published papers resulted from his position as vice-president for international affairs of the Norwegian national union of students in 1951 and a visit to the Soviet Union at the time of Stalin's death with the Norwegian student delegation in early 1953, and his collaboration with Næss and prison experience. Among those first few Norwegian language articles we have titles such as 'What is Pacifism?', 'Alternative Service or Just Conscientious Objection?', 'Gandhi's Way', and 'The Way of Gandhi – Our Way'. Since that time, his writings have continued to include many references to the Mahatma and are clearly informed by Galtung's interpretation of Gandhian philosophy. In describing important sources of inspiration, Galtung has noted that Gandhi is 'the major one . . . and increasingly Buddhism in general'.[37]

---

[32] Galtung, *The Way is the Goal*, p. v; and Johan Galtung, *60 Speeches on War and Peace* (Oslo: PRIO, 1990), p. 158.

[33] Korhonen, *The Geometry of Power*, p. 6.

[34] Korhonen notes that although it is a joint book between Galtung and Næss, 'seen in the light of the course of [Galtung's] later development he might as well have written the book himself.' Korhonen, *The Geometry of Power*, p. 7.

[35] Korhonen, *The Geometry of Power*, p. 10.   [36] Galtung, *The Way is the Goal*, p. vii.

[37] Galtung, *60 Speeches on War and Peace*, p. 280. See also Johan Galtung, 'Introduction', in Johan Galtung, *Essays in Peace Research, volume 5: Peace Problems: Some Case Studies* (Copenhagen: Ejlers, 1975), p. 23, where he makes the Gandhian antecedents of his best known theoretical work most explicit.

Gandhi was as much concerned with exploitation and oppression as he was with war, in fact he construed nonviolence in such a way that its meaning was very wide. His definition included not treating another with less dignity than was warranted by a shared humanity. Not only does dehumanisation pave the way for violence, but dehumanisation *is* violence – and this is closely echoed in Galtung's notion of structural violence. Gandhi made this clear when he spoke of exploitation in economic terms, pointing out that when someone claims as his or her own 'more than the minimum that is really necessary for him' that person is guilty of theft.[38] And this applies in the international sphere as it does at the interpersonal:

If I take anything that I do not need for my immediate use, and keep it, I thieve it from somebody else. I venture to suggest that it is the fundamental law of nature, without exception, that Nature produces enough for our wants from day to day, and if only everybody took enough for himself and nothing more, there would be no pauperism in this world, there would be no dying of starvation in this world. But so long as we have got this inequality, so long we are thieving.[39]

A reading of Gandhi would suggest that he would be happy to push this line of reasoning to its logical conclusion: If aid programmes were not sufficient to reduce this 'theft' then neighbours must be invited to share resources, and, if there is not enough to go around, belts must be tightened in a way that no one who is genuinely in want is excluded.

During his 1969 India trip, Galtung turned his analytical skills to an exploration of Gandhi's philosophy. At the Gandhian Institute of Studies at Rajghat in Varanasi, Galtung refined his ideas about structural and direct violence. In his reading of Gandhi, he noted a person *vs* structure distinction and he defined Gandhi as a 'structuralist' in the sense that he saw 'conflict in the deeper sense as something that was built into social structures, not into the persons . . . Colonialism was a structure and caste was a structure; both of them filled with persons performing their duties according to their roles or statuses . . . The evil was in the structure, not in the person who carried out his obligations.' Galtung added that 'Exploitation is violence, but it is quite clear that Gandhi sees it as a structural relation more than as the intended evil inflicted upon innocent victims by evil men.'[40] This meant that change was to be of structures, 'not mobility of actors in the structure'.[41]

---

[38] Gandhi, *Ashram Observances in Action*, p. 58.
[39] 'Speech on "Ashram Vows" at Y.M.C.A., Madras', *The Indian Review*, February 1916.
[40] Galtung, 'Gandhi and Conflictology', pp. 124, 133–4; and Galtung, *The Way is the Goal*, pp. 57, 68.
[41] Galtung, 'Gandhian Themes', p. 225.

Later that year, the groundbreaking paper 'Violence, Peace and Peace Research', written on the roof terrace of the Gandhian Institute of Studies, was published. Unfortunately, the incisive fifty-page paper on Gandhi, entitled 'Gandhi and Conflictology', which grew out of this and a later visit to India, was not published at the time. In 1974, Galtung's philosophical mentor, Arne Næss, wrote one of the major scholarly works systematising Gandhian ethics. In the preface to *Gandhi and Group Conflict*, which the subtitle explicitly designated as 'the theoretical background', Næss informed readers that it was to be taken as the first volume of a larger work. A sequel, to be written by Galtung, was to complement it by providing the 'practical foreground' dealing with the implementation of Gandhian norms in contemporary societies.[42] While Næss hoped that the second volume would soon be available, it took almost twenty years before the appearance of Galtung's book on Gandhi, *The Way is the Goal: Gandhi Today*, of which the central part is a reworked version of the 'Gandhi and Conflictology' paper. Ironically, much of the original paper and resulting book is, like Næss' work, concerned with philosophical issues. The chapter on 'The Practical Gandhi' is relatively short. In other words, the book provides more of an addition to Næss' theoretical work rather than providing the promised 'practical foreground.' Nevertheless, as the practical terrain has been adequately covered in numerous other books (it was the focus of Krishnalal Shridharani's *War Without Violence*, the first edition of which was published in 1939, and Joan Bondurant's *Conquest of Violence*), and as the theoretical insights of *The Way is the Goal* are considerable and important (giving us a Gandhi who is a constructive worker and spiritual seeker as well as political activist), this perhaps is not such a great loss given that of the many hundreds of books on Gandhi only a handful, and now this one among them, make a serious attempt at an analytical treatment of Gandhi's philosophy in a way that goes beyond the narrowly political. Here Galtung attempts to take the intellectual Gandhi – 'Gandhi the analyst, who cuts every issue a different way because he has other concepts, other ways of looking at the world'[43] – seriously. Gandhi's value is not only that he rejects all forms of violence, including repression and exploitation, but that he does so 'not only in words but by resisting all of them'; and this through a belief in 'humanity and history of Unity-of-man, even Unity-of-life'.[44] This unity is the central theme of the book. In this context, Galtung explores the themes of goals, conflict formation, power, violence, struggle

[42] Naess, *Gandhi and Group Conflict*, p. 10.
[43] Galtung, *The Way is the Goal*, p. ix.   [44] *Ibid.*, p. x.

and coercion in a Gandhian approach to situations of conflict and presents an extremely useful and typically Næssian/Galtungian taxonomic schedule of the norms of satyagraha. Further, much of Galtung's central writings on peace research can be linked to Gandhi through this source.

In recognition for his writings on Gandhi, Johan Galtung was awarded the prestigious Indian Gandhian Jamnalal Bajaj International Prize in 1993 for the promotion of Gandhian values outside India.

A THEORY OF CONFLICT

Galtung often advances his theory of conflict by talking about a Gandhian theory of conflict. He notes that for Gandhi a sharp distinction had to be drawn between conflict and its manifestations, and that Gandhi's injunctions to fight the sin and not the sinner had to be seen in this context. Galtung adds that Gandhi's views about combating evil rather than combating actors presupposes the norm that 'conflicts are to be solved'.[45] This in turn meant that 'Gandhi seems to prefer a disharmonious relationship to no relationship at all, while of course preferring a harmonious one to disharmony.' Because Gandhi was a structuralist, it was easier for him 'to exonerate the actors in a conflict', and focus on patterns of conflict behaviour 'which are both person-preserving and structure-demolishing'.[46] However, it was never Gandhi's aim 'merely to create a new structure, he also wanted his opponent to be a part of this structure, and that he should take part in creating it'.[47] He also makes Gandhi the spokesperson for his formulation of structural violence: 'Gandhi . . . seems to define as violence anything which would impede the individual from self-realization, whether by his progress, or by keeping him at a moral stand-still. Hence the violence of the "evil-doer" includes its effects in setting the "evil-doer" back himself; violence can be self-inflicted, and not just inflicted upon others.'[48] Galtung (and as we have seen, Næss) clearly makes the point that for Gandhi the aim of the process of conflict was not merely to reach a resolution but that the process was about the achievement of self-realization, nothing less. The fundamental principle is that of the unity of existence (or in the more

---

[45] Johan Galtung, 'A Gandhian Theory of Conflict', in David Selbourne (ed.), *In Theory and In Practice: Essays on the Politics of Jayaprakash Narayan* (Delhi: Oxford University Press, 1985), p. 97.

[46] *Ibid.*, pp. 97–8.

[47] Johan Galtung, 'Gandhi's Views on the Political and Ethical Preconditions of a Nonviolent Fighter', in Pran Chopra (ed.), *The Sage in Revolt: A Remembrance* (New Delhi: Gandhi Peace Foundation, 1972), p. 212.

[48] Galtung, 'A Gandhian Theory of Conflict', p. 104.

immediate, unity of humans). People are related to each other in a way that has a transcendental nature and conflict should be seen as a gift providing a rich opportunity, potentially to the benefit of all, to realize a higher self.[49] In fact a conflict 'resolved' that left the parties unchanged was no success because success implied the 'creation of a new social structure as the expression of the resolution of the conflict'; and a higher level of self-purification in both conflicting parties.[50]

Korhonen notes that from the early 1970s onwards, while international and inter-group violence are still important for Galtung, the individual became the ultimate unit for him and 'the fulfillment of individuals the ultimate goal of peace research and peace action – just as the development of the individual spirit was the goal of Gandhi's thought'.[51]

Galtung has made a further contribution to a conflict theory that is intimately tied in with Gandhian nonviolence. It examines the mechanism by which nonviolence might work and therefore how it can be strategically applied in conflict situations at various levels.

The psychologist Carl Rogers noted that life can become existentially dysfunctional if it is 'incongruent', and this, at some stage, will force change in individual behaviour.[52] In a conflict situation, this incongruence is most likely to be initiated by being out of step with third parties who are in a close social relationship with the actors.[53] If one can influence an audience at a closer social distance to the opponent or alter public opinion – the milieu in which the opponent must live – there is a fair chance of influencing the opponent's attitude even when there has been no opportunity for direct communication. Gandhi, quite candidly, claimed that 'the method of reaching the heart is to awaken public opinion. Public opinion, for which one cares, is a mightier force than that of gunpowder.'[54] And this may help the opponent to clearer insights into their own motivation and sense of belonging in a larger reality. In short, conducting conflict in what can be termed a Gandhian context may not only be instrumentally valuable but again, from another angle, may be intrinsically important in an existential sense.

---

[49] Galtung, *The Way is the Goal*, p. 62.
[50] Galtung, 'A Gandhian Theory of Conflict', p. 110; and see also Galtung, *Peace by Peaceful Means*, p. 116; and Galtung, *The Way is the Goal*, p. 88.
[51] Korhonen, *The Geometry of Power*, p. 110.
[52] See Carl Rogers, *On Becoming a Person: A Therapist's View of Psychotherapy* (Boston: Houghton Mifflin, 1961).
[53] Johan Galtung, *Nonviolence and Israel/Palestine* (Honolulu: University of Hawaii Press, 1989), pp. 20–1.
[54] 'Notes', *Young India*, 19 March 1925.

Galtung has examined this sense of incongruence and attempted to plot the mechanism by which it may be brought about in order to achieve a change of heart in an opponent. Gandhi claimed that satyagraha, his principle- (as opposed to policy-) based method of nonviolence was a way of reaching the truth, that it worked through conversion rather than coercion, and that the driving force of conversion was self-suffering on the part of the satyagrahi that could 'melt the heart' of the opponent. Gandhi had great faith in human goodness. For him, the whole notion of conversion rests upon the assumption that the opponent is open to reason, that they have a conscience, that human nature is such that it is bound, or at least likely, to 'respond to any noble and friendly action'.[55]

The role of self-suffering is, in the words of Gandhian theorist Joan Bondurant, to break a deadlock, to 'cut through the rationalised defences of the opponent'.[56] According to Gandhi the aim is to convert an opponent 'by sheer force of character and suffering'.[57] This is because 'Reason has to be strengthened by suffering and suffering opens the eyes of understanding',[58] for an 'appeal of reason is more to the head, but penetration of the heart comes from suffering. It opens up the inner understanding of man.'[59] And, 'Suffering is infinitely more powerful than the law of the jungle for converting the opponent and opening his ears, which are otherwise shut, to the voice of reason.'[60] And even, 'suffering will melt the stoniest heart of the stoniest fanatic',[61] 'Real suffering bravely borne melts even a heart of stone',[62] or 'The hardest heart and the grossest ignorance must disappear before the rising sun of suffering without anger and without malice.'[63]

Miller, a Christian interpreter of nonviolence, in talking of black-rights demonstrators in the United States South, concluded that 'opponents were seldom if ever won over to the side of justice as a result of voluntary suffering or Christian love on the part of the demonstrators'. Instead, it was economic pressure and desires for stability and civil order that led

[55] 'Cow Protection', *Young India*, 4 August 1920.
[56] Joan Bondurant, *The Conquest of Violence: The Gandhian Philosophy of Conflict*, revised edition (Berkeley: University of California Press 1967), p. 228.
[57] 'Notes', *Young India*, 18 September 1924.
[58] 'Talk to Inmates of Satyagraha Ashram, Vykom', *Young India*, 19 March 1925.
[59] Gandhi, quoted in Gene Sharp, *The Politics of Nonviolent Action* (Boston: Porter Sargent, 1973), p. 709.
[60] 'Speech at Birmingham Meeting', *Young India*, 5 November 1931.
[61] 'Vykom', *Young India*, 4 June 1925.
[62] Gandhi, *Satyagraha in South Africa*, p. 32.
[63] 'Vykom Satyagraha', *Young India*, 19 February 1925.

to success. The dormant consciences that were stirred belonged to 'white students, liberals and churchmen', not to the racial supremacists.[64]

In order to touch the heart of the opponent it appears that some form of feeling of identification with the victim is necessary, the social distance must not be too great. However, in situations of self-suffering in the face of violence, especially direct violence, by definition, the social distance is so great that there is a lack of identification. A rapid conversion through reason upon realisation of suffering caused is unlikely. Can conversion then, not merely victory, be achieved by nonviolent action?

The psychological pressure towards congruence is just as great at the interpersonal (and international) level as it is at the intrapersonal. Galtung, while examining the Israel/Palestine conflict, has given a name to the working of indirect conversion brought about by self-suffering. He calls it the 'Great Chain of Nonviolence'. Galtung points out that there is truth in the proposition that Washington lost the Vietnam war in the streets of America, not the jungles of Asia. Conversion comes through those

who are sufficiently close to the oppressors to be seen by them as human beings, and so touch the human nerve in them, if not in sympathy with the victim, at least in response to the demands put upon them by the intervening/interceding group. By the Other in the Self, in other words, since the Self in the Other has been erased.[65]

He summarises the Great Chain hypothesis through an analogy with a theory of classical physics where, for one thing to move another, there must be proximity in space and time, or there must be a field through which energy can be communicated:

Black people suffering nonviolently, making their plight evident, touchable, speakable, would not be enough. The field does not connect blacks with white supremacists. Nonviolence has to be communicated from group to group until it reaches the nucleus of the structure challenged through civil disobedience. And the field through which this operates is not spatial distance but social distance. Via social proximity this age-old principle in physical theory can be translated into social dynamics. The field has to reach all the way for a message to arrive undistorted.[66]

While Gandhi provided a theory of self-suffering induced conversion, Galtung has refined the theory, to come to a clearer understanding of its workings in a way that allows not only peace researchers to be able to plot

---

[64] William Robert Miller, *Nonviolence: A Christian Interpretation* (New York: Association Press, 1964), p. 313.
[65] Galtung, *Nonviolence and Israel/Palestine*, pp. 20–1.   [66] *Ibid.*, p. 25.

the probable outcome of a conflict, but also peacemakers and activists to know where to target their actions in order to maximise the 'this worldly' as well as existential outcomes.

Johan Galtung's peace research is not based on one monumentally significant paper or new paradigm. Although peace research is now a recognised discipline in its own right thanks largely to Galtung, and the concept of 'structural violence' has become part of an almost universally accepted framework for the discipline, Galtung's work and influence have not stopped there. His writing output is prodigious – the 1980 bibliography of his work listed 676 publications while the new bibliography, which covers his work up till 1990,[67] lists close to 1,000 publications including fifty-six books – and there is no evidence that this production has slowed at all since then. In all this Galtung has not been saying the same thing over and over. As Gleditsch has pointed out, Galtung is the 'center of an intellectual movement, constantly coming up with new ideas, throwing them in all directions . . . constantly surprising his adherents or even exasperating them: no sooner have they internalized the ideas of one paper before a whole series of others is published in which the ideas of the first are if not contradicted, at least transcended.'[68]

The same is often more specifically also claimed for his peace research. This however is only true to the extent that the audience of his peace-related writings are not aware of the influence of Mahatma Gandhi on Galtung's growing conception of the discipline of peace research or are not well enough versed in Gandhian philosophy to discern the constant threads. Galtung's peace research is not merely about achieving the negative peace of ending direct violence, especially wars, or even achieving positive peace by ending direct and structural violence. His later development may leave other more conventional peace researchers scratching their heads (or worse). What are they to do when a leading figure in their discipline becomes more interested in the individual than the group or the state? Who could or would want to make the shift from 'enlightened technocrat' to 'karmayogi'? And what, for example, are they to make of the 'Father of Modern Peace Research' talking about those who have studied

---

[67] Johan Galtung, *Bibliography: 1951–90* (Oslo: PRIO, 1990).
[68] Nils Petter Gleditsch, 'The Structure of Galtungism', in Gleditsch *et al* (eds.), *Johan Galtung: A Bibliography*, pp. 64–81 at p. 79.

Gandhi (as he has) seeing the requirements of conflict as being more than making a struggle compatible with goals, and calling for an embracing of conflict as a basic social reality that demands optimism and innovation, and imagination in finding new forms of noncoercive struggle because 'love is invincible'?[69] The goal becomes not just the resolution of the conflict but also 'a higher level of self-purification in all actors',[70] in short something akin to the Gandhian project of realising the Truth. And it is not merely an academic exercise – as Galtung suggests the peace researcher should be a peace educator and peace activist, and truth-seeker as Gandhi was.

[69] Galtung, 'Gandhian Themes', p. 234.   [70] Galtung, *Peace by Peaceful Means*, p. 116.

CHAPTER II

E. F. Schumacher – economics as if people mattered

INTRODUCTION

Early in its history, economics was referred to as the 'dismal science' because it was seen as being devoid of any moral underpinning and because it seemed to be about untold riches for some and abject poverty for others. Modern economists, of course, do not see it this way. They tend to see the market as being a value-neutral mechanism that is quite good at arranging for a wide and relatively equitable distribution of wealth. Some critics, however, point out that now that technology has enabled the production of countless goods for human consumption, it has not only made possible unlimited consumption and greed but also legitimised it. As demand grows, the problem of unfulfilled needs (at least in the affluent world) becomes one of unfulfilled wants. Economic theory, the critics argue, ignores 'social wastefulness as distinguished from market wastefulness'.[1] It neglects questions concerning the right to employment, the state as an institution of violence or the corporate system as an institution of exploitation. They claim that the maximisation of consumption and the continual raising of 'living standards' became the measures of success. The critics further assert that the expansion of production that led to this also leads to environmental problems, and that so-called efficiency leads to unemployment, exploitation and international inequalities. This expansion is not only aimed at satisfying wants but also to creating ever new (material, not spiritual) ones. In short, for these critics 'The Science of Economics ceased to be dismal, it rather became an art of rat race.'[2] The Gandhian economist J. D. Sethi, for example, makes the point that it is little wonder that the beneficiaries of this system push Gandhi 'from the debate and the curricula because of his emphasis on making ethical means the central core of economic

[1] J. D. Sethi, 'Foreword', in Romesh Diwan and Mark Lutz (eds.), *Essays in Gandhian Economics* (New Delhi: Gandhi Peace Foundation, 1985), pp. xiii–xiv.
[2] Sethi, 'Foreword', p. xiii.

theory and practice'. He adds that the questions posed by the consequences of current economic thought and practice make 'the study of Gandhi, his philosophy of economics and his methods' suddenly relevant and urgent.[3]

Soon after Gandhi arrived back in India from South Africa, he gave a lecture titled 'Does economic progress clash with real progress?' to the Muir College Economic Society in Allahabad. In his presentation, he admitted that he knew little of economics the way his audience understood the term. However, he told the listeners that choices had to be made as God and Mammon could not be served concurrently, and because the monster of materialism was crushing society. He pleaded for an economy where there was more truth than gold, where there was more charity than self-love. He added that America may be the envy of other nations and while some may say that American wealth may be obtained while its methods avoided, such an attempt is foredoomed to failure. And, the better part of a century ago, he summed up the situation that formed the basis for the new economic thinking by the likes of E. F. Schumacher:

This land of ours was once, we are told, the abode of the gods. It is not possible to conceive gods inhabiting a land which is made hideous by the smoke and the din of null chimneys and factories and whose roadways are traversed by rushing engines dragging numerous cars crowded with men mostly who know not what they are after, who are often absent-minded, and whose tempers do not improve by being uncomfortably packed like sardines in boxes and finding themselves in the midst of utter strangers who would oust them if they could and whom they would in their turn oust similarly. I refer to these things because they are held to be symbolical of material progress. But they add not an atom to our happiness.[4]

Five years later he added that 'The economics that disregard moral and sentimental considerations are like wax-works that being life-like still lack the life of the living flesh. At every crucial moment these new-fangled economic laws have broken down in practice. And nations or individuals who accept them as guiding maxims must perish.'[5]

Some editions of Schumacher's landmark book, *Small is Beautiful*, had a picture of the Mahatma on the cover, and for many in the West it provided an introduction to the economic ideas of Gandhi. As important as its popular appeal was, that book also introduced Gandhian ideas to economists

---

[3] *Ibid.*, pp. xxii–xxiii.
[4] 'Speech at Muir College Economic Society, Allahabad', 22 December 1916.
[5] 'The Secret of It', *Young India*, 27 October 1921.

and allowed these ideas to become the focus of serious study. Schumacher pre-empted Sethi's challenge and it earned him the title of 'later-day [sic] Gandhi'.[6]

SCHUMACHER AS ECONOMIST

Ernst Friedrich (Fritz) Schumacher was born in Bonn in 1911, the third child of a professor of economics. He studied economics and political sciences at Bonn University and was awarded the first post-war German Rhodes Scholarship which took him to New College in Oxford between 1930 and 1932. Through the Rhodes Trust he was able to go to Colombia University where, by the tender age of twenty-three he was lecturing at the School of Banking. Following his return to Germany in 1935, he worked for an organisation set up by leading industrial and export concerns to foster international trade. That year he also received his country's highest award for life-saving after he had rescued a drowning man. However, he was unhappy with the Nazi government and felt alienated from his own Germanness and in January 1937, with his young wife, he emigrated to England. He worked in investment finance in London until the war broke out. During his brief internment as an enemy alien in 1940 he became friends with a staunch Marxist and this lead him to serious thinking about political economy. During the next three years Schumacher was conditionally freed to work as a farm labourer.

Even before the war had ended he was writing economic articles for leading London journals (under pseudonyms as the editors feared that a German name would offend). By the time that he became a British citizen after the war he had already undertaken practical work in many different economic institutions and had also 'experienced poverty, social injustice and alienation first-hand'.[7] Following the war, he worked back in Germany carrying out a study on the effects of strategic bombing for the Americans and then on the reorganisation of the German coal industry as an economic adviser for the Allied Control Commission. According to his daughter/biographer, Schumacher was already an admirer of Gandhi and was greatly shocked when he learned of his assassination.[8]

---

[6] M. M. Hoda, 'Schumacher: A Profile', in M. M. Hoda (comp. and ed.), *Future is Manageable: Schumacher's Observations on Non-Violent Economics and Technology With A Human Face* (New Delhi: Impex India, 1978), p. 2.

[7] Diana Schumacher, 'Introduction' to E. F. Schumacher, *This I Believe and Other Essays* (Dartington Totnes: Resurgence, 1998), p. 11.

[8] Barbara Wood, *Alias Papa: A Life of Fritz Schumacher* (London: Cape, 1984), p. 243.

In 1950 he began his twenty-year career as Economic Adviser and then Director of Statistics to the British National Coal Board. Schumacher was a prolific reader and in the mid-1950s he began a study of eastern thought, using his train trips to work to further his comparative studies of religions. He attended lectures on eastern philosophy and took up meditation.[9] He read the writings and speeches of Gandhi, noting that the Mahatma's view of economic development was quite different to that of the mainstream and required careful examination.[10]

The various strands of Schumacher's experience and thinking crystallized during an assignment to Burma as a governmental economic adviser in 1955. Later he recalled that,

Within a few weeks of my arrival in Rangoon and after visiting a few villages and towns, I realised that the Burmese needed little advice from a Western economist like me. In fact we Western economists could learn a thing or two from the Burmese. They have a perfectly good economic system which has supported a highly developed religion and culture and produced not only enough rice for their own people but also a surplus for the markets of India.[11]

Schumacher had realised that western economic philosophy could not simply be transferred to Burma because it would merely lead to an introduction of western demands.[12] Further, on that trip, he realised that 'overseas development aid really was a process where you collect money from the poor people in the rich countries, to give it to the rich people in the poor countries'.[13]

What was needed was, in his terms, a 'Buddhist economics'.[14] Following the Burma trip, Schumacher wrote a short paper titled 'Economics in a Buddhist Country' and later expanded it into an article which first appeared in the weighty tome *Asia: A Handbook*[15] and eventually became a chapter in *Small is Beautiful*. This, and another paper, titled 'Non-Violent Economics', published on 21 August 1960 in the 'Weekend Review' of the London *Observer*, were groundbreaking. The original essay was probably Schumacher's 'first critique of the impact of Western economic philosophy on the life and culture of developing countries' and was also 'a critique

[9] Diana Schumacher, 'Introduction', p. 13.   [10] Wood, *Alias Papa*, p. 243.
[11] Quoted in 'Foreword' by Satish Kumar to Schumacher, *This I Believe*, p. 8.
[12] Hoda, 'Schumacher: A Profile', pp. 5–6.
[13] Schumacher quoted in George McRobie, *Small is Possible* (London: Jonathan Cape, 1981), p. 2.
[14] Wood, *Alias Papa*, p. 246.
[15] E. F. Schumacher, 'Buddhist Economics', in Guy Wint (ed.) *Asia: A Handbook* (London: A. Blond, 1965), pp. 695–701. In 1968 it was reproduced in the British journal *Resurgence*, and the following year in the US journal *Manas*.

of the notion of limitless and completely indiscriminate growth, and of the consequences of the inability to distinguish between renewable and non-renewable products'.[16]

The 1955 essay was in effect a vision of an alternative economics 'propounded by the greatest man of our age, Mahatma Gandhi'.[17] Later, with ever increasing global nuclear fears, Schumacher was to explore the link between economics and war in the light of Gandhi's thinking and came to the conclusion that what was needed was a 'non-violent economics'.[18]

As important as his understandings of Gandhi's writings were, there was a more direct link to the Mahatma. Throughout the 1950s and 1960s, Jayaprakash Narayan was one of the early supporters of Schumacher. He also gave the alternatives-seeking economist practical guidance in shaping his ever more radical vision. JP had read Schumacher's early writings and they had met when, in 1959, JP was visiting London to promote Vinoba's Bhoodan movement with which he was deeply involved and which Schumacher supported. In 1960, JP attempted to persuade Schumacher to join the Gandhian Institute of Studies in Varanasi, an institute founded by JP to bring together Gandhian thought and modern social sciences.

JP informed Indian Prime Minister Jawaharlal Nehru of Schumacher's work and in January 1961 Schumacher was invited to be a key speaker at an international seminar on 'Paths to Economic Growth' held in Poona. In his introductory remarks before he presented his paper, Schumacher noted that economic growth through imported technologies may be fine, but it was important not to 'forget that the more you bring in, the greater is the need to compensate its inevitable adverse effects upon the great traditional body which is inhabited by something like 80 per cent of the population of the country'.[19] In his paper, 'Help to Those Who Need it Most', he pointed out that 'Economists have assumed too easily that what works best in an advanced country must be best for economic development. Gandhi never made that mistake,' and added that 'Perhaps the best – perhaps even the only effective slogan for aid is: "Find out what the people are trying to do and help them to do it better."'[20] George McRobie, Schumacher's

[16] George McRobie, 'Against the Destructive Economy', in Selbourne, *In Theory and in Practice*, p. 111.

[17] McRobie, 'Against the Destructive Economy', p. 115.   [18] Wood, *Alias Papa*, p. 292.

[19] E. F. Schumacher, 'Paths to Economic Growth: Introductory Remarks', in E. F. Schumacher, *Roots of Economic Growth* (Varanasi: Gandhian Institute of Studies), p. 21.

[20] E. F. Schumacher, 'Help to Those Who Need it Most: Some Problems of Economic Development', in E. F. Schumacher, *Roots of Economic Growth* (Varanasi: Gandhian Institute of Studies), pp. 40, 42.

assistant, notes that with a paper titled 'Levels of Technology', written for the Gandhian Institute of Studies in July, within six months 'he had virtually arrived' at the now lauded concept of intermediate technology.[21] In that paper he noted that

> In a country in which the opportunity cost of labour is nil – or practically nil – 'high cost' products produced by indigenous labour from indigenous materials are normally very much more advantageous than 'low cost' products produced with the help of highly efficient machinery from special materials which may themselves have been imported or else prepared by a further set of special machinery. It is of course unfortunate that prices, as actually charged, do not and cannot reflect the basic fact that the opportunity costs of labour may be *nil*. Many of the paradoxes of economics result from precisely this divergence between private cost accounting and true social cost. That is why Khadi appears very expensive, while mill cloth appears cheap. Yet as long as Khadi is produced (preponderantly) by labour which would otherwise do nothing at all, it is, for the economy as a whole, the cheapest cloth of all – a fact very clearly appreciated by Gandhi.

He concluded the paper with the maxim 'Study their needs and help them to help themselves.'[22]

Following these early publications, Schumacher was labelled a crank by fellow economists. With his ever present sense of humour, he replied: 'What is wrong with a crank? The crank is the part of the machine which creates revolution and it is very small. I am a small revolutionary! It is a compliment.'[23]

In 1970 he became one of the founders of the Intermediate Technology Development Group, a charitable organisation which aimed to provide skills and education to the poor in rural areas of developing countries. Gradually he became known for this work and his broadcasts and lectures, but recognition, and indeed fame, only came with the publication of his book *Small is Beautiful* in 1973. In this book he not only 'launched a powerful attack on conventional economics and technology, and the value system supporting both', but also 'mapped out a sane route towards a sustainable way of life'.[24] The book sold hundreds of thousands of copies, was translated into fifteen languages, and in 1995 was named as one of

---

[21] McRobie, *Small is Possible*, p. 21; and McRobie, 'Against the Destructive Economy', p112. The word 'intermediate' was not welcomed by all. To some in India it smacked of signifying a second-rate technology and the term 'appropriate' technology was favoured. See Ram K. Vepa, *New Technology: A Gandhian Concept* (New Delhi: Gandhi Book House, 1975), pp. 213, 215.

[22] E. F. Schumacher, 'Levels of Technology: A Key Problem for Underdeveloped Countries', in Schumacher, *Roots of Economic Growth*, pp. 42–3, 56.

[23] Schumacher, *This I Believe*, p. 8.

[24] George McRobie, 'Preface' in E. F. Schumacher, *Good Work* (London: Jonathan Cape, 1979), p. ix.

the 100 most influential books written after the Second World War by the London *Times Literary Supplement*.

SCHUMACHER AS GANDHIAN ECONOMIST

Schumacher realised that economics did not stand alone. As with other disciplines, it derived from a view of the meaning and purpose of life – in this case a purely materialistic one. Gandhi's economic thinking, on the other hand, was based on a spiritual criterion. Schumacher took Gandhi's ideas of swadeshi and khadi and applied them to modern economic problems.[25]

Gandhi claimed that 'True economics never militates against the highest ethical standard just as all true ethics, to be worth its name, must at the same time be also good economics . . . True economics stands for social justice; it promotes the good of all equally, including the weakest and is indispensable for decent life';[26] and that he had to confess that he did not 'draw a sharp or any distinction between economics and ethics'.[27]

Gandhi's notion of revitalising village India through the spinning wheel struck many as anachronistic, but the logic of his arguments took on greater force after his death. Gandhi's economic ideals were not about the destruction of all machinery, but a regulation of their excesses. He noted that that requires decentralisation of production and consumption, which in turn should take place as near as possible to the source of production. Such localisation would do away with the temptation to speed up production regardless of the costs and would alleviate the problems of an inappropriately structured economic system.

In his economics of locally handmade goods, the Mahatma saw the poor as being delivered from the 'bonds of the rich'.[28] His approach was 'wholly different' from ordinary economics which 'takes no note of the human factor'. He added that the 'former wholly concerns itself with the human. The latter is frankly selfish, and the former necessarily unselfish'.[29]

Gandhi's ideas on swadeshi were summed up during his first major Indian struggle and repeated almost verbatim throughout the next thirty years. At a women's meeting in 1919 he was already pointing out to his audience that 'swadeshi is that spirit in them which required them to serve their immediate neighbours before others and to use things produced in their neighbourhood in preference to those more remote. So doing, they served

---

[25] Wood, *Alias Papa*, p. 247.   [26] 'Primary Education in Bombay', *Harijan*, 9 October 1937.
[27] 'The Great Sentinel', *Young India*, 13 October 1921.
[28] 'No and Yes', *Young India*, 17 March 1927.   [29] 'Some Posers', *Young India*, 16 July 1931.

humanity to the best of their capacity. They could not serve humanity neglecting their neighbours.'[30]

In a similar vein, following the Burma trip, Schumacher gives an example of contrasting views on freight rates between the thinking of an economic expert and an economist in the Gandhian tradition or, as he termed it, a 'Buddhist economist'.[31] A traditional economist 'may be inclined to advise that the rates per ton/mile should "taper-off", so that they are the lower the longer the haul. He may suggest that this is simply the "right" system, because it encourages long distance transport, promotes large scale, specialised production, and thus leads to an "optimum use of resources".' The latter would argue the opposite: 'Local, short-distance transportation should receive every encouragement but long hauls should be discouraged because they would promote urbanisation, specialisation beyond the point of human integrity, the growth of a rootless proletariat, – in short, a most undesirable and uneconomic way of life.'[32]

In 1960, he published what was to become his manifesto in the *Observer*:

A way of life that ever more rapidly depletes the power of earth to sustain it and piles up ever more insoluble problems for each succeeding generation can only be called 'violent' . . . In short, man's urgent task is to discover a non-violent way in his economics as well as in his political life . . . Non-violence must permeate the whole of man's activities, if mankind is to be secure against a war of annihilation . . . Present day economics, while claiming to be ethically neutral, in fact propagates a philosophy of unlimited expansionism without any regard to the true and genuine needs of man which are limited.[33]

Nonviolent production meant employing modes of production which both respected ecological principles and attempted to work with nature rather than 'attempting to force their way through natural systems in the conviction that unintended damage and unforseen side-effect can always be undone by the further application of violence. All too often one problem is "solved" by creating several new ones.'[34]

Only months after the publication of the article, through his friendship with Jayaprakash Narayan, Schumacher paid a short visit to India to deliver his address and to examine local economic systems. The crushed spirit of the country he saw led him on a further quest. Following Gandhi, Schumacher

---

[30] 'Speech at Women's Meeting, Godhra', *Young India*, 20 August 1919.
[31] E. F. Schumacher, *Small is Beautiful: A Study of Economics as if People Mattered* (London: Abacus, 1974), p. 49.
[32] Wood, *Alias Papa*, p. 247.
[33] E. F. Schumacher, 'Non-Violent Economics', *Observer*, 21 August 1960.
[34] McRobie, *Small is Possible*, pp. 36–7.

saw the distinction between 'production by the masses' and 'mass production'. The former provides dignity, meaningful contact with others
and is appropriate in a country with a huge population while the latter
is violent, ecologically damaging, self-destructive in its consumption of
non-renewable resources and dehumanising for the individuals involved.[35]
In 1962, following prompting from Nehru, JP invited Schumacher to go
to India for six months as an adviser to the Planning Commission. This
visit allowed him the opportunity to further immerse himself in Gandhian
literature, to have extensive discussions with JP, Vinoba and economists
such as Professor D. R. Gadgil,[36] and to see life in village India first hand.
The Scarfes, then teachers in JP's ashram and later his biographers, escorted
him on a tour of the nearby village when he came to visit JP in November.
Although they argued that even the rural poor were entitled to good medical care rather than quickly trained first-aid workers,[37] during this trip
Schumacher came to the realisation that the key to solving the dilemma
of implementing Gandhi's dream was the development of a level of
technology which would be appropriate to the needs and resources of
the poor with tools and equipment designed to be small, simple, low-
cost, environmentally friendly,[38] and 'compatible with man's need for
creativity'.[39]

Two years later he was back in India at a conference with Indian
economists and it was during this time that the term 'appropriate technology' was first used.[40] At JP's invitation, Schumacher made his final
visit to India in 1973 to deliver the Fourth Gandhi Memorial Lecture at the
Gandhian Institute of Studies and to inaugurate an appropriate technology
development unit at the institute.[41]

GANDHIAN ECONOMICS

As early as 1909, in his important work *Hind Swaraj*, Gandhi was already
writing about the evils of modern civilisation with its abundance of material
goods, where people become factory slaves or slaves to materialism, aban-
doning morality and religion, where rapid railway travel spread plagues and

[35] Schumacher, *Small is Beautiful*, p. 128.
[36] Gadgil was the author of *Planning and Economic Policy in India* (Poona: Gokhale Institute of Politics and Economics, 1961).
[37] See Allan and Wendy Scarfe, *Remembering Jayaprakash* (New Delhi: Siddharth, 1997), p. 193.
[38] Schumacher, *Good Work*, chapter 2.   [39] Schumacher, *Small is Beautiful*, p. 27.
[40] McRobie, 'Against the Destructive Economy', p. 114.
[41] Jayaprakash Narayan, 'Foreword', in Hoda, *Future is Manageable*, p. ix.

prevented people from having a chance to get to meet and establish kindred feelings with their neighbours on long journeys, where educated lawyers further divided rather than reconciled disputing parties, and where doctors treated symptoms so that causes did not need to be tackled.[42] He remarked that the 'mind is a restless bird; the more it gets the more it wants, and still it remains unsatisfied'. He added that while 'a man is not necessarily unhappy because he is rich, or unhappy because he is poor', 'life-corroding competition' and large cities do not further health or happiness.[43]

Several decades later, but still several decades before Schumacher took up the cause, Gandhi had explained that while he was not against machinery per se, he did object to the 'craze for machinery':

The craze is for what they call labour-saving machinery. Men go on 'saving labour' till thousands are without work and thrown on the open streets to die of starvation. I want to save time and labour, not for a fraction of mankind, but for all. I want the concentration of wealth, not in the hands of a few but in the hands of all. To-day machinery merely helps a few to ride on the backs of millions. The impetus behind it all is not the philanthropy to save labour, but greed.[44]

This leads to what Gandhi termed 'parasitism':

Man is made to obey the machine. The wealthy and middle classes become helpless and parasitic upon the working classes. And the latter become so specialized that they also become helpless. The ordinary city-dweller cannot make his own clothing or produce or prepare his own food. The cities become parasitic upon the country. Industrial nations upon agricultural nations. Those who live in temperate climates are increasingly parasitic upon tropical peoples. Governments upon the peoples they govern. Armies upon civilians. People even become parasitic and passive in regard to their recreation and amusements.[45]

And, of course, this is unsustainable. Gandhi, in a now famous saying, told his secretary that the 'Earth provides enough to satisfy every man's need but not for every man's greed.'[46]

Schumacher's book *Small is Beautiful* is subtitled 'A Study of Economics as if People Mattered' and echoed this message. In it he pointed out that there are two types of mechanisation: the use of tools which enhance skill and power, and the use of machines which turn work over to mechanical

[42] See Gandhi, *Hind Swaraj*, chapter 6 'Civilization', chapter 9 'The Condition of India: Railways', chapter 11 'The Condition of India: Lawyers', and chapter 12 'The Condition of India: Doctors',
[43] Gandhi, *Hind Swaraj*, chapter 13 'What is True Civilization'.
[44] 'Discussion with G. Ramachandran', *Young India*, 13 November 1924.
[45] 'Notes', *Young India*, 15 April 1926.
[46] Quoted in Pyarelal, *Mahatma Gandhi, volume X: The Last Phase, Part-II* (Ahmedabad: Navajivan, 1958), p. 552.

slaves and then leave the worker in a position of having to tend the slave.[47] Further, he notes that we are moving ever more rapidly into a world dominated by the large-scale; complexity; high capital intensity which eliminates the human factor; and violence. In order to ensure survival he recommended new guidelines which point towards smallness rather than giantism, simplification rather than complexity ('any fool can make things complicated, it requires a genius to make things simple'[48]), capital saving rather than labour saving – and towards nonviolence.[49] The profit motive throws humanity and the planet out of equilibrium. The emphasis has to be shifted back to the person rather than the product, capital has to serve humans rather than humans remaining the slaves of capital. Costs have to be measured in human terms by taking cognisance of happiness, beauty, health and the protection of the planet.

In his 1973 Gandhi Memorial Lecture, following close on the heels of the oil crisis and the Club of Rome's *Limits to Growth* report, Schumacher noted that the affluence of a small part of the world was pushing the whole world into the three concurrent crises concerning resources, ecology and alienation. He explained that the modern world finds itself in trouble and that this would not have come as a surprise to Gandhi. Voicing his debt to the economic thought of the Mahatma, Schumacher noted that Gandhi enunciated his economic position in the language of the people, rather than that of academic economists: 'And so the economists never noticed that he was, in fact, a very great economist in his own right, and as things have been developing these last twenty-five years, it may well emerge that he was the greatest of them all.'

As he continued his lecture, he made this point even more explicit:

The story goes that a famous German conductor was once asked: 'Whom do you consider the greatest of all composers?' 'Unquestionably Beethoven,' he replied . . . 'Would you not even consider Mozart?' 'Forgive me,' he said, 'I thought you were referring only to the others.' The same initial question may one day be put to an economist. 'Who, in our lifetime is the greatest?' And the answer might come back, 'Unquestionably Keynes.' . . . 'Would you not even consider Gandhi?' . . . 'Forgive me, I thought you were referring only to the others.'[50]

He then summarised the fundamentals of a Gandhian prescription that rejected an economics in which people did not really matter, one that was

---

[47] Schumacher, *Small is Beautiful*, p. 46.

[48] Quoted in Satish Kumar 'You Are, Therefore I Am', *Life Positive Plus* 1 (2002), p. 69.

[49] E. F. Schumacher, 'Small is Beautiful', in Hoda (ed.), *Future is Manageable*, p. 25.

[50] *Ibid.*, pp. 14, 16, 18.

at the foundation of his own economics: First, that all economic reasoning should start from the genuine needs of the people, and that economic and social practice should help the poor to help themselves. Second, that not only agriculture as such, but also all possible productive, non-agricultural activities in the rural areas, should be revitalised and fostered. Third, that trends towards the further, excessive concentration of populations in large cities should be resisted. And fourth, that systematic policies – based on the best of available knowledge – should be developed for the mobilisation of India's resources, the greatest of which is the population itself.[51]

A few years later, commenting on this analysis, JP pointed out that 'Taking a cue from Gandhi, he proposed three remedies for the maladies of modern society, namely, small-ness, simplicity and non-violence',[52] and for India he added two more: capital saving and a rural-based, self-reliant and employment-oriented economy.[53] For Schumacher smallness meant reuniting small-scale production and small-scale consumption, thus minimising transport as transport added cost without adding anything of real value to goods. The economics of scale which were a nineteenth-century truth had been shown to be a twentieth century myth.[54] He also affirmed Gandhi's dictum that 'high-thinking is inconsistent with complicated material life', noting that 'all real human needs were essentially simple, therefore only frivolities and extravagances like supersonic transport were invariably complex'.[55] He believed that the crises of resource depletion, ecological destruction and personal alienation suffered by the modern world could be overcome with 'Gandhian work with a spirit of truth and non-violence which inspired Gandhi'.[56] Capital had to be saved so that people did not simply become minders of very expensive machines, diminished in personality development and robbed of creative spirit. And finally, noting Gandhi's vision for a rural-based India (one which was not based on an inherently violent factory civilisation built on exploitation, but on a rural-minded nonviolence), he called Gandhi a nonviolent social revolutionary.[57]

Gandhi's vision of an India composed of self-sufficient but interlinked rural republics with decentralised small-scale economic structures and participatory democracy was quickly dispensed with in the newly independent country bent on industrialisation. Gandhian economics was perceived as reactionary, now here was an eminent economist praising it.[58] This lead

---

[51] *Ibid.*, p. 23.   [52] Narayan, 'Foreword', in Hoda, *Future is Manageable*, p. x.
[53] Surur Hoda, 'Schumacher on Gandhi', in Manmohan Choudhuri and Ramjee Singh (eds.), *Mahatma Gandhi: 125 Years* (Varanasi: Sarva Seva Sangh/Gandhian Institute of Studies, 1995), p. 98.
[54] *Ibid.*, pp. 101–2.   [55] *Ibid.*, pp. 99–100.   [56] *Ibid.*, p. 99.
[57] *Ibid.*, pp. 102–3.   [58] *Ibid.*, p. 95.

to a feedback loop of sorts in the relationship between the Gandhians in India and Schumacher. They supported his ideas and helped him to understand Gandhi in his context. He supported the efforts of the Gandhians in their quest for appropriate technology and gave legitimacy to their ideas, in fact he was acclaimed as 'the man who could interpret Gandhi to the Indians.'[59] And of course the loop was not a closed one, Schumacher's ideas had great resonance outside Gandhian circles. The concept of intermediate technology,[60] following initial criticisms by the economic community, was eventually taken up by UN agencies, governments and non-governmental organisations around the world and led to a proliferation of studies in Gandhian economics.

ECONOMICS AND SPIRITUALITY

Gandhi's admission that he had not made a study of the great economic thinkers did not concern Schumacher, who himself had turned his back on traditional orthodoxy. Gandhi's ultimate goal of self-realisation naturally carried over into his economic thinking. It meant more than an identification with the mere personal ego, it required a merging with a greater self. This could not come about through exploitation, but demanded social justice and the good of all. For Gandhi, economics was an economics of nonviolence. Towards the end of his life he wrote:

I will give you a talisman. Whenever you are in doubt or when the self becomes too much for you, apply the following test. Recall the face of the poorest and weakest man whom you have seen, and ask yourself if the step you contemplate is going to be of any use to him. Will he gain anything by it? Will it restore him to a control over his own life and destiny? In other words, will it lead to Swaraj for the hungry and spiritually starving millions? Then you will find your doubt and your self melting away.[61]

This had resonance in Schumacher's own world view. In *Small is Beautiful* he points out that 'While the materialist is mainly interested in goods, the Buddhist is mainly interested in liberation.' The keynotes of Buddhist

---

[59] Wood, *Alias Papa*, p. 322.

[60] Intermediate technology implies a choice of technology that does not assume that what is best in conditions of affluence is necessarily the best in conditions of poverty, and that technologies that are most likely to be appropriate to conditions of poverty are presumably going to be 'intermediate' between tools such as the hoe and the tractor. See McRobie, *Small is Possible*, pp. 33–4.

[61] Reproduced in D. G. Tendulkar, *Mahatma: Life of Mohandas Karamchand Gandhi* (New Delhi: Publications Division, Ministry of Information and Broadcasting, Government of India, 1960–1963), vol. VIII, between pp. 288–9.

economics are simplicity and nonviolence, while for modern economists who measure 'standards of living' by amounts of consumption, this is difficult to understand. In modern economics consumption is the end and purpose of economic activity, in Buddhist economics, on the other hand, ownership and consumption are merely means to an end.[62]

Just before his own death, Schumacher mapped out his personal philosophy of the meaning of human life. In the book *Guide for the Perplexed*, without explicitly mentioning Gandhi, he talks of the transformation of the inner self through 'inner work' in ways reminiscent of Gandhi and Næss' views of self-realisation. In an earlier essay on this topic he did include references to Gandhi.[63] And, in language that could have come straight from the Mahatma, in a film, *On the Edge of the Forest*, Schumacher explained that the 'religion' of economics is the enemy of all the things that really matter – beauty, sympathy and harmony; it is, in fact, uneconomical because it produces waste. In this 'religion' the only thing considered worthy of economising is human labour – paradoxically the very thing that is free and of which there is plenty. Schumacher emphasised that we are part of the environment, that if we win the fight against nature we will find ourselves on the losing side and, finally, that if we do not develop an economics of permanence then we are too 'clever' to survive, that we can be classified as a species in danger of extinction[64] – again sentiments familiar to anyone who is versed in Gandhi's economic writings.

In Schumacher's journey through life, notes his daughter, 'his changing economic and metaphysical views (which sometimes seemed contradictory) chronologically mirrored his own spiritual struggles and developments. His speeches, articles and projects likewise reflected these changes from Marxism through Buddhism and eventually to Christianity.'[65] Six years before he died, much to the surprise of his Marxist and Buddhist friends, he became a Roman Catholic. 'It was a formal renouncement of his previously cherished views of the supremacy of the intellect and reason over the Christian virtues of compassion, forgiveness, unconditional love, the acknowledgement of a Divine Creator, and the integrity of all creation.'[66] If these sentiments came as a surprise to Marxists and Buddhist, they would not have done so to Gandhi or the Gandhians.

---

[62] Schumacher, *Small is Beautiful*, pp. 47–8.
[63] See E. F. Schumacher, 'The Economics of Permanence', in Ted Dunn (ed.), *Foundations of Peace and Freedom: The Ecology of a Peaceful World* (Swansea: Davies, 1975), pp. 102–6.
[64] E. F. Schumacher, *On the Edge of the Forest*, a film directed by Barrie Oldfield, 1977.
[65] Diana Schumacher, 'Introduction', p. 13.   [66] *Ibid.*

CHAPTER 12

Gene Sharp – nonviolence becomes a political method

INTRODUCTION

For those interested in nonviolence theory, the politics of nonviolent activism, the ethics of civil disobedience or people-power social movements, or indeed for those who are activists and go to training workshops, look for inspiration or want help in selecting appropriate tactics, Gene Sharp is usually the starting point. Through his near definitive work *The Politics of Nonviolent Action*, Sharp provides the theory and examples which form the basis of countless political actions, pre-action nonviolence training workshops, and academic studies of nonviolent political activism.

Gene Sharp is an internationally known scholar whose works on nonviolent direct action and civilian-based defence have been translated into almost thirty languages and even used by government defence planners in Estonia, Latvia and Lithuania in formulating strategies to ensure that the Soviet Union did not regain control over the newly independent states. Besides his deserved reputation in nonviolent activist circles, based on *The Politics of Nonviolent Action*, he has also been portrayed as the 'Machiavelli of nonviolence' because of his pragmatic approach to nonviolent activism, and been hailed as the 'Clausewitz of nonviolent warfare' for his writings on nonviolent defence and people power.[1]

In his major area of work, Gene Sharp was perhaps even more singularly influenced by Gandhi than were Næss, Galtung and Schumacher yet, unlike them, he has spent a good deal of his later intellectual life trying to distance himself from his source of inspiration. While Sharp started his life's work as an idealistic seeker after Gandhi, his later work is characterised by hard-bitten realism. The older Sharp champions a 'technique approach' to nonviolent action, arguing that it is used, and should be used,

---

[1] Ralph Summy, 'One Person's Search for a Functional Alternative to Violence', *Gandhi Marg* 5 (1983), p. 26.

'for pragmatic reasons [rather] than for religious or ethical ones'.[2] A 'Biographical Profile' of Sharp on his website claims that 'He is convinced that pragmatic, strategically planned, nonviolent struggle can be made highly effective for application in conflicts to lift oppression and as a substitute for violence.' Gandhi, too, was concerned about lifting oppression and finding a substitute for violence. However his reasons for doing so had more to do with a perceived intrinsic, rather than merely an instrumental, value in nonviolence. For some people this different direction taken by Gene Sharp, has moved nonviolence beyond Gandhi, making it a more practically available method of struggle. For others, he has diminished Gandhi's philosophy in action by divorcing it from its fundamental underpinnings.

THE YOUNG SHARP: GANDHI AND MORAL POWER

Gene Sharp was born in 1928 in Ohio in the United States.[3] At Ohio State University he completed a BA in social sciences in 1949, with his senior honours thesis on war, and an MA in sociology in 1951, with a dissertation titled 'Non-violence: A Sociological Study'. After going through several incarnations, a chapter of the MA dissertation appeared as a book chapter under the title 'A Study of the Meanings of Nonviolence'.[4] Here Sharp noted that, largely thanks to Gandhi, the ideals of nonviolence and methods of nonviolent social action had risen to 'sufficient prominence that they must be reckoned with in world thinking and events'.[5] He also pointed out that despite this awareness there is much confusion surrounding the term and set out to 'clarify, classify and define'[6] various forms of nonviolence in a value-neutral way. However, in the three-page table illustrating the characteristics of his nine types of generic nonviolence and in the introductory sections of the paper, there is a progression in the way the categories are listed. Sharp states that the classification is roughly 'in the order of increasing activity',[7] but the tone of the work also implies Sharp's increasing approval, and the methods of Gandhi and his later followers seem to be the ones Sharp favours most.

---

[2] Roger Powers, 'Gene Sharp (b. 1928)', in Powers and Vogele, *Protest, Power, and Change*, p. 467.
[3] This information is based on the brief biographical sketch by Powers in Powers and Vogele, *Protest, Power, and Change*, pp. 467–9.
[4] Gene Sharp, 'A Study of the Meanings of Nonviolence,' in G. Ramachandran and T. K. Mahadevan (eds.), *Gandhi: His Relevance for our Times* (Berkeley: World Without War Council, circa 1971), pp. 21–66.
[5] Sharp, 'A Study of the Meanings of Nonviolence', p. 22.   [6] *Ibid.*, p. 55.   [7] *Ibid.*, p. 28.

During the next few years, following his formal studies, Sharp supported himself with part-time jobs while studying Gandhian thought and examining Gandhi's political struggles in India more closely. This led in 1953, when he was only twenty-five years old, to the completion of his first book manuscript. Although Albert Einstein was a firm supporter of the youthful conscientious objector, wrote a foreword for the work and tried to get it published, *Gandhi Wields the Weapon of Moral Power* did not appear between covers until 1960.

In order to replace violent forms of social conflict with nonviolent ones, Sharp tells us, we must study Gandhi's methods of combating evil because they are the 'greatest contribution to their development'.[8] In the book, he tries to demonstrate Gandhian techniques in action by presenting a Gandhi who is not impractical or idealistic, but one who tried to 'combine the influence of moral power, love, integrity and goodness with non-violent strategy and techniques which resulted in providing an active, dynamic method of struggle'. He also notes that Gandhi's nonviolence and the 'presently developing thinking' that incorporates much of Gandhi's approach (presumably led by Gandhi's spiritual heir Vinoba Bhave and his land gift movement, and later Jayaprakash Narayan and his 'Total Revolution') are 'seeking to develop a way and a programme which is capable of meeting the crisis of our age'. He adds, in quite Gandhian language, that 'We must become integrated, loving individuals. Unless people can sense in our lives that of which we speak, it is useless for us to talk of a new way of life.'[9] Indeed, he explains that it is important to see Gandhi's 'method of fighting evil in the perspective of Gandhi's whole philosophy, for this weapon is an expression of a way of looking at life and a way of living'.[10]

This is the book of a young Gandhi disciple and it is obvious from it that Sharp includes himself among those who 'believe in changing society by love',[11] and when he informs the reader that 'in Gandhi's thinking, means and ends should be equally pure. The end growing out of the means is just as logical as the tree growing from the seed,' and 'what is attained by love is retained for all time, while what is obtained by violence has within it the seeds of its own destruction',[12] he is doing it from conviction. The same would seem to apply to his summary of what satyagraha entails:

The satyagrahi, a believer in satyagraha, constantly seeks to live a life of truth and love. He always seeks to 'turn the searchlight inward' and to so live that he does

---

[8] Gene Sharp, *Gandhi Wields the Weapon of Moral Power [Three Case Histories]* (Ahmedabad: Navajivan, 1960), p. xiv.
[9] *Ibid.*, pp. xii–xiii.   [10] *Ibid.*, p. 4.   [11] *Ibid.*, p. 9.   [12] *Ibid.*, p. 5.

no wrong to his fellow men through exploitation, oppression, violence or other means. The satyagrahi looks upon all as his brothers. He believes that the practice of love and self-suffering will bring about a change of heart in his opponent. The satyagrahi tries to change both individuals and institutions. He believes that the power of love, if pure, is great enough to melt the stoniest heart of an evil doer.[13]

Only weeks after completing *Gandhi Wields the Weapon of Moral Power*, Sharp was sentenced to two years imprisonment as a conscientious objector during the Korean War. After serving nine months of the sentence he briefly worked as secretary to the American pacifist A. J. Muste and then as an assistant editor of *Peace News* in London and as a research scholar in Oslo under the tutelage of Arne Næss. As a doctoral student at Oxford University, in 1964 Sharp helped to organise an international Civilian Defence Study Conference which three years later led to the publication of Adam Roberts' edited book *The Strategy of Civilian Defence* and sowed the seeds for a different focus for Sharp's thinking on nonviolence.

During the 1960s Gene Sharp was still writing consistently on Gandhi as the basis for his work on nonviolence and in 1979 many of his papers from this period were collected together in his book *Gandhi as a Political Strategist*. In one of these papers, written in 1962, Sharp states his position regarding power – on which his notion of nonviolent activism rests – by noting that 'hierarchical systems ultimately depend upon assistance of the underlings',[14] using a collection of quotations from the Mahatma to make the case. Sharp notes that 'Gandhi was probably the first consciously to formulate over a period of years a major system of resistance based upon this assumption.'[15]

Sharp also devoted a great deal of time in this phase of his life to examining Gandhi as a national defence strategist and the way that the 'technique' of nonviolence could be adopted on a widespread scale for political ends and to remove political violence. The India/China border war provided him with a case in point. Rather than face the invaders nonviolently, in 1962 India fought a brief border war with China. Many saw this as a betrayal of Gandhi. Sharp claimed that western pacifists merely moralised about what not to do in such circumstances or forwarded 'quite incomplete and sometimes naive proposals'.[16] He noted that it is not enough to call for

---

[13] *Ibid.*, p. 4.
[14] Gene Sharp, 'Gandhi on the Theory of Voluntary Servitude,' in Gene Sharp, *Gandhi as a Political Strategist: With Essays on Ethics and Politics* (Boston: Porter Sargent, 1979), pp. 43–59 at p. 44.
[15] *Ibid.*, p. 57.
[16] Gene Sharp, 'India's Lesson for the Peace Movement', in Sharp, *Gandhi as a Political Strategist*, pp. 121–9 at 127.

India to be true to Gandhi or 'to save the world'. What is needed is the development of a realistic and powerful alternative way of both defending borders and internal threats to freedom.

Sharp notes that since the time of Gandhi, nonviolent action 'has spread throughout the world at an unprecedented rate'. While some of this was stimulated by Gandhi, the technique, Sharp reminds us, 'was modified in new cultural and political settings' and that in these cases 'it has already moved beyond Gandhi'.[17] It seems that Sharp is referring to his own work here. He used Gandhi as a staging point for his own more 'realistic' approach to civilian-based defence, which, with a noticeable lack of references to Gandhi in the later works, has been the main focus of much of his work in the past three decades.

THE MATURE SHARP: GANDHI AS POLITICAL STRATEGIST

Among Gene Sharp's last recorded papers specifically on Gandhi is a review essay of Erik Erikson's acclaimed book *Gandhi's Truth*. Here Sharp questions the long-held orthodoxy that Gandhi discovered nonviolence because of an ethical imperative. Sharp comes to the conclusion that, rather than reasoning from the ethical to the political, Gandhi was aware of many recent historical examples of nonviolent resistance before the much touted 1906 meeting in the Empire Theatre in Johannesburg. In fact, in Sharp's new insight, Gandhi's knowledge of a long history of nonviolent struggle meant that 'to a considerable extent Gandhi reasoned directly from the political to the political'.[18] This line of thinking was foreshadowed in a slightly earlier paper where Sharp argued that while Gandhi concluded that if actions were in tune with ethical principles they would eventually be proved to be the most practical, this reasoning would more than likely only appeal to those who already believed in a system which is based on an ethic of nonviolence. Sharp moves to champion a different form of reasoning, one that starts with determining the most practical course of action which enables one to reach the desired goals in the long run. In short, he posits the questions of whether nonviolence as a political technique can be separated from nonviolence as a moral principle and whether the ethical and the practical are related or in

---

[17] Gene Sharp, 'The Technique of Non-violent Action', Adam Roberts (ed.), *Civilian Resistance as a National Defence: Non-violent Action Against Aggression* (Harmondsworth: Penguin, 1969), pp. 107–27 at p. 118.

[18] Gene Sharp, 'Origins of Gandhi's Use of Nonviolent Struggle: A Review-Essay on Erik Erikson's "Gandhi's Truth"', in Sharp, *Gandhi as a Political Strategist*, pp. 23–41 at p. 26.

fact opposed to each other.[19] He seems to be moving towards the position, which he later adopts, that, as far as nonviolent action is concerned, belief systems and techniques are separable. He observes that 'the practice of calling both such beliefs and the technique of struggle by the single word 'nonviolence' was already becoming common and continues today. It's a bad choice of terminology because it is confusing.'[20]

In another of these late papers, Sharp goes to great lengths to examine Gandhi's distinction between 'nonviolence of the brave,' that is nonviolence undertaken as a matter of principle (or as a creed), and 'nonviolence of the weak', that is nonviolence practised as an expedient (or as a policy).[21] He shows that at times the Mahatma, who championed 'nonviolence of the brave,' contradicted himself by advocating nonviolence as a mere practical substitute for violence when it was expedient for an immediate political goal.

In these papers Sharp is questioning Gandhi in a way he did not in his earliest works. His analysis is far more sophisticated and it now presents a more faltering and undecided Mahatma who cannot be held up quite as easily to show that Sharp's own increasing 'realism' is a deviation from established principles of nonviolence.

Eventually even this reinterpreted Gandhi is dispensed with. Nonviolence and Gandhi are largely divorced in his later writings – in his foreword to Ackerman and Kruegler's *Strategic Nonviolent Conflict*, Sharp manages to avoid mentioning Gandhi even once. And in general, in his books on civilian defence, Gandhi is completely missing. As Gandhi is 'secularised' and then dispensed with, the definition of nonviolent action is also secularised. In a 1989 film by Ilan Ziv called *People Power*, speaking of the Palestinian *Intifada*, Gene Sharp makes the point that 'It is not a question, is this violent or nonviolent. It is not a question, is it morally right or morally wrong. It is not a question, is it justified or unjustified. Those are the ways it is usually argued among Palestinians. The question is, what are its consequences?' In Gandhi's philosophy the consequences of actions cannot be known in advance and that is precisely why the means, over which there is control, must be kept pure. Sharp has moved a long way from the

[19] Gene Sharp, 'Nonviolence: Moral Principle or Political Technique? – Clues from Gandhi's Thought and Experience', in Sharp, *Gandhi as a Political Strategist*, pp. 273–309 at pp. 293, 305.
[20] Gene Sharp, 'Conducting Conflicts Without Violence', *Peace Magazine* 23 (1997), available at www.peacemagazine.org
[21] Gene Sharp, 'Gandhi's Evaluation of Indian Nonviolent Action', in Sharp, *Gandhi as a Political Strategist*, pp. 87–120.

position he had adopted in his earliest Gandhian writings which he now seems to downplay: 'I had done some earlier studies on what might be called principled nonviolence – ethical or religious nonviolence, or various types of pacifism. And those are important; but I concluded after minimal study that they were a separate phenomenon from what was now called nonviolent action.'[22]

FROM IDEALISM TO PRAGMATISM: POLITICAL POWER WITHOUT GANDHI

In an article originally published in the Gandhian studies journal *Gandhi Marg* in 1965, Gene Sharp writes about 'Gandhi's political significance today'. Here Sharp is worried by Gandhi's eccentricities and religious symbolism and language which 'more often confuses than clarifies'.[23] He sees that for westerners generally, and Americans in particular, this may cause a problem in adequately evaluating the Mahatma's political significance. He tries to make Gandhi palatable by a process of 'secularisation'. He does this even though he warns us that 'Gandhi must be evaluated on the basis of his own outlook and his own policies, not those of others.'[24] He aims to strip the Gandhian message of elements which allow westerners to engage in rationalisations that enable them to avoid considering the Gandhian experiments seriously. Sharp ends up doing something similar, reevaluating Gandhi in his own terms. At first he 'secularises' Gandhi and his message so that both can be taken seriously and eventually, because ultimately Sharp's life work becomes one of promoting his own brand of nonviolence not Gandhi or Gandhi's satyagraha, Sharp more or less abandons the Mahatma. For him the most important task becomes one of discovering a nonviolent alternative to war, one that is realistic and pragmatic – and in the end, for him too, in this task Gandhi seems to have become a liability rather than an asset.

When he was specifically asked to address the links between Gandhi and nonviolence, as he was for a lecture marking the fiftieth anniversary of Gandhi's assassination at McMaster University in 1997, Sharp noted that the Mahatma 'tried to convince people who did not believe in *ahimsa* on ethical grounds to adopt nonviolent methods as a practical expedient, a technique that works'.[25] In his foreword to a later edition of Krishnalal

---

[22] Sharp, 'Conducting Conflicts Without Violence.'

[23] Gene Sharp, 'Gandhi's Political Significance', in Sharp, *Gandhi as a Political Strategist*, pp. 1–21, at p. 2.

[24] *Ibid.*, p. 5.　　[25] Reported in *Peace Research Abstract Journal* 36 (1999), p. 157.

Shridharani's 1939 classic study of Gandhi's satyagraha, Sharp makes it clear that he is much less interested in the extreme religious pacifist and moral arguments approach to nonviolence, which emphasises conversion, preferring instead a 'technique approach'.[26] In a recent interview, Sharp, in the words of the reviewer, sees nonviolent action as 'a strategy for imperfect people in an imperfect world'.[27] Sharp notes that many people understand that nonviolent action provides the best chance for achieving their objectives and that nonviolence is not there to resolve the conflict or eliminate the conflict but as a way of conducting conflict. This, of course, does not mean that Sharp now believes it to be wrong to be a 'moral pacifist', merely that one must operate in a context that 'enables the rest of the population to adopt nonviolent means without that commitment'.[28]

Sharp's best-known work is his three-volume magnum opus, *The Politics of Nonviolent Action*. Here he writes at length about the notion of power, historical examples of nonviolent struggle, catalogues 198 different methods of nonviolent action, and examines the dynamics of nonviolent action, including action against violent and repressive opponents. He states that nonviolent action 'consists of acts of protest and persuasion, noncooperation and nonviolent intervention designed to undermine the sources of power of the opponent in order to bring about change'.[29] All the Gandhian references aside, this is a work without the 'feel' of Gandhi as presented by those that can be called exponents of 'ideological', 'principled', 'conscientious', or 'positive' nonviolence.

Nonviolence is a complex phenomenon and theorists have provided differing definitions of it. Gene Sharp, for example, has distinguished nine types of 'generic nonviolence', and Robert Burrowes has attempted to locate nonviolence on a matrix with axes indicating continua from principled to pragmatic and strategic to tactical. However, even before Gene Sharp became known as the pre-eminent theorist of nonviolent activism, it was already acknowledged that, broadly speaking, there appeared to be two main approaches to nonviolence. These approaches were most clearly set out by Judith Stiehm in a perceptive essay titled 'Nonviolence is Two'. One strand, based on human harmony and a moral rejection of violence and coercion, she termed 'conscientious'. The other strand, which sees conflict as normal

---

[26] Reprinted in Sharp, *Gandhi as a Political Strategist*, pp. 315–18, as 'Shridharani's Contribution to the Study of Gandhi's Technique'.

[27] *New Internationalist* interview with Gene Sharp by Noreen Shanahan, November 1997, available at *www.newint.org/issue296/interview.htm*

[28] Gene Sharp, 'People "don't need to believe right"', *National Catholic Reporter* 20 (7 September 1984), p. 11.

[29] Gene Sharp, *The Politics of Nonviolent Action* (Boston: Porter Sargent, 1973), p. 109.

and the rejection of violence as an effective way of challenging power, she called 'pragmatic'. She noted that they 'are different in their motivation, their assumptions, and their implications'[30] and therefore may in some ways be incompatible. Failure to distinguish between the two strands can lead to a diminution in the effectiveness of nonviolent action and cause confusion among the audience. Ralph Summy notes that while debates over this dichotomy may be viewed in academic circles as 'an exhausted, sterile and futile exercise', to peace movement votaries the issue of the choice of approach to nonviolence is vital.[31]

For Sharp, the key feature is power rather than ethical principle: 'Nonviolent action is a technique by which people who reject passivity and submission, and who see struggle as essential, can wage their conflict without violence. Nonviolent action is not an attempt to avoid or ignore conflict. It is one response to the problem, of how to act effectively in politics, especially how to wield power effectively.'[32] He often refers to nonviolence as an 'alternative weapons system'[33] and even describes it as a 'means of combat, as is war. It involves the matching of forces and the waging of "battles", it requires wise strategy and tactics, employs numerous "weapons" and demands of its "soldiers" courage, discipline, and sacrifice.'[34] The central dynamic operates in the realm of power politics rather than morals.

This, to others is 'negative' or 'pragmatic' nonviolence where nonviolent action is used because it is believed to be the most effective method available in the circumstances. Conflict is viewed as a relationship between antagonists with incompatible interests, and the goal is to defeat the opponent.[35] The stream which adheres more closely to Gandhian values, relies on a religious or ethical objection to violence. It is concerned with re-establishing communication and, through self-suffering if necessary, attempts to convince the opponent of the error of their ways, of converting rather than coercing them.[36] Or, according to Burrowes, those with a principled approach 'choose [nonviolent action] for ethical reasons and believe in the unity of means and ends. They view the opponent as a partner in the struggle to satisfy the needs of all; if anyone suffers, it is

---

[30] Judith Stiehm, 'Nonviolence is Two', *Social Inquiry* 38 (1968), p. 23.

[31] Summy, 'One Person's Search', p. 35.

[32] Sharp, *The Politics of Nonviolent Action*, p. 64.   [33] *Ibid.*, pp. 112–14, 452–3.

[34] Gene Sharp, *Civilian-Based Defense: A Post-Military Weapons System* (Princeton University Press, 1990), p. 37.

[35] Robert J. Burrowes, *The Strategy of Nonviolent Defense* (State University of New York Press, 1996), p. 99.

[36] See Stiehm, 'Nonviolence is Two', p. 25.

the practitioner of nonviolence. More fundamentally, this practitioner may view nonviolence as a way of life.'[37]

Sharp notes that this may be fine 'if it occurs', but the simple assertion that nonviolence must be adopted as an ethical principle 'ignores the social reality in which we must operate'. As long as violent sanctions are accepted, violence cannot be removed from political societies by 'witnessing against it or denouncing it on moral grounds' (this is what he seems to have reduced principled nonviolence to). He states that, first, nonviolence must reach the position where it is seen as an alternative form of sanction, and 'once that major changeover has been completed', or at least 'well under way', then people can 'consider and deal with the finer ethical problems which arise in the application of nonviolent sanctions'.[38] In short, be realistic, start with what is most easily achievable.

In relation to himself, echoing Emerson's well-known dictum, Gandhi once noted that 'Foolish consistency is the hobgoblin of little minds.'[39] Sharp, too, must be given room to mature and for his vision to grow. It is not unreasonable that, as is the case for many of the rest of us, Sharp the youthful idealist should develop into a more seasoned and possibly practically minded adult. But perhaps there is more to the story. The young Sharp was a pacifist and worked with well-known pacifists and on well-known pacifist papers. In 1963, while studying at Oxford, he wrote an essay for the London Quakers titled 'Morality, Politics, and Political Technique'. In this article he proclaimed his 'personal belief in "nonviolence as a principle" and a "philosophy of life"'.[40] It is quite clear from the, angry does not seem to be too strong a word, additional introductory note when the essay was eventually reprinted in *Gandhi as a Political Strategist* that Sharp was frustrated with principled pacifists who were more interested in gaining 'individual converts to personal pacifism', than in trying to 'replace violent sanctions with nonviolent ones in society'.[41]

It appears that the essay was ignored by its intended audience and when, two years later, it was published by *Reconciliation Quarterly* it came out, without Sharp's permission, in a truncated form that dropped sections critical of pacifists and their intermittent hostility to the 'nonviolent technique of action' because it might compromise principles. In this essay Sharp, the

---

[37] Burrowes, *The Strategy of Nonviolent Defense*, p. 99.

[38] Gene Sharp, *Social Power and Political Freedom* (Boston: Porter Sargent, 1980), pp. 395–6.

[39] 'My Inconsistencies', *Young India*, 13 February 1930.

[40] Gene Sharp, 'Morality, Politics, and Political Technique', in *Gandhi as a Political Strategist*, pp. 251–71 at p. 252.

[41] *Ibid.*, p. 252.

principled practitioner of nonviolence, was trying to marry the 'moral' and the 'practical', the 'other worldly' and the 'this worldly'. The reaction to this work appears to have been a turning point for him – he states that 'This article was my last major such effort to seek to achieve these changes within pacifist groups.'[42]

While there is too little evidence available to determine whether Sharp's shift in position arose more from finding fault with Gandhi's approach to nonviolence or because his disillusionment with western pacifist thinking and organisations had reached a personal tipping point, it does seem that this experience not only altered the choices he made as to which groups he would work with, but also altered the message itself. Later he was able to say of this principled pacifist period that 'I changed a lot of ideas; sometimes I reversed them. I found that people didn't need to *believe* right to engage in nonviolent struggle,' and of himself he could observe that 'I (now) don't agree with myself then.'[43]

SHARP'S NONVIOLENCE *VS* GANDHI'S NONVIOLENCE

Is the nonviolence of Sharp and Gandhi really at odds here? Gandhi, of course, used nonviolent action on a mass scale, being aware of the use of power while attempting to maintain the principled base for the actions. The Mahatma proclaimed that 'Somehow or other the wrong belief has taken possession of us that ahimsa is pre-eminently a weapon for individuals and its use therefore should be limited to that sphere. In fact that is not the case. Ahimsa is definitely an attitude of society.'[44] He added: 'It is blasphemy to say that nonviolence can only be practiced by individuals and never by nations which are composed of individuals.'[45] The question remains as to whether such proclamations are adequate, and whether they stand up in the face of empirical investigation. Certainly, principled action is more likely among committed individuals, and as activist groups grow larger it becomes increasingly difficult to maintain the purity of means, generally leading to a more pragmatic phase of the struggle. Sharp, in effect, may be accusing Gandhi of wishful thinking. And, if the ends sought by the two men were similar, perhaps Sharp would be right in such an assessment. The point, however, is that the ends are not necessarily the same.

Sharp sees success through nonviolent action being achieved in three possible ways: accommodation (where the opponent does not believe in

---

[42] *Ibid.*   [43] Sharp, 'People "Don't Need to Believe Right"', p. 11.

[44] 'Equal Distribution', *Harijan*, 25 August 1940.

[45] 'Why Not Great Powers?', *Harijan*, 12 November 1938.

the changes made but nevertheless believes that it is best to give in on some or all points to gain peace or to cut losses), nonviolent coercion (where the opponent wants to continue the struggle but cannot because they have lost the sources of power and means of control), and conversion (where the opponent has changed inwardly to the degree that they want to make the changes desired by the nonviolent activist).[46] In his detailed typology of the many varying types of nonviolence, the Gandhian 'technique' of satyagraha seems to contain an ambiguity over whether, while attempting conversion, it is permissible to couple nonviolent resistance with direct action that may force a policy change on the opponent even though their attitudes may not have been changed first. The reason for this ambiguity stems from Sharp's categorisation of satyagraha as being completely 'this' as opposed to 'other worldly'.[47] Satyagraha in its ideal *does* have a very pronounced 'other worldly' underpinning, and in its ideal operation employs no coercive tactics.

Generally, as interpreted, the term 'other worldly' contains an element of world-renunciation or, in its extreme form, a preoccupation with the world to come. It may imply ignoring evil as much as possible and suffering without resisting evil, even by nonviolent means, as part of religious duty. The concern is generally with consistency of beliefs and individual integrity rather than with social reconstruction.[48] However, Johan Galtung is correct when he notes that generally the 'mundane Kingdom' and the 'transcendental Kingdom' are 'two separate components in an ideological space', yet in Gandhi's 'kingdom' the components are combined.[49] A question remains as to whether this is an artificial construct that entails an unresolvable contradiction. In an insightful article, philosopher Smith argues that there is an ambiguity in nonviolence being seen both as an appeal to moral principle and as an effective practical device for achieving a given goal. He adds that

Those who practice nonviolence are forced to oscillate between these two poles. On the one hand, nonviolence as a form of response is adopted because it is dictated by a principle, the principle that violence is always to be avoided because in itself it is 'wrong' and perpetuates the very divisiveness we are trying to overcome. On the other hand, nonviolence is not chosen for this reason alone. It is chosen because, as a matter of actual fact derived from past experience, this method has been shown to be more *effective* than violence in accomplishing certain objectives.[50]

---

[46] Sharp, *The Politics of Nonviolent Action*, p. 706.
[47] Sharp, 'A Study of the Meaning of Nonviolence', see table p. 64.   [48] *Ibid.*, p. 29.
[49] Galtung, 'Gandhi and Conflictology', p. 116.
[50] John E. Smith, 'The Inescapable Ambiguity of Nonviolence', *Philosophy East and West* 19 (1969), p. 157.

Sharp wants to popularise nonviolence as a political weapon to fight tyranny and as a substitute for war. While early on he discovered ambiguities in Gandhi's actions, allowing him a secularised interpretation of Gandhi as a political activist, now ambiguities are hindrances to him. Instead of trying to 'combine kingdoms', Sharp declares Gandhian nonviolence to be 'this worldly', and the aim of nonviolence to be victory not conversion. Arguments about principles and the relationship of ends and means disappear, to be overtaken by those based solely on effectiveness. In fact an insistence on principles may alienate potential practitioners of nonviolence and thus 'impede rather than promote the substitution of nonviolent for violent means'.[51]

Sharp may be of the view that not all conflicts can be or should be resolved, that some should be won. Gandhian satyagraha, at least at a theoretical level, rejects this on at least two grounds. First, in Gandhi's approach, attempts should be made to resolve all conflicts and attempts should be made to convert all opponents so that the parties end up 'on the same side'. If, however, this is not possible, it provides a way of fighting for justice that minimises the possibility of excluding the chance of later conversion taking place. Second, while winning is not totally rejected the main aim of conducting conflict may be something beyond winning or losing, or even beyond a win-win resolution of the dispute at hand – it may have more to do with an existential transformation of the individuals involved. The Gandhian conflict process also goes well beyond conflict resolution to personal integration (or transformation) at a deeper level.[52] For the pragmatic Sharp, this is utopian. Gone is the talk of changing society by love and becoming integrated, loving individuals.

However, as already discussed in the Galtung chapter, for the Mahatma the process was nothing short of a striving for self-realisation. According to Gandhian practice, conflict stems from unmet needs and in order for needs to be met they must first be understood, and this requires true self-awareness. For Gandhi, the discovery of Self was the primary task of life. In Gandhi's vision, satyagraha was not only a useful technique for the resolution of conflicts, and the satyagrahi was far more than a mere practitioner of a certain skill. The satyagrahi was the embodiment of an ideal and the satyagrahi lifestyle was the lifestyle worth living. Sharp does not emphasise the potential positively transformative effect of nonviolent action (for example

---

[51] Sharp, *The Politics of Nonviolent Action*, p. 635.
[52] See Weber, 'Gandhian Philosophy, Conflict Resolution Theory and Practical Approaches to Negotiation'.

in terms of empowerment, openness, participation, gaining of skills) on either the activists themselves or on others, more or less limiting its use to a tool for achieving extrinsic goals.[53]

When writing about the meaning of 'success' in nonviolent action, Sharp takes a far more 'objective' view than would many other nonviolent activists. The important questions are: were the opponent's objectives frustrated, what factors in the social or political situation allowed the opponent to be defeated,[54] and were the stated goals of the nonviolent group achieved because of the struggle?[55] The subjective, and we could say existential, pay-offs that are so important to exponents of principled nonviolence are not considered. Interestingly, in Sharp's second book, dealing with civilian defence, there is an essay by Theodor Ebert in which Gandhian concepts are applied to this area in ways that Sharp was no longer countenancing. Ebert talks of the pay-offs for defending a country with nonviolence as being not only fewer casualties and possibly greater "success" in the narrow meaning of the term, but also 'emerging purified and strengthened from the conflict'.[56] Stiehm notes that such considerations are 'by no means unimportant', the most positive effect of nonviolent action being 'its effect on the participants themselves'. She adds that 'No matter what his adversary does, the nonviolent resister can always achieve his own humanity.'[57]

While Sharp is concerned with social and political freedom, Gandhi's focus is on a search for Truth, and, according to Hayes, this means that in 'a theoretical-practical sense, Gandhi's ideals can be seen to be directly aimed at addressing many of the existential effects of being dominated, and of being a dominator', and 'what nonviolent actors might be or become as a result of their struggle.'[58]

A friend of Sharp's has pointed out that this debate must be seen in context. Summy notes that Sharp is trying to promote nonviolence in a highly acquisitive capitalist society and adds that Gandhi would be the first to proclaim that 'a satyagraha that discounted the views and passions rife

---

[53] Brian Martin and Wendy Varney, *Nonviolence Speaks: Communicating Against Repression* (Cresskill, NJ: Hampton Press, 2003).

[54] See for example, Gene Sharp, 'The Technique of Non-violent Action', in Roberts, *Civilian Resistance*, p. 127.

[55] Sharp, *The Politics of Nonviolent Action*, p. 766. However it should be added that, in this work which deals with nonviolent action more generally than with civilian defence, Sharp does include as a potential criterion of success possible 'additional subtle and indirect effects'. See p. 765.

[56] Theodor Ebert, 'Final Victory', in T. K. Mahadevan, Adam Roberts and Gene Sharp (eds.), *Civilian Defence: An Introduction* (New Delhi: Gandhi Peace Foundation, 1967), p. 209.

[57] Stiehm, *Nonviolent Power*, p. 59.

[58] Mark D. Hayes, 'Domination and Peace Research,' unpublished Ph.D. dissertation, Griffith University (1995), part 2, chapter 2, 'Domination and Nonviolence'.

in its society and proceeded blindly on its own purist path was tantamount to pursuing merely personal redemption and not societal change'.[59] However, many do see a distinction between approaches to nonviolence and for some of them the seeming need to get things done here and now, to achieve immediate political goals, points to a preference for the older more pragmatic Sharp over Sharp the young Gandhian. And for some of these people this pragmatic approach *is* nonviolence. Ackerman and Duvall claim that Gene Sharp is 'the great theoretician of nonviolent power'[60] and Ackerman and Kruegler quite rightly note that 'anyone undertaking to write about nonviolent action necessarily stands on the shoulders of Gene Sharp.'[61] In the same way Gene Sharp necessarily stood on the shoulders of Mohandas Gandhi.

[59] Ralph Summy, personal communication, 29 March 2001.
[60] Peter Ackerman and Jack Duvall, *A Force More Powerful: A Century of Nonviolent Conflict* (New York: St Martin's Press, 2000), p. 8.
[61] Peter Ackerman and Christopher Kruegler, *Strategic Nonviolent Conflict: The Dynamics of People Power in the Twentieth Century* (Westport, CT: Praeger, 1994), p. xvii.

CHAPTER 13

The bottom of the hourglass: Gandhi's influence

GANDHI AND HIS DISCIPLES

For many westerners, and increasingly Indians as well, Gandhism stopped with the Mahatma. Jayaprakash Narayan and Vinoba Bhave are unknown or distantly remembered as Gandhi-following politicians or social reformers. Although many of the Mahatma's leading co-workers wrote autobiographies, or had biographies written about them, and Vinoba Bhave's Bhoodan movement and Jayaprakash Narayan's Total Revolution have received considerable attention, especially by Indian scholars, books about, and studies of, the rest of the Gandhi-inspired post-Gandhians have been rare.

In 1977, highly successful books by Ved Mehta[1] and V. S. Naipaul[2] appeared in which Gandhi and his disciples were portrayed in most unsympathetic ways. Ten years later, American writer Mark Shepard produced an uplifting book on Gandhi's disciples. In this book, *Gandhi Today*, Shepard asked the question about the status of the Gandhian tradition in India, whether it had died away, and what had become of the constructive workers that Gandhi sent to the villages. He concluded that with the passing of Vinoba and JP, 'it is unlikely that the Sarvodaya Movement will again be a major force on a national level'. He noted, however, that there are still Gandhians who are a 'vital force' in the communities they have settled in, and it is 'in these enclaves . . . that the main strength of the Sarvodaya Movement is found today.'[3]

Shepard profiled Gandhi's spiritual heir Vinoba Bhave and his political heir JP, along with a host of other inspiring older Indian Gandhians and had very brief sketches of Gandhi-influenced people and institutions in other parts of the world including Cesar Chavez, Lanza del Vasto, Danilo Dolci and the Sarvodaya Shramadana movement in Sri Lanka. In a more

---

[1] Mehta, *Mahatma Gandhi and his Apostles.*
[2] V. S. Naipaul in *India: A Wounded Civilisation* (London: Andre Deutsch, 1977).
[3] Shepard, *Gandhi Today*, p. 39.

recent book, *Gandhians in Contemporary India*,[4] while more detailed and analytical in setting the scene, Ishwar Harris covers basically similar ground to Shepard's work. And like it, it is an extremely positive account of the work and life of some leading contemporary Gandhians, those whose efforts are said to constitute the main strength of the Sarvodaya movement. In other words, Gandhi's influence was great, leading to a legion of post-Gandhi Gandhians to work in the villages of India. However, as both Shepard and Harris note, as they age and disappear, the influence (while not necessarily the inspiration[5]) of Gandhi seems to be disappearing with them. A *Directory of Gandhian Constructive Workers*, published in the mid-1990s, lists less than ninety who can be identified as being younger than sixty and only five less than forty years old among the almost 700 entries.[6] And although many Indian politicians still wear khadi, including those most antithetical to the philosophy of the Mahatma, not too many objective observers would claim that any sizeable proportion of them were working and living in a way that clearly showed they were influenced by the Father of the Nation.

Gandhi was sceptical about the value of his writings as a source of influence and maintained that his writings should be cremated with his body.[7] He believed that his active achievements would live after him and that his example, as it directly touched those around him, would effect change in the world rather than his words: 'My Life is my message',[8] he claimed. Of course everyone could not be touched by his personal experience in the way that Prasad, Patel, Vinoba and Shantidas were. Others, like Bahuguna, lived in a world that was still heavily permeated by his presence. For others, whose lives of Gandhian activism came after the death of the Mahatma, it had to be primarily the written word. And as a counter to his desire to see his writings destroyed, Gandhi did state that 'I flatter myself with the belief that some of my writings will survive me and will be of service to the causes for which they have been written.'[9] It seems that the personal example of Gandhi's deeds and the influence of his writings did not carry the weight that he may have hoped. However, on the other hand, Gandhi has been declared one of the most important persons of the twentieth century and his writings have been collected, annotated and analysed by many. They

---

[4] Harris, *Gandhians in Contemporary India*, 1998.
[5] See Thomas Weber, 'Gandhi is Dead. Long Live Gandhi: The Post-Gandhi Gandhian Movement in India', *Gandhi Marg* 18 (1996), pp. 160–92.
[6] K. Balasubramanian (comp.), *Directory of Gandhian Constructive Workers* (New Delhi: Gandhi Peace Foundation, 1996).
[7] See 'Speech at Gandhi Seva Sangh Meeting, Hudli', 16 April 1937.
[8] Quoted in Tendulkar, *Mahatma*, vol. VIII, p. 111.
[9] 'The Jewish Question', *Harijan*, 27 May 1939.

are available to those who were not touched by his personal example. And those words did work in powerful ways with Kaunda, King, Næss, Galtung, Schumacher and Sharp, and through them many others.

THE INFLUENCE OF THE POLITICAL GANDHI OR THE WHOLE GANDHI?

As Michael True says, 'For almost every civil disobedient for justice in the twentieth century, Gandhi . . . has been a presence, a person to be contended with, either challenged or imitated.'[10] When some of the imitators reached the pinnacles of political power in their own right, they felt the need to challenge their past adherence to a strongly Gandhian formulation and then felt the need to justify their actions. As Deputy Prime Minister and President and Commander-in-Chief of the new republic, Patel and Prasad succumbed to the pressure to temper their idealist Gandhian positions and adopt far more realist ones (a process Nehru never had to go through). Kaunda did the same and presented the most lengthy justification for his abandonment of Gandhian nonviolence in government. They all claimed that practical realities had to trump philosophy when they became wielders of political power as opposed to being exponents in the employment of moral power. Probably, such shifts are inevitable because, as Gandhi clearly saw, the state itself is an instrument of violence.

While the influence of the political Gandhi is apparently represented in some of the major political leaders (such as Albert Luthuli, Kwame Nkrumah, Julius Nyerere, Kenneth Kaunda, Nelson Mandela, Martin Luther King Jr., Aung San Suu Kyi, the Dalai Lama and Lech Walesa) who contended in a more imitative way with his techniques of nonviolent action in their attempts to liberate their people from various forms of oppression (not the least of which was colonialism), perhaps the greatest legacy of the political Gandhi can be seen in the many young activists who either know something of the life of Gandhi or who, at least in the West, more often have been inspired by the writings of Gene Sharp.

Sharp started off working with what I have called the 'whole Gandhi' but gradually came to the realisation that the satyagrahi Gandhi was the most important given the dangers of war, and the imperatives of defence, as well as civil disobedience campaigns against oppressors and injustice. Satyagraha was an excellent tool to defeat opponents rather than a vehicle

---

[10] Michael True, *Justice Seekers Peace Makers: 32 Portraits in Courage* (Mystic, CT: Twenty-Third Publications, 1985), p. 122.

for more spiritual ends. Where Gandhi remained at all, he became relatively one-dimensional, a political actor who, stripped of his more confusing trimmings, became palatable for his western audience, his moral jiu-jitsu[11] replaced by a political one where, instead of the moral balance being shifted, the political power of the opponent was undermined. While under Gandhi's influence, although philosophically he saw it as far more, King used nonviolence as a political tool to combat a repressive regime. Lanza del Vasto also engaged in political nonviolent direct action but for him this was an outgrowth of trying to live out the spiritual dimensions of Gandhi's philosophy.

There is of course substantially more to the influence of Gandhi in areas that are not within the narrowly defined political arena. As pointed out in the second half of this book, he also had a large influence on at least branches of the disciplines of ecology, peace research and economics through his profound influence on their founders. Often the connection with Gandhi is played down or overlooked by some of the later promoters of the fields in the way that the founders never did, or, as the founders came to an ever deeper understanding of the whole Gandhi, the promoters tended to maintain their focus on the earlier, more secular and less confusing (or disturbing?) writings of the founders. For example, where there is any awareness of them at all, cow protection and khadi production may have seemed even more anachronistic and irrelevant (and indeed bizarre) to western audiences than they did to some of Gandhi's English educated political co-workers. Ironically these very practices, or at least the philosophy behind them, were examined rather than discarded out of hand by some and even touched profound chords in western thinkers such as Næss and Schumacher, and went into the formulation of deep ecology and appropriate technology and human-centred economics.

THE LEGACY AND RELEVANCE OF THE WHOLE GANDHI

Why did so many of the others see many of Gandhi's experiments in truth as not relevant to them? The ascetic Gandhi seems to be dropped even by

---

[11] Gregg's term 'moral jiu-jitsu' was formulated to explain how self-suffering is supposed to induce conversion by causing an opponent to lose their ethical balance: 'He suddenly and unexpectedly loses the moral support which the usual violent resistance of most victims would render him. He plunges forward, as it were, into a new world of values. He feels insecure because of the novelty of the situation and his ignorance of how to handle it. He loses his poise and self-confidence. The victim not only lets the attacker come, but, as it were, pulls him forward by kindness, generosity and voluntary suffering, so that the attacker loses his moral balance.' See Richard B. Gregg, *The Power of Non-Violence* (London: James Clarke and Co., 1960), p. 44.

most of his closest followers. Is this because disciples always diminish the importance of the philosophy of the master as they find difficulty in living up to the principles (especially when they are not in close physical contact with him or her), or because they want to expand the sect/organisation and this may entail making it palatable to a larger audience? Does the asceticism of Gandhism need to be maintained to preserve the integrity of the philosophy, or can at least some parts of it be eliminated without doing too much damage to the central idea?

Almost all of those influenced by personal contact with Gandhi went on to get married, and most to have children (with Vinoba, of course, being the most notable exception, and although Kallenbach never married, it was probably not for reasons of brahmacharya). Gandhi's somewhat idiosyncratic concerns with celibacy (which spiritual seekers often seem to exhibit) may have had a strong connection with his early sexuality and the death of his father. Bramacharya, with which Maganlal Gandhi and Bajaj struggled, does not seem to have outlived the Mahatma as a lasting part of his legacy even among many of his immediate followers. Further, if we note Gandhi's change of heart about the joyful experiments in diet that he conducted with Kallenbach by way of seeking new and ever tastier healthy vegetarian food, and his later realisation that appeal to the palate is a religious trap,[12] or if we note how quickly King dismissed the idea of doing without technology or dressing in more simple ways that he was contemplating following his return from India, we see that at least these aspects of Gandhian asceticism did not outlast Gandhi.

Gandhi seems almost to have had a habit of leaving his family and friends when a geographical relocation was called for in his life. He did this when he moved back to the city from Phoenix in order to be better able to provide leadership for the Indians' struggle and to maintain his legal work. He did this again when he established Tolstoy Farm, when he left Sabarmati and when he attempted to live alone in Sevagram. While some core members may have accompanied him in the original move, eventually many others, often because of obsessive desires, drifted back into his immediate orbit. For others the philosophy or activism was more important than the personality, or perhaps they merely had far stronger sense of their own selves. They could take what they desired from the philosophy and apply it elsewhere without having to be physically serving the master at all times. Prasad, and more particularly, Patel and Shantidas are good examples here.

---

[12] Gandhi, *An Autobiography*, 1940, p. 237.

And those who were not touched by Gandhi's direct personal influence through any long-term relationship, yet who took Gandhism beyond India, also did not accept the complete corpus of Gandhi's beliefs without question. Although they may not have actively criticised Gandhi, they were content to leave certain aspects of his philosophy behind either as apparently irrelevant, or at least irrelevant to the new settings in which they were to be applied, or at times even as positively counterproductive. Shantidas, for example, cleaved to Gandhian ideals but his communities maintained a sense of joy centred on music, dance and crafts. Schumacher was concerned with beauty rather than merely with function. King showed no interest in an ascetic and sexually abstemious lifestyle. Sharp came to see the whole of Gandhian spirituality as confusing and limiting, something that repelled rather than attracted followers to nonviolence. In the case of Kaunda, when push came to shove, with much self-justification, nonviolence became a matter of policy rather than creed. By examining the parts of Gandhi's philosophy in action which lived beyond him, we can make some judgement about Gandhian relevance, about the parts of his philosophy which had (and have) the power to influence. A narrow reading would certainly give us a political technique with which to challenge repressive power, a wider reading shows that Gandhi's spiritual quest and ideas about the unity of life are not necessarily irrelevant or confusing to many.

CONCLUSION

In his biography of the Mahatma, John Haynes Holmes, American clergyman and Gandhi's friend and promoter, talks of Gandhi in terms of the "immortality of influence". He reminds us that most of us live on in the minds of family and friends, but as they disappear so too does our "immortality". However, he also points out that some have far-reaching influence and touch 'so many lives, that they take on genuine immortality'[13] – the bottom of the hourglass rather than spout of the funnel. Where did this power to influence in Gandhi's case come from?

In his lifetime Gandhi was commonly revered as a saint, and there are not too many almost universally recognised saints that grace any given generation. But then again saints are often worshiped and they appear to have very little direct influence on the life of the masses. Although

---

[13] John Haynes Holmes, *My Gandhi: A Personal Portrait of a Man Who Shook the World* (London: George Allen and Unwin, 1954), p. 136.

Gandhi was something of a charismatic leader and has been characterised as one of the outstanding persons of the last century, he still lives in our collective consciousness and his faults (a poor father, at times intolerant and inconsistent, prone to anger, often unreasonable in his demands and baffling in his arguments etc.) and sense of humour are remembered and they humanise him. Even if we just look at Gandhi the political activist or Gandhi the saint we still see someone with great power to influence others. While George Orwell thought that Gandhi's basic aims were reactionary and that his political methods could not have worked against extremely repressive regimes, he still managed to conclude that, 'regarded simply as a politician, and compared with other leading political figures of our time, how clean a smell he has managed to leave behind!'[14]

If, however, we look at the whole Gandhi, instead of just Gandhi the clean-smelling politician or beyond-reproach saint, we see a person struggling very publicly to discern the meaning of life, someone who not only knew that there was something more to human existence than the mundane, but had the courage to reach out for it and admit to failure. Perhaps some of Gandhi's biographers best pinpointed his power to influence in these terms. Louis Fischer perceptively remarked that it 'lay in doing what everyone could do but doesn't',[15] and George Woodcock noted that the Mahatma, 'with an extraordinary persistence . . . made and kept himself one of the few free men or our time.'[16] Saints are easier to contend with than truly free individuals. Sainthood tends to neutralises the message of the saint – after all, as mere mortals, how can we even aspire to be in the same league or, in he words of Thomas à Kempis, to imitate Christ?

In Gandhi's relationships with Polak, Kallenbach, Maganlal Gandhi and Bajaj, we see a very human Mohandas Gandhi, one who struggles with the same existential questions about what it is that constitutes a good and worthwhile life that so many of the rest of humanity at times feels the necessity to confront. And many, including Næss, Galtung, Schumacher and Sharp, have asked (and still do ask) these questions when they try to discern their place in the larger world, or when they ponder the meaning of peace, when they even perhaps dimly perceive that having may not be as important as being, when they see their lives dominated by machines which were supposed to be their servants, when they realise that so-called

[14] George Orwell, 'Reflections on Gandhi', in *The Collected Essays, Journalism and Letters of George Orwell, volume 4: In Front of Your Nose* (Harmondsworth: Penguin, 1970), p. 531.
[15] Louis Fischer, 'Miscellaneous Notes from a House Guest', in Norman Cousins (ed.), *Profiles of Gandhi: America Remembers a World Leader* (New Delhi: Indian Book Co., 1969), p. 61.
[16] Woodcock, *Gandhi*, p. 6.

progress is diminishing the habitability of the planet, their only home, or when they see injustice in the world and ask why it exists. Perhaps this leaves the sneaking suspicion that may be, just may be, the person hailed as a mahatma could have been right when he said that 'All mankind in essence are alike. What is, therefore, possible for me, is possible for everyone',[17] and in this lies a large measure of the power of Gandhi's influence.

[17] 'Discussion with Abdul Ghaffar Khan', 19/20 October 1938.

Bibliography

Ackerman, Peter, and Jack Duvall, *A Force More Powerful: A Century of Nonviolent Conflict* (New York: St Martin's Press, 2000).

Ackerman, Peter, and Christopher Kruegler, *Strategic Nonviolent Conflict: The Dynamics of People Power in the Twentieth Century* (Westport: Praeger, 1994).

Ahluwalia, B. K., *Sardar Patel: A Life* (New Delhi: Sagar, 1974).

Aiyar, S. P., 'Gandhi, Gokhale and the Moderates', in Ray, *Gandhi, India and the World*, pp. 99–118.

Anand, Mulk Raj, *Homage to Jamnalal Bajaj: A Pictorial Biography* (Ahmedabad: Allied Publishers, 1988).

Anker, Peder, 'Ecosophy: An Outline of its Megaethics', *The Trumpeter* 15 (1998), available at http://trumpeter.athabascau.ca/contents/v15.1/anker.html

Ansbro, John J., *Martin Luther King, Jr.: The Making of a Mind* (Maryknoll, NY: Orbis, 1983).

The Ark: Elements of a Non-Violent World, pamphlet, (n.p., n.d.).

Aryal, Manisha, 'Axing Chipko', *Himal* 7 (1994), pp. 8–23.

Ashe, Geoffrey, *Gandhi: A Study in Revolution* (London: Heinemann, 1968).

Bahuguna, Sunderlal, 'Gandhi's Betis', in Chipko Information Centre, *Save Himalaya*, pp. 1–4.

Bajaj, Jamnalal, 'In Search of a Guru', in Kalelkar, *To a Gandhian Capitalist*, pp. 9–12.

Bajaj, Savitri, *I Write as I Feel* (Bombay: Sevak, 1977).

Balasubramanian, K. (comp.), *Directory of Gandhian Constructive Workers* (New Delhi: Gandhi Peace Foundation, 1996).

Baldwin, Lewis V., *There is a Balm in Gilead: The Cultural Roots of Martin Luther King, Jr.* (Minneapolis: Fortune Press, 1991).

Balvantsinha, *Bapuka Ashram Parivar* (Ahmedabad: Navajivan, 1972).

Under the Shelter of Bapu (Ahmedabad: Navajivan, 1962).

Bandyopadhyay, J., and Vandana Shiva, 'Chipko', *Seminar* (February 1987), pp. 33–8.

Bandyopadhyay, Jayanta, and Vandana Shiva, 'Chipko: Rekindling India's Forest Culture', *The Ecologist* 17 (1987), pp. 26–34.

Barash, David P., *Introduction to Peace Studies* (Belmont, CA: Wadsworth, 1991).

Bartolf, Christian (ed.), *Letter to a Hindoo: Taraknath Das, Leo Tolstoi and Mahatma Gandhi* (Berlin: Gandhi Informations Zentrum, 1997).

Baruah, Upendra Kumar, *Portrait of a Gandhian: Biography of Dr. Martin Luther King, Jr.* (Gauhati: the author, 1985).

Bennet, Brad, 'Larzac (France), 1971–1981', in Powers and Vogele, *Protest, Power, and Change*, pp. 301–2.

Benoit, Madhu, 'The Mahatma and the Poet', *Gandhi Marg* 19 (1997), pp. 304–23.

Berning, Gillian, *Gandhi Letters: From Upper House to Lower House* (n.p.: Local History Museum, 1994).

Bhana, Surendra, 'The Tolstoy Farm: Gandhi's Experiment in "Cooperative Commonwealth"', *South African Historical Journal* (1975), available at www.anc.org.za/andocs/history/people/gandhi/bhana.htm

Bhave, Vinoba, *Bhoodan Yagna* (Ahmedabad: Navajivan, 1957).
  Moved by Love: The Memoirs of Vinoba Bhave, (trans. Marjorie Sykes from a Hindi text prepared by Kalindi) (Dartington Totnes: Resurgence, 1994).
  Swaraj Sastra [The Principles of a Non-Violent Political Order] (Varanasi: Sarva Seva Sangh, 1973).
  Third Power (A New Dimension) (Varanasi: Sarva Seva Sangh, 1972).
  'Wherein Lies Real Revolution', *Sarvodaya* 13 (1963), pp. 126–9.

Bishop, Peter D., *A Technique for Loving: Non-violence in Indian and Christian Traditions* (London: SMC Press, 1981).

Bondurant, Joan V., *Conquest of Violence: The Gandhian Philosophy of Conflict*, revised edition (Berkeley: University of California Press, 1967).

Bose, Amalendu, 'Gandhi and Ruskin: Ideological Affinities', in C. D. Narasimhaiah (ed.), *Gandhi and the West* (University of Mysore, 1969), pp. 128–44.

Boulding, Kenneth E., 'Twelve Friendly Quarrels with Johan Galtung', *Journal of Peace Research* 14 (1977), pp. 75–86.

Branch, Taylor, *Parting the Waters: America in the King Years 1954–63* (New York: Simon and Schuster, 1988).

Brown, Judith M., *Gandhi: Prisoner of Hope* (New Haven: Yale University Press, 1989).
  Gandhi's Rise to Power: Indian Politics 1915–1922 (London: Cambridge University Press, 1972).

Burrowes, Robert J., *The Strategy of Nonviolent Defense* (State University of New York Press, 1996).

Caldecott, Leonie and Stephanie Leland (eds.), *Reclaim the Earth: Women Speak out for Life on Earth* (London: Women's Press, 1983).

Carson, Clayborne (ed.), *The Autobiography of Martin Luther King, Jr.* (London: Little Brown and Company, 1999).

Carson, Rachel, *Silent Spring* (Harmondsworth: Penguin, 1962).

Chatterjee, Margaret, *Gandhi and his Jewish Friends* (London: Macmillan, 1992).

Chipko Information Centre, pamphlet *Save Himalaya* (Silyara, n.d.).

Church, Roderick, 'Vinoba and the Origins of Bhoodan', *Gandhi Marg* 5 (1983), pp. 469–91.
  'Vinoba Bhave, Jayaprakash Narayan and Indian Democracy', *Gandhian Perspectives* 2 (1980), pp. 89–129.

Desai, Mahadev, 'Apartim Sadhak', in Navajivan Trust, *Ashram No Pran*, pp. 50–67.

Day to Day with Gandhi: Secretary's Diary, 9 vols. (Rajghat, Varanasi: Sarva Seva Sangh, 1968–74).

The Story of Bardoli: Being a History of the Bardoli Satyagraha of 1928 and Its Sequel (Ahmedabad: Navajivan, 1929).

Desai, Narayan, *My Gandhi* (Ahmedabad: Navajivan, 1999).

The Fire and the Rose [Biography of Mahadevbhai] (Ahmedabad: Navajivan, 1995).

Deshpande, Nirmala, *Vinoba* (New Delhi: National Book Trust, 2001).

Devanesen, D. S., *The Making of the Mahatma* (New Delhi: Orient Longmans, 1969).

Devdutt, 'Vinoba and the Gandhian Tradition', *Gandhi Marg* 5 (1983), pp. 600–15.

Diamond, Irene and Gloria Feman Orenstein (eds.), *Reweaving the World: The Emergence of Ecofeminism* (San Fransico: Sierra Club, 1990).

Dogra, Bharat, *Living for Others: Vimla and Sunderlal Bahuguna* (New Delhi: Bharat Dogra, 1993).

Doke, Joseph J., *M. K. Gandhi: An Indian Patriot in South Africa* (The London Indian Chronicle, 1909).

Dyson, Michael Eric, *I May Not Get There With You: The True Martin Luther King Jr.* (New York: The Free Press, 2000).

Ebert, Theodor, 'Final Victory', in T. K. Mahadevan, Adam Roberts and Gene Sharp (eds.), *Civilian Defence: An Introduction* (New Delhi: Gandhi Peace Foundation, 1967), pp. 194–211.

Eide, Kjell, 'Note on Galtung's Concept of "Violence"', *Journal of Peace Research* 8 (1971), pp. 71–2.

Erikson, Erik H., *Gandhi's Truth: On the Origins of Militant Nonviolence* (New York: Norton, 1969).

Life History and the Historical Moment (New York: Norton, 1975).

Ferguson, Niall, 'Introduction', in Naill Ferguson (ed.), *Virtual History: Alternatives and Counterfactuals* (London: Papermac, 1988), pp. 1–90.

Fischer, Louis, *The Life of Mahatma Gandhi* (New York: Collier, 1962).

'Miscellaneous Notes from a House Guest', in Norman Cousins (ed.) *Profiles of Gandhi: America Remembers a World Leader* (New Delhi: Indian Book Co., 1969), pp. 54–64.

Fitzgerald, Jeffrey M., David C. Hickman and Richard L. Dickins, 'A Preliminary Discussion of the Definitional Phase of the Dispute Process', unpublished paper presented at the 1980 Conference of the 'Law and Society' Association in Madison, Wisconsin.

Foreman, Dave (ed.), *Ecodefense: A Field Guide to Monkeywrenching* (Tuscon: A Ned Ludd Book, 1985).

Gaard, Greta (ed.), *Ecofeminism: Women, Animals, Nature* (Philadelphia: Temple University Press, 1993).

Gadgil, D. R., *Planning and Economic Policy in India* (Poona: Gokhale Institute of Politics and Economics, 1961).

Galtung, Johan, *Bibliography: 1951–90* (Oslo: PRIO, 1990).

Buddhism: A Quest for Unity and Peace (Honolulu: Dae Won Sa Buddhist Temple, 1988).

'Cultural Violence', *Journal of Peace Research* 27 (1990), pp. 291–305.

'Gandhi and Conflictology', *Papers: A Collection of Works Previously Available Only in Manuscript or Very Limited Circulation Mimeographed or Photo-copied Editions, volume 5: Papers in English 1968–1972* (Oslo: PRIO, 1980), pp. 107–58.

'Gandhian Themes', in Ingemund Gullvåg and Jon Wetlesen (eds.), *In Sceptical Wonder: Inquiries into the Philosophy of Arne Naess on the Occasion of his 70th Birthday* (Oslo: Universitetsforlaget, 1982), pp. 220–36.

'A Gandhian Theory of Conflict', in Selbourne, *In Theory and In Practice*, pp. 95–110.

'Gandhi's Views on the Political and Ethical Preconditions of a Nonviolent Fighter', in Pran Chopra (ed.), *The Sage in Revolt: A Rememberance* (New Delhi: Gandhi Peace Foundation, 1972), pp. 203–16.

'Introduction', in Johan Galtung, *Essays in Peace Research, volume 1, Peace: Research–Education–Action* (Copenhagen: Ejlers, 1975), pp. 19–28.

'Introduction', in Johan Galtung, *Essays in Peace Research, volume 5: Peace Problems: Some Case Studies* (Copenhagen: Ejlers, 1975), pp. 23–4.

Nonviolence and Israel/Palestine (Honolulu: University of Hawaii Press, 1989).

'Pacifism from a Sociological Point of View', *Journal of Conflict Resolution* 3 (1959), pp. 67–84.

Peace by Peaceful Means: Peace and Conflict, Development and Civilisation (London: Sage, 1996).

'A Structural Theory of Imperialism', *Journal of Peace Research* 18 (1971), pp. 81–118.

The Way is the Goal: Gandhi Today (Ahmedabad: Gujarat Vidyapith Peace Research Centre, 1992).

'Twenty-five Years of Peace Research: Ten Challenges and Some Responses', *Journal of Peace Research* 22 (1985), pp. 141–58.

'Violence, Peace and Peace Research', *Journal of Peace Research* 6 (1969), pp. 167–91.

60 Speeches on War and Peace (Oslo: PRIO, 1990).

Galtung, Johan, and Daisaku Ikeda, *Choose Peace: A Dialogue between Johan Galtung and Daisaku Ikeda* (trans. and ed. Richard Gage) (London: Pluto, 1995).

Galtung, Johan, and Arne Næss, *Gandhis Politiske Ettik* (Oslo: Tanum, 1955).

Gandhi, Arun, and Sunanda Gandhi, *The Forgotten Woman: The Untold Story of Kastur Gandhi, Wife of Mahatma Gandhi* (Huntsville, AR: Ozark Mountain Publishers, 1998).

Gandhi, M. K., *An Autobiography Or The Story of My Experiments With Truth* (Ahmedabad: Navajivan, 1940).

Ashram Observances in Action (Ahmedabad: Navajivan, 1955).

Bapu's Letters to Mira [1924–1948] (Ahmedabad: Navajivan, 1949).

Collected Works of Mahatma Gandhi, vols. 1–100 (New Delhi: Publications Division, Government of India, 1958–91); and CD-ROM version (New Delhi: Publications Division, Government of India, 1999).

Constructive Programme: Its Meaning and Place (Ahmedabad: Navajivan, 1941).

From Yeravda Mandir (Ahmedabad: Navajivan, 1932).

Hind Swaraj or Indian Home Rule (Ahmedabad: Navajivan, 1939).

Ruskin: Unto This Last: A Paraphrase (Navajivan: Ahmedabad, 1951).

Sarvodaya (The Welfare of All) (Navajivan: Ahmedabad, 1954).

Satyagraha in South Africa (Madras: S. Ganesan, 1928).

Gandhi, Prabhudas, 'Magankaka', in Navajivan Trust, *Ashram No Pran*, pp. 4–41.

My Childhood With Gandhi (Ahmedabad: Navajivan, 1957).

Gandhi, Rajmohan, *Patel: A Life* (Ahmedabad: Navajivan, 1991).

Garrow, David J., *Bearing the Cross: Martin Luther King, Jr., and the Southern Christian Leadership Conference* (New York: William Morrow, 1986).

Gay, Peter, *Freud for Historians* (New York: Oxford University Press, 1985).

Gillion, K. L., *Ahmedabad: A Study in Indian Urban History* (Canberra: Australian National University Press, 1969).

Gladwell, Malcolm, *The Tipping Point: How Little Things Can Make a Big Difference* (London: Abacus, 2000).

Gleditsch, Nils Petter, 'The Structure of Galtungism', in Gleditsch *et al, Johan Galtung: A Bibliography*, pp. 64–81.

Gleditsch, Nils Petter, Odvar Leine, Hans-Henrik Holm, Tord Høvik, Arne Martin Klausen, Erik Rudeng and Håkan Wiberg (eds.), *Johan Galtung: A Bibliography of his Scholarly and Popular Writings 1951–1980* (Oslo: PRIO, 1980).

Green, Martin, *The Challenge of the Mahatmas* (New York: Basic Books, 1978).

Gandhi: Voice of a New Age Revolution (New York: Continuum, 1993).

The Origins of Nonviolence: Tolstoy and Gandhi in their Historical Settings (University Park: Pennsylvania State University Press, 1986).

Gregg, Richard B., *A Discipline for Non-Violence* (Ahmedabad: Navajivan, 1941).

The Power of Nonviolence (London: James Clarke and Co., 1960).

Guha, Ramchandra, 'Radical American Environmentalism and Wilderness Preservation: A Third World Critique', in Witoszek and Brennan, *Philosophical Dialogues*, pp. 313–24.

The Unquiet Woods: Ecological Change and Peasant Resistance in the Himalaya (Berkeley: University of California Press, 1989).

Hall, Richard, *The High Price of Principles: Kaunda and the White South* (Harmondsworth: Penguin, 1973).

Kaunda: Founder of Zambia (London: Longmans, 1964).

Handa, R. L., *Rajendra Prasad: Twelve Years of Triumph and Despair* (New Delhi: Sterling, 1978).

Hanigan, James P., *Martin Luther King, Jr. and the Foundations of Nonviolence* (Lanham: University of America Press, 1984).

Harris, Ishwar C., *Gandhians in Contemporary India: The Vision and the Visionaries* (Lewiston, NY: The Edwin Mellen Press, 1998).

Hatch, John, *Two African Statesmen: Kaunda of Zambia and Nyerere of Tanzania* (London: Secker and Warburg, 1976).

Hay, Stephen N., 'Jain Influences on Gandhi's Early Thought', in Ray, *Gandhi, India and the World*, pp. 29–38.

Hayes, Mark D., 'Domination and Peace Research', unpublished Ph.D. dissertation, Griffith University (1995).

Hendrick, George, 'Gandhi and Dr Martin Luther King', *Gandhi Marg* 3 (1959), pp. 18–22.

'Influence of Thoreau and Emerson on Gandhi's Satyagraha', *Gandhi Marg* 3 (1959), pp. 165–78.

'Influence of Thoreau's "Civil Disobedience" on Gandhi's Satyagraha', *New England Quarterly* 29 (1956), pp. 462–71.

Herman, Ted, 'Adding Gandhi to Galtung for Peace Work', *Peace, Environment and Education* 5 (1994), pp. 23–7.

Hermann, A. L., 'Satyagraha: A New Indian Word for Some Old Ways of Western Thinking', *Philosophy East and West* 19 (1969), pp. 123–42.

Hingorani, Anand T., and Ganga A. Hingoraini, *The Encyclopedia of Gandhian Thoughts* (New Delhi: AICC(I), 1985).

Hoda, M. M., (comp. and ed.), *Future is Manageable: Schumacher's Observations on Non-Violent Economics and Technology with a Human Face* (New Delhi: Impex India, 1978).

'Schumacher: A Profile', in Hoda, *Future is Manageable*, pp. 1–13.

Hoda, Surur, 'Schumacher on Gandhi', in Manmohan Choudhuri and Ramjee Singh (eds.), *Mahatma Gandhi: 125 Years* (Varanasi: Sarva Seva Sangh/Gandhian Institute of Studies, 1995), pp. 95–105.

Holm, Hans-Henrik, 'Johan Galtung and the Science of Human Fulfilment: From Petal-Picking to Mega Research', in Gleditsch *et al.*, *Johan Galtung: A Bibliography*, pp. 27–50.

Holmes, John Haynes, *My Gandhi: A Personal Portrait of a Man Who Shook the World* (London: George Allen and Unwin, 1954).

Hope, Marjorie and James Young, *The Struggle for Humanity: Agents of Nonviolent Change in a Violent World* (Maryknoll, NY: Orbis, 1977).

Horsburgh, H. J. N., 'Nonviolence and Impatience', *Gandhi Marg* 12 (1968), pp. 355–60.

Hunt, James D. 'Experiments in Forming a Community of Service: The Evolution of Gandhi's First Ashrams, Phoenix and Tolstoy Farm', in K. L. Seshagiri Rao and Henry O. Thompson (eds.) *World Problems and Human Responsibility: Gandhian Perspectives* (Barrytown, NY: Unification Theological Seminary, 1988), pp. 177–203.

Gandhi and the Nonconformists: Encounters in South Africa (New Delhi: Promilla, 1986).

'Gandhi and the Theosophists', in V. T. Patil (ed.), *Studies on Gandhi* (New Delhi: Sterling, 1983), pp. 163–76.

Gandhi in London (New Delhi: Promilla, 1978).

'The Kallenbach Papers and Tolstoy Farm', unpublished working paper presented to the Association for Asian Studies meeting in Washington, DC, 6–9 April 1995.

'Suffragettes and Satyagraha', *Indo-British Review* 9 (1981), pp. 65–76.

'Thoreau and Gandhi: a Re-evaluation of the Legacy', *Gandhi Marg* 14 (1970), pp. 325–32.

Ingram, Catherine, *In the Footsteps of Gandhi: Conversations with Spiritual Social Activists* (Berkeley: Parallax, 1990).

Jack, Homer A., 'Henry S. L. Polak', *Gandhi Marg* 3 (1959), pp. 289–92.

Jacobsen, Knut A., 'Bhagavadgita, Ecosophy T, and Deep Ecology', *Inquiry* 39 (1996), pp. 219–38.

James, William, *The Varieties of Religious Experience: A Study in Human Nature* (Glasgow: Collins, 1960).

Joshi, Chhaganlal, *Satyagraha Ashram ane Gandhi Parivar* (Ahmedabad: Sabarmati Ashram Suraksha ane Smarak Trust, 1975).

Kakar, Sudhir, *Intimate Relations: Exploring Indian Sexuality* (The University of Chicago Press, 1989).

Kalelkar, Kaka, 'Jamnalalji as I Knew Him', in Kalelkar, *To a Gandhian Capitalist*, pp. 13–20.

Stray Glimpses of Bapu (Ahmedabad: Navajivan, 1960).

'Tapasvi Jivan', in Navajivan Trust, *Ashram No Pran*, pp. 78–82.

(ed.), *To a Gandhian Capitalist* (Bombay: Sevak Prakashan, 1979).

Kamath, M. V., *Gandhi's Coolie: Life and Times of Ramakrishna Bajaj* (Ahmedabad: Allied Publishers, 1988).

Kapur, Sudarshan, *Raising Up a Prophet: The African-American Encounter with Gandhi* (Boston: Beacon Press, 1992).

Kaunda, Kenneth, *Zambia Shall be Free: An Autobiography* (London: Heinemann, 1962).

Kaunda, Kenneth David, *Kaunda on Violence* (London: Sphere, 1980).

Kelman, Herbert C., 'Reflections on the History and Status of Peace Research', *Conflict Management and Peace Science* 5 (1981), pp. 95–110.

King, Coretta Scott, *My Life with Martin Luther King, Jr.* (London: Hodder and Stoughton, 1969).

King, Jr., Martin Luther, 'Nonviolence and Racial Justice', *Christian Century* 74 (6 February 1957), pp. 165–7.

The Papers of Martin Luther King, Jr.: Volume IV: Symbol of the Movement, January 1957–December 1958 (Berkeley: University of California Press, 2000).

'The Power of Nonviolence', *Intercollegian* (May 1958), p. 8.

Stride Towards Freedom (New York: Harper and Row, 1958).

A Testament of Hope: The Essential Writings of Martin Luther King, Jr. (ed. James Melvin Washington) (San Francisco: HarperCollins, 1986).

Kohut, Heinz, 'Creativeness, Charisma, Group Psychology: Reflections on the Self-Analysis of Freud', in Paul H. Ornstein (ed.), *The Search for Self: Selected Writings of Heinz Kohut, 1950–1978* (New York: International Universities Press, 1990), vol. II, pp. 793–843.

Korhonen, Pekka, *The Geometry of Power: Johan Galtung's Conception of Power* (Tampere Peace Research Institute, 1990).

Krishna, B., *Sardar Vallabhbhai Patel: India's Iron Man* (New Delhi: HarperCollins, 1996).

Kumar, Satish, 'You Are, Therefore I Am', *Life Positive Plus* 1 (2002), pp. 68–70.

LaChapelle, Dolores, *Earth Wisdom* (Silverton, CO: International College, 1978).

Lal, Vinay, 'Nakedness, Non-Violence and the Negation of Negation: Gandhi's Experiments in *Brahmacharya* and Celibate Sexuality', *South Asia* 22 (1999), pp. 63–94.

Lannoy, Richard, *The Speaking Tree: A Study of Indian Culture and Society* (London: Oxford University Press, 1971).

Lanza del Vasto, J. J., *Gandhi to Vinoba: The New Pilgrimage* (London: Rider, 1956).

Les Enfances d'une Pensée (Paris: Denoël, 1970).

Return to the Source (London: Rider, 1971).

Warriors of Peace: Writings on the Technique of Nonviolence (New York: Knopf, 1974).

Lawler, Peter, *A Question of Values: Johan Galtung's Peace Research* (Boulder, CO: Lynne Reinner, 1995).

Little, Graham, *Political Ensembles: A Psychosocial Approach to Politics and Leadership* (Melbourne: Oxford University Press, 1958).

Lok Sabha Secretariate, *Eminent Parliamentarians Monograph Series: Dr. Rajendra Prasad* (New Delhi: Lok Sabha Secretariate, 1990).

Lovelock, James, *Gaia: A New Look at Life on Earth* (New York: Oxford, 1979).

Macpherson, Fergus, *Kenneth Kaunda of Zambia: The Times and the Man* (Lusaka: Oxford University Press, 1974).

Macquarrie, John, *The Concept of Peace* (London: SCM, 1973).

Mahadevan, T. K., (ed.), *Truth and Nonviolence: A UNESCO Symposium on Gandhi* (New Delhi: Gandhi Peace Foundation, 1970).

The Year of the Phoenix: Gandhi's Pivotal Year (New Delhi: Arnold-Heinemann, 1982).

Mandela, Nelson, 'The Sacred Warrior: The Liberator of South Africa Looks at the Seminal Work of the Liberator of India', *Time*, 31 December 1999.

Martin, Brian, and Wendy Varney, *Nonviolence Speaks: Communicating Against Repression* (Cresskill, NJ: Hampton Press, 2003).

Mashruwala, Kishorlal G., *In Quest of Truth* (Ahmedabad: Shravana, 1983).

McLaughlin, Elizabeth T., *Ruskin and Gandhi* (Cranbury, NJ: Associated University Presses, 1974).

McNeish, James, *Fire Under the Ashes: The Life of Danilo Dolci* (London: Hodder and Stoughton, 1965).

McRobie, George, 'Against the Destructive Economy', in Selbourne, *In Theory and in Practice*, pp. 111–23.

'Preface' in Schumacher, *Good Work*, pp. vii–xi.

Small is Possible (London: Jonathan Cape, 1981).

Meadows, Donella H., Dennis L. Meadows, Jørgen Randers and William W. Behrens III, *The Limits to Growth: A Report for the Club of Rome's Project on the Predicament of Mankind* (New York: Universe, 1972).

Mehta, Digish, *Shrimad Rajchandra–A Life* (Ahmedabad: Shrimad Rajchandra Janama Shatabdi Mandal, 1978).

Mehta, Ved, *Mahatma Gandhi and his Apostles* (London: Andre Deutsch, 1977).

Merchant, Carolyn, *Radical Ecology: The Search for a Livable World* (New York: Routledge, 1992).

Merriman John, M. (ed.), *For Want of a Horse: Choice and Chance in History* (Lexington: The Stephen Green Press, 1985).

Miller, William Robert, *Nonviolence: A Christian Interpretation* (New York: Association Press, 1964).

Mira Behn, 'Something Wrong in the Himalaya' (Chipko Information Centre, *Save Himalaya*), pp. 5–10.

Mira Behn [Madeleine Slade], *The Spirit's Pilgrimage* (London: Longmans, 1960).

Mishra, Anupam, and Satyendra Tripathi, *Chipko Movement: Uttarkhand women's bid to save forest wealth* (New Delhi: People's Action for Development with Justice, 1978).

Moore, Thomas, *Soul Mates: Honoring the Mysteries of Love and Relationship* (New York: Harper Perennial, 1994).

Morris, Collin M., and Kenneth D. Kaunda, *A Humanist in Africa: Letters to Colin M. Morris from Kenneth D. Kaunda President of Zambia* (Nashville: Abingdon, 1966).

Murthi, R. K., *Sardar Patel: The Man and His Contemporaries* (New Delhi: Sterling, 1976).

Naess, Arne, 'Comments on Guha's "Radical American Environmentalism and Wilderness Preservation: A Third World Critique"', in Witoszek and Brennan, *Philosophical Dialogues*, pp. 325–33.

'Environmental Ethics and Spinoza's Ethics: Comments on Genevieve Lloyd's Article', *Inquiry* 23 (1980), pp. 313–25.

Gandhi and Group Conflict: An Exploration of Satyagraha (Oslo: Universitetsforlaget, 1974).

Gandhi and the Nuclear Age (Totowa, NJ: The Bedminster Press, 1965).

'How My Philosophy Seemed to Develop', in Andre Mercier and Maja Svilar (eds.), *Philosophers on their Own Work* (Bern: Peter Lang, 1982), vol. x, pp. 209–26.

'Identification as a Source of Deep Ecological Attitudes', in Michael Tobias (ed.), *Deep Ecology* (San Diego: Avant Books, 1984), pp. 256–70.

'Is the Deep Ecology Vision a Deep Vision or is it Multicolored like the Rainbow? An Answer to Nina Witoszek', in Witoszek and Brennan, *Philosophical Dialogues*, pp. 466–72.

'Letter to Dave Foreman, 23 June 1988', in Witoszek and Brennan, *Philosophical Dialogues*, pp. 225–31.

'Modesty and the Conquest of Mountains', in Michael Tobias (ed.) *The Mountain Spirit* (New York: Overlook, 1979), pp. 13–16.

'*Self-*Realisation: An Ecological Approach to Being in the World', in John Seed, Joanna Macy, Pat Fleming and Arne Naess (eds.), *Thinking Like a Mountain: Towards a Council of All Beings* (Philadelphia: New Society Publishers, 1988), pp. 19–30.

'The Shallow and the Deep, Long-Range Ecology Movement. A Summary', *Inquiry* 16 (1973), pp. 95–100.

Arne Næss, Alfred Ayer and Fons Elders, 'The Glass is on the Table: The Empiricist versus Total View', quoted in Witoszek and Brennan, *Philosophical Dialogues*, pp. 10–28.

Naess, Arne and George Sessions, 'Platform Principles of the Deep Ecology Movement', in Bill Deval and George Sessions, *Deep Ecology: Living as if Nature Mattered* (Salt Lake City, UT: Gibbs Smith, 1985), pp. 54–63.

Nag, Kalidas, *Tolstoy and Gandhi* (Patna: Pustak Bhandar, 1950).

Naipaul, V. S., *India: A Wounded Civilisation* (London: Andre Deutsch, 1977).

Nanda, B. R., *Gokhale, Gandhi and the Nehrus: Studies in Indian Nationalism* (London: Allen and Unwin, 1974).

In Gandhiji's Footsteps: The Life and Times of Jamnalal Bajaj (New Delhi: Oxford University Press, 1990).

In Search of Gandhi: Essays and Reflections (New Delhi: Oxford University Press, 2002).

Mahatma Gandhi: A Biography (London: Oxford University Press, 1981).

Nanurkar, G. M. (ed.), *Sardar Patel–In Tune with the Millions–II* (Ahmedabad: Sardar Vallabhbhai Patel Smarak Bhavan, 1976).

Narayan, Jayaprakash, 'Foreword', in Hoda, *Future is Manageable*, pp. ix–x.

Narayan, Shriman. *Jamnalal Bajaj: Gandhiji's Fifth Son* (New Delhi: Publications Division, Ministry of Information and Broadcasting, Government of India, 1974).

Vinoba: His Life and Work (Bombay: Popular Prakashan, 1970).

Nargolkar, Vasant, *The Creed of Saint Vinobha* (Bombay: Bharatiya Vidya Bhavan, 1963).

'Vinoba and Satyagraha', *Gandhi Marg* 2 (1981), pp. 661–72.

Nash, Roderick, *The Rights of Nature: A History of Environmental Ethics* (Madison: University of Wisconsin Press, 1989).

Navajivan Trust (ed.), *Ashram No Pran* (Ahmedabad: Navajivan, 1993).

Nayar, Sushila, *Mahatma Gandhi, volume IV: Satyagraha at Work* (Ahmedabad: Navajivan, 1989).

Mahatma Gandhi, volume V: India Awakened (Ahmedabad: Navajivan, 1993).

Mahatma Gandhi, volume VI: Salt Satyagraha: The Watershed (Ahmedabad: Navajivan, 1995).

Orwell, George, 'Reflections on Gandhi', in *The Collected Essays, Journalism and Letters of George Orwell, volume 4: In Front of Your Nose* (Harmondsworth: Penguin, 1970), pp. 523–31.

Ostergaard, Geoffrey, *Nonviolent Revolution in India* (New Delhi: Gandhi Peace Foundation, 1985).

'Vinoba's "Gradualist" Versus Western "Immediatist" Anarchism', *Gandhi Marg* 5 (1983), pp. 509–30.

Pardesi, Ghanshyam, 'Editor's Introduction', in Ghanshyam Pardesi (ed.), *Contemporary Peace Research* (Brighton: Harvester, 1982), pp. 1–29.

Parel, Anthony J., 'Editor's introduction' to M. K.Gandhi, *Hind Swaraj and Other Writings* (Cambridge University Press, 1997), pp. xiii–lxii.

'Gandhi and Tolstoy', in Puri, *Mahatma Gandhi and His Contemporaries*, pp. 36–51.

Parikh, Narhari D., *Sardar Vallabhbhai Patel* (Ahmedabad: Navajivan, 1953), vol. 1.

Parvate, T. V., *Jamnalal Bajaj [A Brief Study of his Life and Character]* (Ahmedabad: Navajivan, 1962).

Payne, Robert, *The Life and Death of Mahatma Gandhi* (London: The Bodley Head, 1969).

Plant, Judith (ed.), *Healing the Wounds: The Promise of Ecofeminism* (Philadelphia: New Society, 1989).

Polak, H. S. L. 'Appendix II' in M. K. Gandhi, *Speeches and Writings of M. K. Gandhi* (Madras: Natesan, 1922), Appendicies, pp. 38–44.

'Satyagraha and its Origin in South Africa', in Kshitis Roy (ed.), *Gandhi Memorial Peace Number* (Shantiniketan: The Visva-Bharati Quarterly, 1949), pp. 111–120.

'Some South African Reminiscences', in Shukla, *Incidents of Gandhiji's Life*, pp. 230–247.

Polak, H. S. L., H. N. Brailsord and Lord Pethick-Lawrence, *Mahatma Gandhi* (London: Odhams Press, 1949).

Polak, Millie Graham, *Mr. Gandhi: The Man* (London: Allen and Unwin, 1931).

'In the South African Days', in Shukla, *Incidents of Gandhiji's Life*, pp. 247–51.

Popenoe, Oliver and Cris Popenoe, *Seeds of Tomorrow: New Age Communities that Work* (San Francisco: Harper and Rowe, 1984).

Power, Shahed, 'Gandhi and Deep Ecology: Experiencing the Nonhuman Environment', unpublished PhD thesis, Environmental Resources Unit, University of Salford (1991).

Powers, Roger, 'Gene Sharp (b.1928),' in Powers and Vogele, *Protest, Power, and Change*, pp. 467–9.

Powers, Roger, and William Vogele (eds.), *Protest, Power, and Change: An Encylopedia of Nonviolent Action from ACT-UP to Women's Suffrage* (New York and London: Garland, 1997).

Pradhan, Benudhar, *The Socialist Thought of Mahatma Gandhi*, vol. 1 (Delhi: GDK, 1980).

Prasad, C. Shambu, 'Gandhi and Maganlal: Khadi Science and the Gandhian Scientist', in Puri, *Mahatma Gandhi and His Contemporaries*, pp. 228–51.

Prasad, Rajendra, *At the Feet of Mahatma Gandhi* (Westport, CT: Greenwood, 1971).

Rajendra Prasad: Autobiography (New Delhi: National Book Trust, 1994).

Satyagraha in Champaran (Ahmedabad: Navajivan, 1949).

Punjabi, Kewal L., *Rajendra Prasad: First President of India* (London: Macmillan, 1960).

Puri, Bindu (ed.), *Mahatma Gandhi and His Contemporaries* (Shimla: Indian Institute of Advanced Study, 2001).

Pyarelal, *Mahatma Gandhi, volume I: The Early Phase* (Ahmedabad: Navajivan, 1965).

    Mahatma Gandhi, volume II: Discovery of Satyagraha–On the Threshold (Bombay: Sevak Prakashan, 1980).

    Mahatma Gandhi, volume III: The Birth of Satyagraha: From Petitioning to Passive Resistance (Ahmedabad: Navajivan, 1986).

    Mahatma Gandhi, volume X: The Last Phase, Part-II (Ahmedabad: Navajivan, 1958).

Pyarelal and Sushila Nayar, *In Gandhiji's Mirror* (Delhi: Oxford University Press, 1991).

Radhakrishnan, S., (ed.), *Mahatma Gandhi: Essays and Reflections on his Life and Work* (Bombay: Jaico, 1956).

Ram, Suresh, *Vinoba and His Mission [Being an account of the rise and growth of the Bhoodan Yajna Movement]* (Varanasi: Akil Bharat Sarva Seva Sangh, 1962).

Ramachandran, G., and T. K. Mahadevan (eds.), *Nonviolence After Gandhi: A Study of Martin Luther King, Jr.* (New Delhi: Gandhi Peace Foundation, 1968).

Rambo, Lewis R., 'Conversion', in Mircea Eliade (ed.), *Encyclopedia of Religion* (New York: Macmillan, 1987), vol. IV, pp. 73–9.

Rao, P. Kodanda, 'Gokhale and Gandhi', in G. Ramachandran and T. K. Mahadevan (eds.), *Quest for Gandhi* (New Delhi: Gandhi Peace Foundation, 1970), pp. 343–51.

Rao, U. S. Mohan, 'Introduction', in Kalelkar, *To a Gandhian Capitalist*, pp. 23–64.

Rawlinson, Roger, *Larzac–A Victory for Nonviolence* (London: Quaker Peace and Service, 1983).

Ray, Sibnarayan (ed.), *Gandhi, India and the World* (Melbourne: The Hawthorn Press, 1970).

Reed, Peter, and David Rothenberg (eds.), *Wisdom in the Open Air: The Norwegian Roots of Deep Ecology* (Minneapolis: University of Minnesota Press, 1993).

Roberts, Adam, untitled essay in Ramachandran and Mahadevan, *Nonviolence After Gandhi*, pp. 66–77.

Rogers, Carl, *On Becoming a Person: A Therapist's View of Psychotherapy* (Boston: Houghton Mifflin, 1961).

Rolland, Romain, *Mahatma Gandhi: The Man who Became One with the Universal Being* (London: Allen and Unwin, 1924).

Rothenberg, David, *Is it Painful to Think?: Conversations with Arne Naess father of deep ecology* (Sydney: Allen and Unwin, 1993).

Rudolph, Lloyd I., and Susanne Hoeber Rudolph, *The Modernity of Tradition: Political Developments in India* (The University of Chicago Press, 1967).

Sarid, Isa, and Christian Bartolf, *Hermann Kallenbach: Mahatma Gandhi's Friend in South Africa* (Berlin: Gandhi Informations Zentrum, 1997).

Sastri, V. S. Srinivasa, *My Master Gokhale* (Madras: Model Publications, 1946).

Scarfe, Allan and Wendy Scarfe, *Remembering Jayaprakash* (New Delhi: Siddharth, 1997).

Schumacher, Diana, 'Introduction' to Schumacher, *This I Believe*, pp. 10–18.

Schumacher, E. F., 'Buddhist Economics', in Guy Wint (ed.), *Asia: A Handbook* (London: A. Blond, 1965), pp. 695–701.

'The Economics of Permanence', in Ted Dunn (ed.), *Foundations of Peace and Freedom: The Ecology of a Peaceful World* (Swansea: Davies, 1975), pp. 104–6.

Good Work (London: Cape, 1979).

A Guide for the Perplexed (London: Cape, 1977).

'Help to Those Who Need it Most: Some Problems of Economic Development', in Schumacher, *Roots of Economic Growth*, pp. 29–42.

'Levels of Technology: A Key Problem for Underdeveloped Countries', in Schumacher, *Roots of Economic Growth*, pp. 49–56.

'Non-Violent Economics', *Observer*, 21 August 1960.

On the Edge of the Forest, A film directed by Barrie Oldfield, 1977.

'Paths to Economic Growth: Introductory Remarks', in Schumacher, *Roots of Economic Growth*, pp. 14–28.

Roots of Economic Growth (Varanasi: Gandhian Institute of Studies, 1962).

'Small is Beautiful', in Hoda, *Future is Manageable*, pp. 14–29.

Small is Beautiful: A Study of Economics as if People Mattered (London: Abacus, 1974).

This I Believe and Other Essays (Dartington Totnes: Resurgence, 1998).

Selbourne, David (ed.), *In Theory and In Practice: Essays on the Politics of Jayaprakash Narayan* (Delhi: Oxford University Press, 1985).

Semelin, Jacques, 'Lanza del Vasto, Joseph Jean (1901–1981)', in Powers and Vogele, *Protest, Power, and Change*, p. 300.

Seshachari, C., *Gandhi and the American Scene: An Intellectual History and Inquiry* (Bombay: Nachiketa, 1969).

Sessions, George, 'Arne Naess and the Union of Theory and Practice', in Alan Drengson and Yuich Inoue (eds.), *The Deep Ecology Movement: An Introductory Anthology* (Berkeley: North Atlantic Books, 1995), pp. 54–63.

Sethi, J. D., 'Foreword', in Romesh Diwan and Mark Lutz (eds.), *Essays in Gandhian Economics* (New Delhi: Gandhi Peace Foundation, 1985), pp. xiii–xiv.

Shah, Kanti, *Vinoba: Life and Mission* (Varanasi: Sarva Seva Sangh, 1979).

(ed.), *Vinoba on Gandhi* (Varanasi: Sarva Seva Sangh, 1985).

Sharp, Gene, *Civilian-Based Defense: A Post-Military Weapons System* (Princeton University Press, 1990).

'Conducting Conflicts Without Violence', *Peace Magazine* 23 (1997), available at www.peacemagazine.org

'Foreword', in Ackerman and Kruegler, *Strategic Nonviolent Conflict*, pp. ix–xiii.

Gandhi as a Political Strategist: With Essays on Ethics and Politics (Boston: Porter Sargent, 1979).

'Gandhi's Political Significance Today', *Gandhi Marg* 9 (1965), pp. 47–56.

Gandhi Wields the Weapon of Moral Power [Three Case Histories] (Ahmedabad: Navajivan, 1960).

'People "don't need to believe right"', *National Catholic Reporter* 20 (September 1984), p. 11.

The Politics of Nonviolent Action (Boston: Porter Sargent, 1973).

Social Power and Political Freedom (Boston: Porter Sargent, 1980).

'A Study of the Meanings of Nonviolence', in G. Ramachandran and T. K. Mahadevan (eds.), *Gandhi: His Relevance for our Times* (Berkeley: World Without War Council, circa 1971), pp. 21–66.

'The Technique of Non-violent Action', in Adam Roberts (ed.), *Civilian Resistance as a National Defence: Non-violent Action Against Aggression* (Harmondsworth: Penguin, 1969), pp. 107–27.

Shepard, Mark, *The Community of the Ark* (Arcata, CA: Simple Productions, 1990).

Gandhi Today: A Report on Mahatma Gandhi's Successors (Arcata, CA: Simple Productions, 1987).

Shifman, Alexander, *Tolstoy and India* (New Delhi: Sahitya Akademi, 1969).

Shiva, Vandana, and Jayanto Bandhyopadhyay, *Chipko: India's Civilisational Response to the Forest Crisis*, pamphlet (New Delhi: The Indian National Trust for Art and Cultural Heritage, 1986).

Shridharani, Krishnalal, *War Without Violence: A Study of Gandhi's Method and its Accomplishments* (New York: Harcourt, Brace and Co., 1939).

Shukla, Chandrashanker (ed.), *Incidents of Gandhiji's Life* (Bombay: Vora, 1949).

Smith, Donald H., 'An Exegesis of Martin Luther King, Jr.'s Social Philosophy', in David J. Garrow (ed.), *Martin Luther King, Jr.: Civil Rights Leader, Theologian, Orator* (Brooklyn: Carlson, 1989), vol. III, pp. 829–37.

Smith, John E. 'The Inescapable Ambiguity of Nonviolence', *Philosophy East and West* 19 (1969), pp. 155–8.

Smith, Kenneth L., and G. Zepp Jr., *Search for the Beloved Community: The Thinking of Martin Luther King, Jr.* (Valley Forge: Judson Press, 1974).

Sørensen, Georg, 'Utopianism in Peace Research: The Gandhian Heritage', *Journal of Peace Research* 29 (1992), pp. 135–44.

Spodek, Howard, 'On the Origins of Gandhi's Political Methodology: The Heritage of Kathiawad and Gujarat', *Journal of Asian Studies* 30 (1970–1), pp. 361–72.

Stiehm, Judith, 'Nonviolence is Two', *Social Inquiry* 38 (1968), pp. 23–30.

Summy, Ralph, 'One Person's Search for a Functional Alternative to Violence', *Gandhi Marg* 5 (1983), pp. 26–44.

Sutherland, Bill, and Matt Meyer, *Guns and Gandhi in Africa: Pan African Insights on Nonviolence, Armed Struggle and Liberation in Africa* (Trenton, NJ: Africa World Press, 2000).

Swan, Maureen, *Gandhi: The South African Experience* (Johannesburg: Ravan Press, 1985).

Sykes, Marjorie, *The Story of Nai Talim: Fifty Years of Education at Sevagram 1937–1987* (Wardha: Nai Talim Samiti, 1988).

Tahmankar, D. V., *Sardar Patel* (London: Allen and Unwin, 1970).

Tandon, Vishwanath, 'The Bhoodan-Gramdan Movement (1951–74) – A Review', *Gandhi Marg* 5 (1983), pp. 492–500.

'Vinoba and Satyagraha', *Gandhi Marg* 2 (1980), pp. 385–94.

Taylor, Richard, *Axing the Himalayas*, film made for the BBC *The World Around Us*, 1981.

Tendulkar, D. G., *Mahatma: Life of Mohandas Karamchand Gandhi*, 8 vols. (New Delhi: Publications Division, Ministry of Information and Broadcasting, Government of India, 1960–3).

Thomson, Mark, *Gandhi and His Ashrams* (Bombay: Popular, 1993).

Thoreau, Henry David, *Walden and Civil Disobedience* (New York: Harper and Row, 1965).

True, Michael, *Justice Seekers Peace Makers: 32 Portraits in Courage* (Mystic, CT: Twenty-Third Publications, 1985).

Vepa, Ram K., *New Technology: A Gandhian Concept* (New Delhi: Gandhi Book House, 1975).

Vine, John C., 'Interview with Mrs. Millie Graham Polak', 2 May 1960, in S. Durai Raja Singam, 'They Were Ready to Talk About Gandhi', unpublished manuscript (n.d), pp. 16–20.

Walker, Charles C., 'Nonviolence in Eastern Africa 1962–4: The World Peace Brigade and Zambian Independence', in A. Paul Hare and Herbert H. Blumberg (eds.), *Liberation Without Violence: A Third Party Approach* (Totowa, NJ: Rowman and Littlefield, 1977), pp. 157–77.

Watson, Francis and Hallam Tennyson, *Talking of Gandhi* (New Delhi: Sangam, 1976).

Weber, Max, *The Theory of Social and Economic Organisations* (New York: The Free Press, 1964).

Weber, Thomas, 'A Brief History of the Shanti Sena as Seen through the Changing Pledges of the Shanti Sainik', *Gandhi Marg* 13 (1991), pp 316–26.

    Conflict Resolution and Gandhian Ethics (New Delhi: Gandhi Peace Foundation, 1991).

    'Gandhi, Deep Ecology, Peace Research and Buddhist Economics', *Journal of Peace Research* 36 (1999), pp. 349–61.

    'Gandhian Philosophy, Conflict Resolution Theory and Practical Approaches to Negotiation', *Journal of Peace Research* 38 (2001), pp. 493–513.

    'Gandhi is Dead. Long Live Gandhi: The Post-Gandhi Gandhian Movement in India', *Gandhi Marg* 18 (1996), pp. 160–92.

    'Gandhi's "Living Wall" and Maude Royden's "Peace Army"', *Gandhi Marg* 10 (1988), pp. 199–212.

    Gandhi's Peace Army: The Shanti Sena and Unarmed Peacekeeping (Syracuse University Press, 1996).

    'Gandhi's Salt March as Living Sermon', *Gandhi Marg* 22 (2001), pp. 417–35.

    Hugging the Trees The Story of the Chipko Movement (New Delhi: Penguin, 1989).

    'Legal Ethics/Gandhian Ethics', *Gandhi Marg* 7 (1986), pp. 592–706.

    'Nonviolence is Who? Gene Sharp and Gandhi', *Peace and Change* 28 (2003), pp. 250–70.

    On the Salt March: The Historiography of Gandhi's March to Dandi (New Delhi: HarperCollins, 1997).

West, Albert, 'In the Early Days with Gandhi', *The Illustrated Weekly of India*, 3 October 1965, pp. 30–1, 33.

Willner, Ann R., *The Spellbinders: Charismatic Political Leadership* (New Haven: Yale University Press, 1984).

Witoszek, Nina, 'Arne Næss and the Norwegian Nature Tradition', in Witoszek and Brennan, *Philosophical Dialogues*, pp. 451–65.

Witoszek, Nina, and Andrew Brennan (eds.), *Philosophical Dialogues: Arne Næss and the Progress of Ecophilosophy* (Lanham, MD: Rowman and Littlefield, 1999).

Wolfenstein, E. Victor, *The Revolutionary Personality: Lenin, Trotsky, Gandhi* (Princeton University Press, 1971).

Wolpert, Stanley, *Tilak and Gokhale: Revolution and Reform in the Making of Modern India* (Berkeley: University of California Press, 1962).

Wood, Barbara, *Alias Papa: A Life of Fritz Schumacher* (London: Cape, 1984).

Woodcock, George, *Gandhi* (London: Fontana, 1972).

Yungblut, June J., untitled essay, in Ramachandran and Mahadevan, *Nonviolence After Gandhi*, pp. 51–7.

Zunes, Stephen, 'The Role of Nonviolent Action in the Collapse of Apartheid', *Gandhi Marg* 20 (1999), pp. 398–429.

Index

Lightning Source UK Ltd.
Milton Keynes UK
UKOW04f1054061013

218536UK00004B/140/P